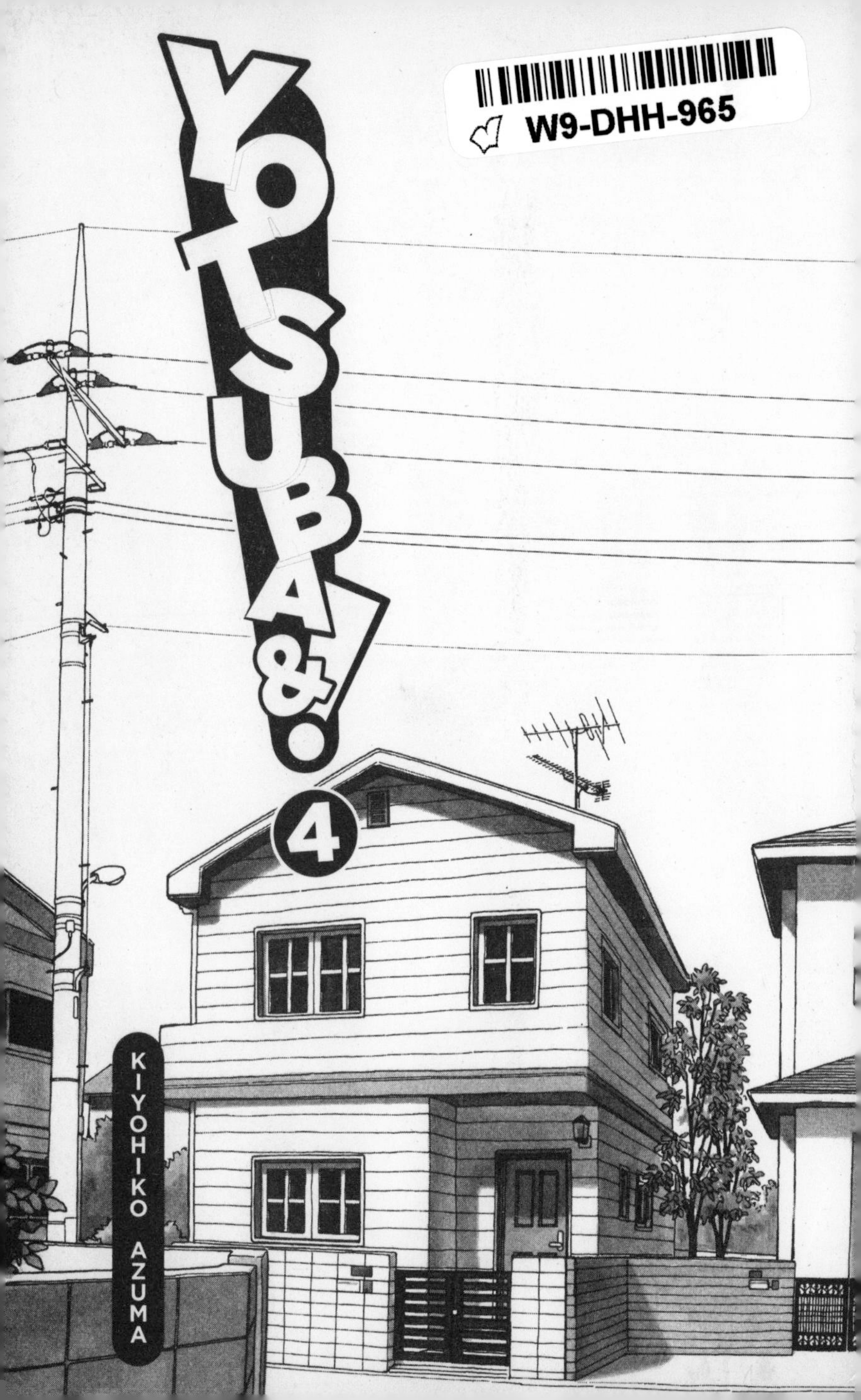
YOTSUBA&!
4
KIYOHIKO AZUMA

TABLE OF CONTENTS

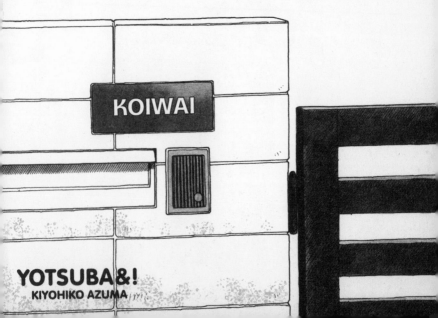

KOIWAI

YOTSUBA&!
KIYOHIKO AZUMA

YOTSUBA& CHALLENGES

CHAPTER 22

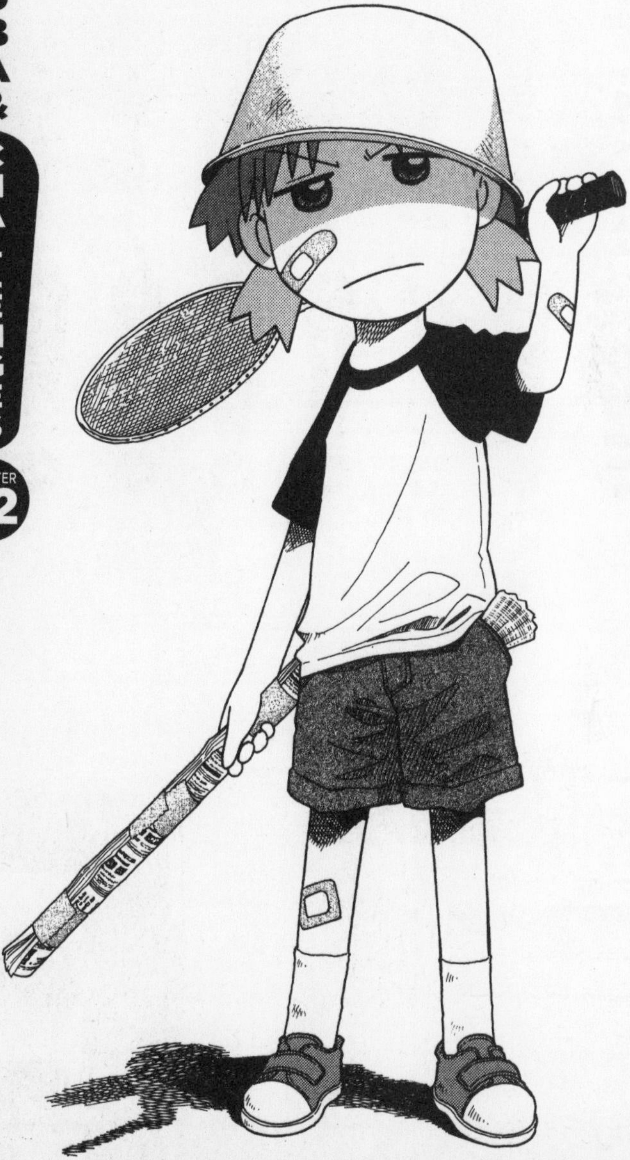

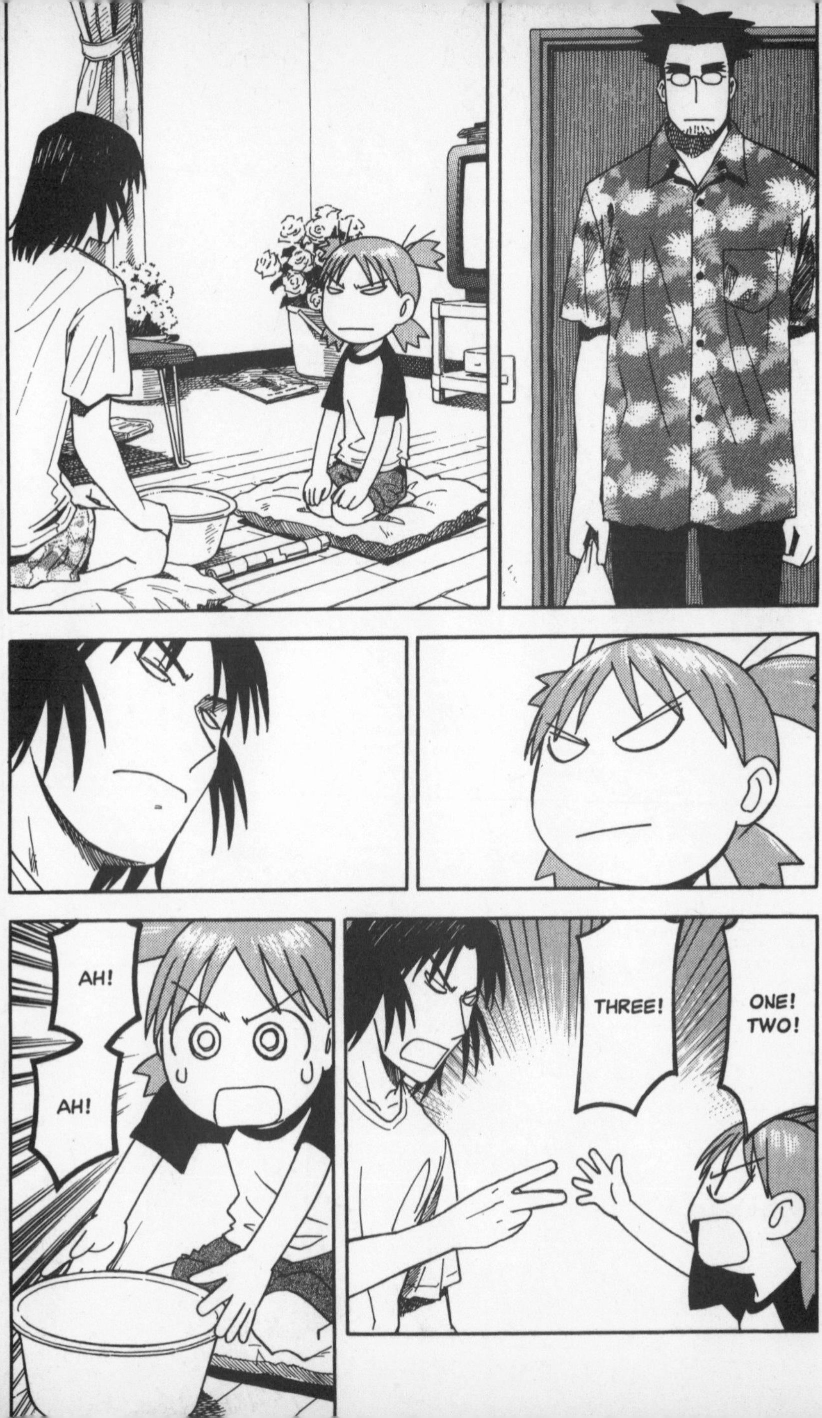
ONE! TWO!
THREE!
AH!
AH!

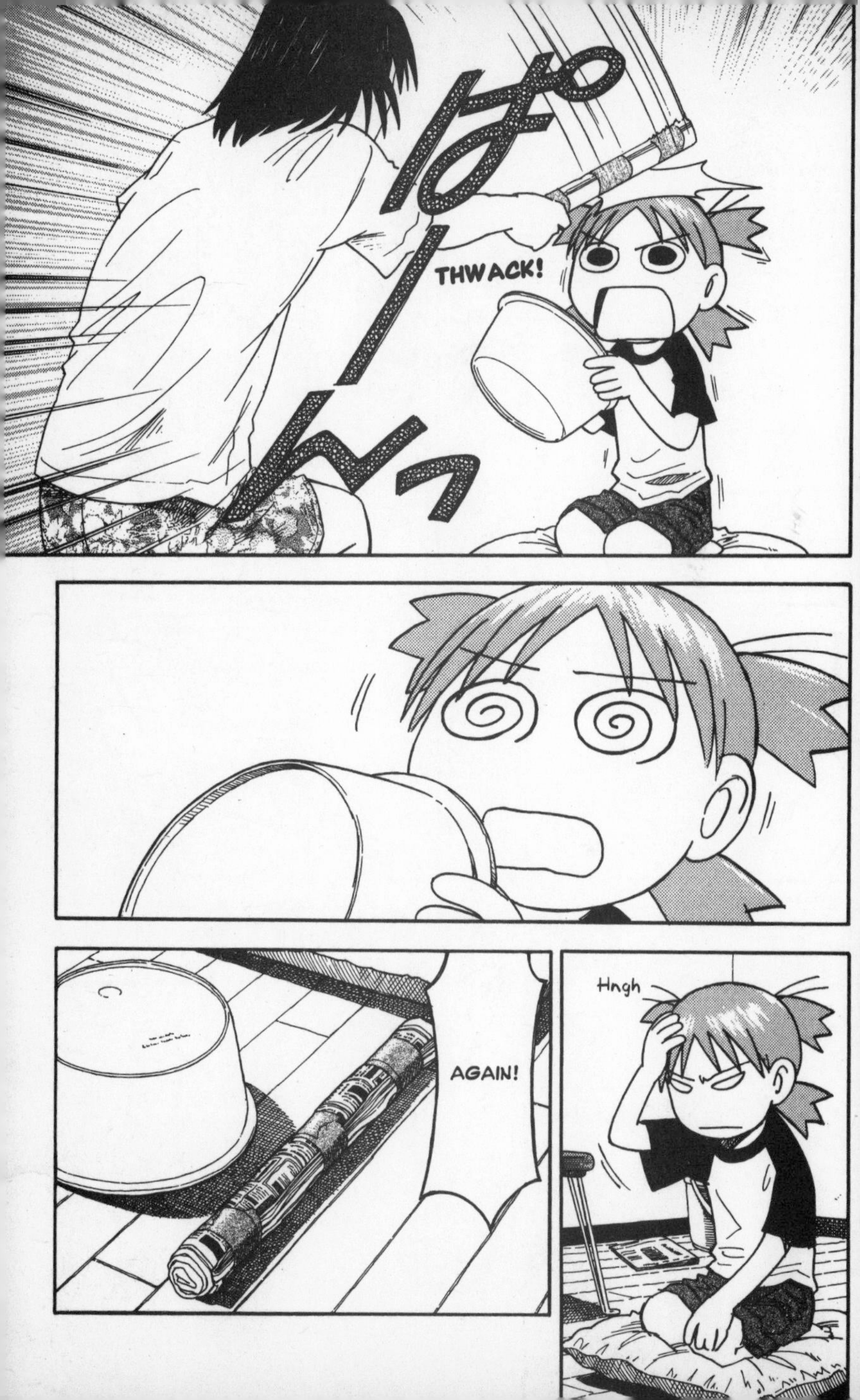

ぱーんっ
THWACK!
Hngh
AGAIN!

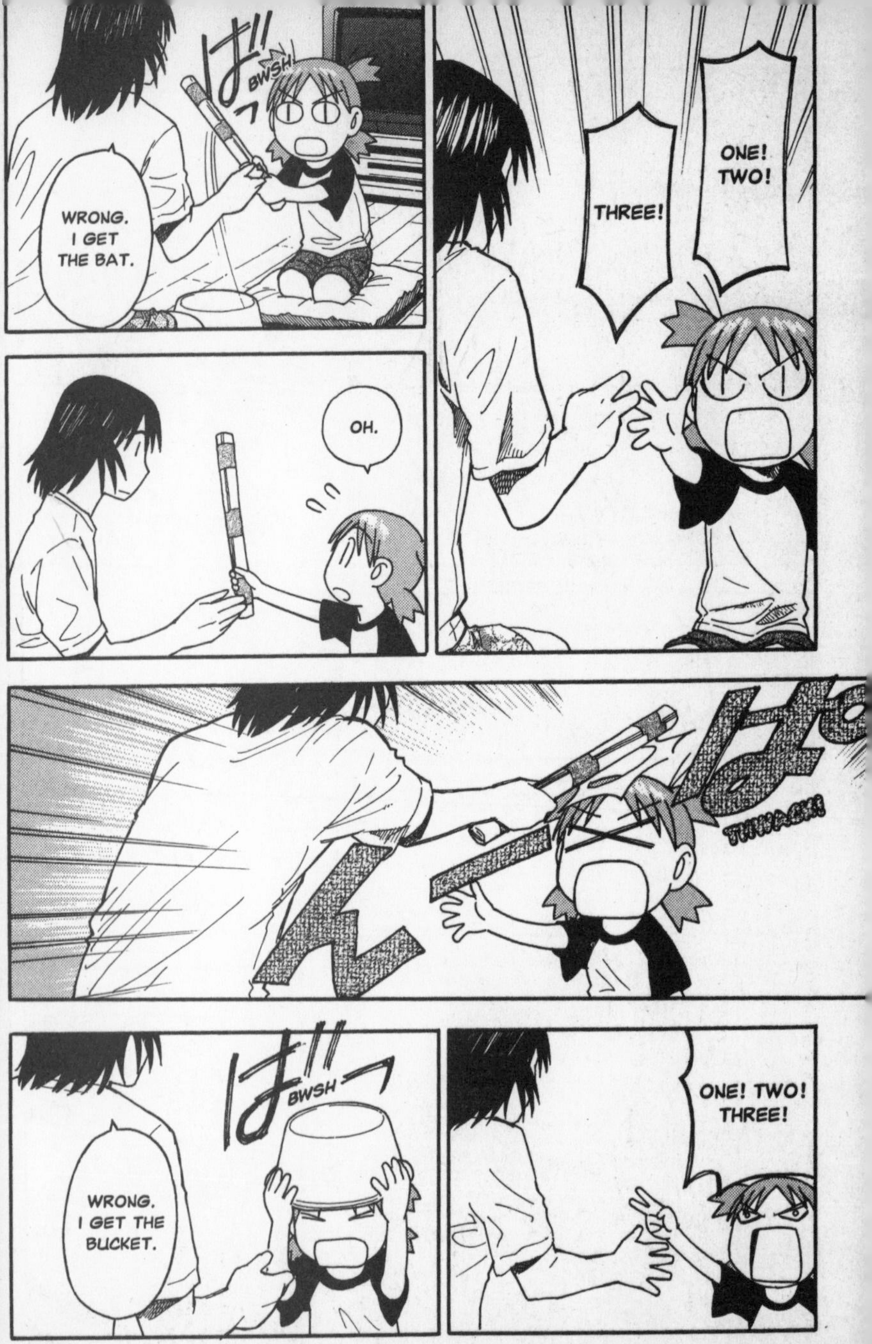
ONE! TWO!
THREE!
BWSH!
WRONG. I GET THE BAT.
OH.
THWACK!
ONE! TWO! THREE!
BWSH
WRONG. I GET THE BUCKET.

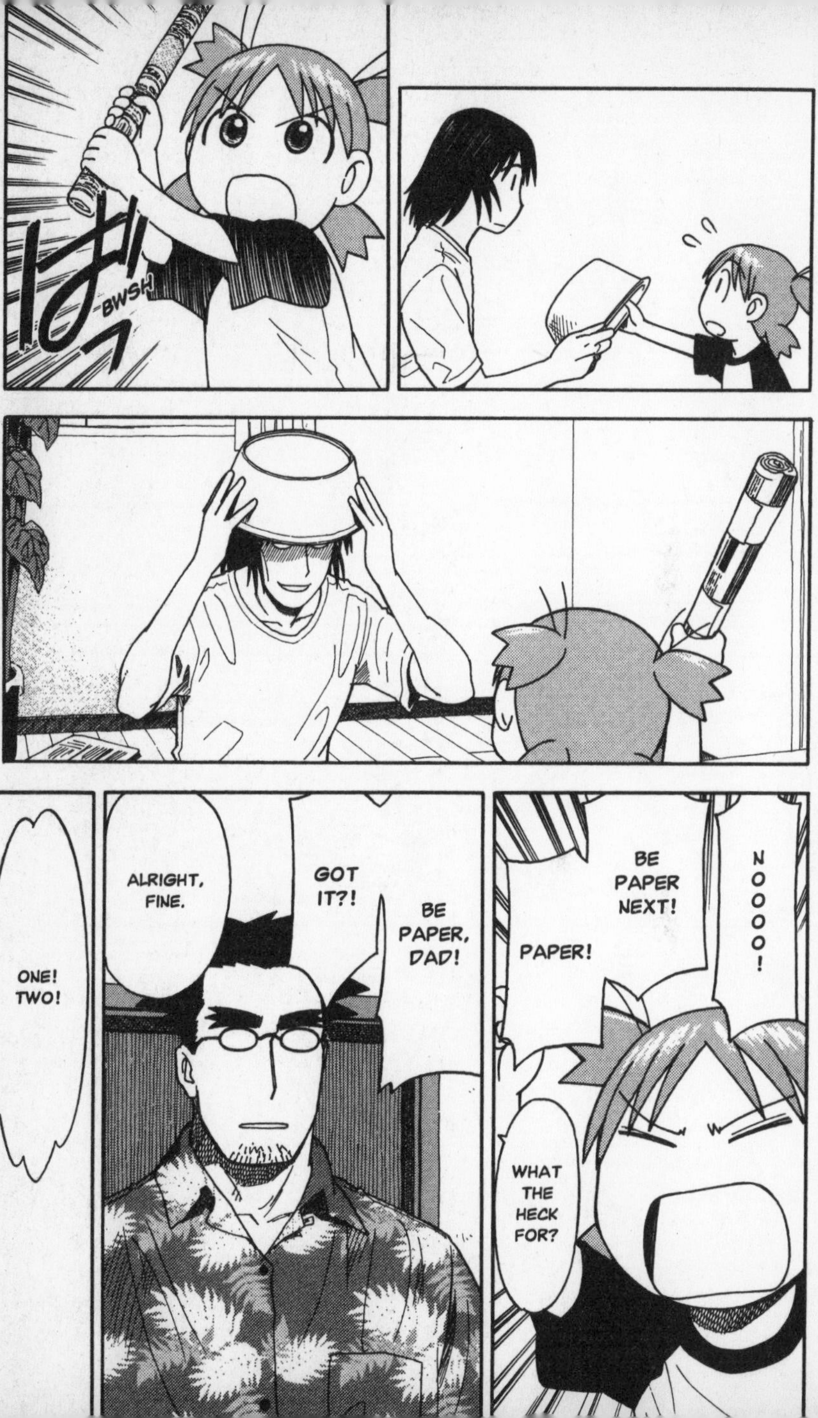
BWSH
NOOOOO!
BE PAPER NEXT!
PAPER!
WHAT THE HECK FOR?
BE PAPER, DAD!
GOT IT?!
ALRIGHT, FINE.
ONE! TWO!

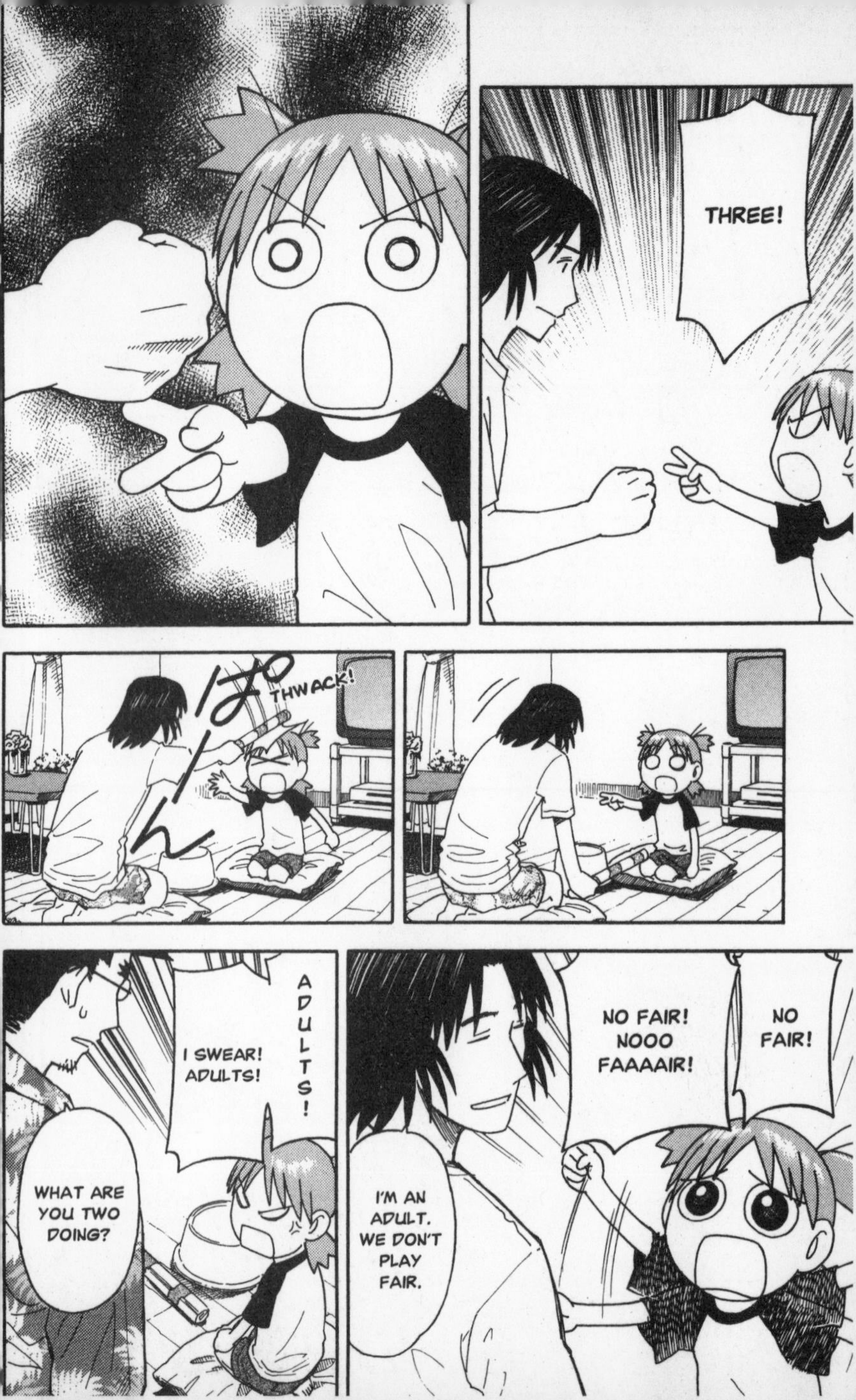
THREE!
THWACK!
ぱーん
NO FAIR!
NO FAIR! NOOO FAAAAIR!
I'M AN ADULT. WE DON'T PLAY FAIR.
ADULTS!
I SWEAR! ADULTS!
WHAT ARE YOU TWO DOING?

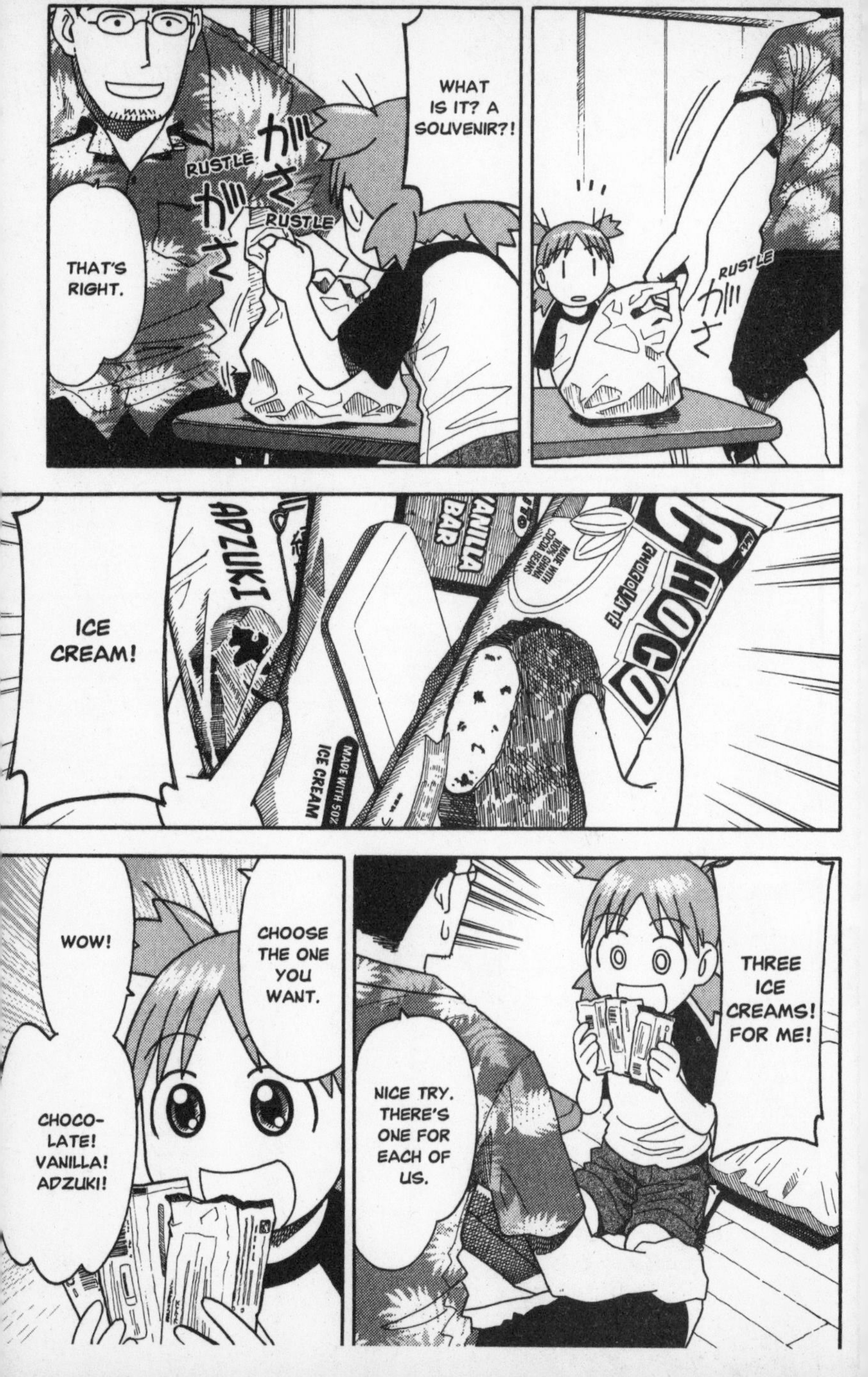
RUSTLE
がさ
WHAT IS IT? A SOUVENIR?!
RUSTLE
がさ
がさ
RUSTLE
THAT'S RIGHT.
ICE CREAM!
CHOCO
CHOCOLATE
MADE WITH 100% GHANA COCOA BEANS
VANILLA BAR
ADZUKI
MADE WITH 50% ICE CREAM
THREE ICE CREAMS! FOR ME!
NICE TRY. THERE'S ONE FOR EACH OF US.
CHOOSE THE ONE YOU WANT.
WOW!
CHOCO-LATE! VANILLA! ADZUKI!

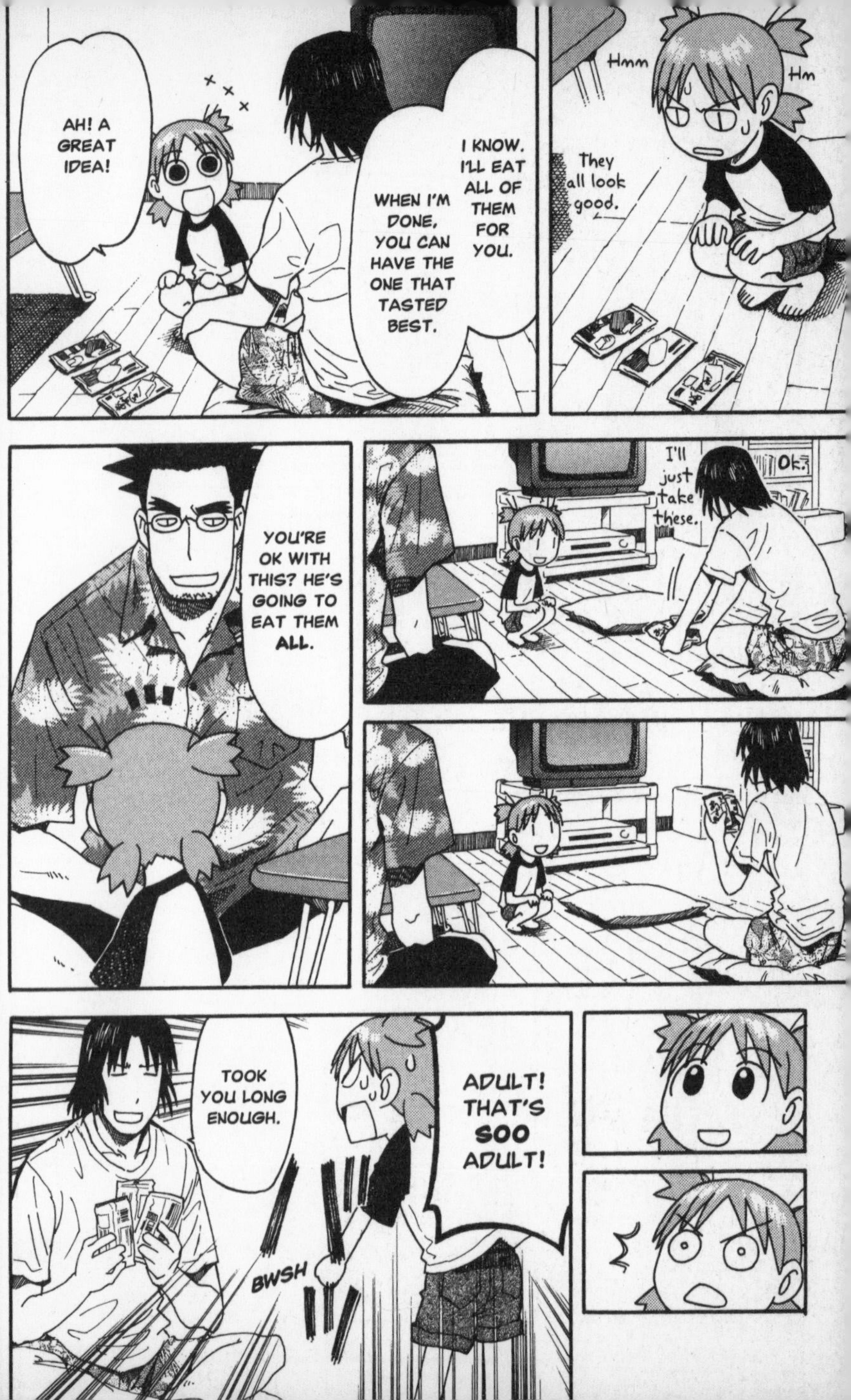
Hmm
Hm
They all look good.
I KNOW. I'LL EAT ALL OF THEM FOR YOU.
WHEN I'M DONE, YOU CAN HAVE THE ONE THAT TASTED BEST.
AH! A GREAT IDEA!
I'll just take these.
Ok.
YOU'RE OK WITH THIS? HE'S GOING TO EAT THEM **ALL**.
ADULT! THAT'S **SOO** ADULT!
TOOK YOU LONG ENOUGH.
BWSH

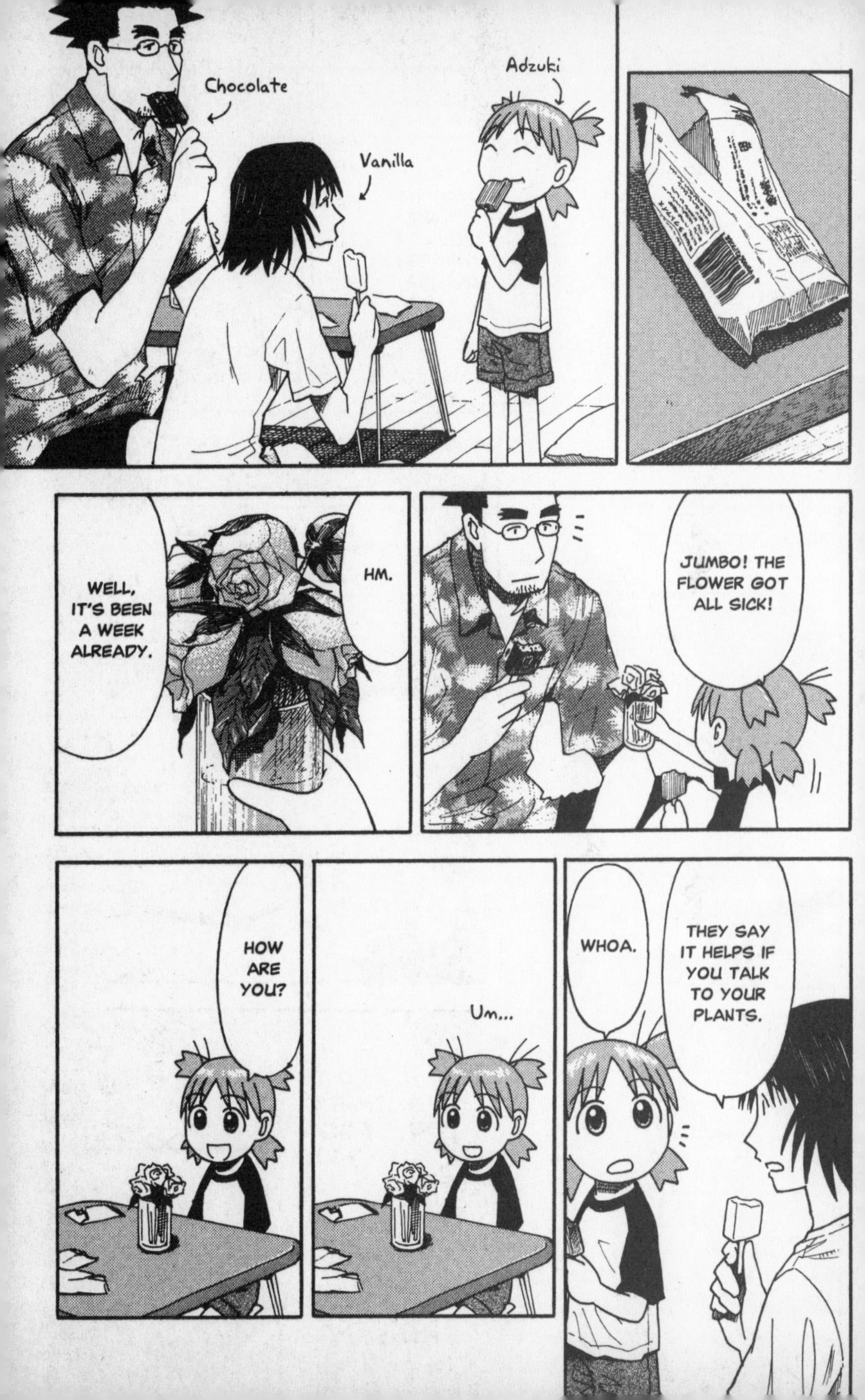
Adzuki
Vanilla
Chocolate
JUMBO! THE FLOWER GOT ALL SICK!
HM.
WELL, IT'S BEEN A WEEK ALREADY.
THEY SAY IT HELPS IF YOU TALK TO YOUR PLANTS.
WHOA.
Um...
HOW ARE YOU?

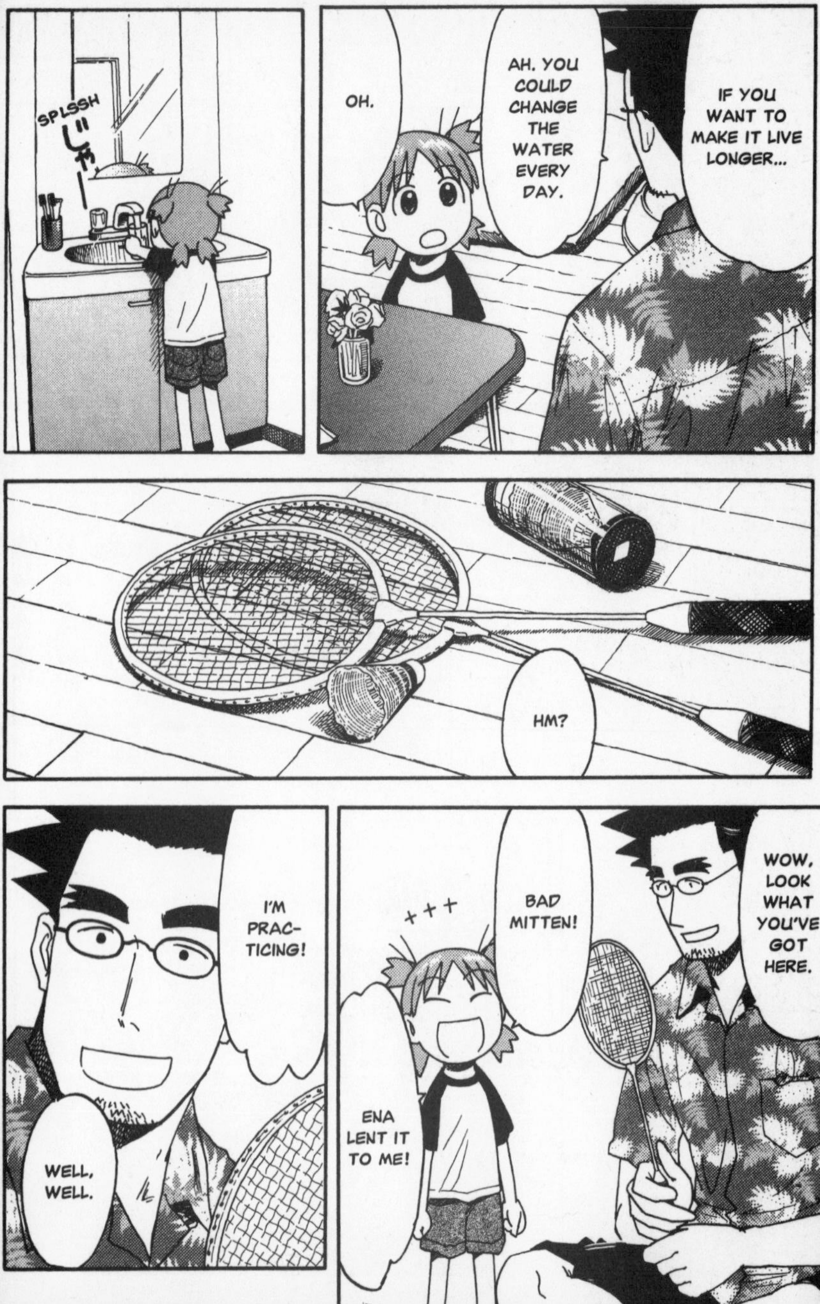
IF YOU WANT TO MAKE IT LIVE LONGER...
AH. YOU COULD CHANGE THE WATER EVERY DAY.
OH.
SPLSSH
しゃー
HM?
WOW, LOOK WHAT YOU'VE GOT HERE.
BAD MITTEN!
ENA LENT IT TO ME!
I'M PRAC-TICING!
WELL, WELL.

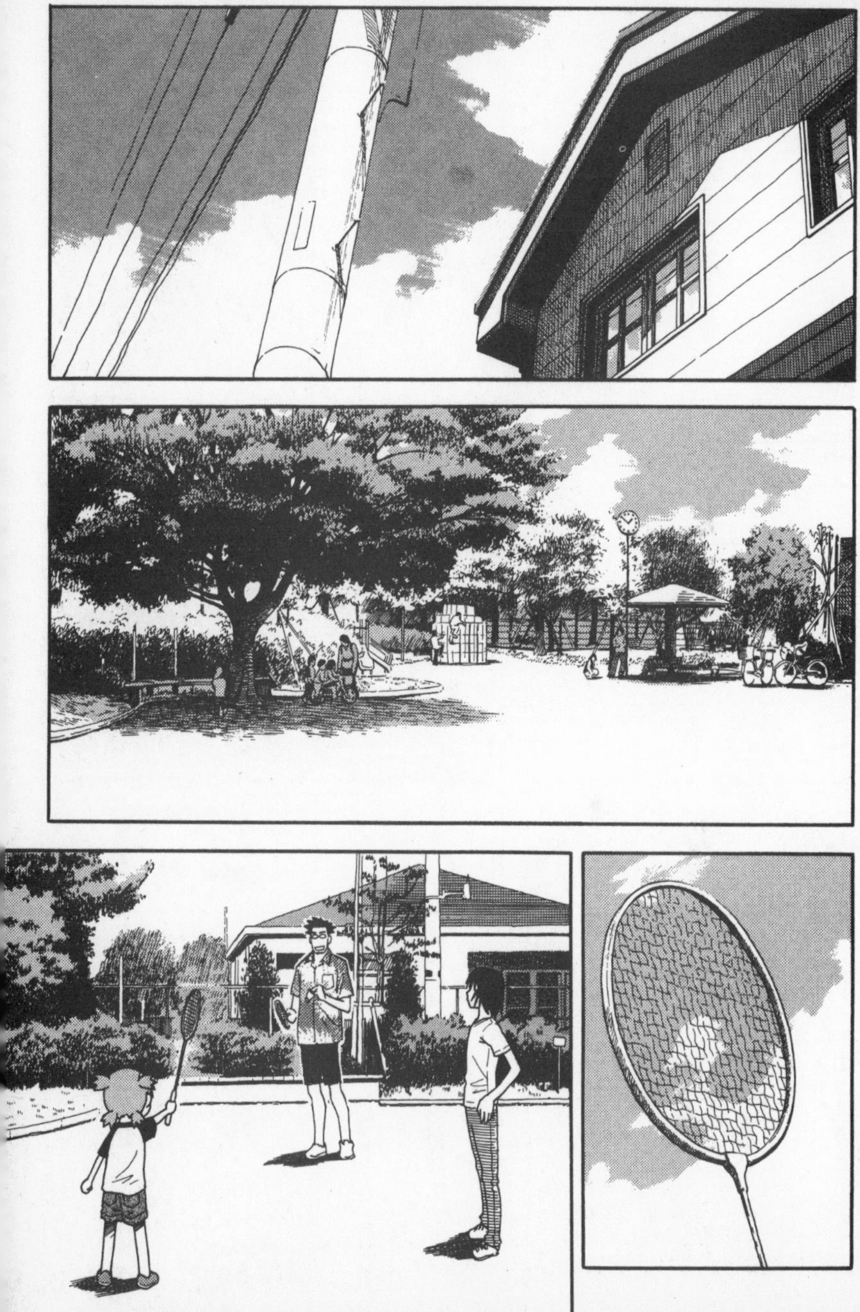

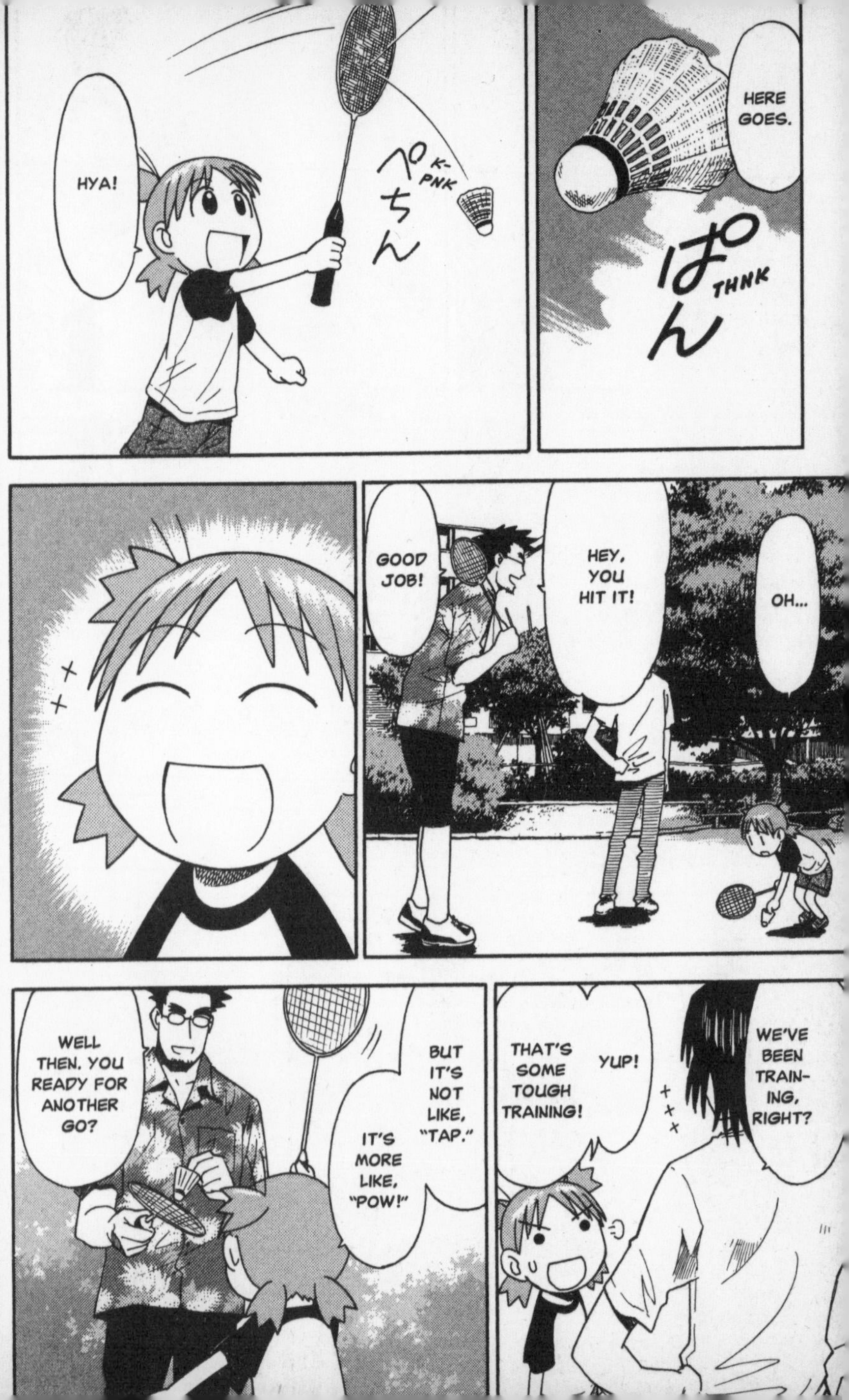
HERE GOES.
ぱん
THNK
HYA!
ぺちん
K-PNK
OH...
HEY, YOU HIT IT!
GOOD JOB!
WE'VE BEEN TRAINING, RIGHT?
YUP!
THAT'S SOME TOUGH TRAINING!
BUT IT'S NOT LIKE, "TAP."
IT'S MORE LIKE, "POW!"
WELL THEN. YOU READY FOR ANOTHER GO?

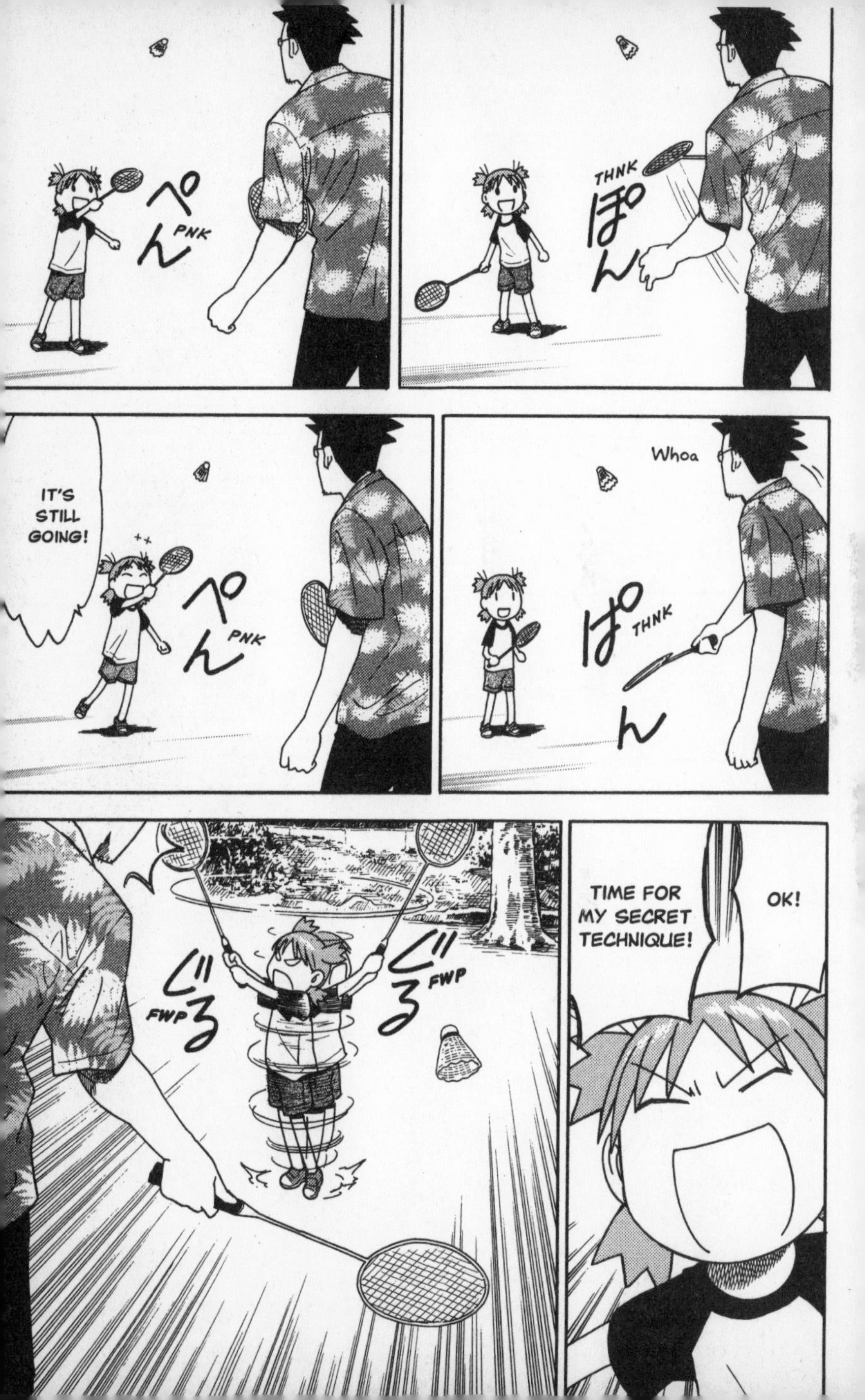
THNK
ぽん
ぺん
PNK
Whoa
ぱん
THNK
IT'S STILL GOING!
ぺん
PNK
OK!
TIME FOR MY SECRET TECHNIQUE!
ぐる
FWP
ぐる
FWP

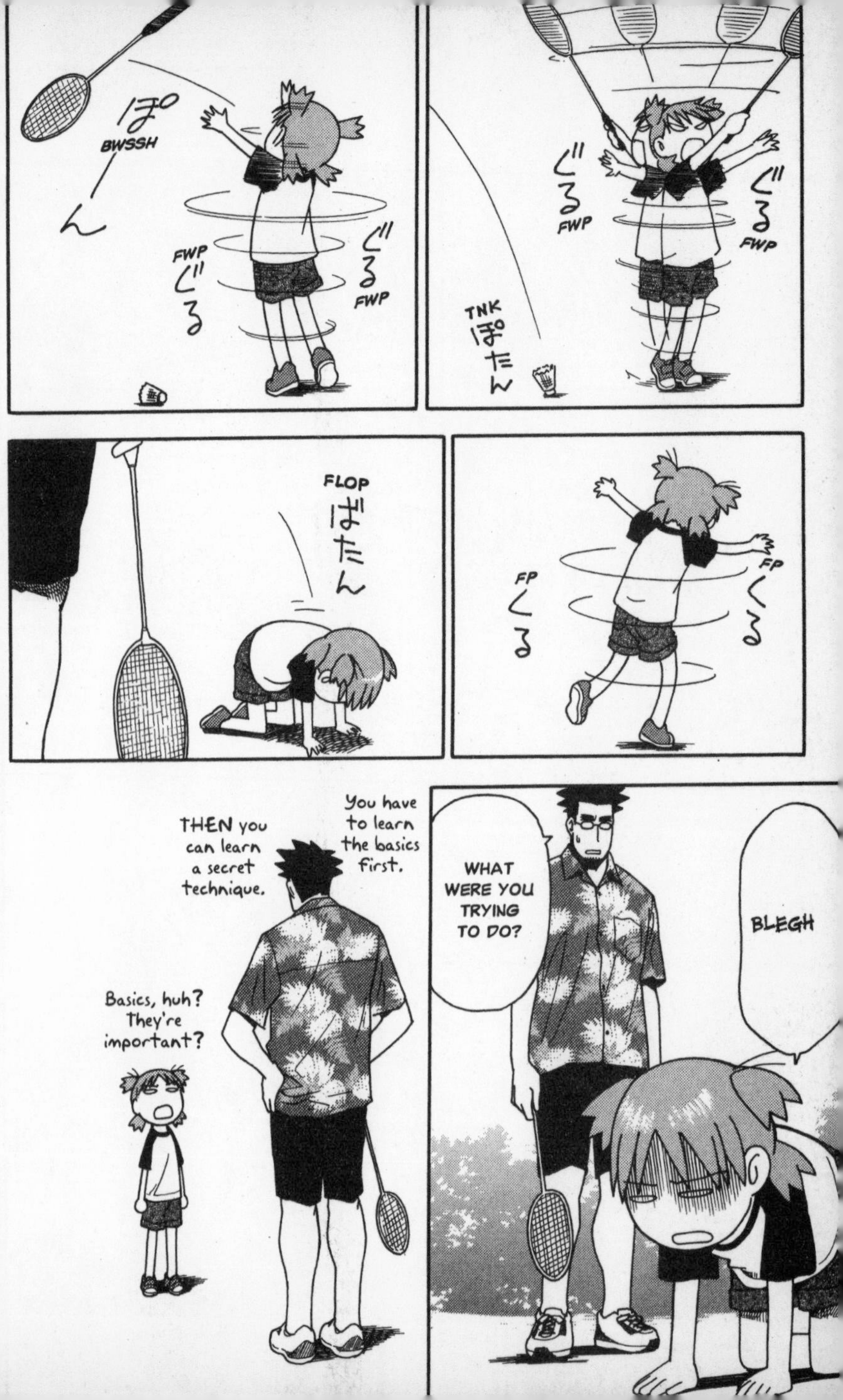
ぐる
FWP
ぐる
FWP
TNK
ぽたん
ぐる
FWP
FWP
ぐる
ぽ
BWSSH
ーん
FP
くる
FP
くる
FLOP
ばたん
BLEGH
WHAT WERE YOU TRYING TO DO?
You have to learn the basics first.
THEN you can learn a secret technique.
Basics, huh? They're important?

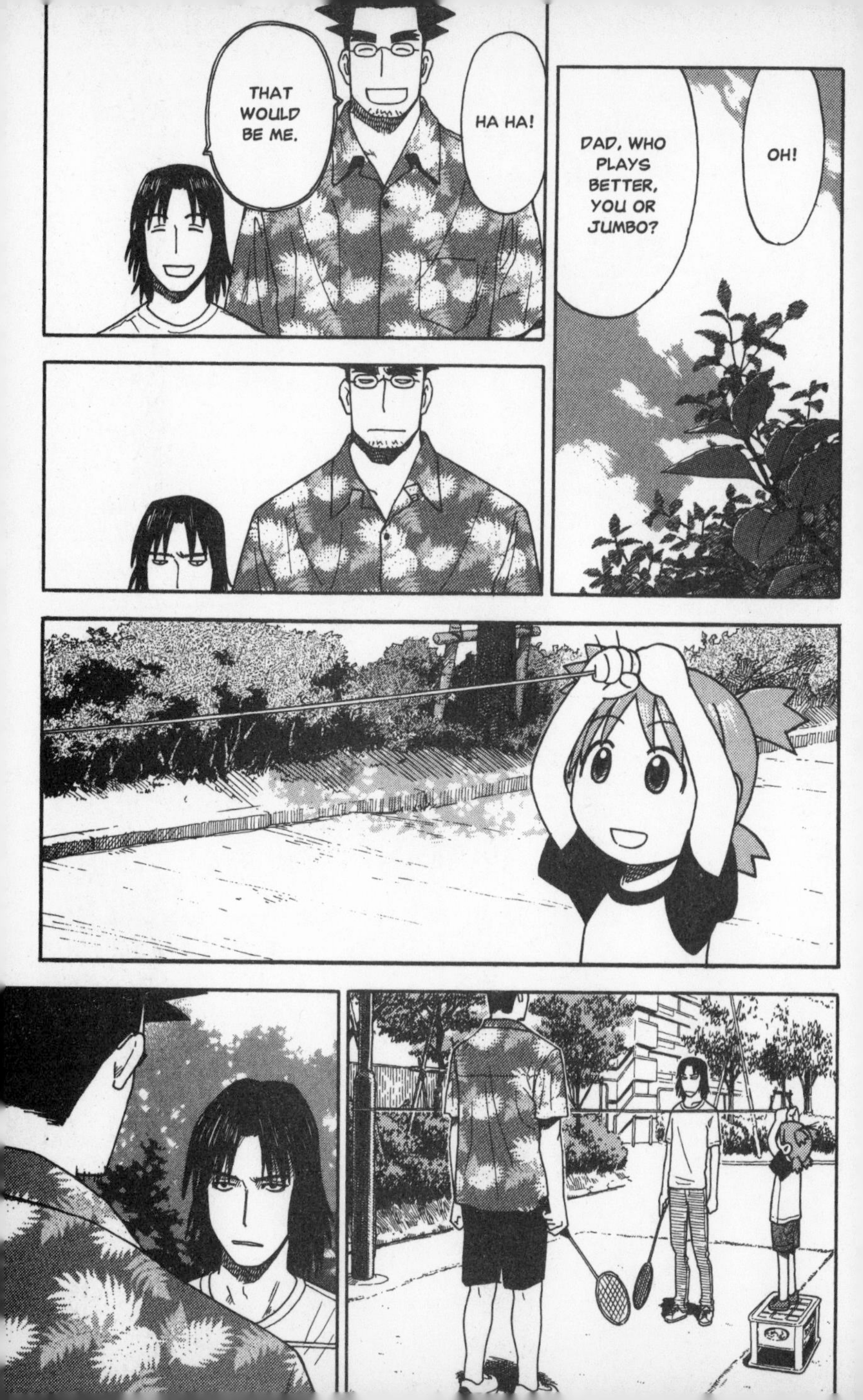
OH!
DAD, WHO PLAYS BETTER, YOU OR JUMBO?
HA HA!
THAT WOULD BE ME.

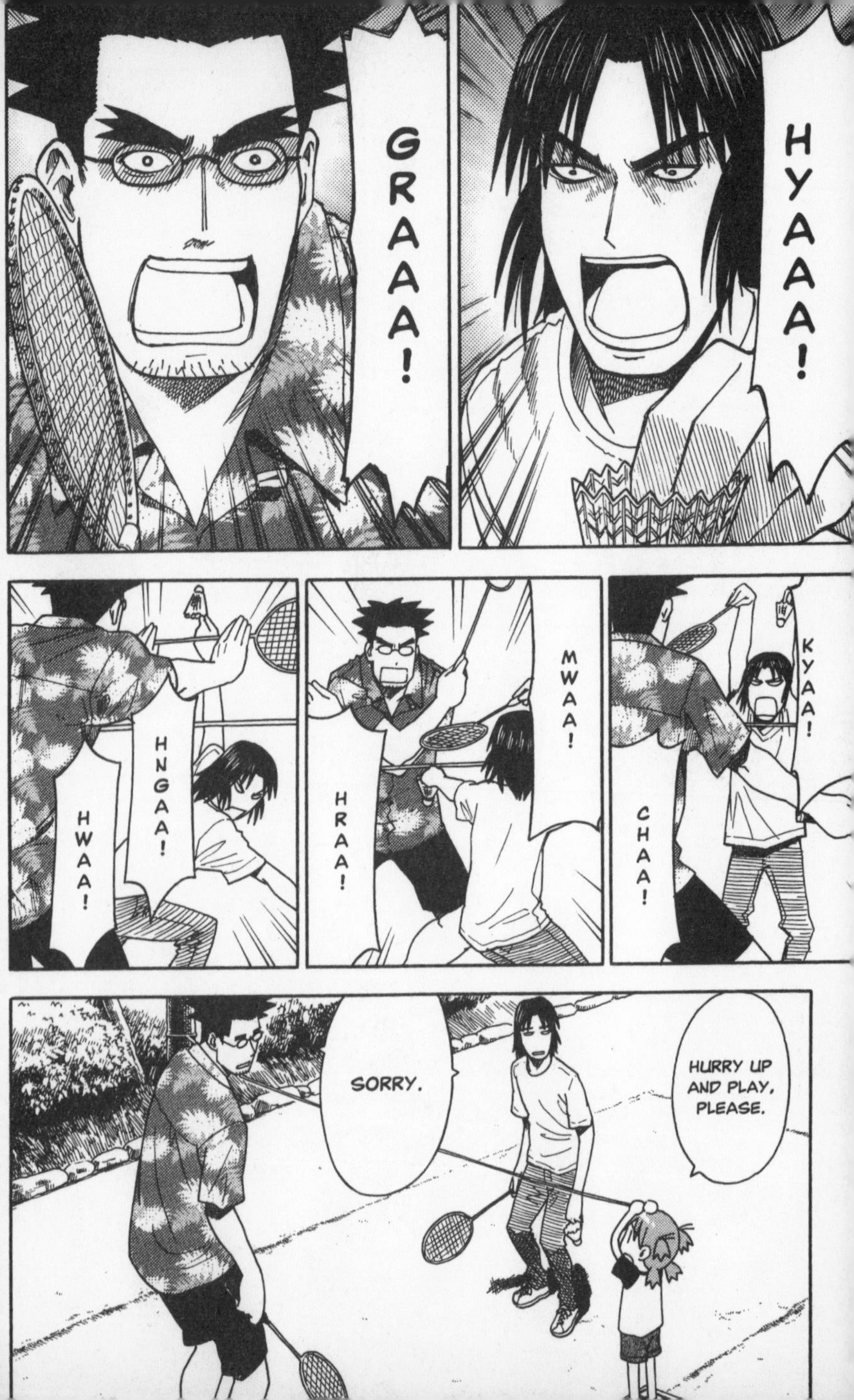
HYAAAA!
GRAAAA!
KYAAA!
CHAAA!
MWAA!
HRAA!
HNGAA!
HWAA!
HURRY UP AND PLAY, PLEASE.
SORRY.

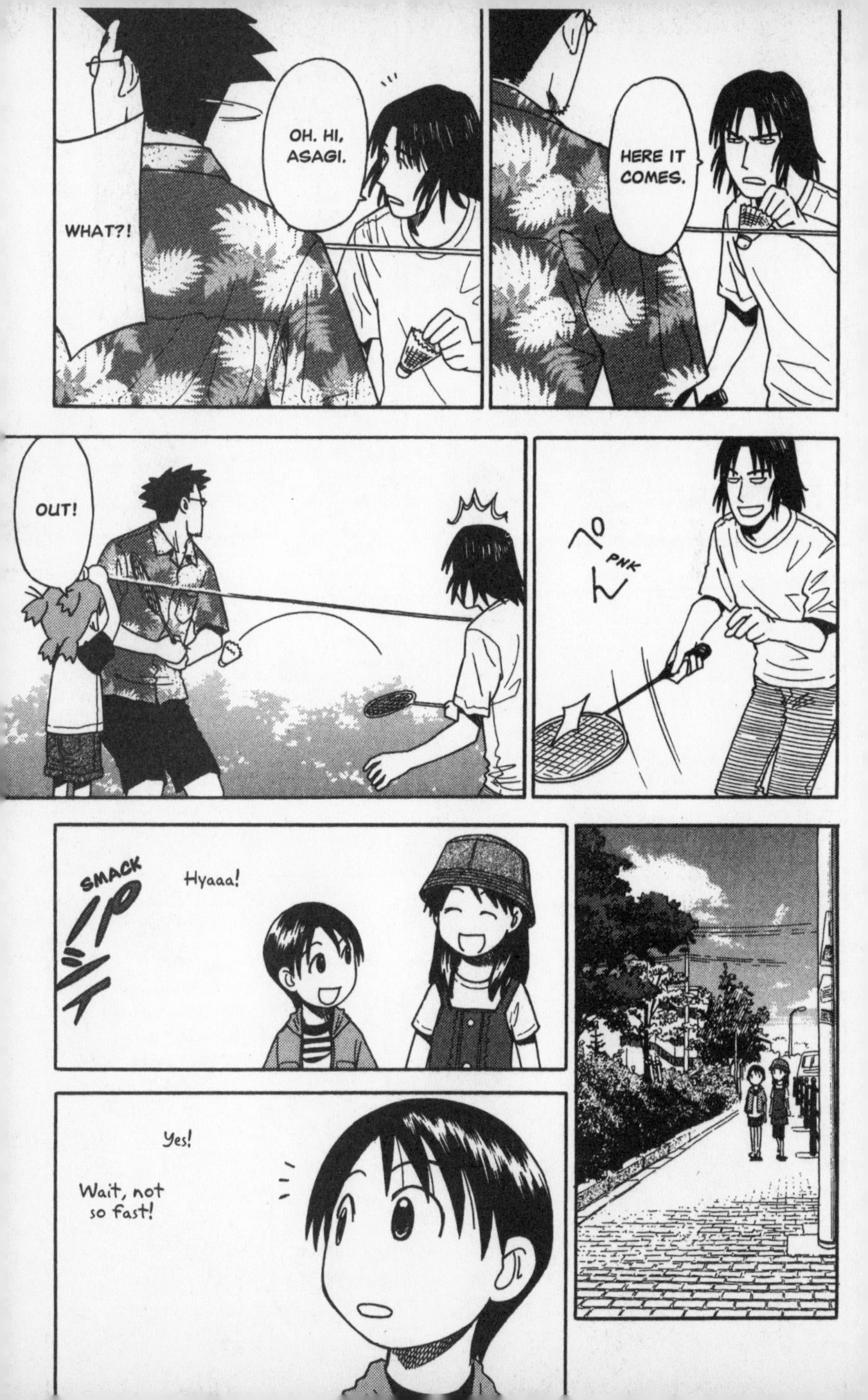
HERE IT COMES.
OH. HI, ASAGI.
WHAT?!
PNK
OUT!
Hyaaa!
SMACK
Yes!
Wait, not so fast!

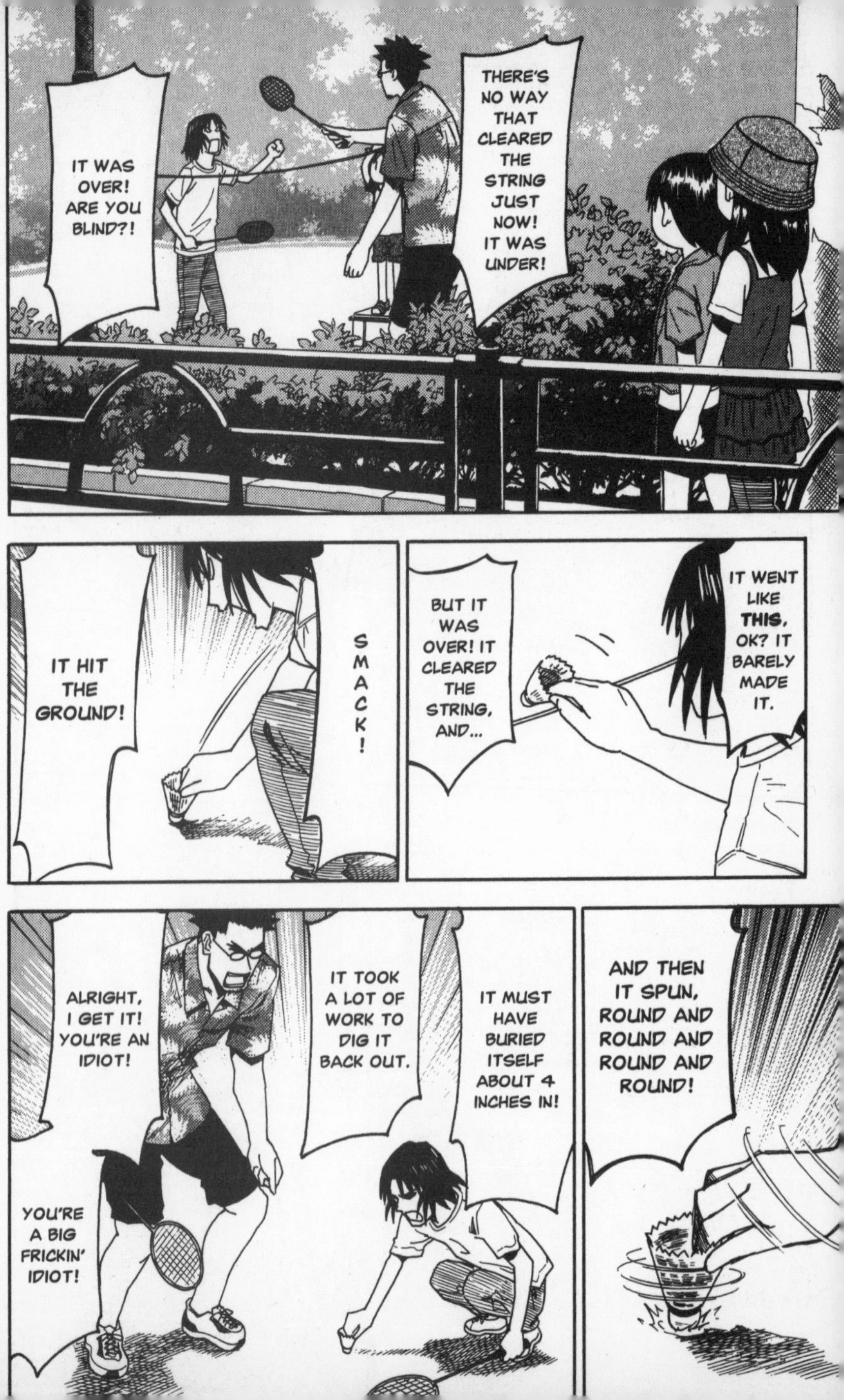
THERE'S NO WAY THAT CLEARED THE STRING JUST NOW! IT WAS UNDER!
IT WAS OVER! ARE YOU BLIND?!
IT WENT LIKE **THIS**, OK? IT BARELY MADE IT.
BUT IT WAS OVER! IT CLEARED THE STRING, AND...
SMACK!
IT HIT THE GROUND!
AND THEN IT SPUN, ROUND AND ROUND AND ROUND AND ROUND!
IT MUST HAVE BURIED ITSELF ABOUT 4 INCHES IN!
IT TOOK A LOT OF WORK TO DIG IT BACK OUT.
ALRIGHT, I GET IT! YOU'RE AN IDIOT!
YOU'RE A BIG FRICKIN' IDIOT!

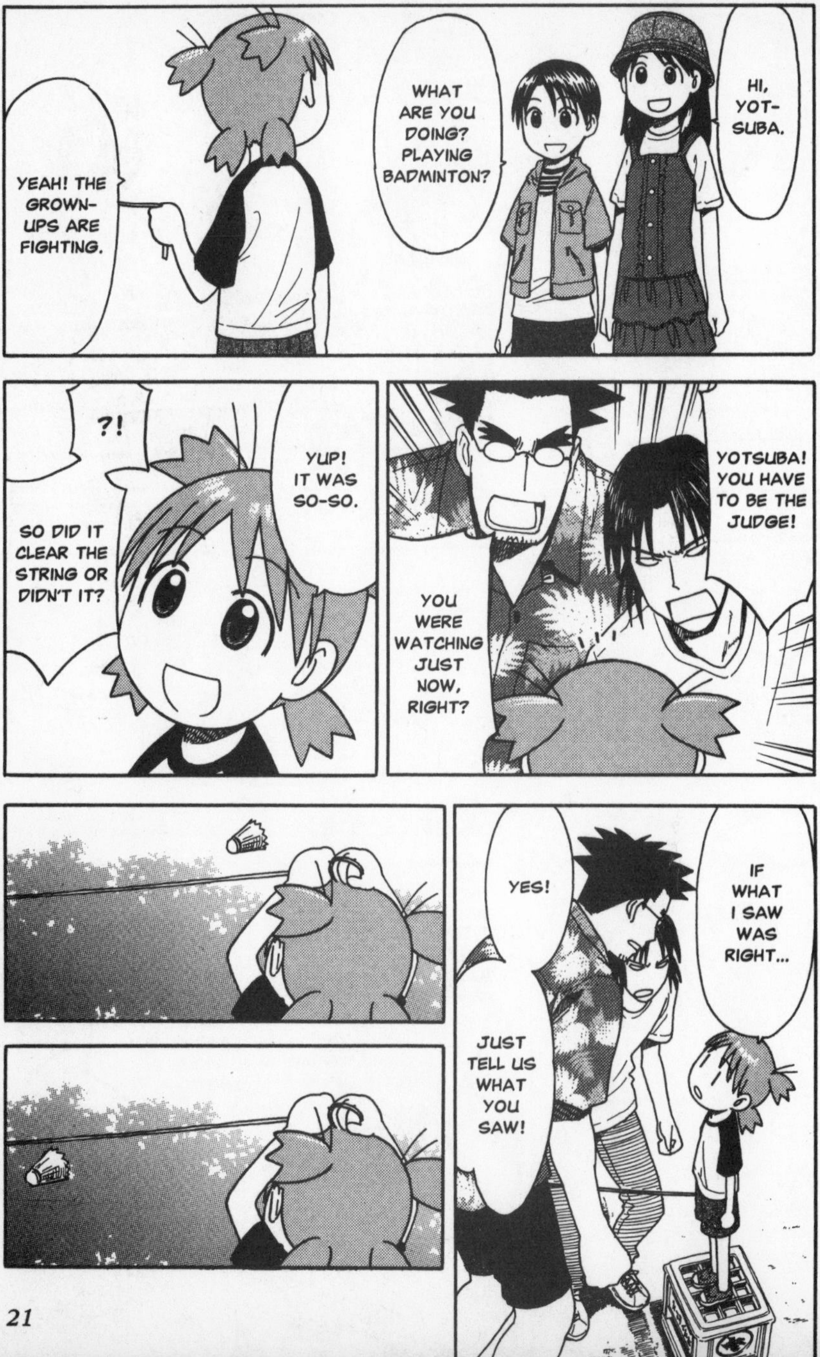
HI, YOT-SUBA.
WHAT ARE YOU DOING? PLAYING BADMINTON?
YEAH! THE GROWN-UPS ARE FIGHTING.
YOTSUBA! YOU HAVE TO BE THE JUDGE!
YOU WERE WATCHING JUST NOW, RIGHT?
YUP! IT WAS SO-SO.
?!
SO DID IT CLEAR THE STRING OR DIDN'T IT?
IF WHAT I SAW WAS RIGHT...
YES!
JUST TELL US WHAT YOU SAW!

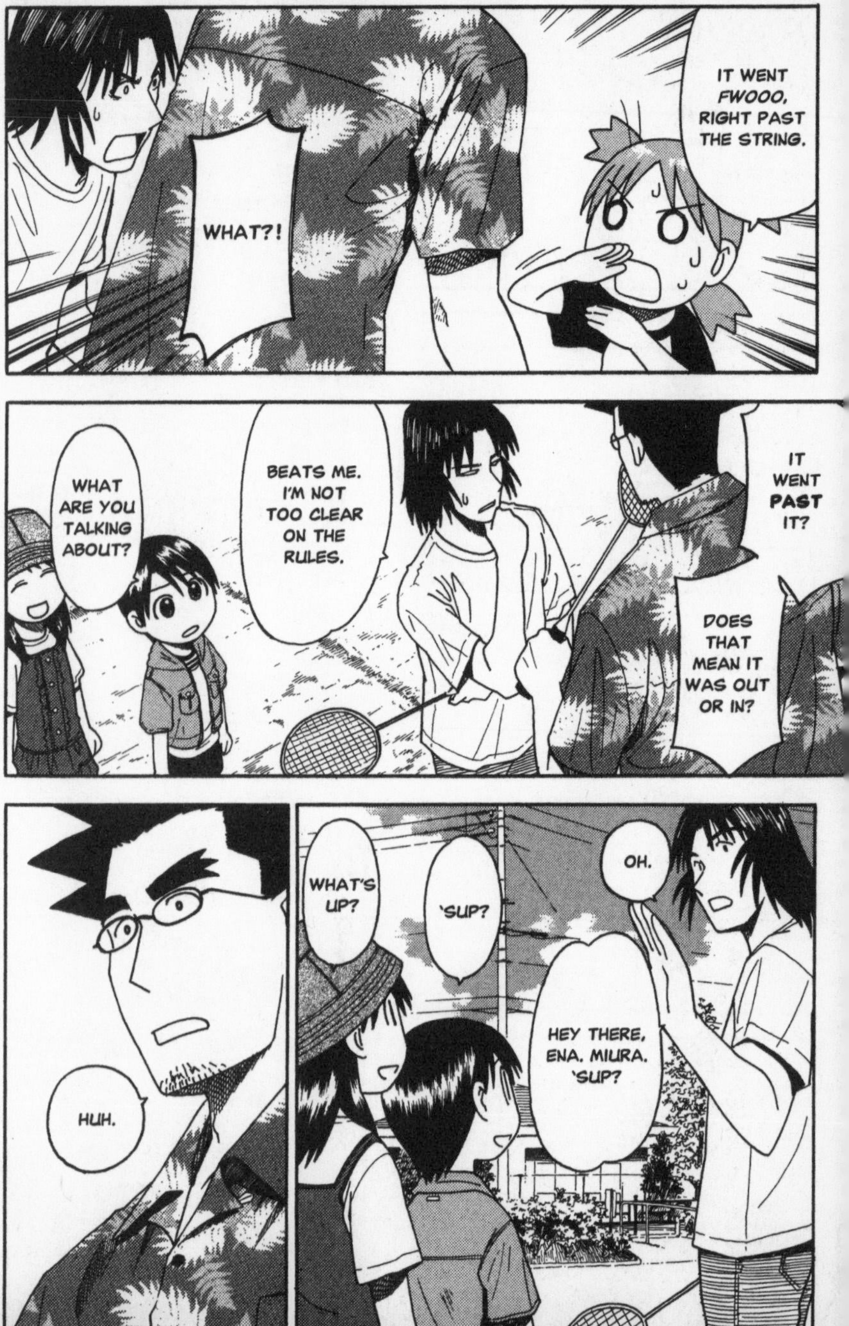
IT WENT FWOOO, RIGHT PAST THE STRING.
WHAT?!
IT WENT PAST IT?
DOES THAT MEAN IT WAS OUT OR IN?
BEATS ME. I'M NOT TOO CLEAR ON THE RULES.
WHAT ARE YOU TALKING ABOUT?
OH.
HEY THERE, ENA. MIURA. 'SUP?
'SUP?
WHAT'S UP?
HUH.

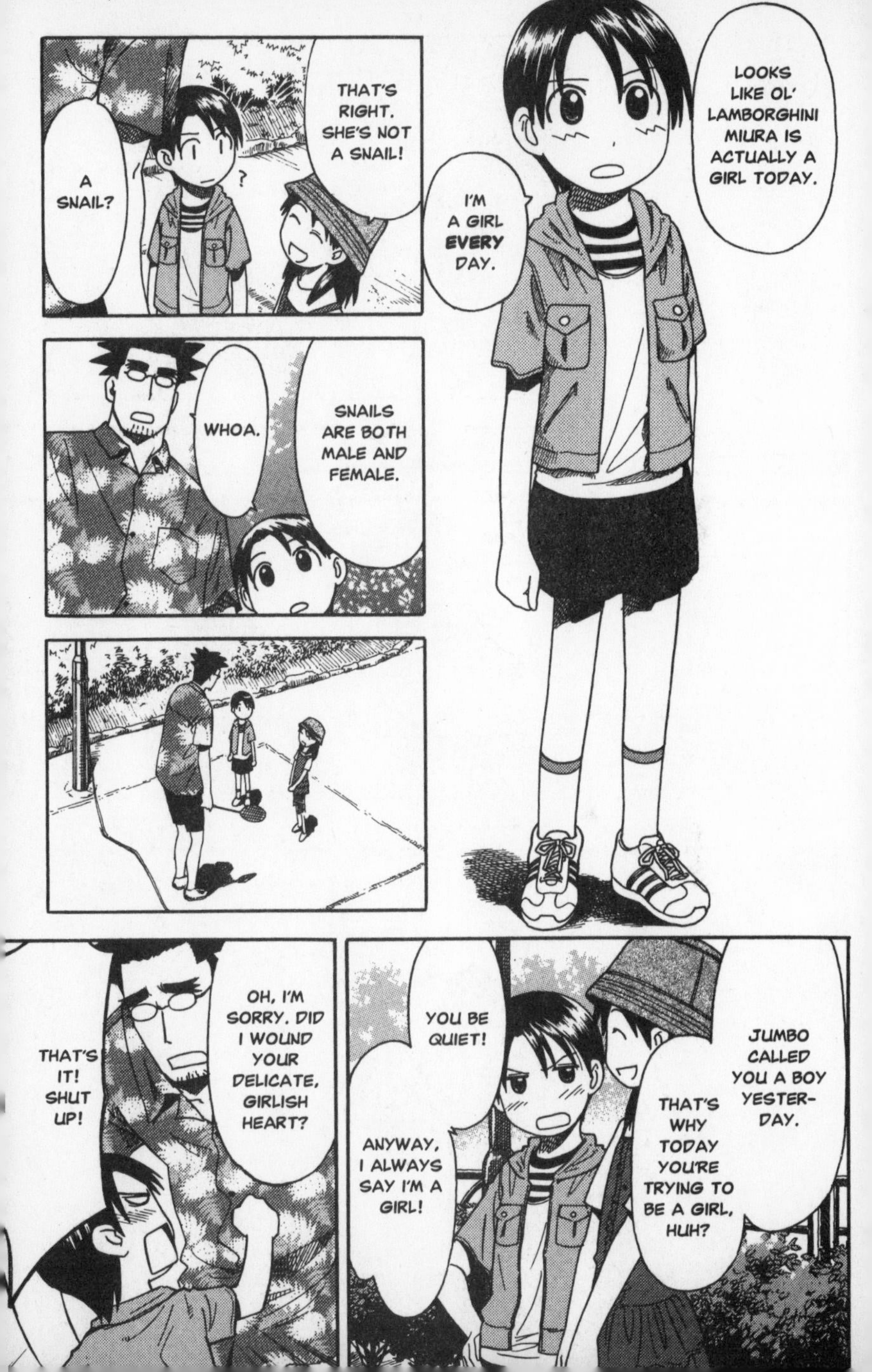
LOOKS LIKE OL' LAMBORGHINI MIURA IS ACTUALLY A GIRL TODAY.
I'M A GIRL **EVERY** DAY.
THAT'S RIGHT. SHE'S NOT A SNAIL!
A SNAIL?
?
SNAILS ARE BOTH MALE AND FEMALE.
WHOA.
JUMBO CALLED YOU A BOY YESTERDAY.
THAT'S WHY TODAY YOU'RE TRYING TO BE A GIRL, HUH?
YOU BE QUIET!
ANYWAY, I ALWAYS SAY I'M A GIRL!
OH, I'M SORRY. DID I WOUND YOUR DELICATE, GIRLISH HEART?
THAT'S IT! SHUT UP!

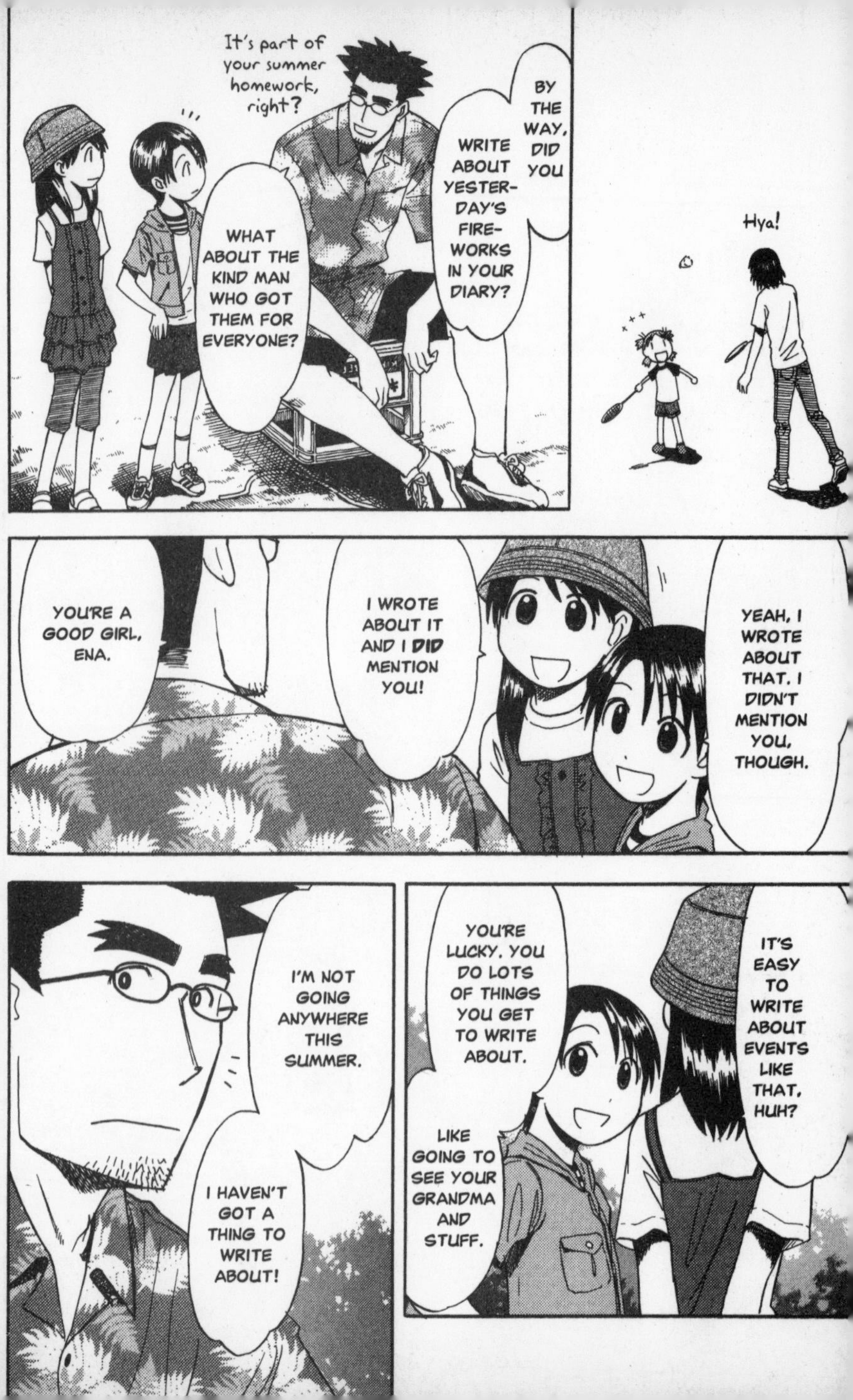
Hya!
BY THE WAY, DID YOU WRITE ABOUT YESTERDAY'S FIREWORKS IN YOUR DIARY?
It's part of your summer homework, right?
WHAT ABOUT THE KIND MAN WHO GOT THEM FOR EVERYONE?
YEAH, I WROTE ABOUT THAT. I DIDN'T MENTION YOU, THOUGH.
I WROTE ABOUT IT AND I DID MENTION YOU!
YOU'RE A GOOD GIRL, ENA.
IT'S EASY TO WRITE ABOUT EVENTS LIKE THAT, HUH?
YOU'RE LUCKY. YOU DO LOTS OF THINGS YOU GET TO WRITE ABOUT.
LIKE GOING TO SEE YOUR GRANDMA AND STUFF.
I'M NOT GOING ANYWHERE THIS SUMMER.
I HAVEN'T GOT A THING TO WRITE ABOUT!

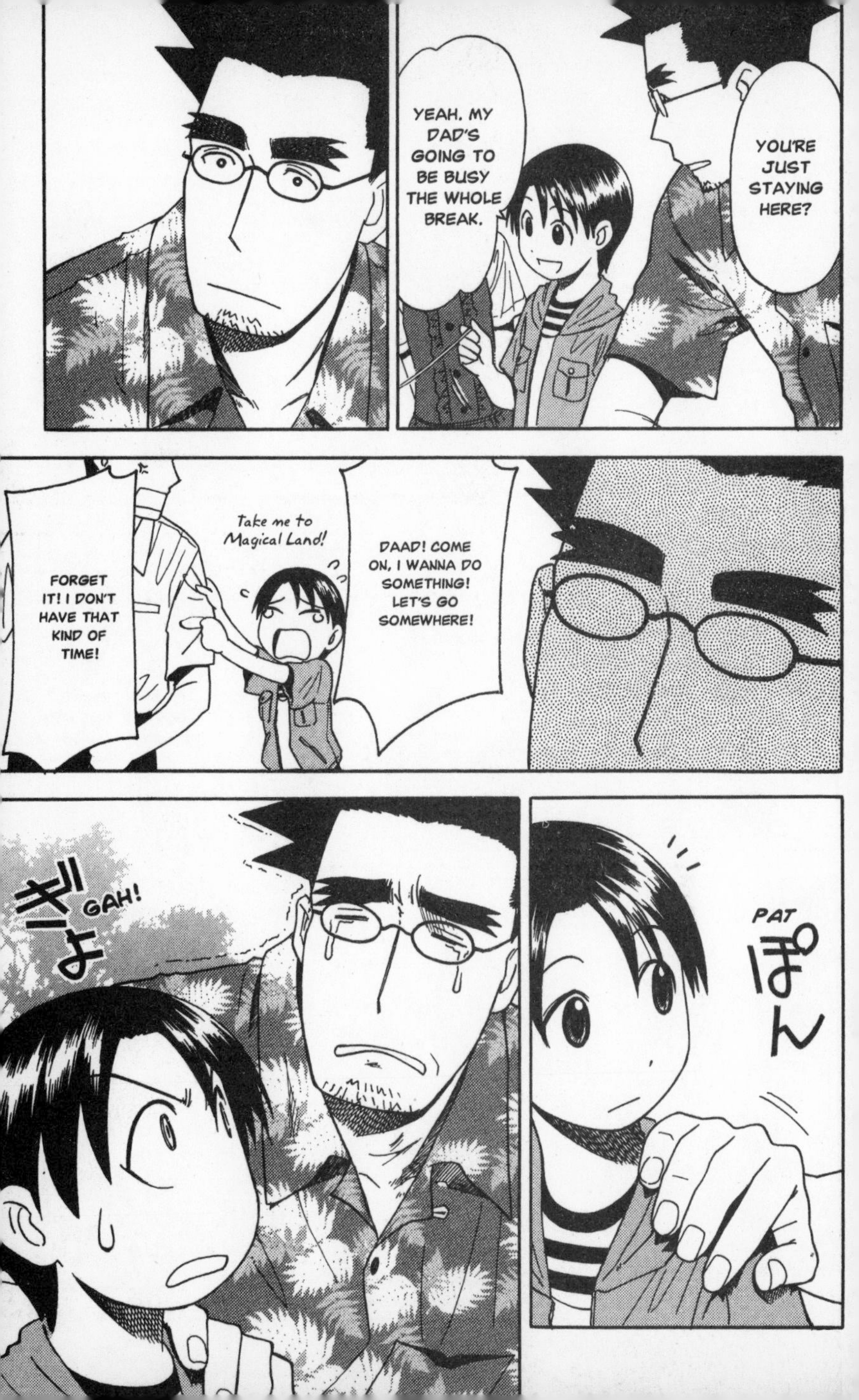
YOU'RE JUST STAYING HERE?
YEAH. MY DAD'S GOING TO BE BUSY THE WHOLE BREAK.
DAAD! COME ON, I WANNA DO SOMETHING! LET'S GO SOMEWHERE!
Take me to Magical Land!
FORGET IT! I DON'T HAVE THAT KIND OF TIME!
PAT
ぽん
ぎーよ
GAH!

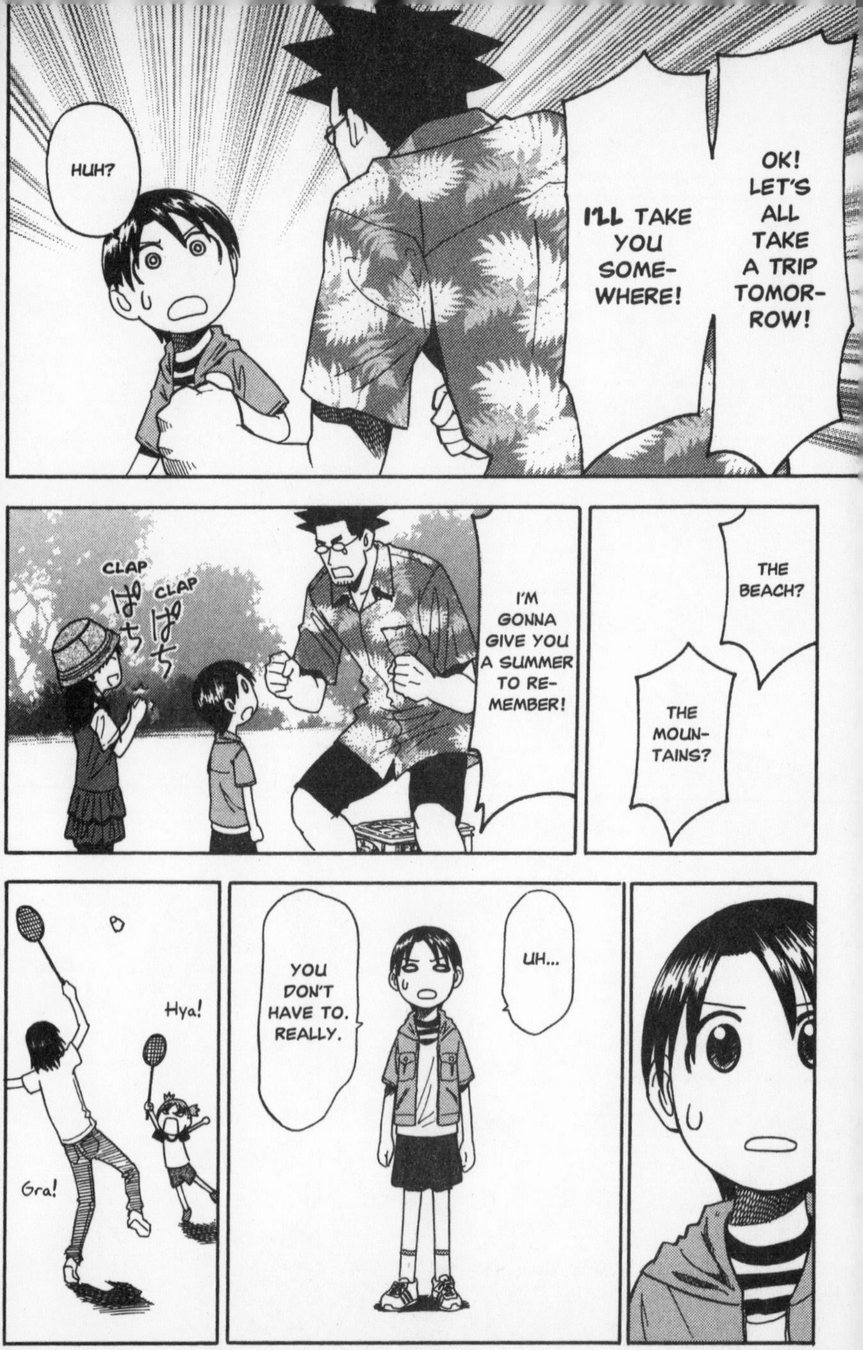
OK! LET'S ALL TAKE A TRIP TOMORROW!
I'LL TAKE YOU SOME-WHERE!
HUH?
THE BEACH?
THE MOUN-TAINS?
I'M GONNA GIVE YOU A SUMMER TO RE-MEMBER!
CLAP ぱち
CLAP ぱち
UH...
YOU DON'T HAVE TO. REALLY.
Hya!
Gra!

YOTSUBA&!

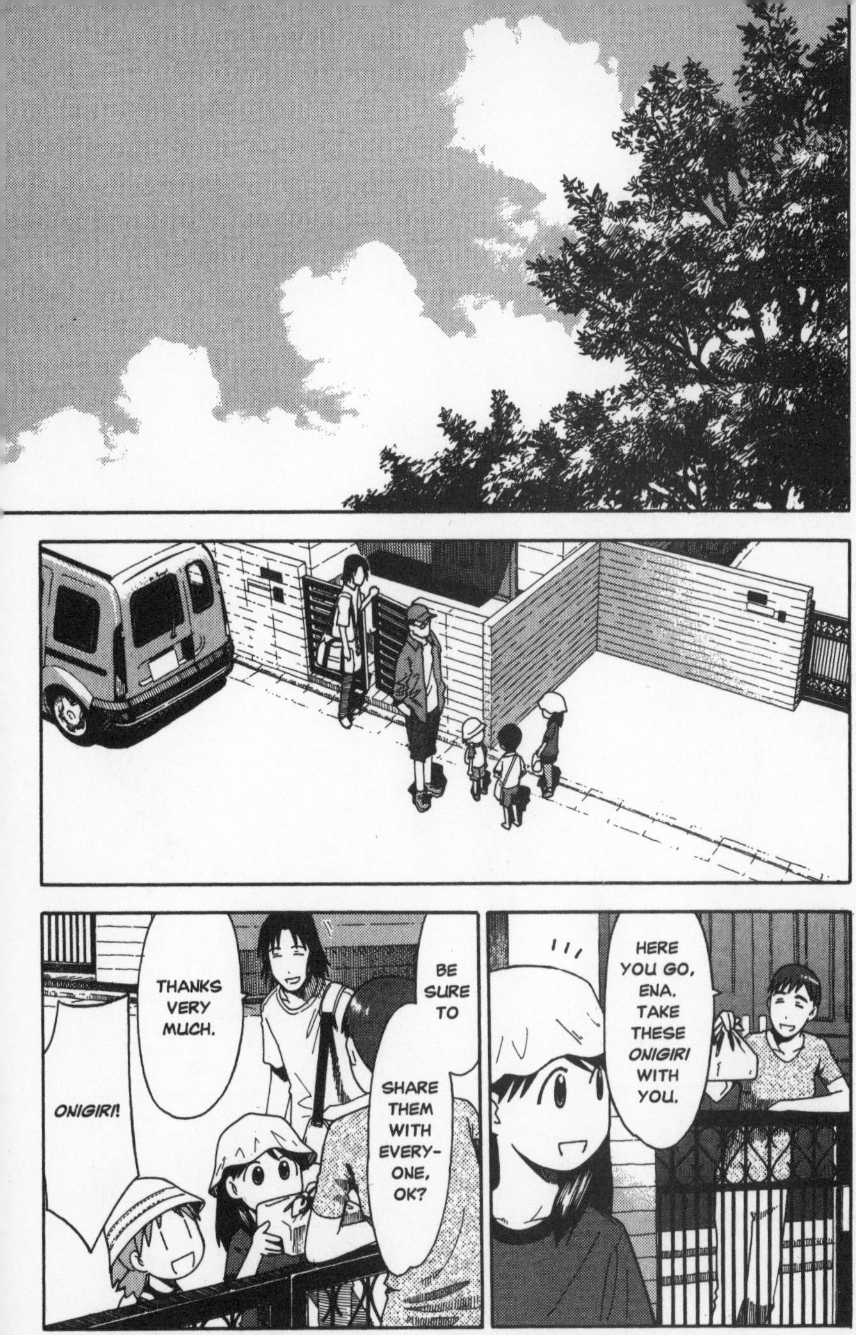
HERE YOU GO, ENA. TAKE THESE ONIGIRI WITH YOU.
BE SURE TO
SHARE THEM WITH EVERY-ONE, OK?
THANKS VERY MUCH.
ONIGIRI!

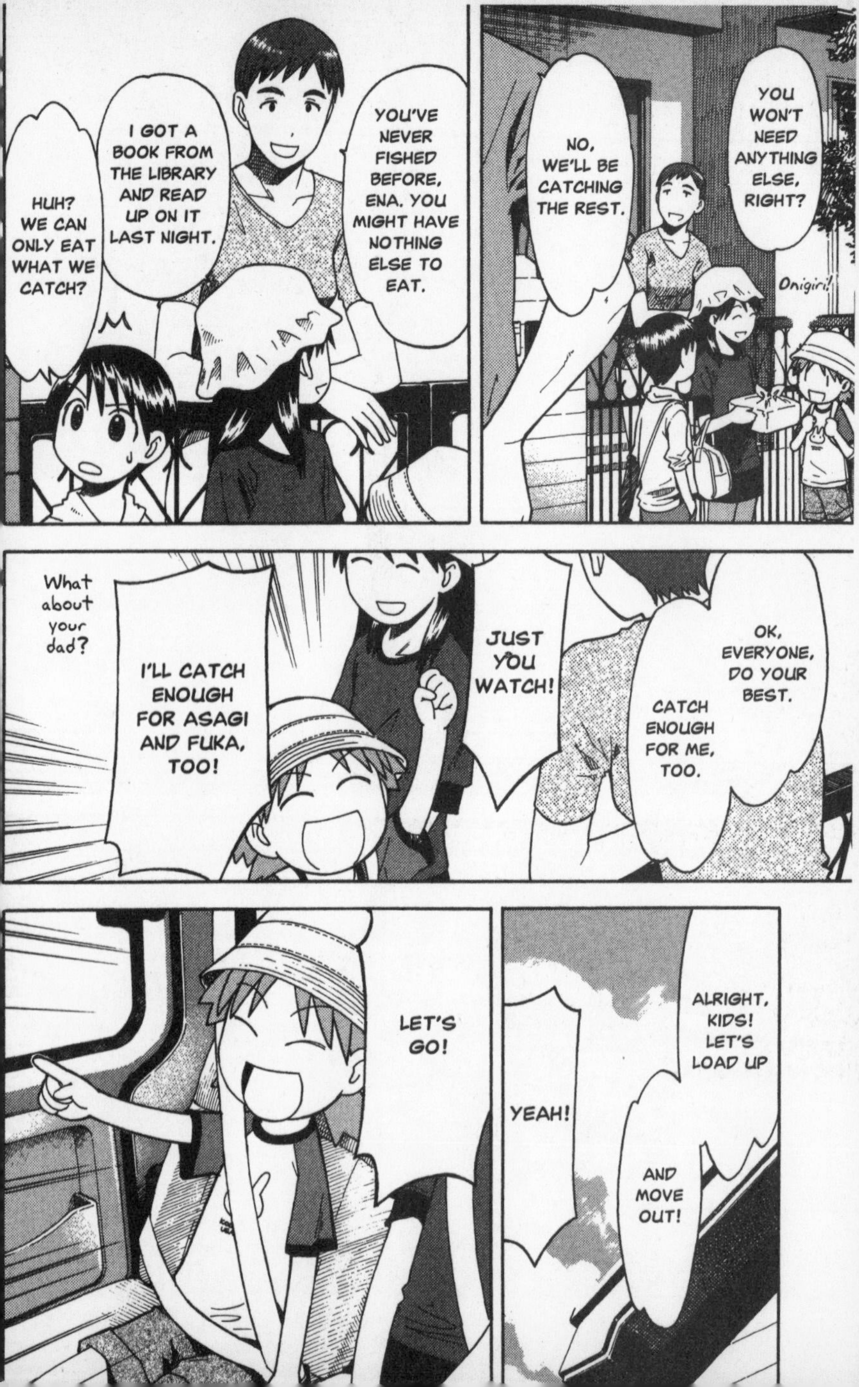
YOU WON'T NEED ANYTHING ELSE, RIGHT?
Onigiri!
NO, WE'LL BE CATCHING THE REST.
YOU'VE NEVER FISHED BEFORE, ENA. YOU MIGHT HAVE NOTHING ELSE TO EAT.
I GOT A BOOK FROM THE LIBRARY AND READ UP ON IT LAST NIGHT.
HUH? WE CAN ONLY EAT WHAT WE CATCH?
OK, EVERYONE, DO YOUR BEST.
CATCH ENOUGH FOR ME, TOO.
JUST YOU WATCH!
I'LL CATCH ENOUGH FOR ASAGI AND FUKA, TOO!
What about your dad?
ALRIGHT, KIDS! LET'S LOAD UP
AND MOVE OUT!
YEAH!
LET'S GO!

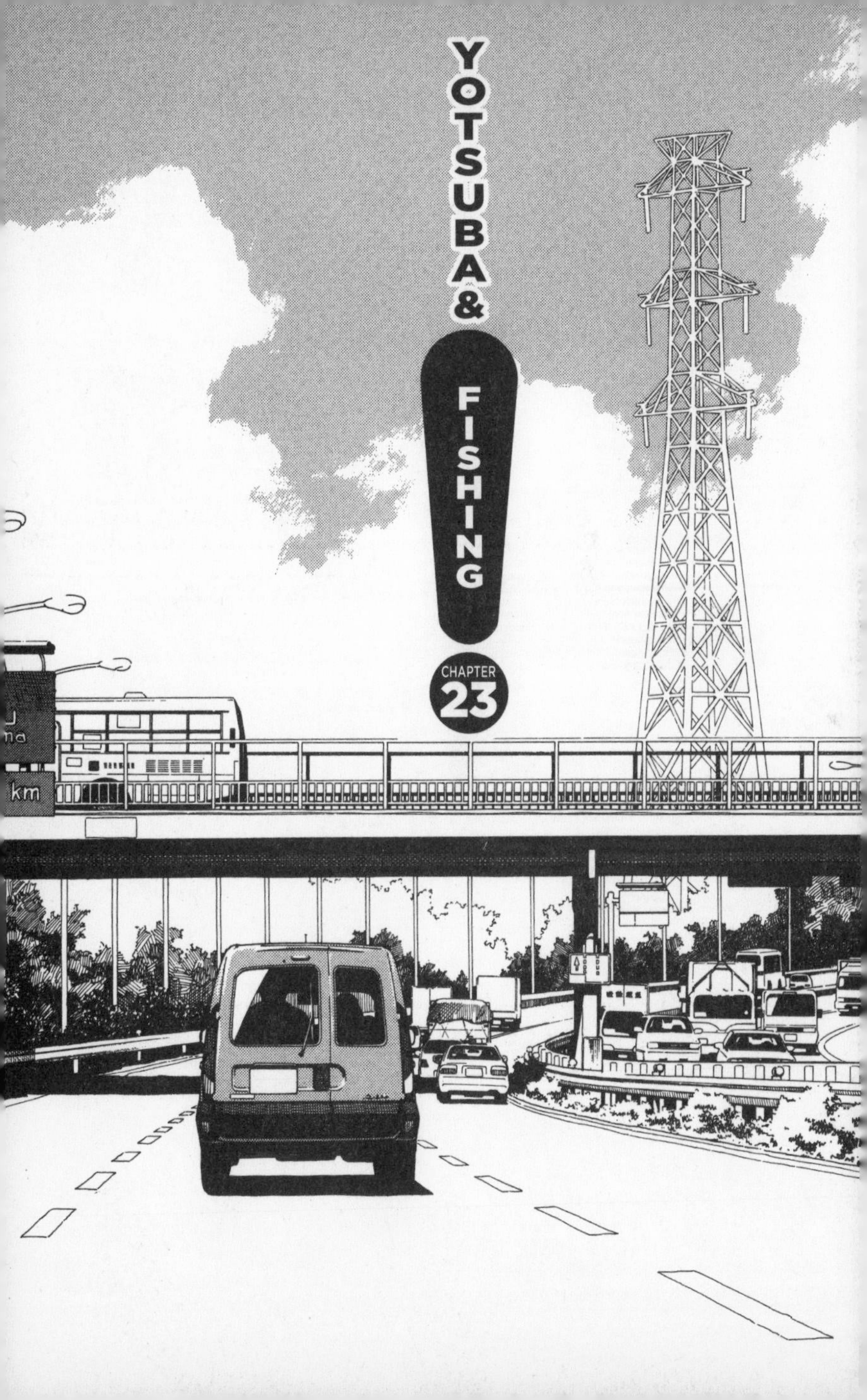
YOTSUBA&
FISHING
CHAPTER 23
km

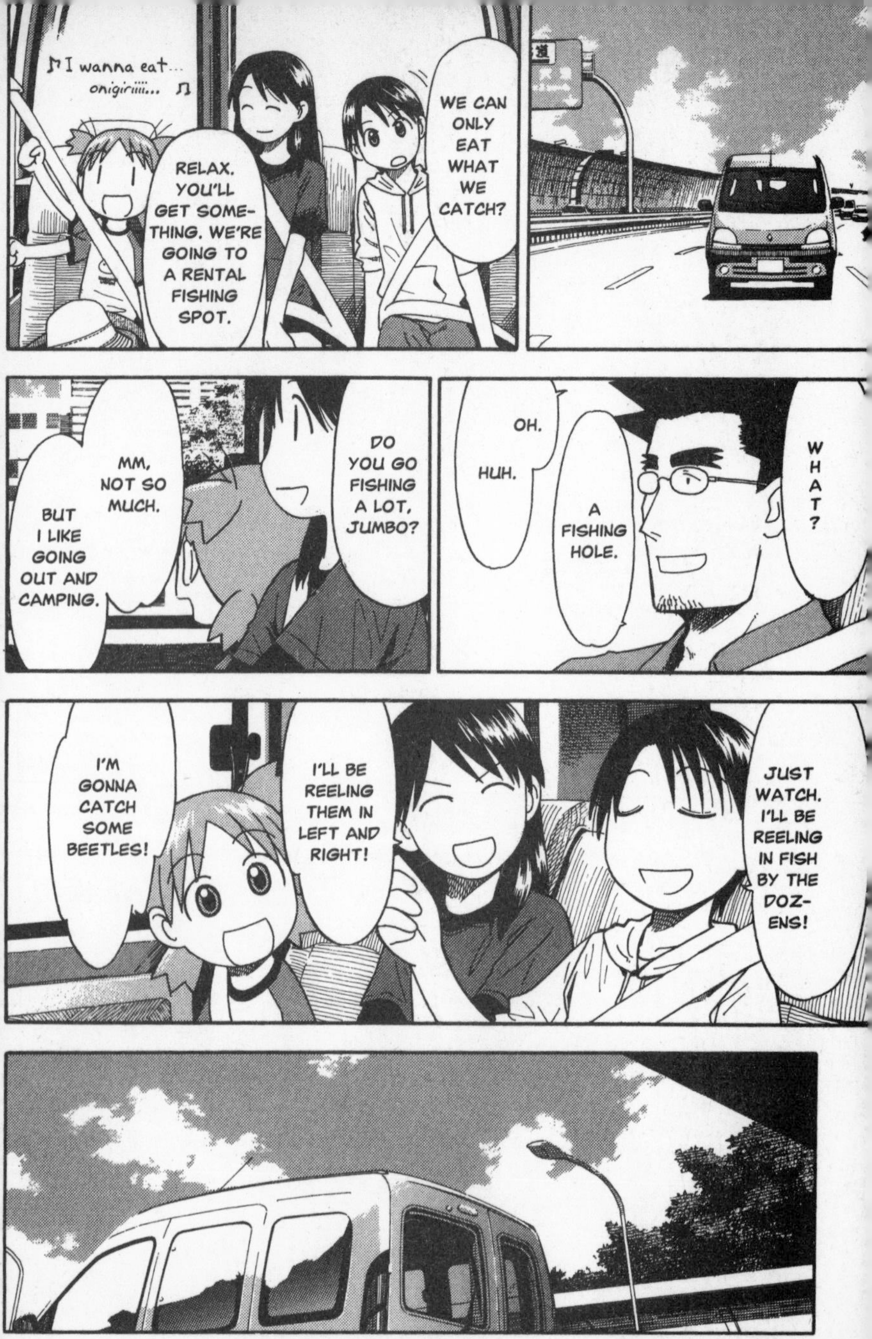
WE CAN ONLY EAT WHAT WE CATCH?
RELAX. YOU'LL GET SOMETHING. WE'RE GOING TO A RENTAL FISHING SPOT.
♪I wanna eat... onigiriiii... ♪
WHAT?
OH. HUH.
A FISHING HOLE.
DO YOU GO FISHING A LOT, JUMBO?
MM, NOT SO MUCH.
BUT I LIKE GOING OUT AND CAMPING.
JUST WATCH. I'LL BE REELING IN FISH BY THE DOZENS!
I'LL BE REELING THEM IN LEFT AND RIGHT!
I'M GONNA CATCH SOME BEETLES!

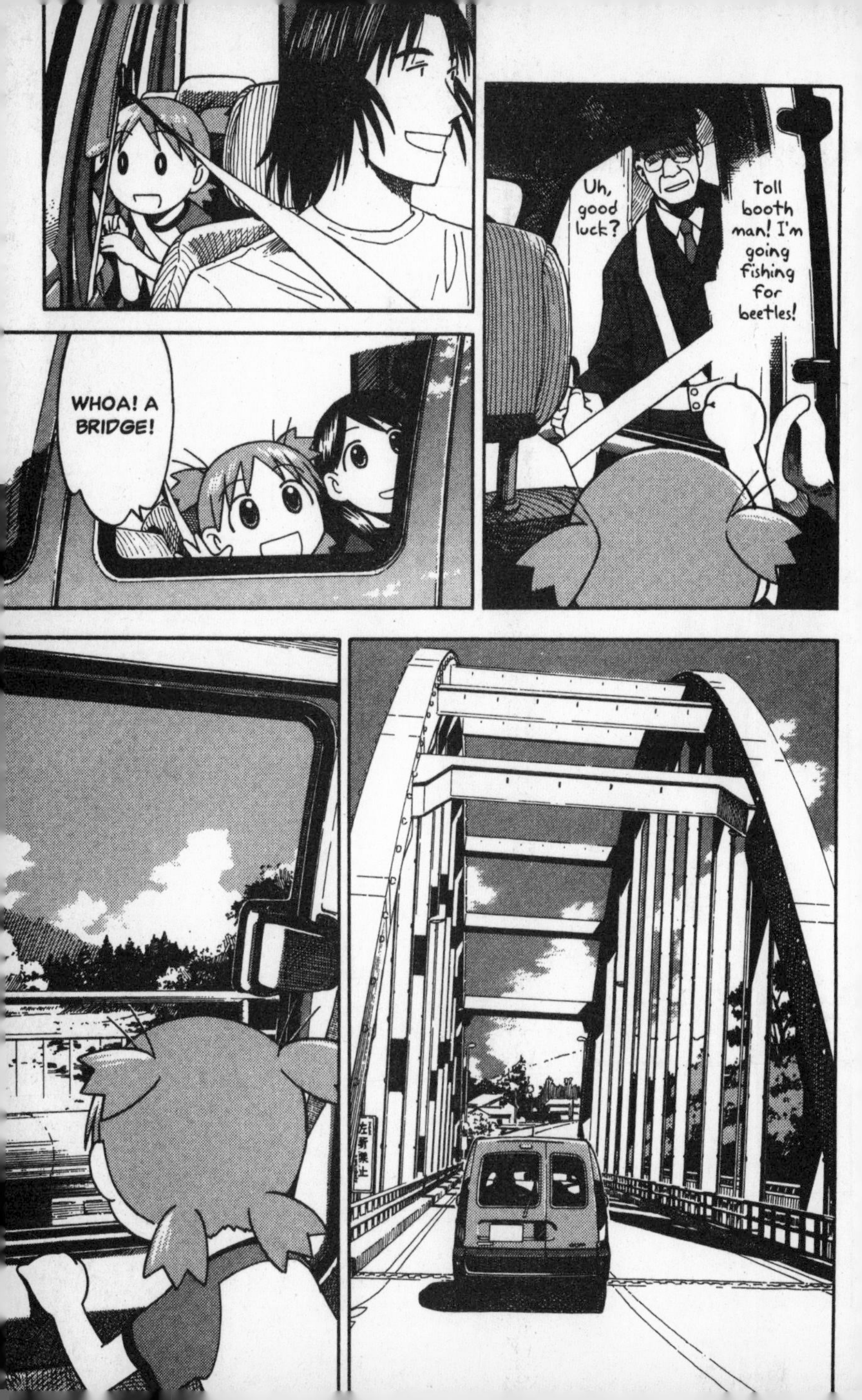
Toll booth man! I'm going fishing for beetles!
Uh, good luck?
WHOA! A BRIDGE!
左折禁止

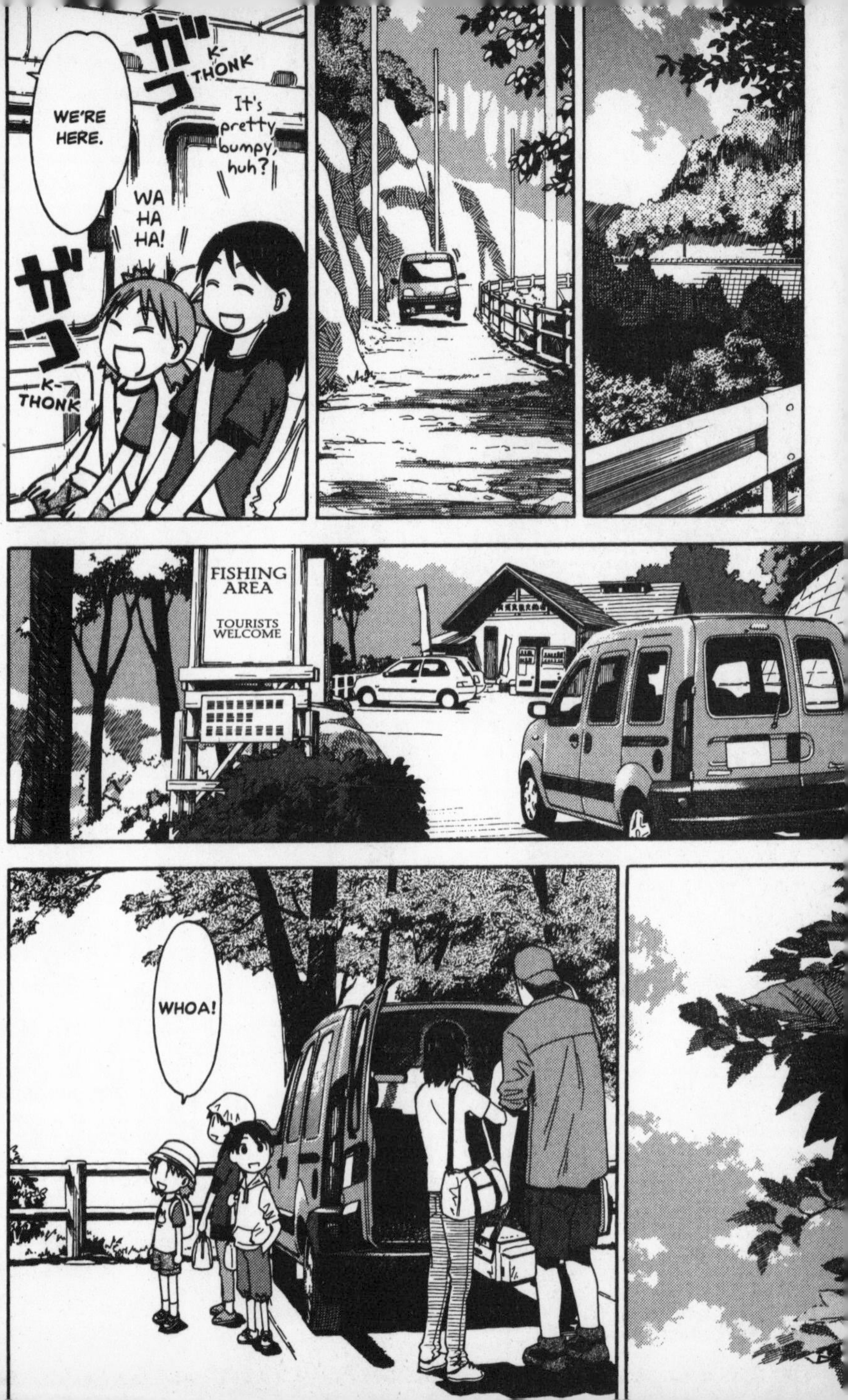

ガコ
K-THONK
It's pretty bumpy, huh?
WE'RE HERE.
WA HA HA!
ガコ
K-THONK
FISHING AREA
TOURISTS WELCOME
WHOA!

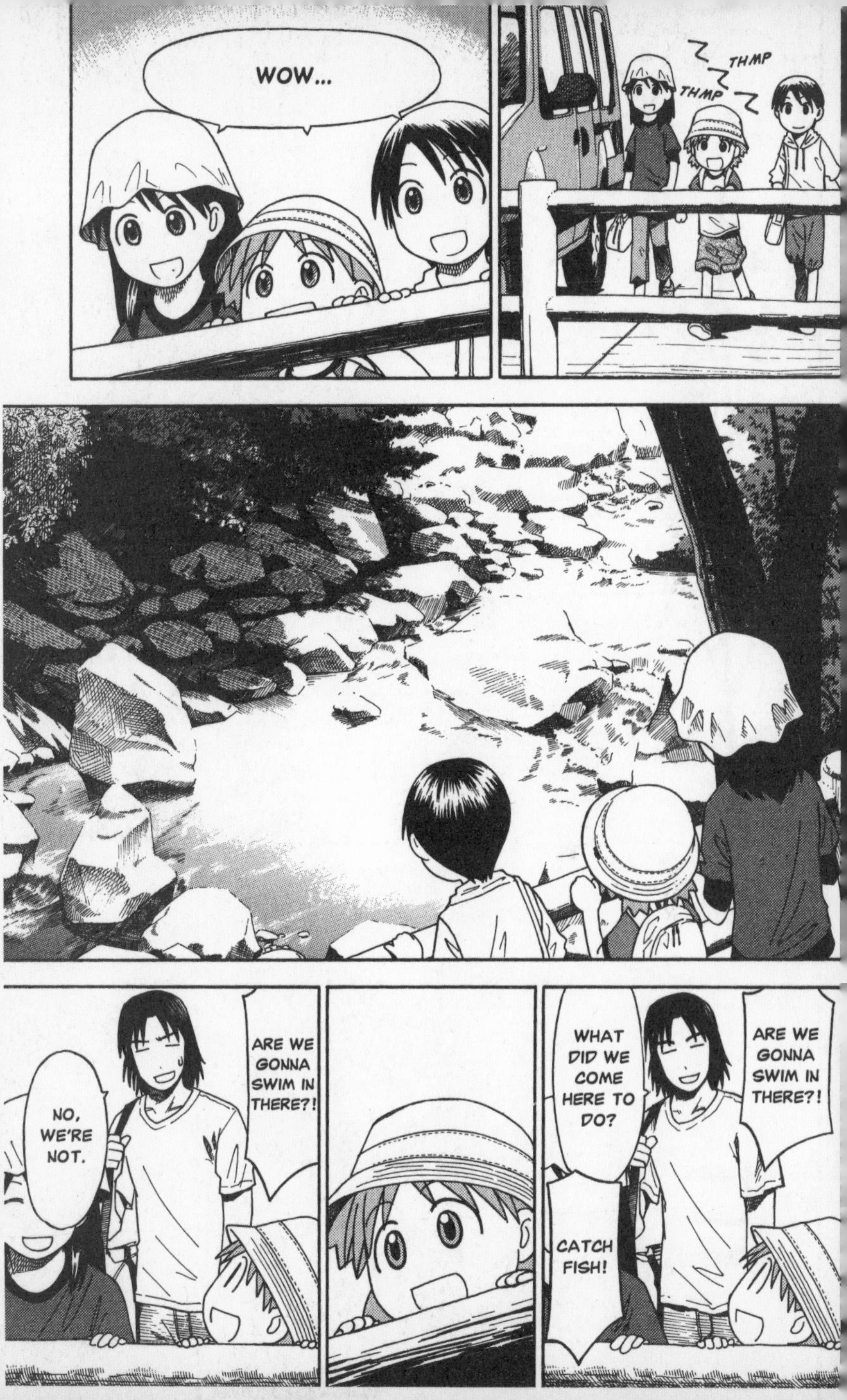
THMP
THMP
WOW...
ARE WE GONNA SWIM IN THERE?!
WHAT DID WE COME HERE TO DO?
CATCH FISH!
ARE WE GONNA SWIM IN THERE?!
NO, WE'RE NOT.

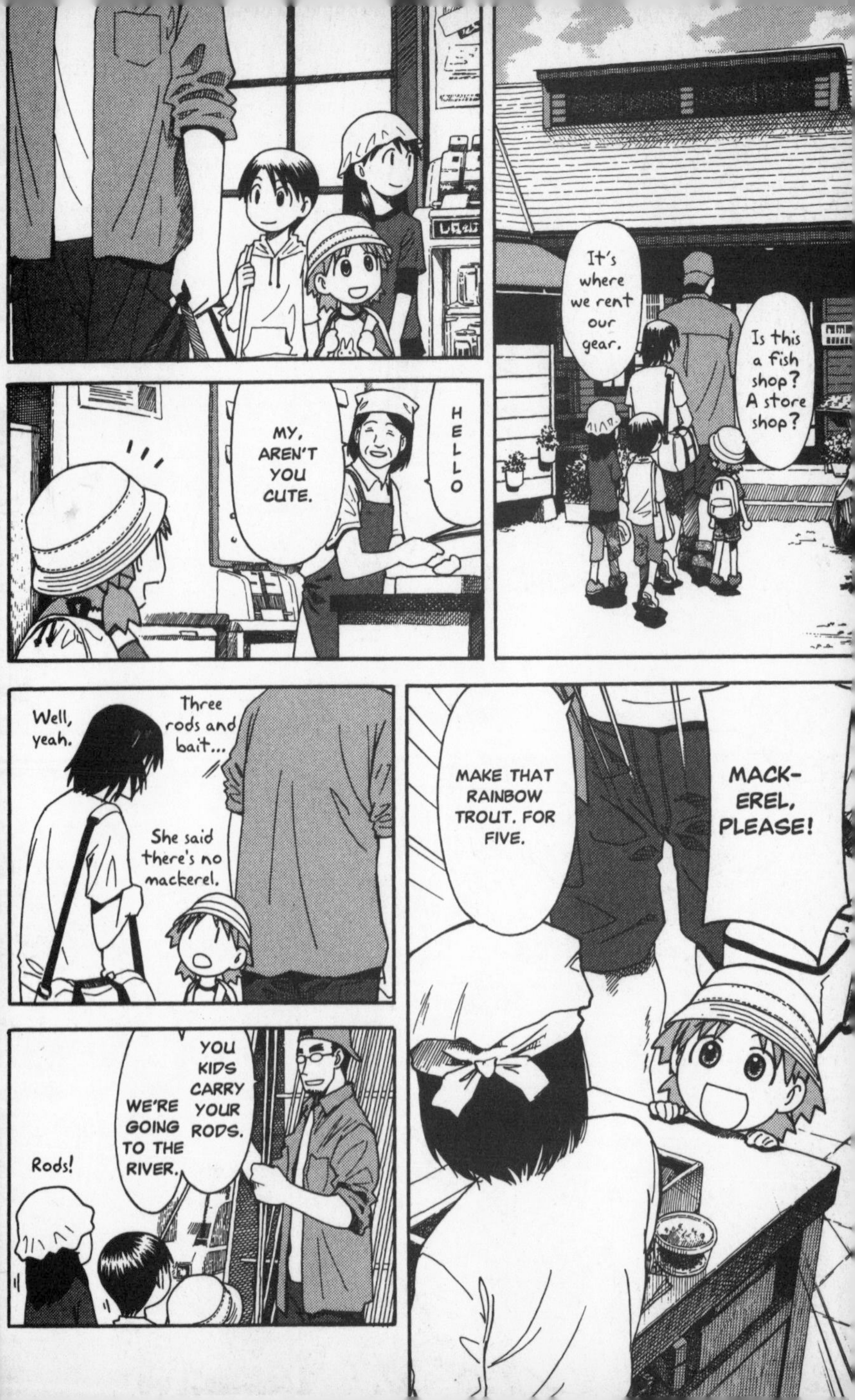

Is this a fish shop? A store shop?
It's where we rent our gear.
HELLO
MY, AREN'T YOU CUTE.
MACK-EREL, PLEASE!
MAKE THAT RAINBOW TROUT. FOR FIVE.
Three rods and bait...
Well, yeah.
She said there's no mackerel.
YOU KIDS CARRY YOUR RODS.
WE'RE GOING TO THE RIVER.
Rods!

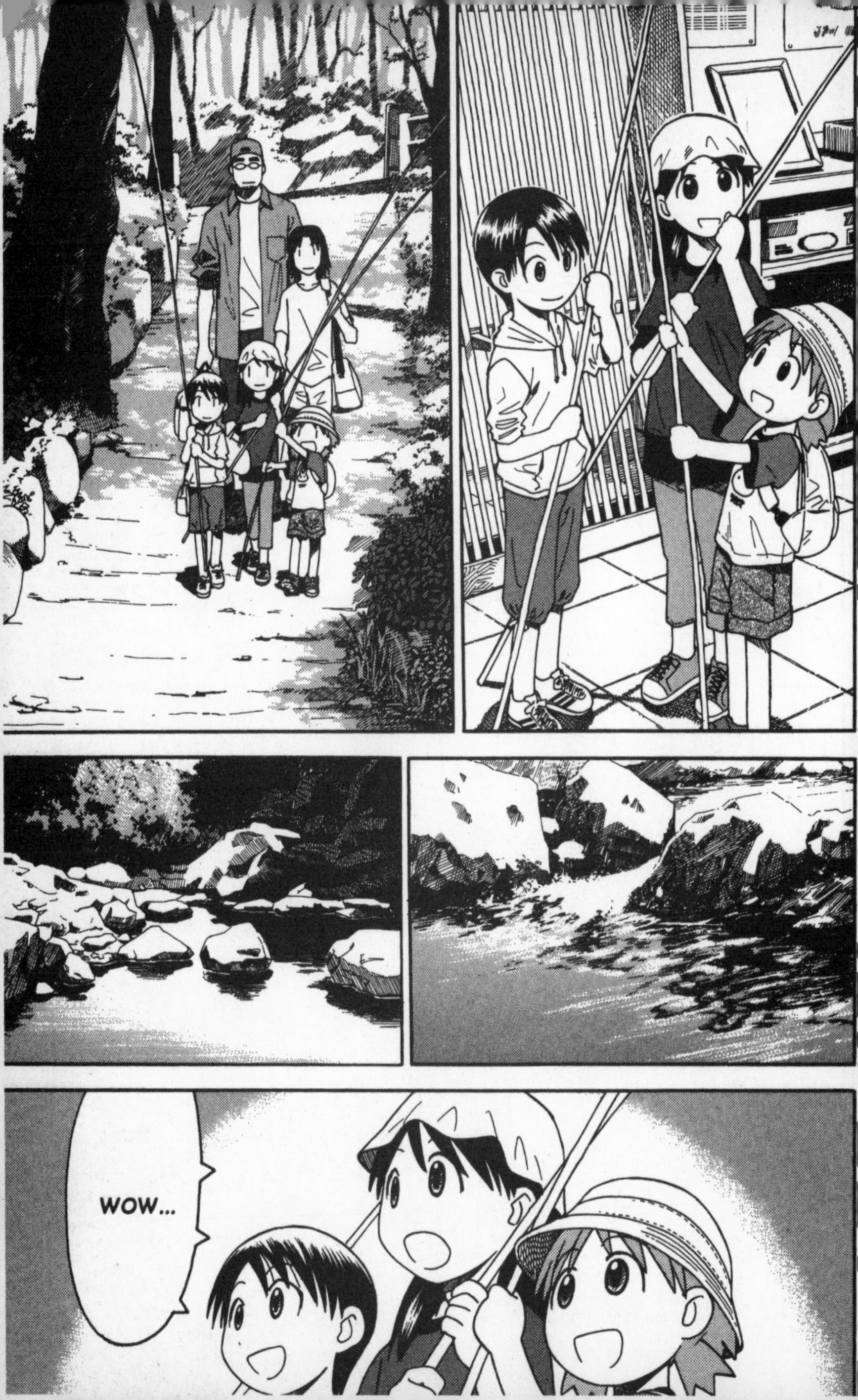
WOW...

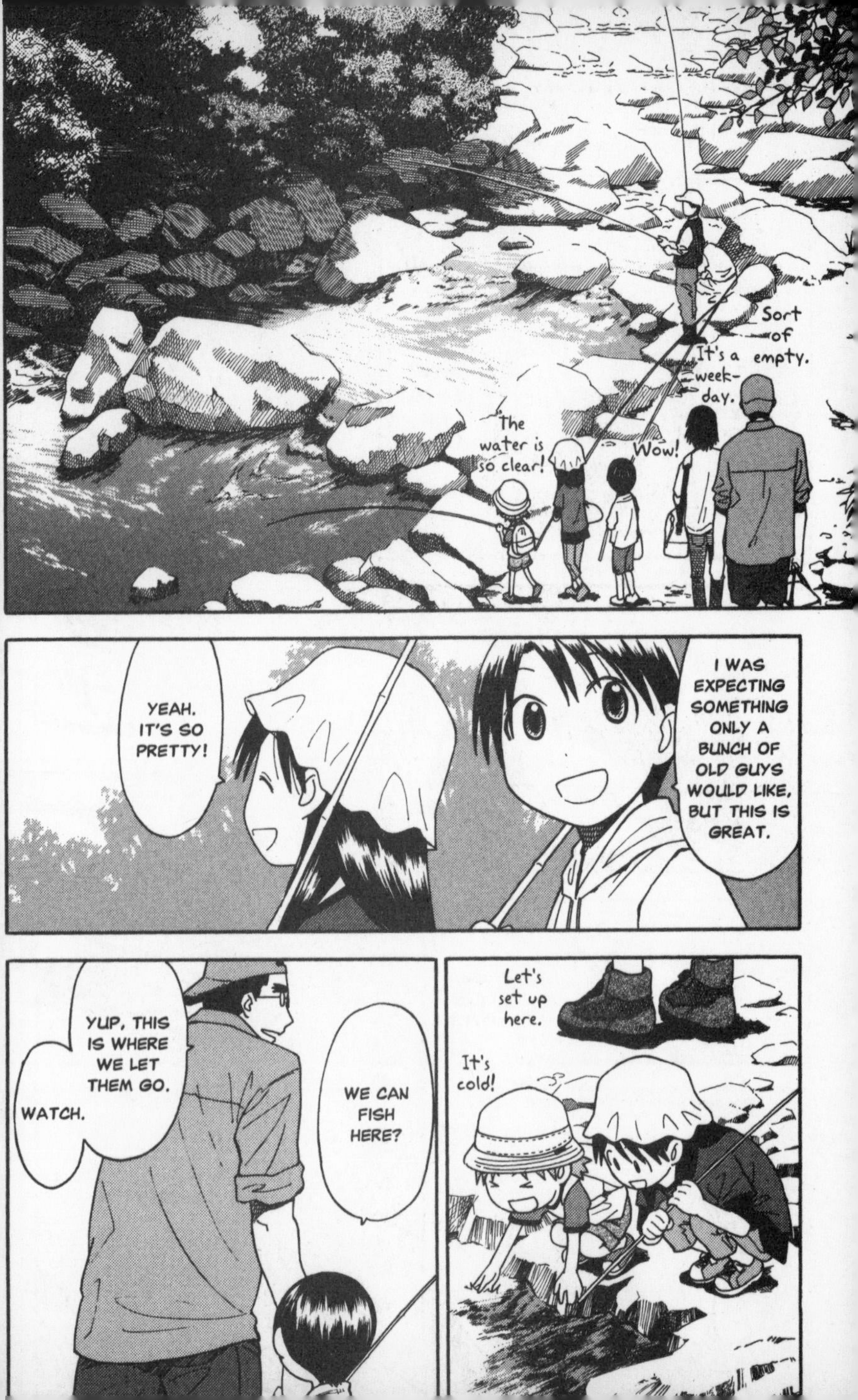

Sort of empty.
It's a week-day.
Wow!
The water is so clear!
I WAS EXPECTING SOMETHING ONLY A BUNCH OF OLD GUYS WOULD LIKE, BUT THIS IS GREAT.
YEAH. IT'S SO PRETTY!
Let's set up here.
It's cold!
WE CAN FISH HERE?
YUP, THIS IS WHERE WE LET THEM GO.
WATCH.

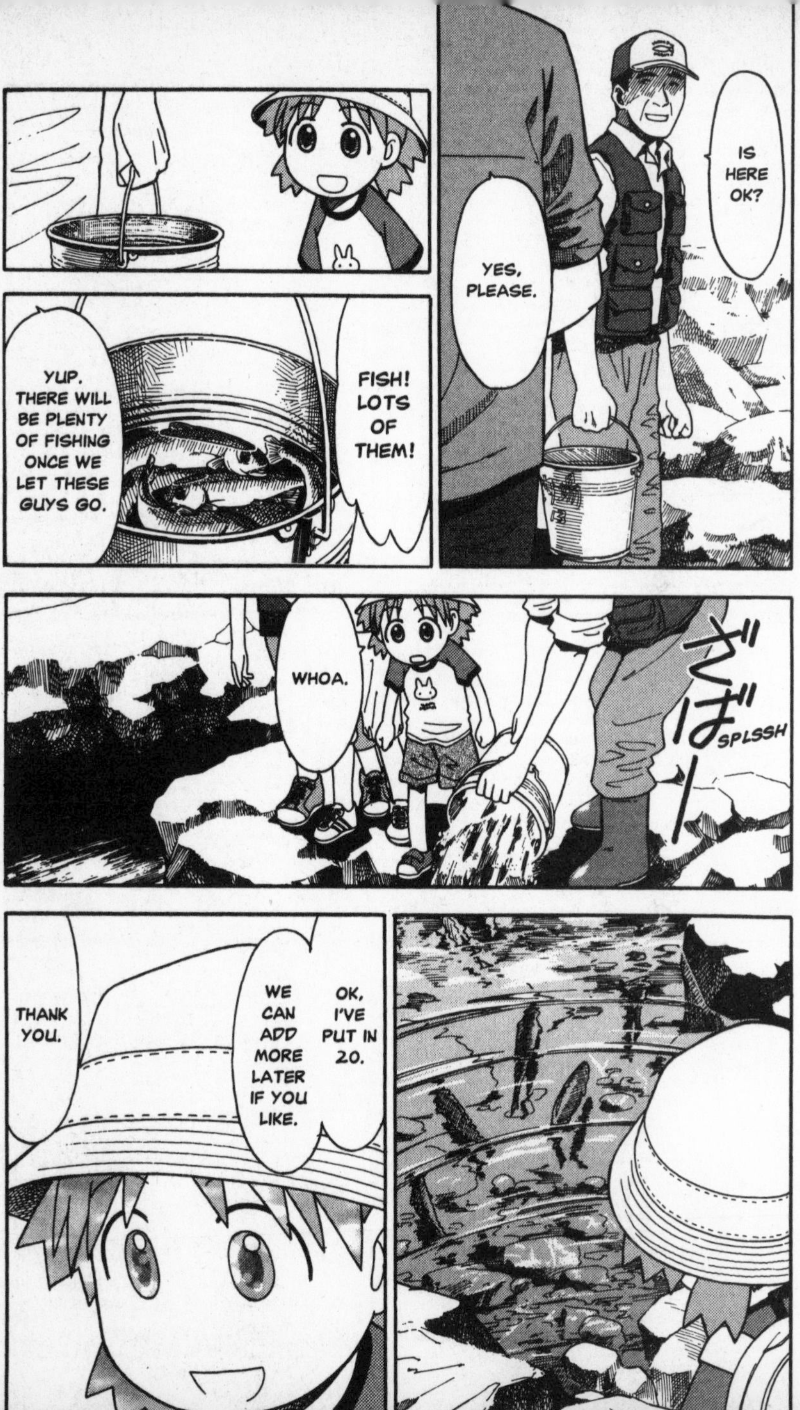
IS HERE OK?
YES, PLEASE.
FISH! LOTS OF THEM!
YUP. THERE WILL BE PLENTY OF FISHING ONCE WE LET THESE GUYS GO.
ざばー
SPLSSH
WHOA.
OK, I'VE PUT IN 20.
WE CAN ADD MORE LATER IF YOU LIKE.
THANK YOU.

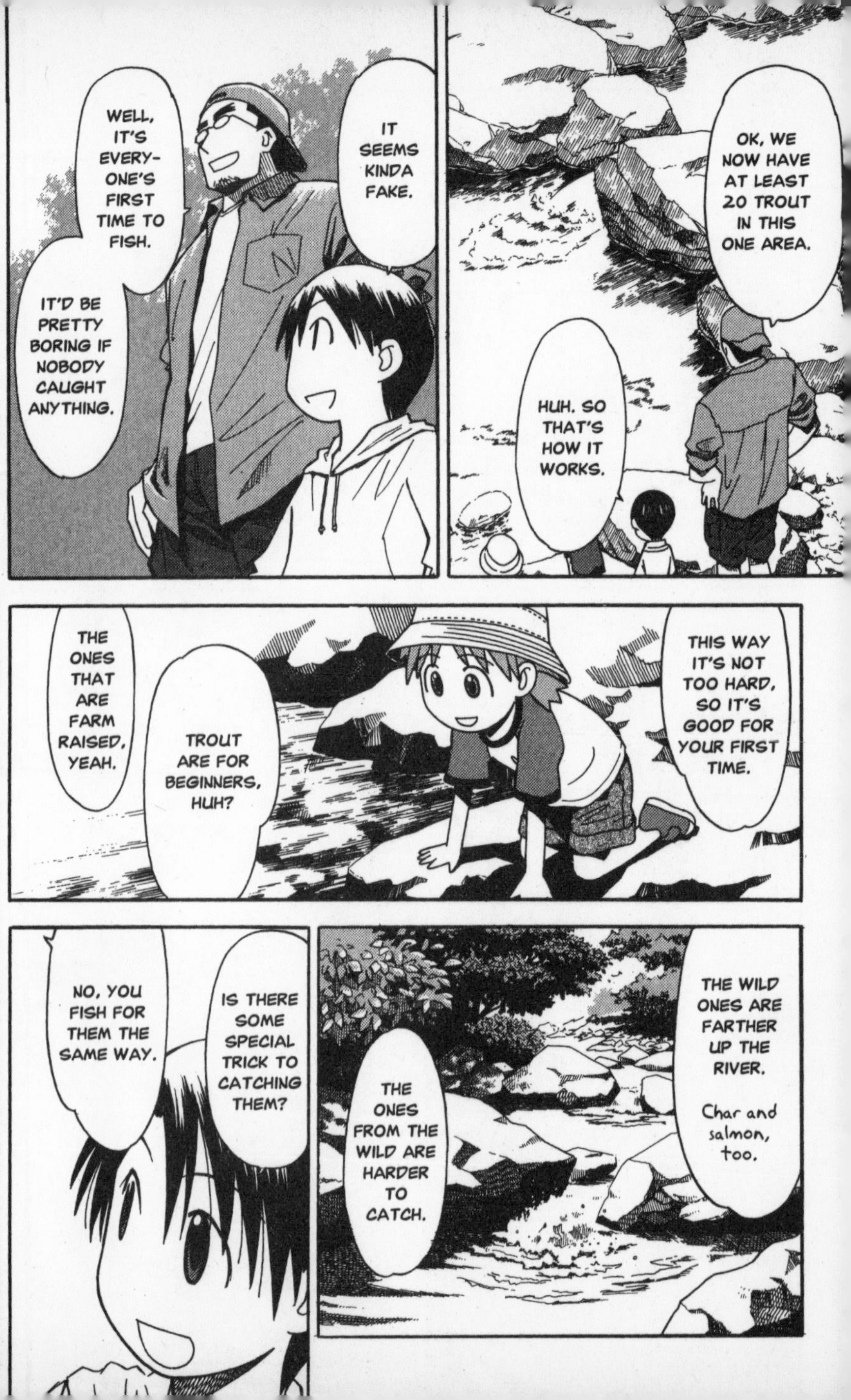
OK, WE NOW HAVE AT LEAST 20 TROUT IN THIS ONE AREA.
HUH. SO THAT'S HOW IT WORKS.
IT SEEMS KINDA FAKE.
WELL, IT'S EVERY-ONE'S FIRST TIME TO FISH.
IT'D BE PRETTY BORING IF NOBODY CAUGHT ANYTHING.
THIS WAY IT'S NOT TOO HARD, SO IT'S GOOD FOR YOUR FIRST TIME.
TROUT ARE FOR BEGINNERS, HUH?
THE ONES THAT ARE FARM RAISED, YEAH.
THE WILD ONES ARE FARTHER UP THE RIVER.
Char and salmon, too.
THE ONES FROM THE WILD ARE HARDER TO CATCH.
IS THERE SOME SPECIAL TRICK TO CATCHING THEM?
NO, YOU FISH FOR THEM THE SAME WAY.

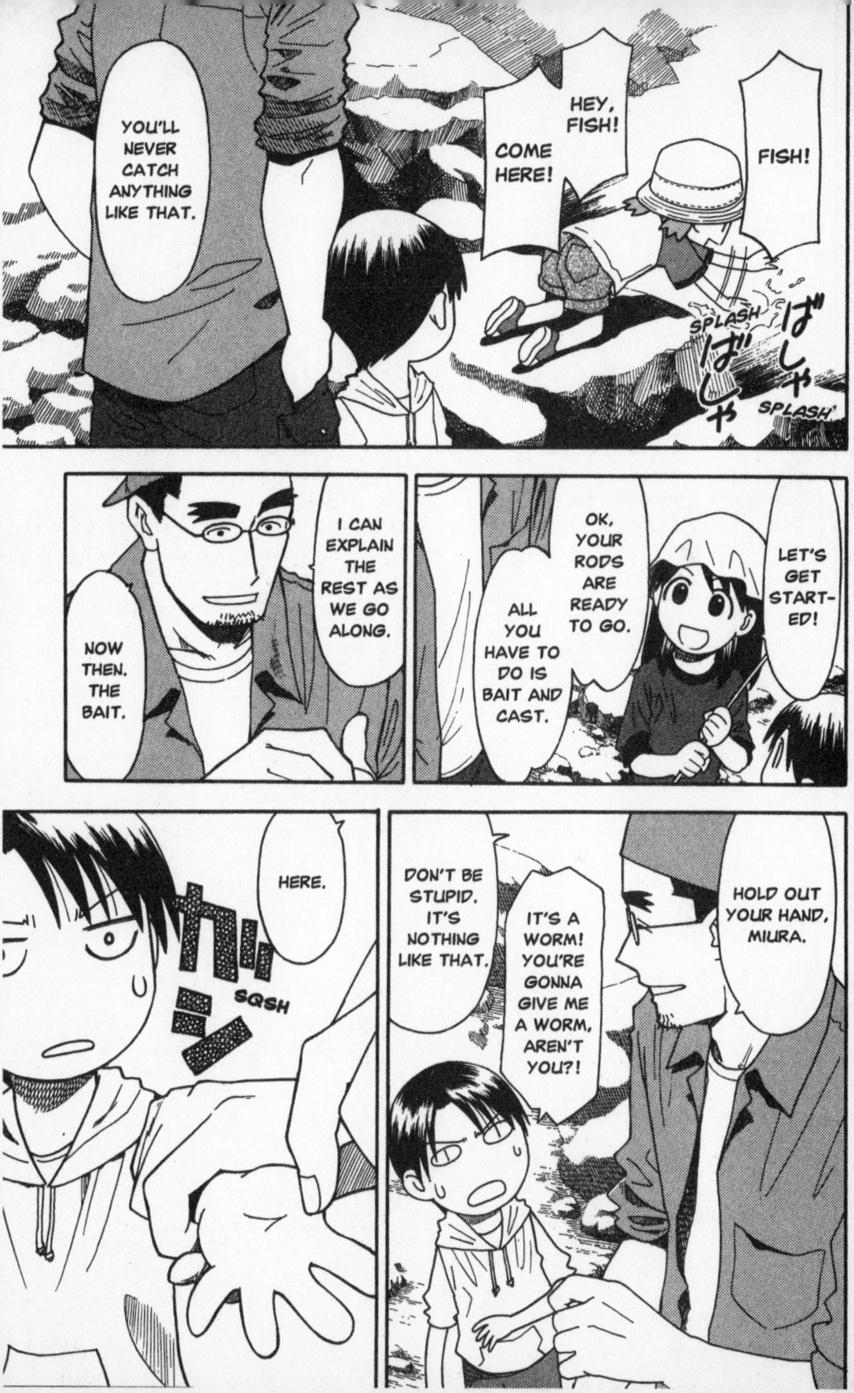
FISH!
HEY, FISH!
COME HERE!
ばしゃ SPLASH
ばしゃ SPLASH
YOU'LL NEVER CATCH ANYTHING LIKE THAT.
LET'S GET START-ED!
OK, YOUR RODS ARE READY TO GO.
ALL YOU HAVE TO DO IS BAIT AND CAST.
I CAN EXPLAIN THE REST AS WE GO ALONG.
NOW THEN. THE BAIT.
HOLD OUT YOUR HAND, MIURA.
IT'S A WORM! YOU'RE GONNA GIVE ME A WORM, AREN'T YOU?!
DON'T BE STUPID. IT'S NOTHING LIKE THAT.
HERE.
SQSH

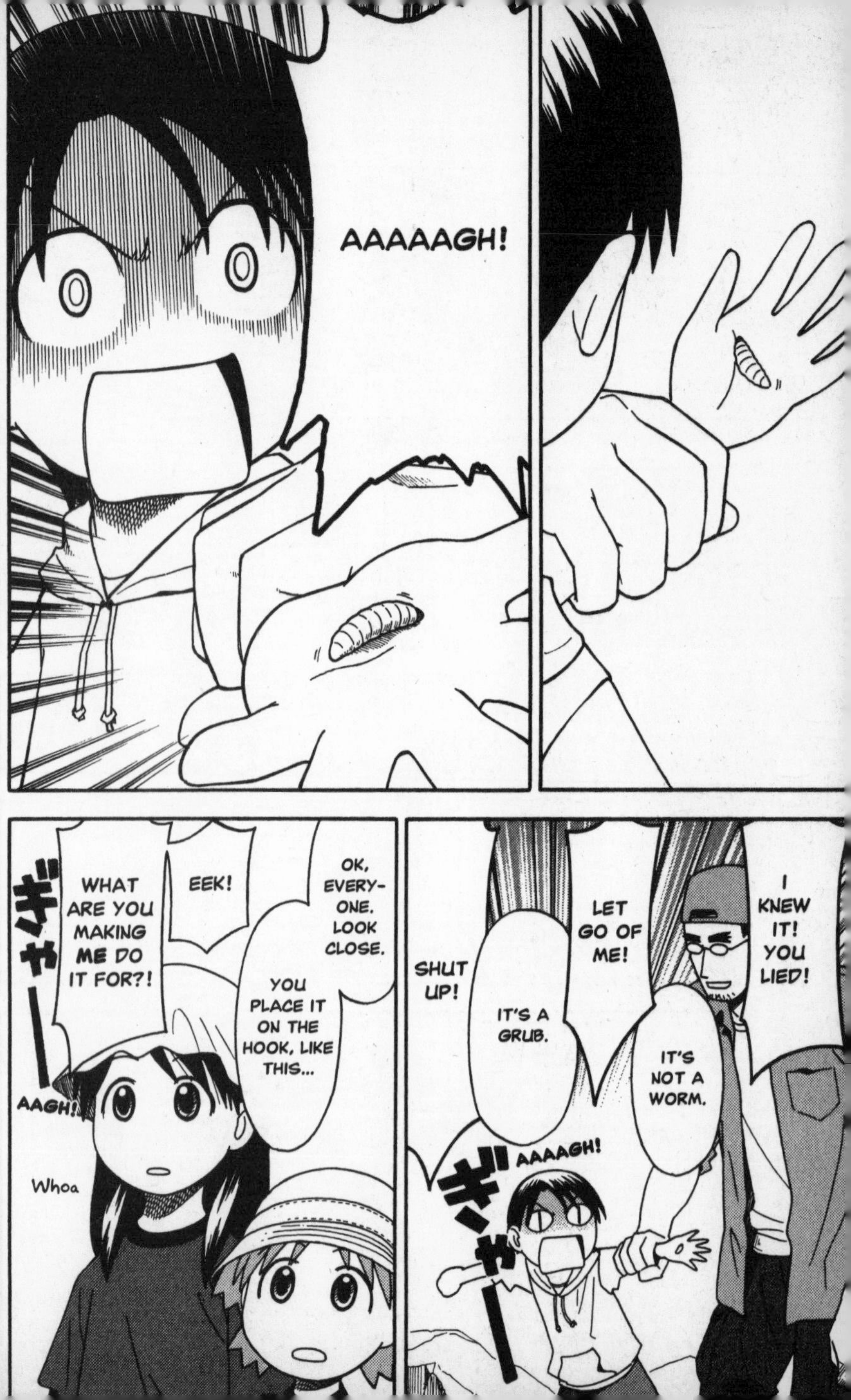
AAAAAGH!
I KNEW IT! YOU LIED!
LET GO OF ME!
IT'S NOT A WORM.
IT'S A GRUB.
SHUT UP!
ギャー
AAAAGH!
OK, EVERY-ONE. LOOK CLOSE.
YOU PLACE IT ON THE HOOK, LIKE THIS...
EEK!
WHAT ARE YOU MAKING ME DO IT FOR?!
ギャー
AAGH!
Whoa

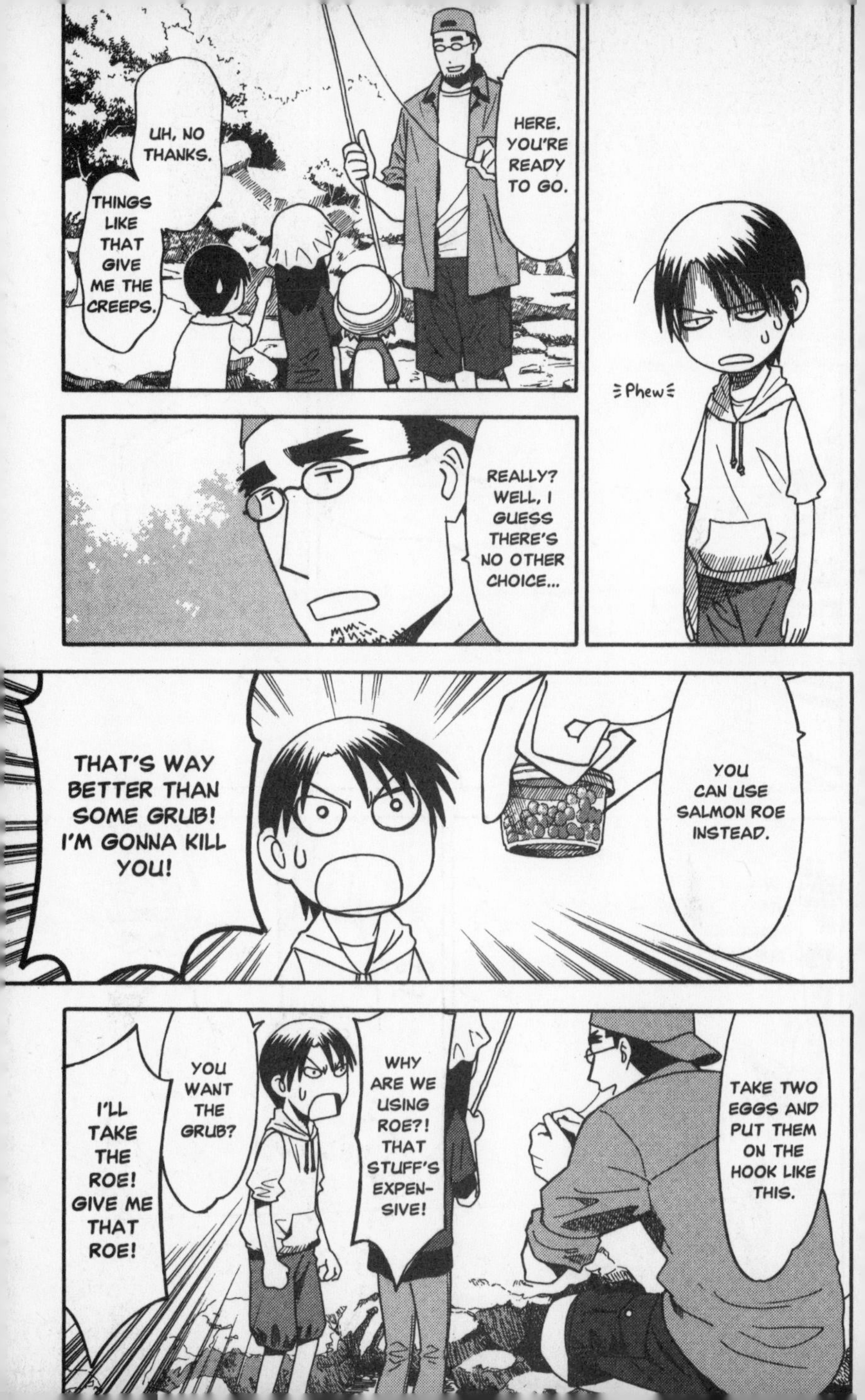

Phew
HERE. YOU'RE READY TO GO.
UH, NO THANKS.
THINGS LIKE THAT GIVE ME THE CREEPS.
REALLY? WELL, I GUESS THERE'S NO OTHER CHOICE...
YOU CAN USE SALMON ROE INSTEAD.
THAT'S WAY BETTER THAN SOME GRUB! I'M GONNA KILL YOU!
TAKE TWO EGGS AND PUT THEM ON THE HOOK LIKE THIS.
WHY ARE WE USING ROE?! THAT STUFF'S EXPEN-SIVE!
YOU WANT THE GRUB?
I'LL TAKE THE ROE! GIVE ME THAT ROE!

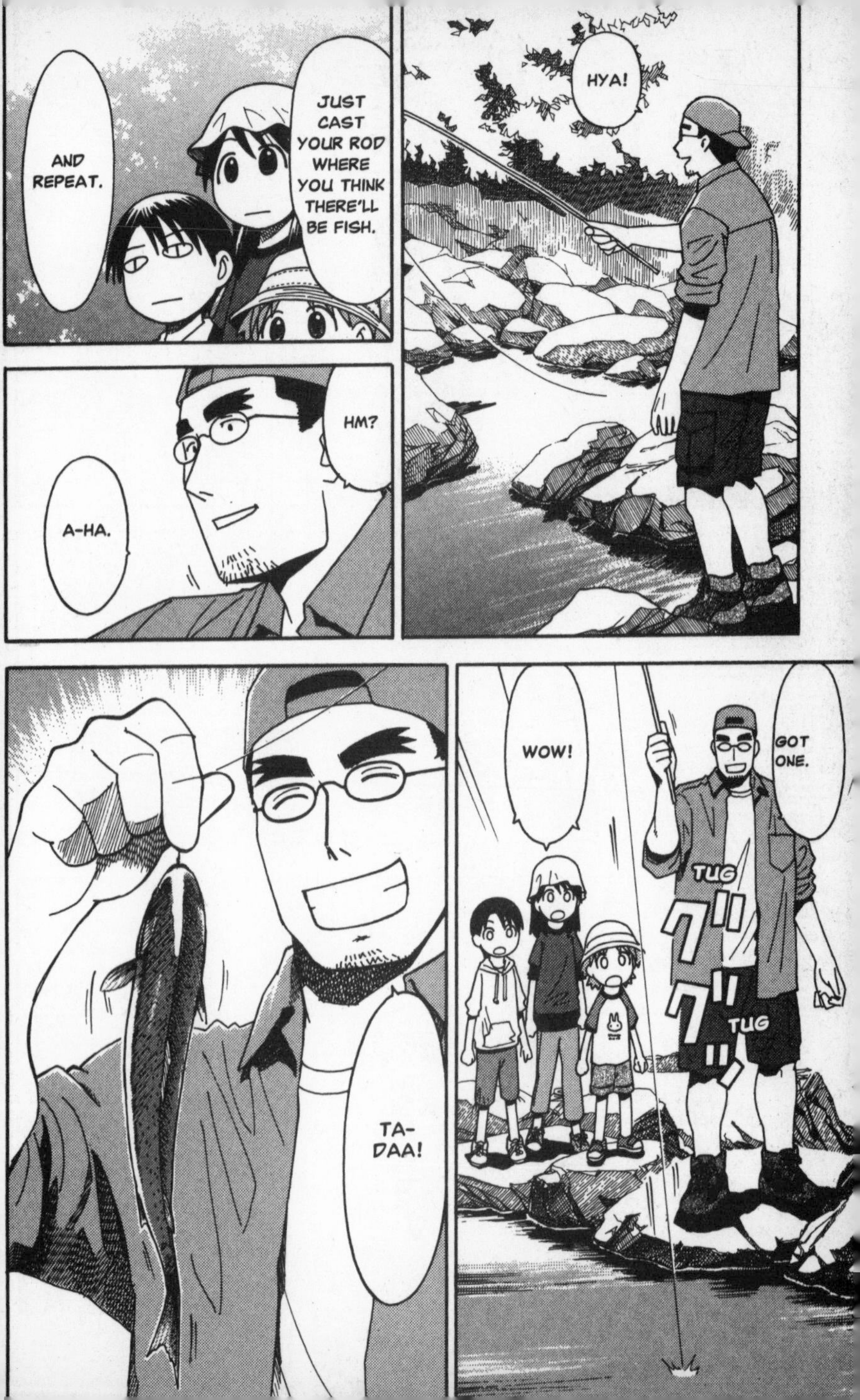
HYA!
JUST CAST YOUR ROD WHERE YOU THINK THERE'LL BE FISH.
AND REPEAT.
HM?
A-HA.
GOT ONE.
TUG
TUG
WOW!
TA-DAA!

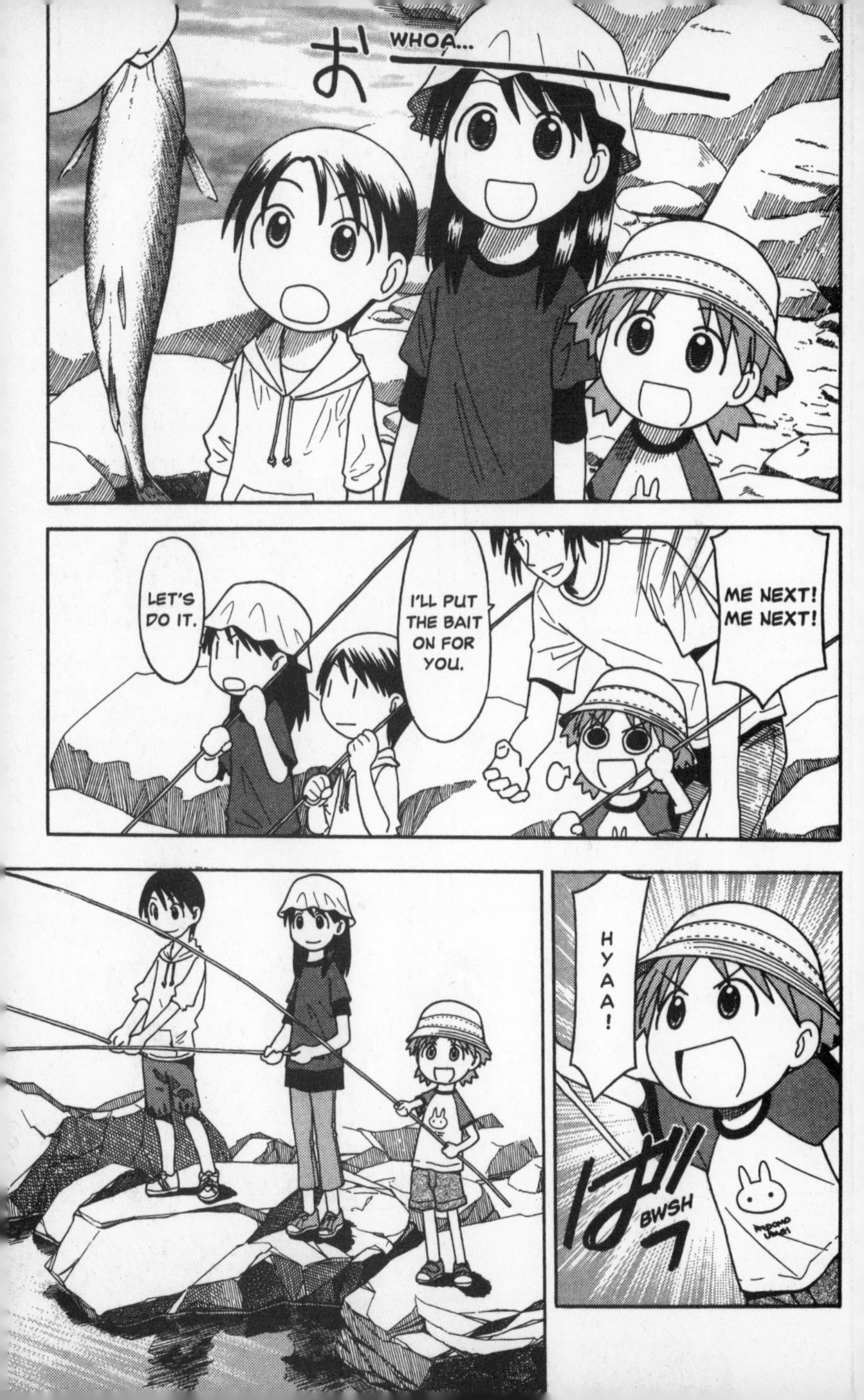
お
WHOA...
ME NEXT! ME NEXT!
I'LL PUT THE BAIT ON FOR YOU.
LET'S DO IT.
HYAA!
ぱっ
BWSH

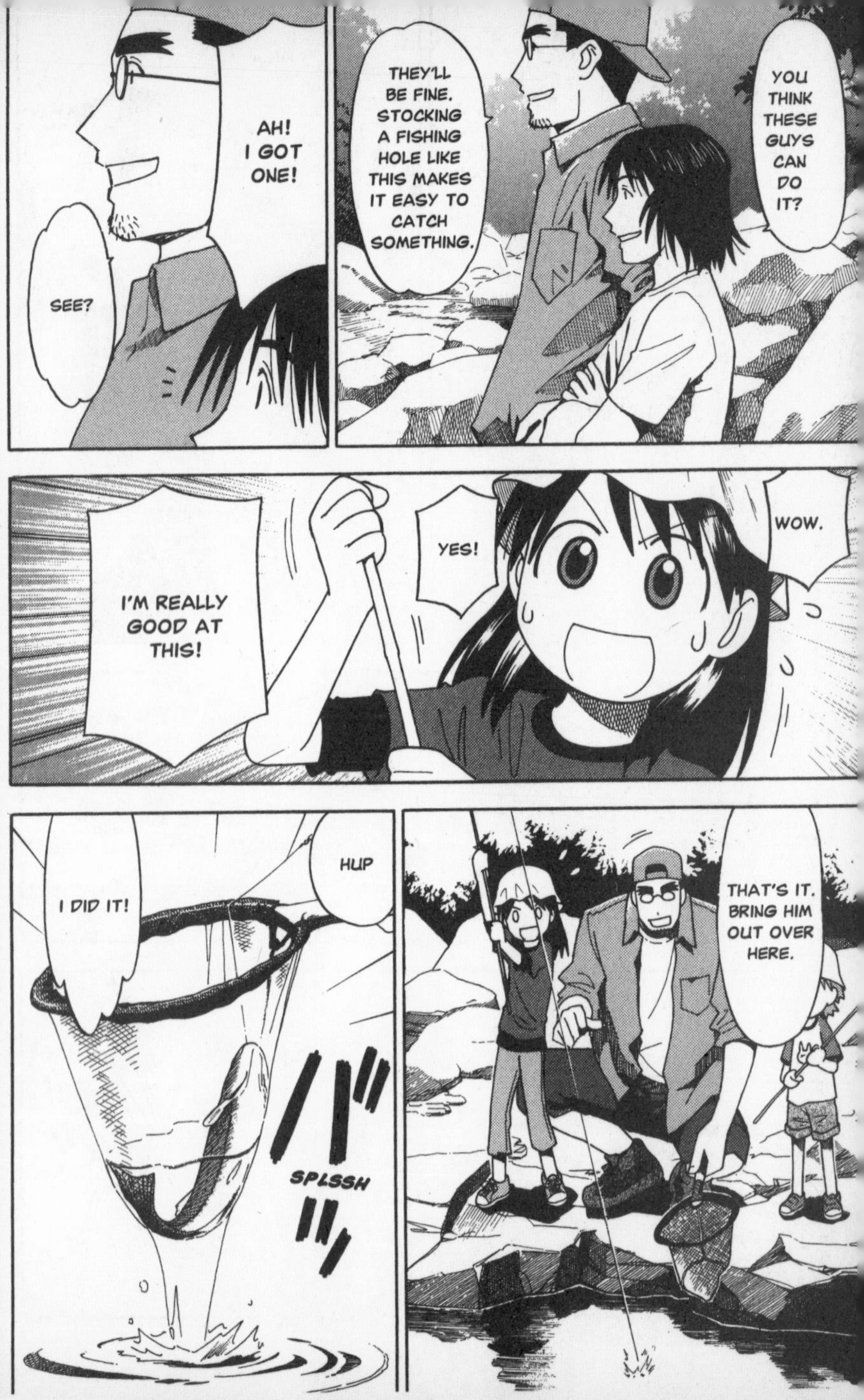
YOU THINK THESE GUYS CAN DO IT?
THEY'LL BE FINE. STOCKING A FISHING HOLE LIKE THIS MAKES IT EASY TO CATCH SOMETHING.
AH! I GOT ONE!
SEE?
WOW.
YES!
I'M REALLY GOOD AT THIS!
THAT'S IT. BRING HIM OUT OVER HERE.
HUP
I DID IT!
SPLSSH

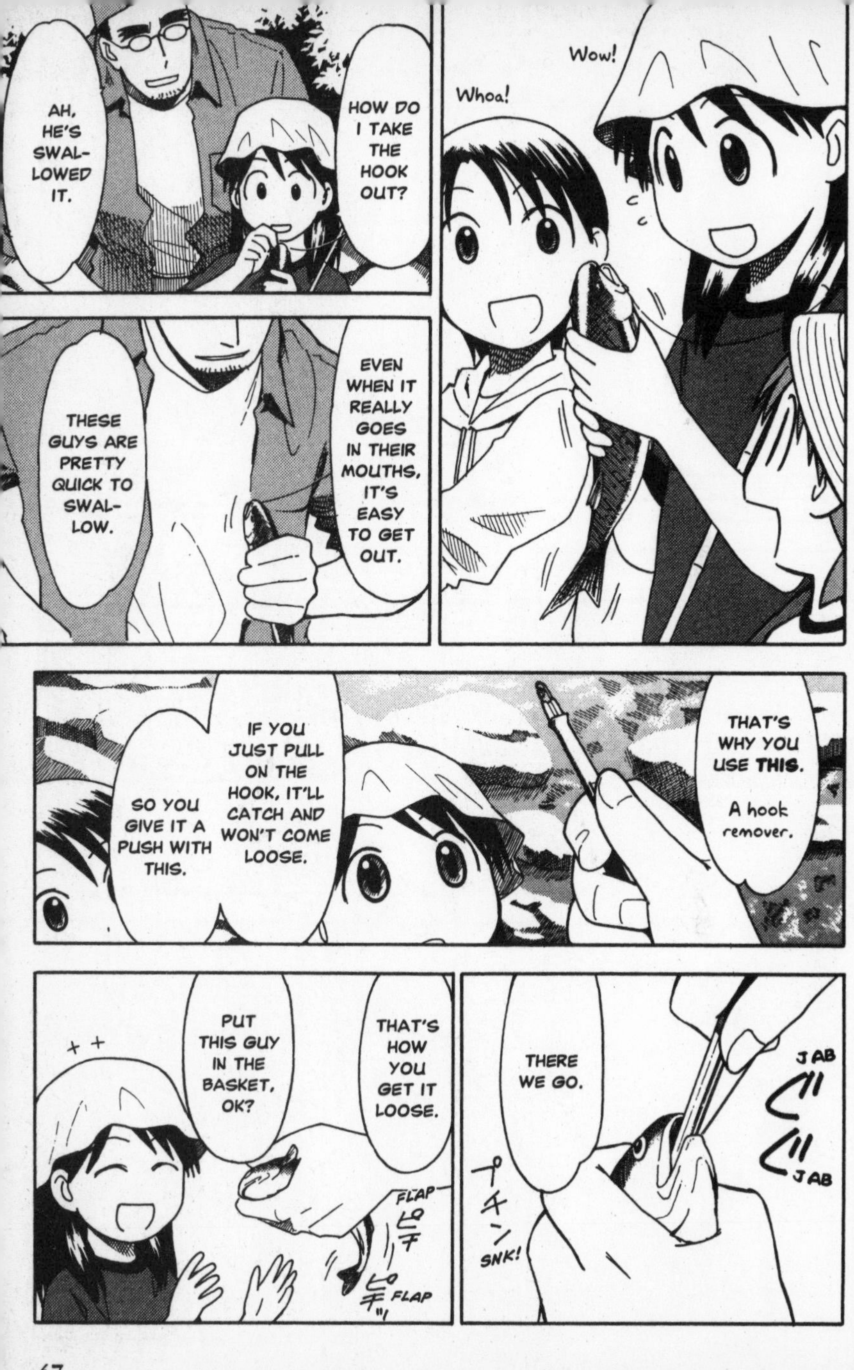
Wow!
Whoa!
HOW DO I TAKE THE HOOK OUT?
AH, HE'S SWAL-LOWED IT.
EVEN WHEN IT REALLY GOES IN THEIR MOUTHS, IT'S EASY TO GET OUT.
THESE GUYS ARE PRETTY QUICK TO SWAL-LOW.
THAT'S WHY YOU USE **THIS.**
A hook remover.
IF YOU JUST PULL ON THE HOOK, IT'LL CATCH AND WON'T COME LOOSE.
SO YOU GIVE IT A PUSH WITH THIS.
JAB
JAB
THERE WE GO.
プチン
SNK!
THAT'S HOW YOU GET IT LOOSE.
PUT THIS GUY IN THE BASKET, OK?
FLAP
ピチ
ピチッ
FLAP

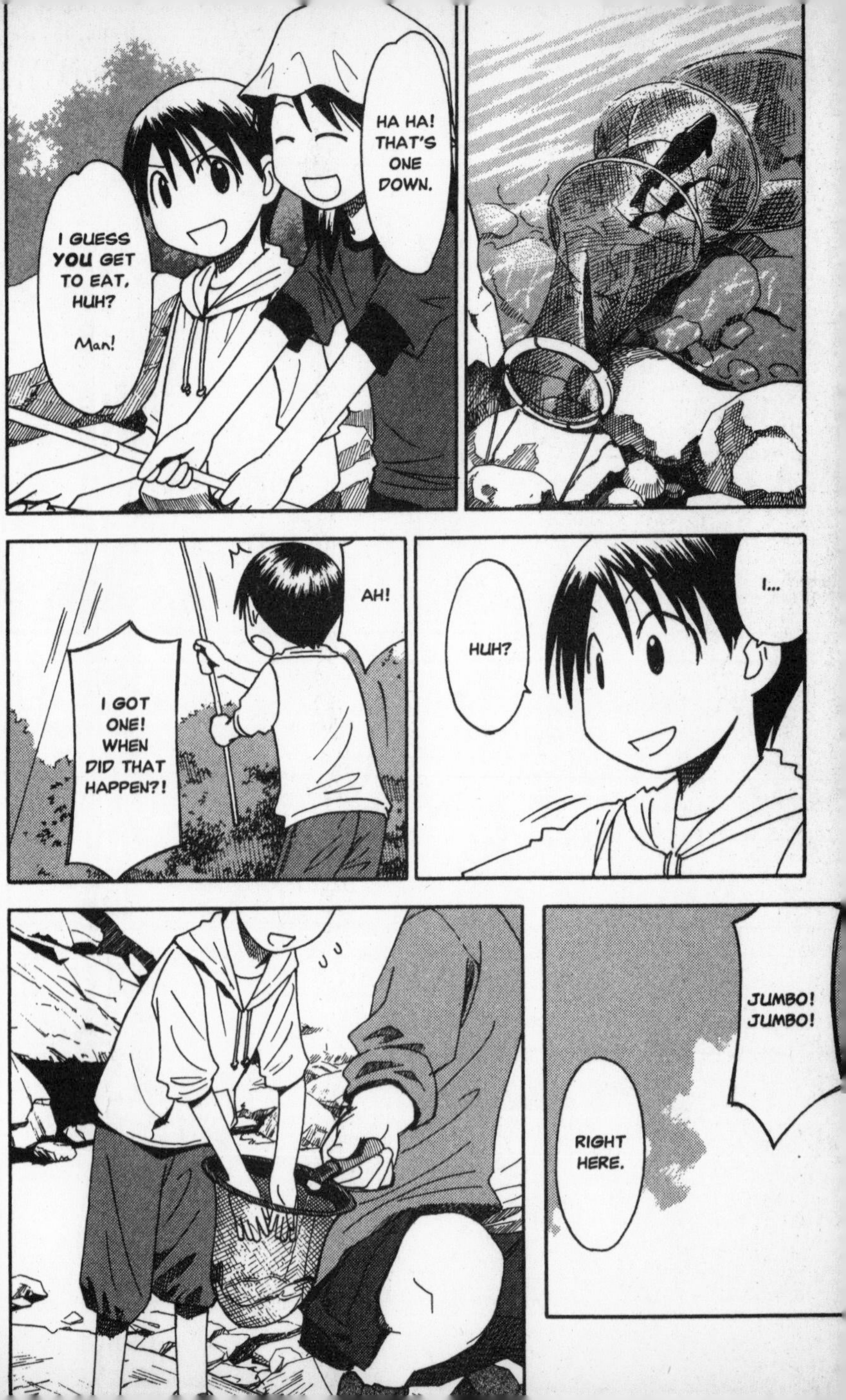
HA HA! THAT'S ONE DOWN.
I GUESS **YOU** GET TO EAT, HUH?
Man!
I...
HUH?
AH!
I GOT ONE! WHEN DID THAT HAPPEN?!
JUMBO! JUMBO!
RIGHT HERE.

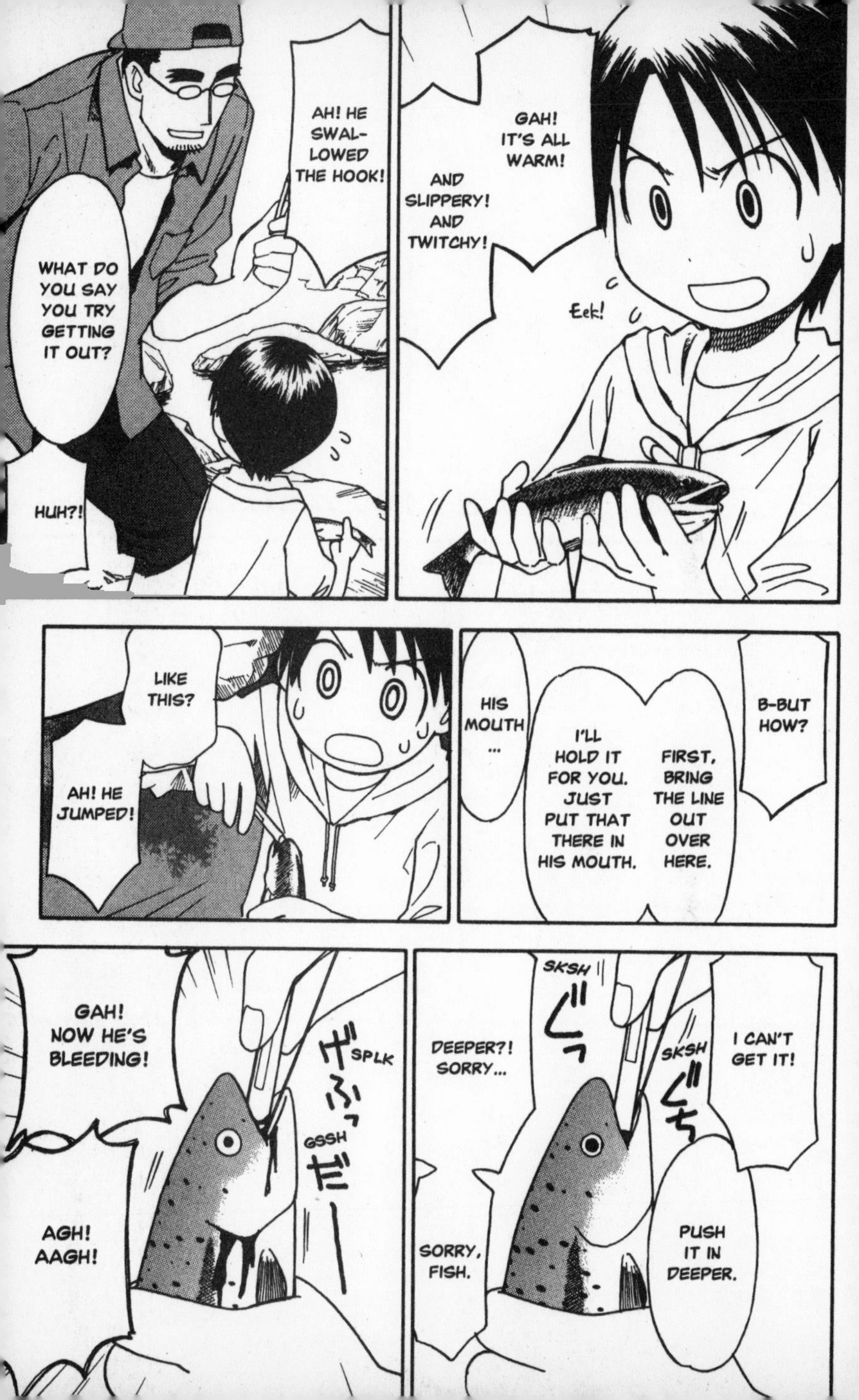
GAH! IT'S ALL WARM!
AND SLIPPERY! AND TWITCHY!
Eek!
AH! HE SWAL-LOWED THE HOOK!
WHAT DO YOU SAY YOU TRY GETTING IT OUT?
HUH?!
B-BUT HOW?
FIRST, BRING THE LINE OUT OVER HERE.
I'LL HOLD IT FOR YOU. JUST PUT THAT THERE IN HIS MOUTH.
HIS MOUTH ...
LIKE THIS?
AH! HE JUMPED!
I CAN'T GET IT!
SKSH
SKSH
PUSH IT IN DEEPER.
DEEPER?! SORRY...
SORRY, FISH.
GAH! NOW HE'S BLEEDING!
SPLK
GSSH
AGH! AAGH!

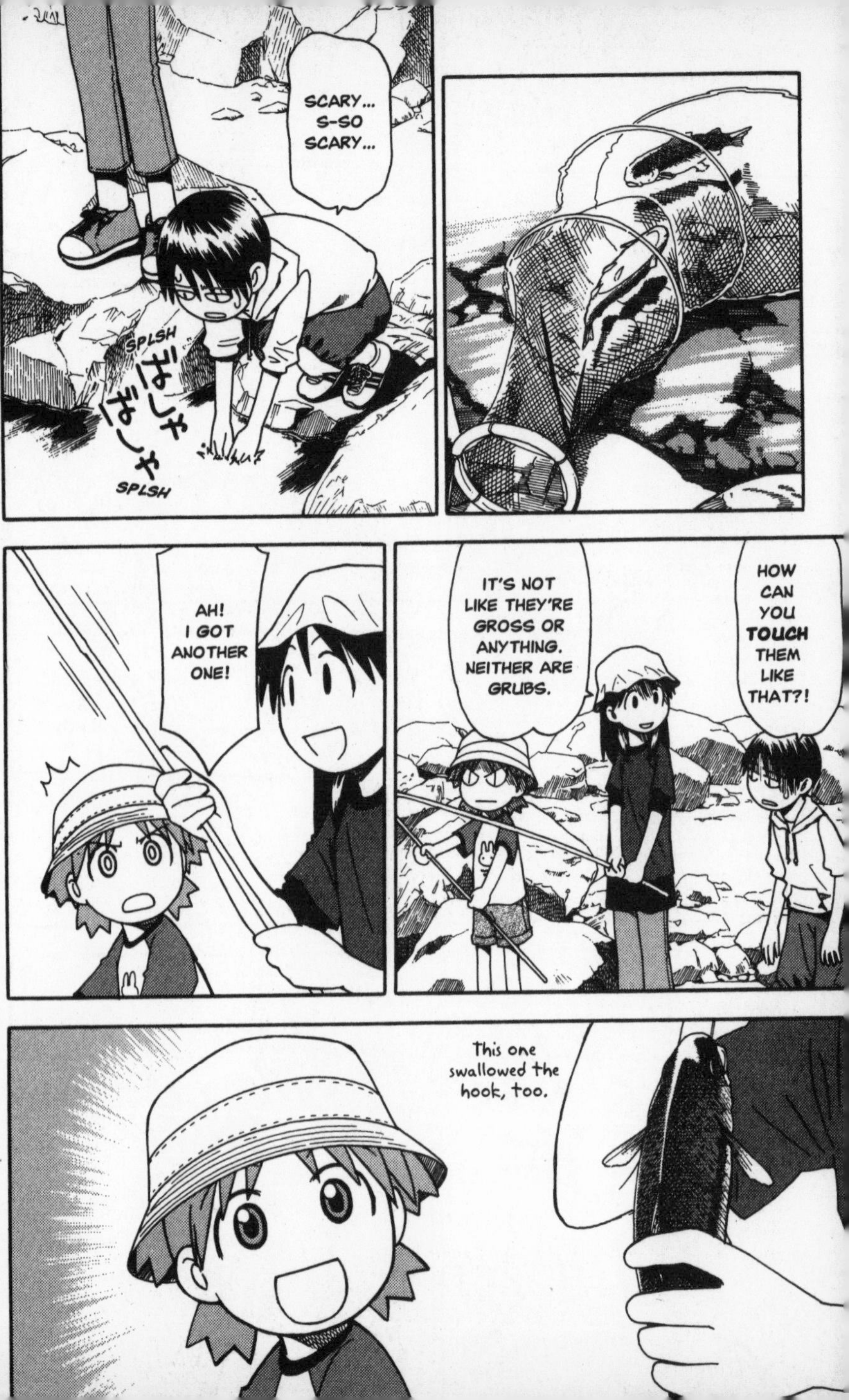
SCARY... S-SO SCARY...
SPLSH ばしゃ
ばしゃ SPLSH
HOW CAN YOU **TOUCH** THEM LIKE THAT?!
IT'S NOT LIKE THEY'RE GROSS OR ANYTHING. NEITHER ARE GRUBS.
AH! I GOT ANOTHER ONE!
This one swallowed the hook, too.

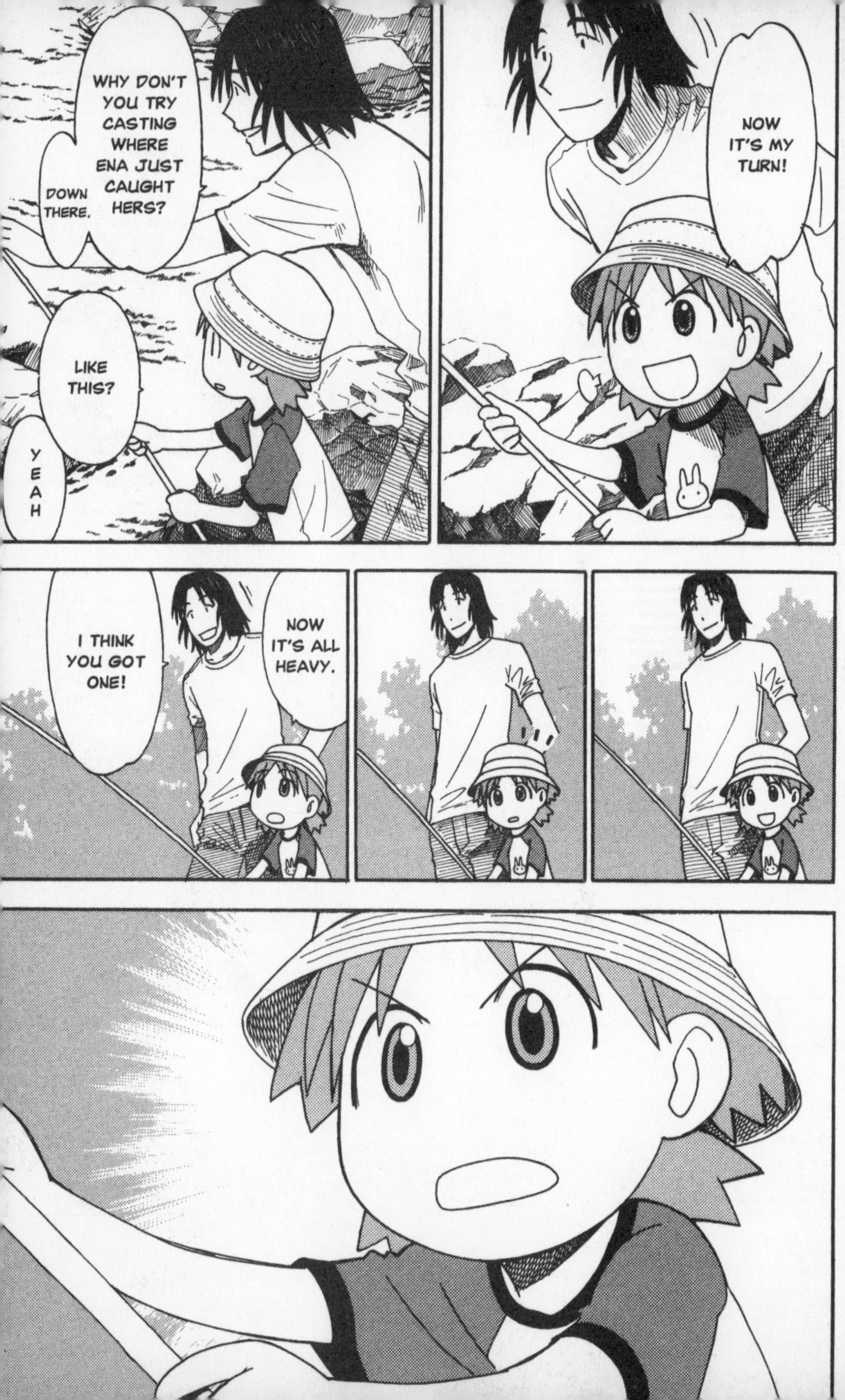
NOW IT'S MY TURN!
WHY DON'T YOU TRY CASTING WHERE ENA JUST CAUGHT HERS?
DOWN THERE.
LIKE THIS?
YEAH
NOW IT'S ALL HEAVY.
I THINK YOU GOT ONE!

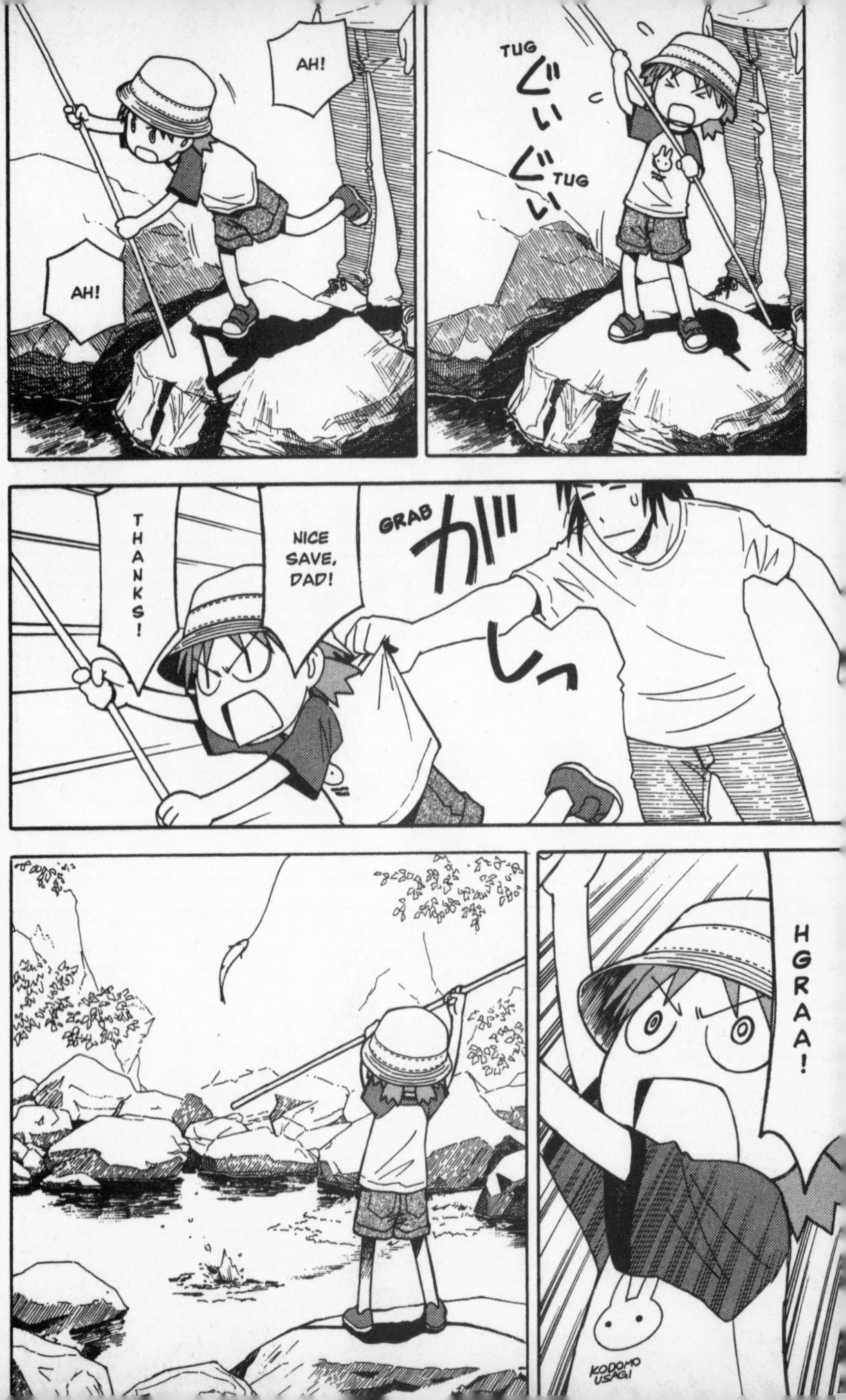
TUG
ぐい
ぐい
TUG
AH!
AH!
GRAB
が
NICE SAVE, DAD!
THANKS!
しっ
HGRAA!
KODOMO USAGI

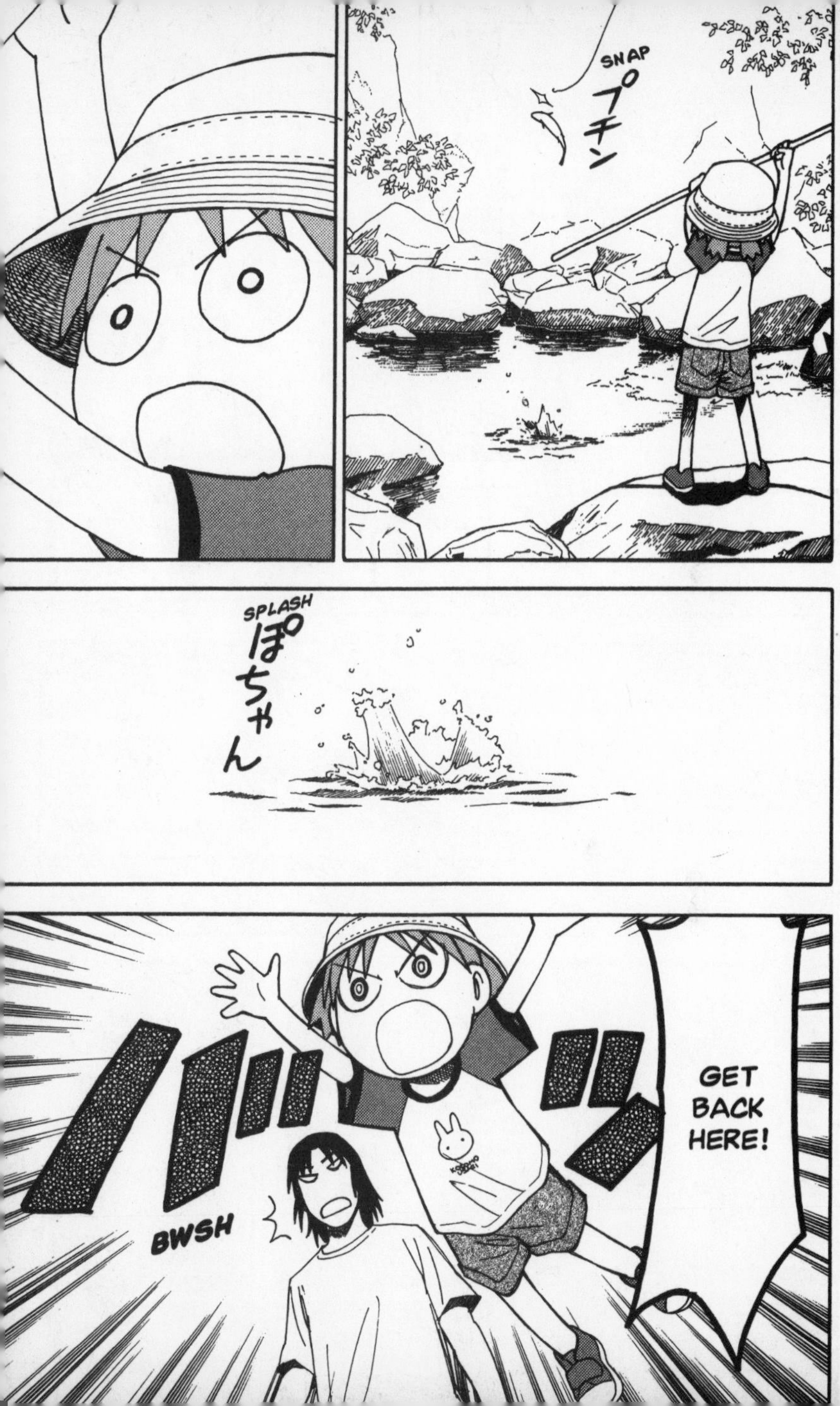
SNAP
プチン
SPLASH
ぽちゃん
GET BACK HERE!
BWSH

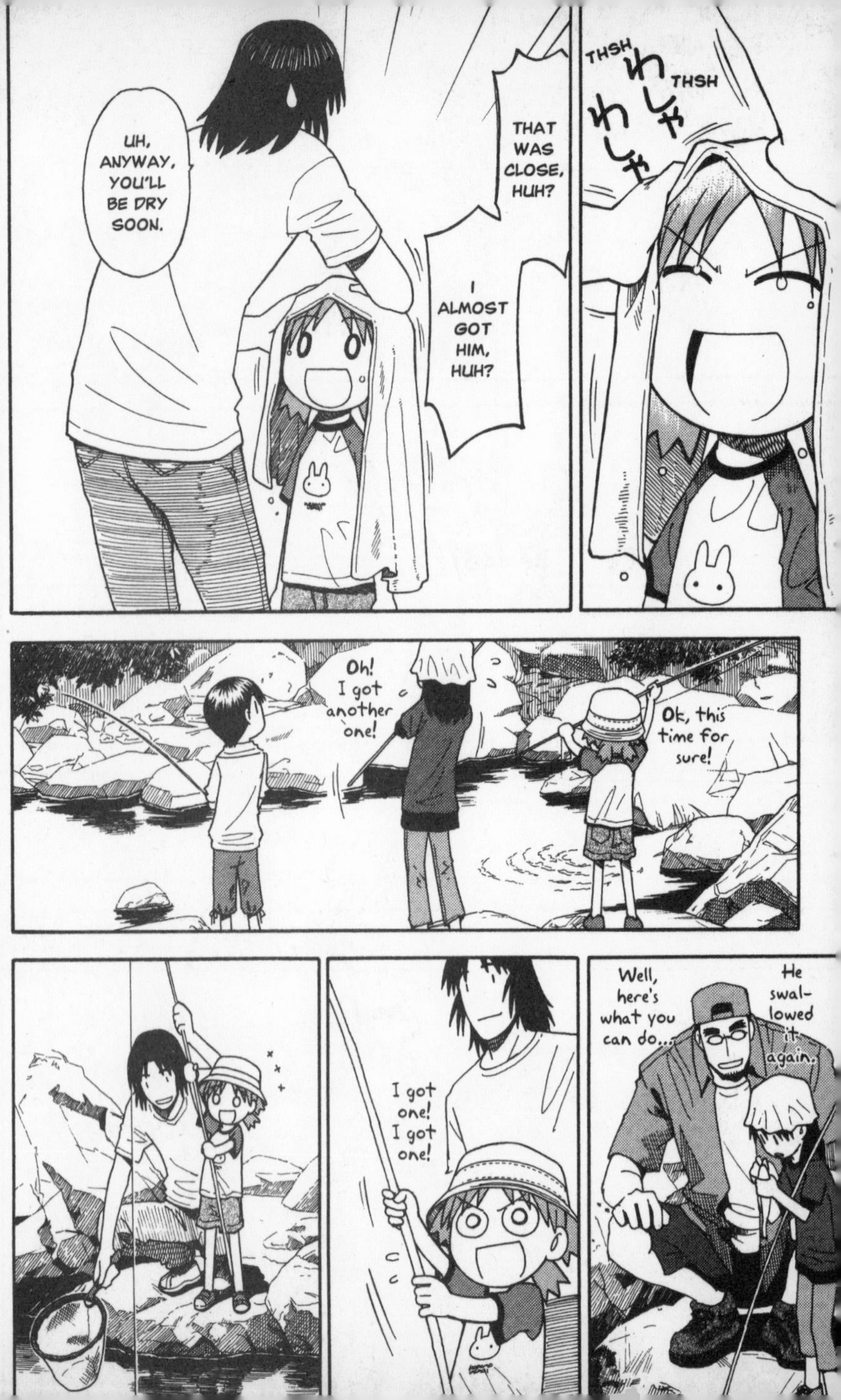

THSH わしゃ
THSH わしゃ
THAT WAS CLOSE, HUH?
I ALMOST GOT HIM, HUH?
UH, ANYWAY, YOU'LL BE DRY SOON.
Ok, this time for sure!
Oh! I got another one!
He swal-lowed it again.
Well, here's what you can do...
I got one! I got one!

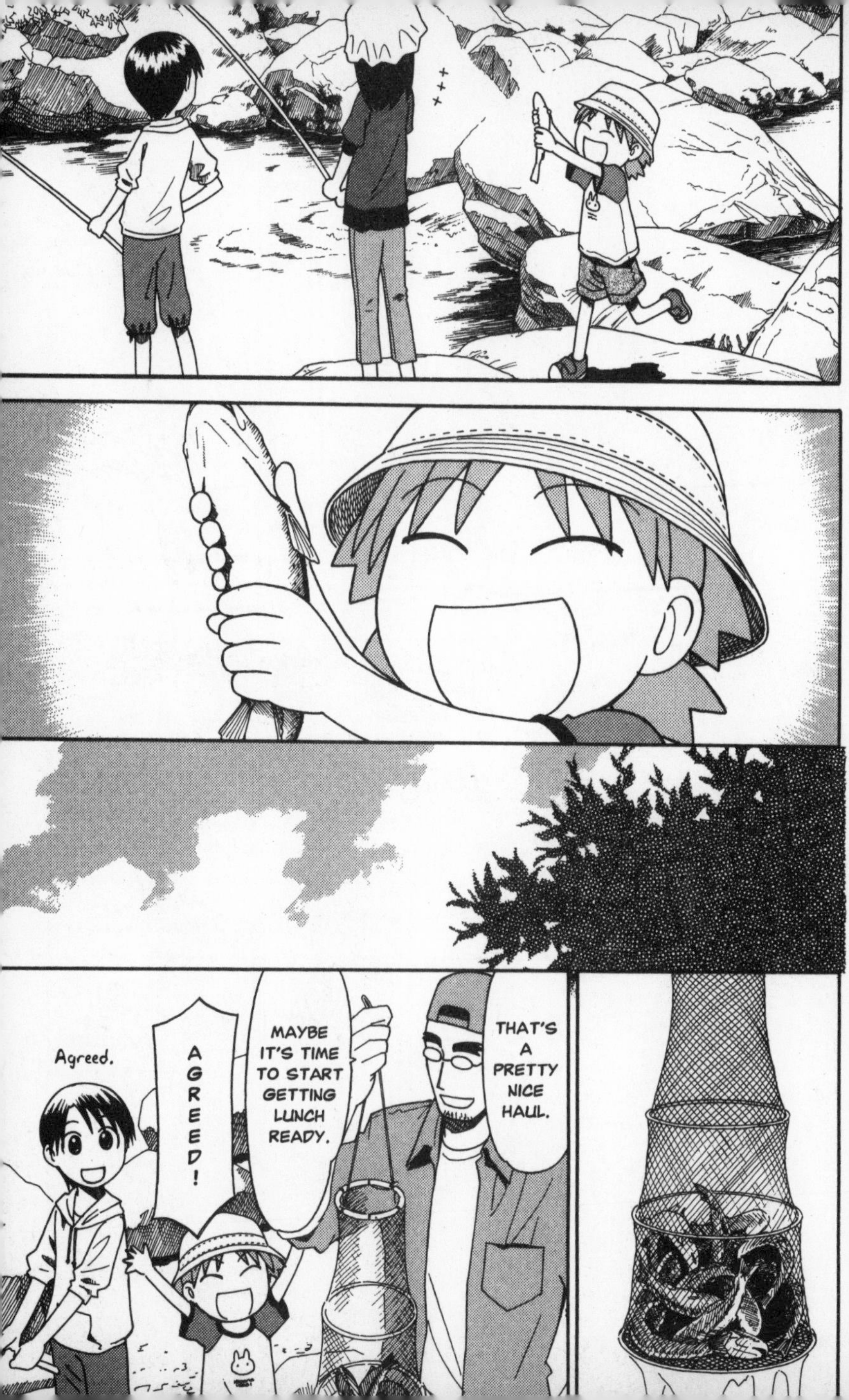
THAT'S A PRETTY NICE HAUL.
MAYBE IT'S TIME TO START GETTING LUNCH READY.
AGREED!
Agreed.

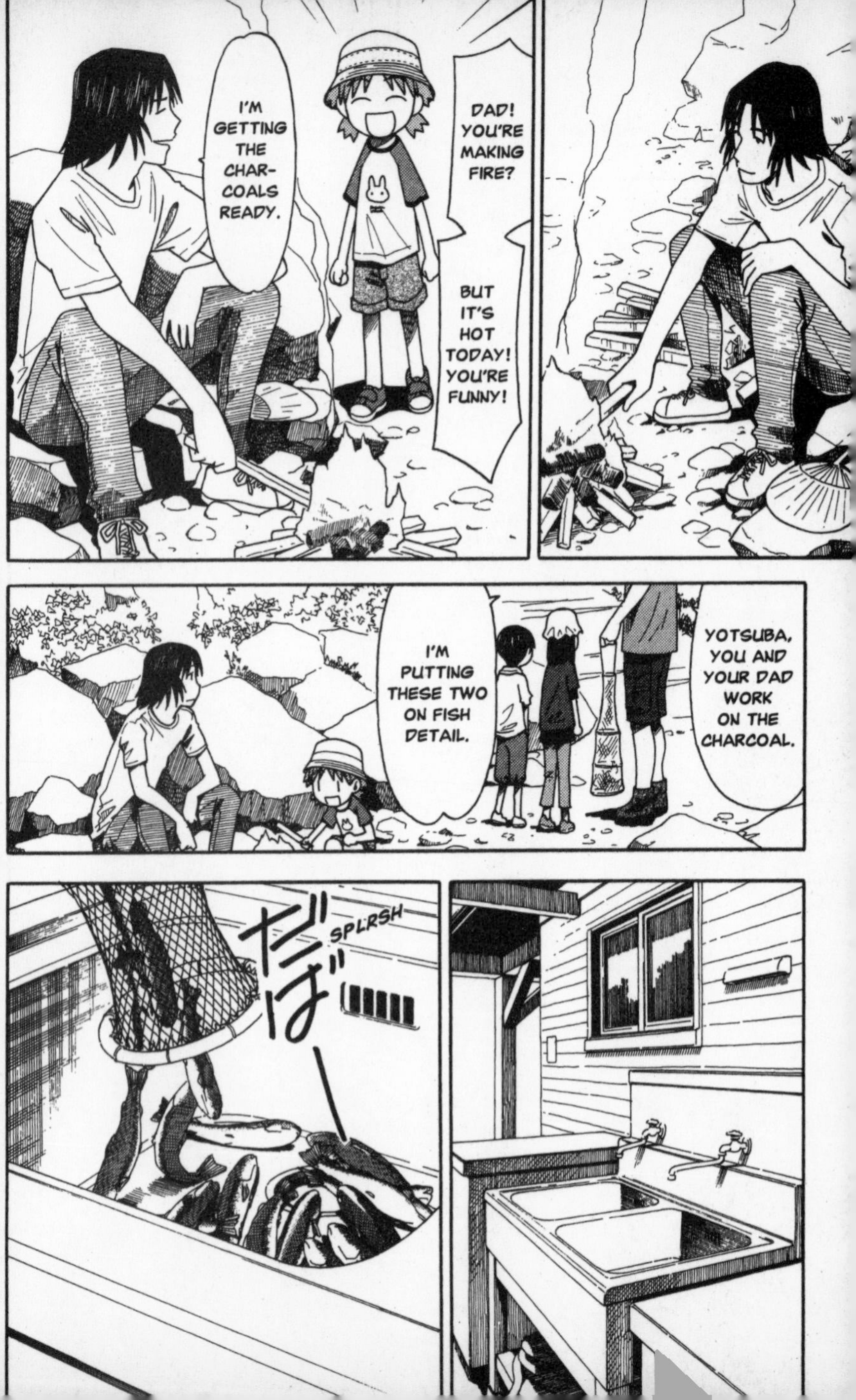
DAD! YOU'RE MAKING FIRE?
I'M GETTING THE CHAR-COALS READY.
BUT IT'S HOT TODAY! YOU'RE FUNNY!
YOTSUBA, YOU AND YOUR DAD WORK ON THE CHARCOAL.
I'M PUTTING THESE TWO ON FISH DETAIL.
だばー
SPLRSH

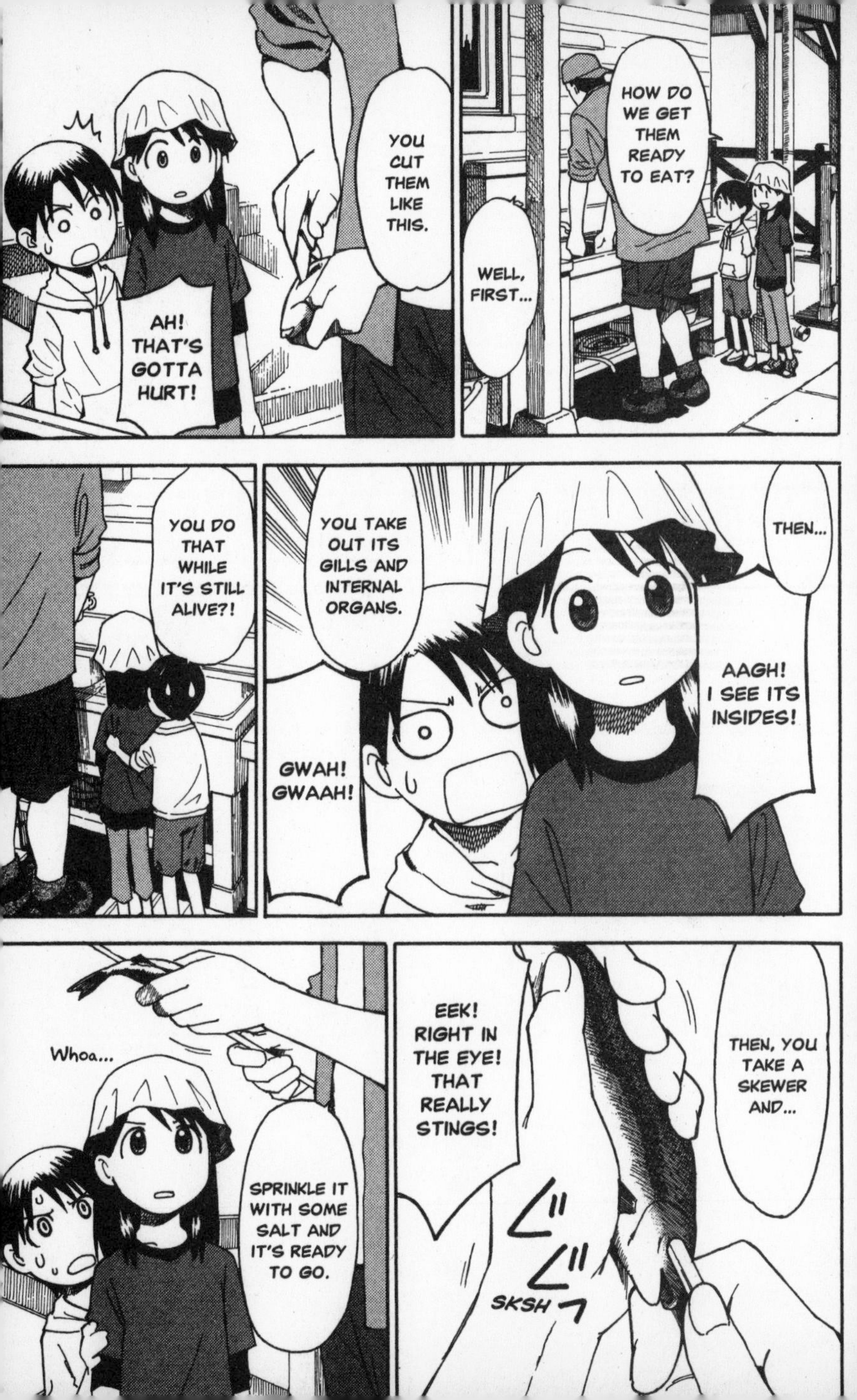
HOW DO WE GET THEM READY TO EAT?
WELL, FIRST...
YOU CUT THEM LIKE THIS.
AH! THAT'S GOTTA HURT!
THEN...
YOU TAKE OUT ITS GILLS AND INTERNAL ORGANS.
AAGH! I SEE ITS INSIDES!
GWAH! GWAAH!
YOU DO THAT WHILE IT'S STILL ALIVE?!
THEN, YOU TAKE A SKEWER AND...
EEK! RIGHT IN THE EYE! THAT REALLY STINGS!
SKSH
SPRINKLE IT WITH SOME SALT AND IT'S READY TO GO.
Whoa...

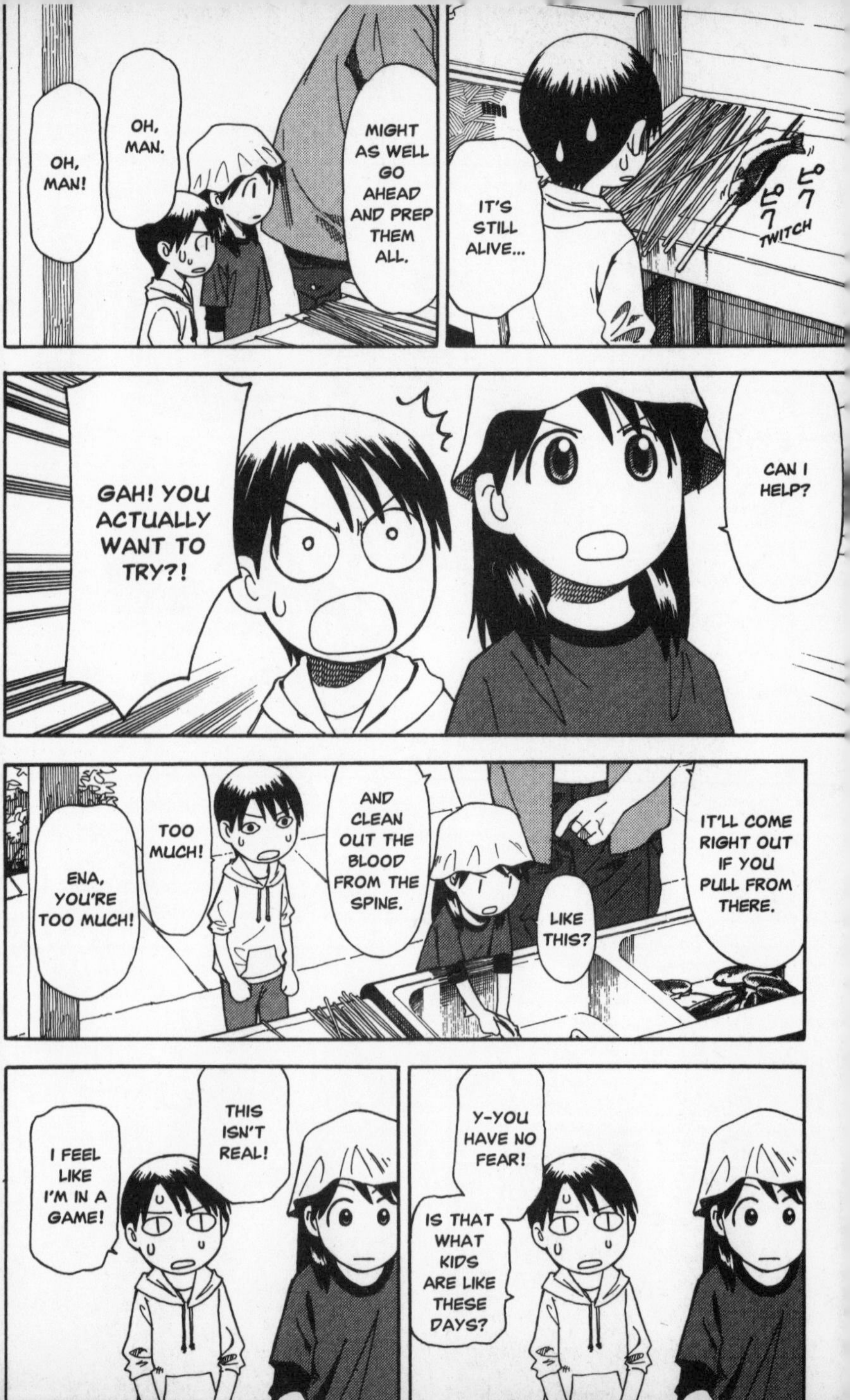
ピク ピク
TWITCH
IT'S STILL ALIVE...
MIGHT AS WELL GO AHEAD AND PREP THEM ALL.
OH, MAN.
OH, MAN!
CAN I HELP?
GAH! YOU ACTUALLY WANT TO TRY?!
IT'LL COME RIGHT OUT IF YOU PULL FROM THERE.
LIKE THIS?
AND CLEAN OUT THE BLOOD FROM THE SPINE.
TOO MUCH!
ENA, YOU'RE TOO MUCH!
Y-YOU HAVE NO FEAR!
IS THAT WHAT KIDS ARE LIKE THESE DAYS?
THIS ISN'T REAL!
I FEEL LIKE I'M IN A GAME!

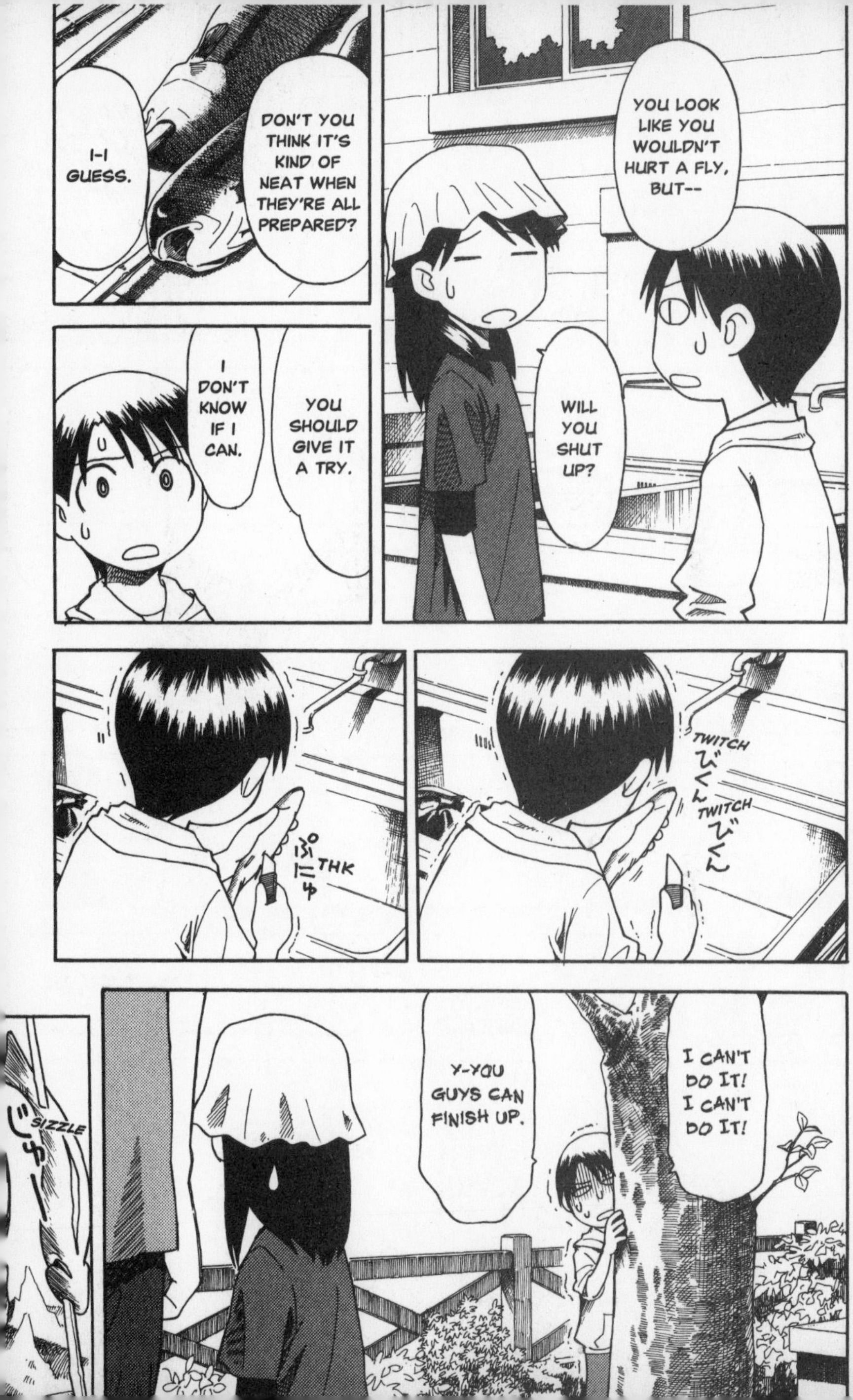
YOU LOOK LIKE YOU WOULDN'T HURT A FLY, BUT--
WILL YOU SHUT UP?
DON'T YOU THINK IT'S KIND OF NEAT WHEN THEY'RE ALL PREPARED?
I-I GUESS.
YOU SHOULD GIVE IT A TRY.
I DON'T KNOW IF I CAN.
TWITCH
びくん
TWITCH
びくん
ぷにゅ
THK
I CAN'T DO IT! I CAN'T DO IT!
Y-YOU GUYS CAN FINISH UP.
じゅー
SIZZLE

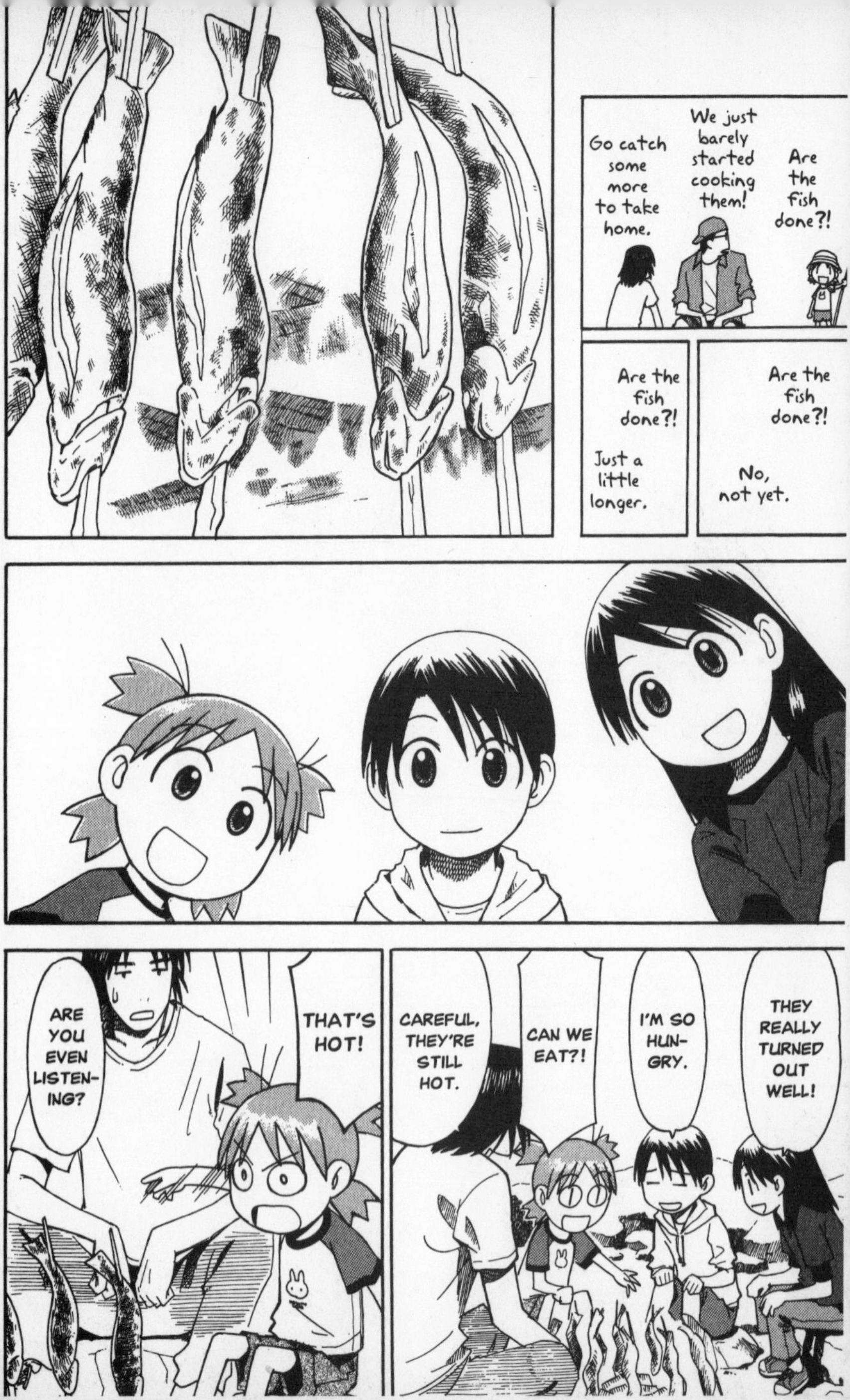
Are the fish done?!
We just barely started cooking them!
Go catch some more to take home.
Are the fish done?!
No, not yet.
Are the fish done?!
Just a little longer.
THEY REALLY TURNED OUT WELL!
I'M SO HUN-GRY.
CAN WE EAT?!
CAREFUL, THEY'RE STILL HOT.
THAT'S HOT!
ARE YOU EVEN LISTEN-ING?

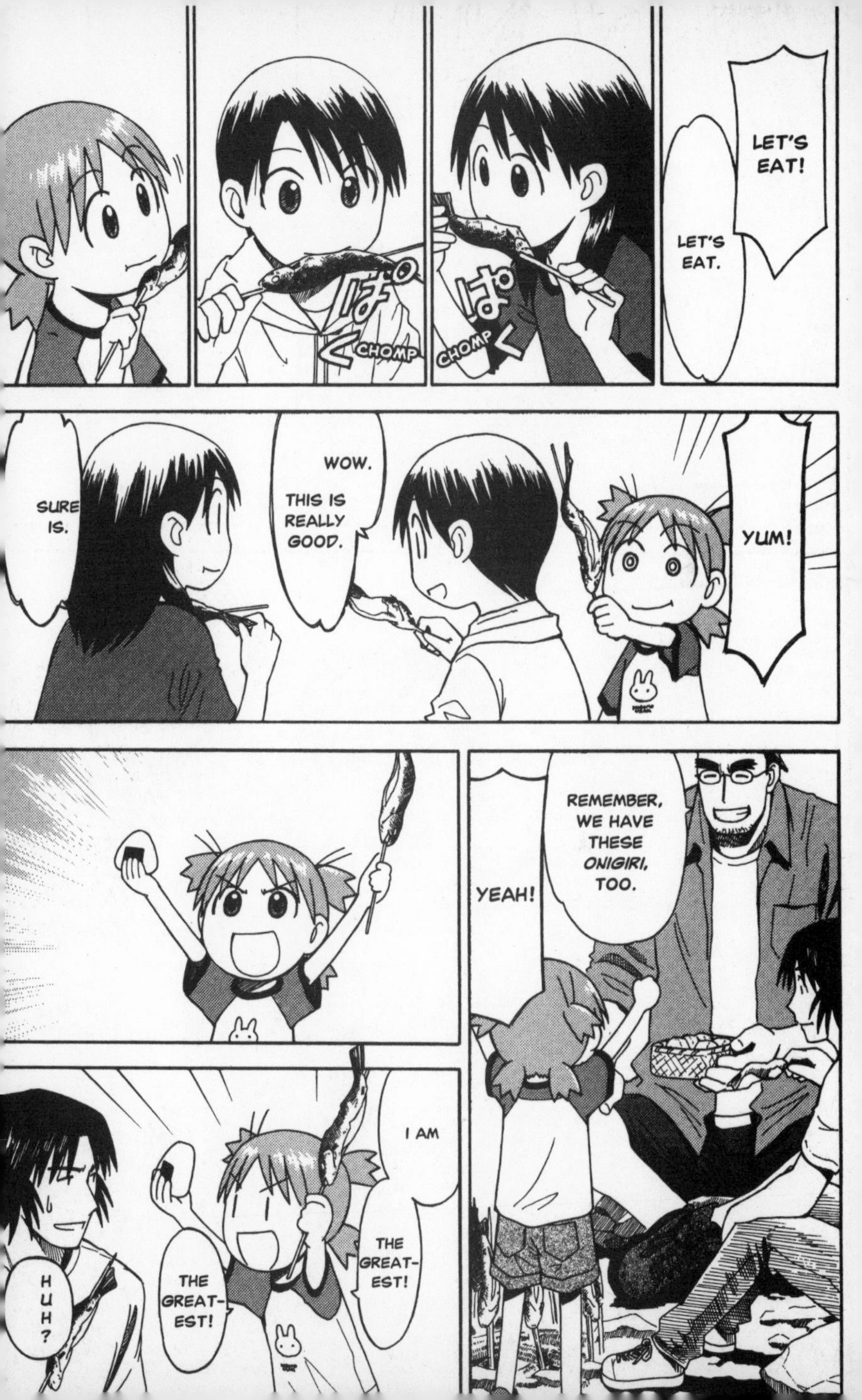
LET'S EAT!
LET'S EAT.
ぱく
CHOMP
ぱく
CHOMP
YUM!
WOW.
THIS IS REALLY GOOD.
SURE IS.
REMEMBER, WE HAVE THESE ONIGIRI, TOO.
YEAH!
I AM
THE GREAT-EST!
THE GREAT-EST!
HUH?

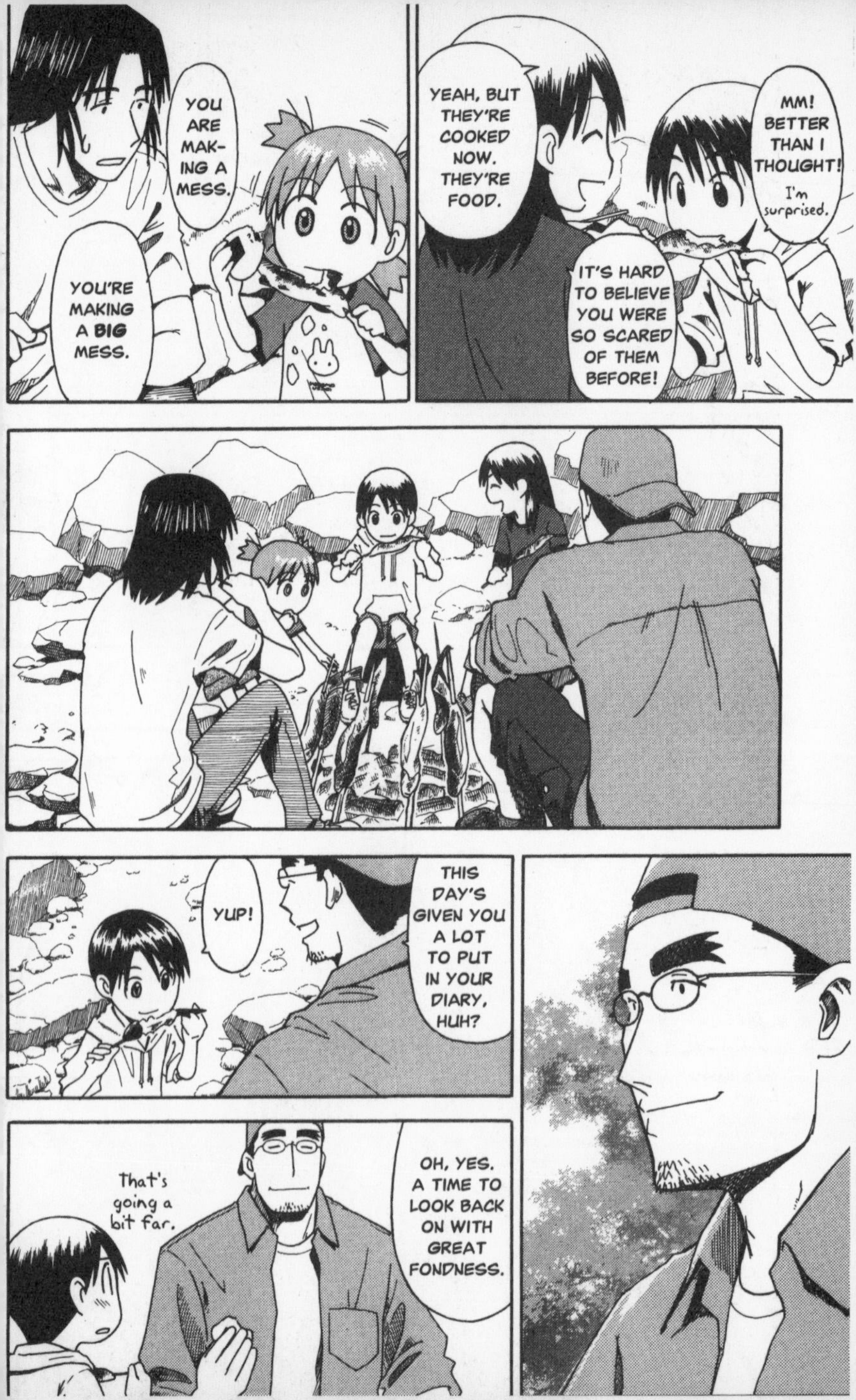
MM! BETTER THAN I THOUGHT!
I'm surprised.
IT'S HARD TO BELIEVE YOU WERE SO SCARED OF THEM BEFORE!
YEAH, BUT THEY'RE COOKED NOW. THEY'RE FOOD.
YOU ARE MAKING A MESS.
YOU'RE MAKING A **BIG** MESS.
THIS DAY'S GIVEN YOU A LOT TO PUT IN YOUR DIARY, HUH?
YUP!
OH, YES. A TIME TO LOOK BACK ON WITH GREAT FONDNESS.
That's going a bit far.

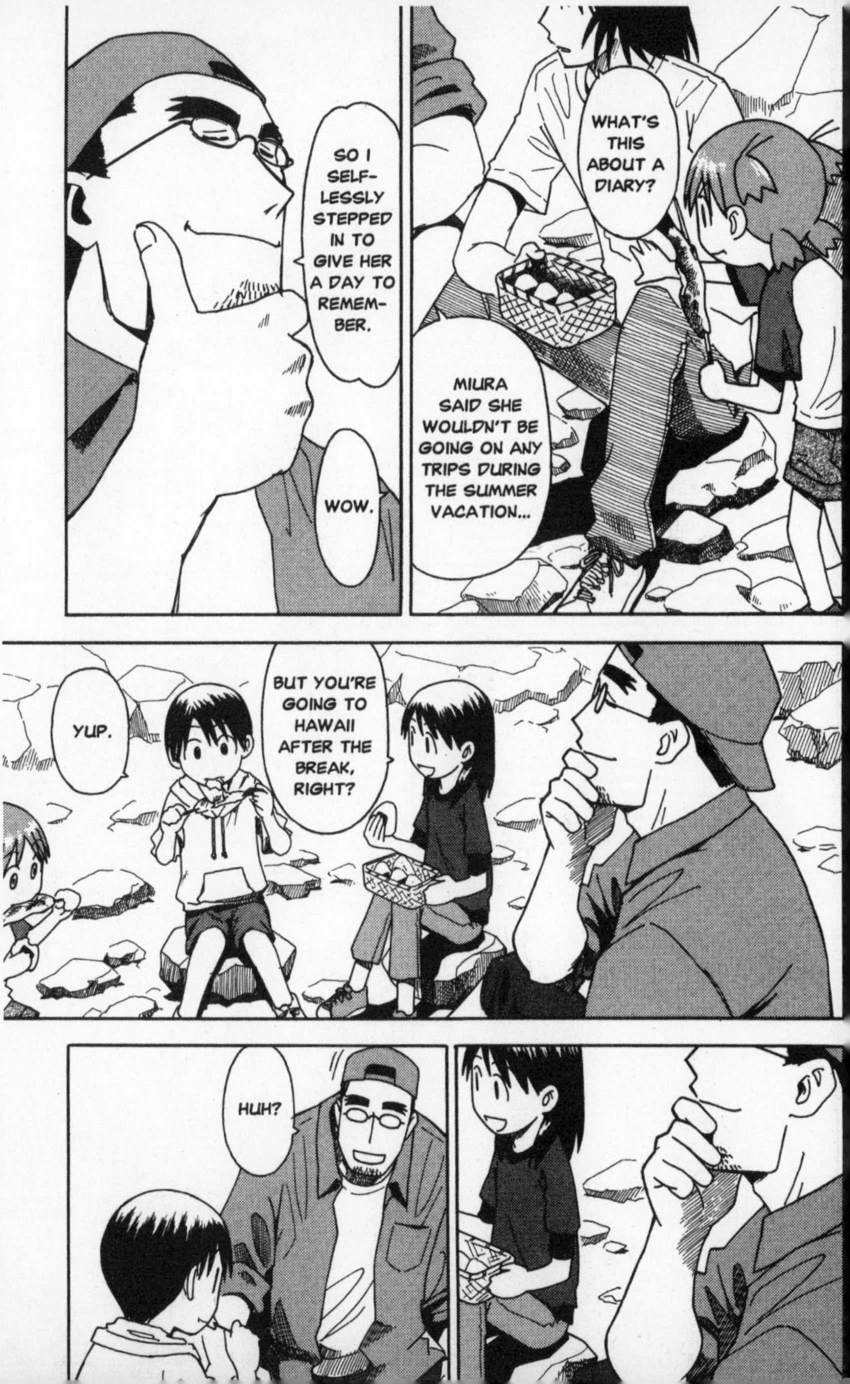
WHAT'S THIS ABOUT A DIARY?
MIURA SAID SHE WOULDN'T BE GOING ON ANY TRIPS DURING THE SUMMER VACATION...
SO I SELF-LESSLY STEPPED IN TO GIVE HER A DAY TO REMEMBER.
WOW.
BUT YOU'RE GOING TO HAWAII AFTER THE BREAK, RIGHT?
YUP.
HUH?

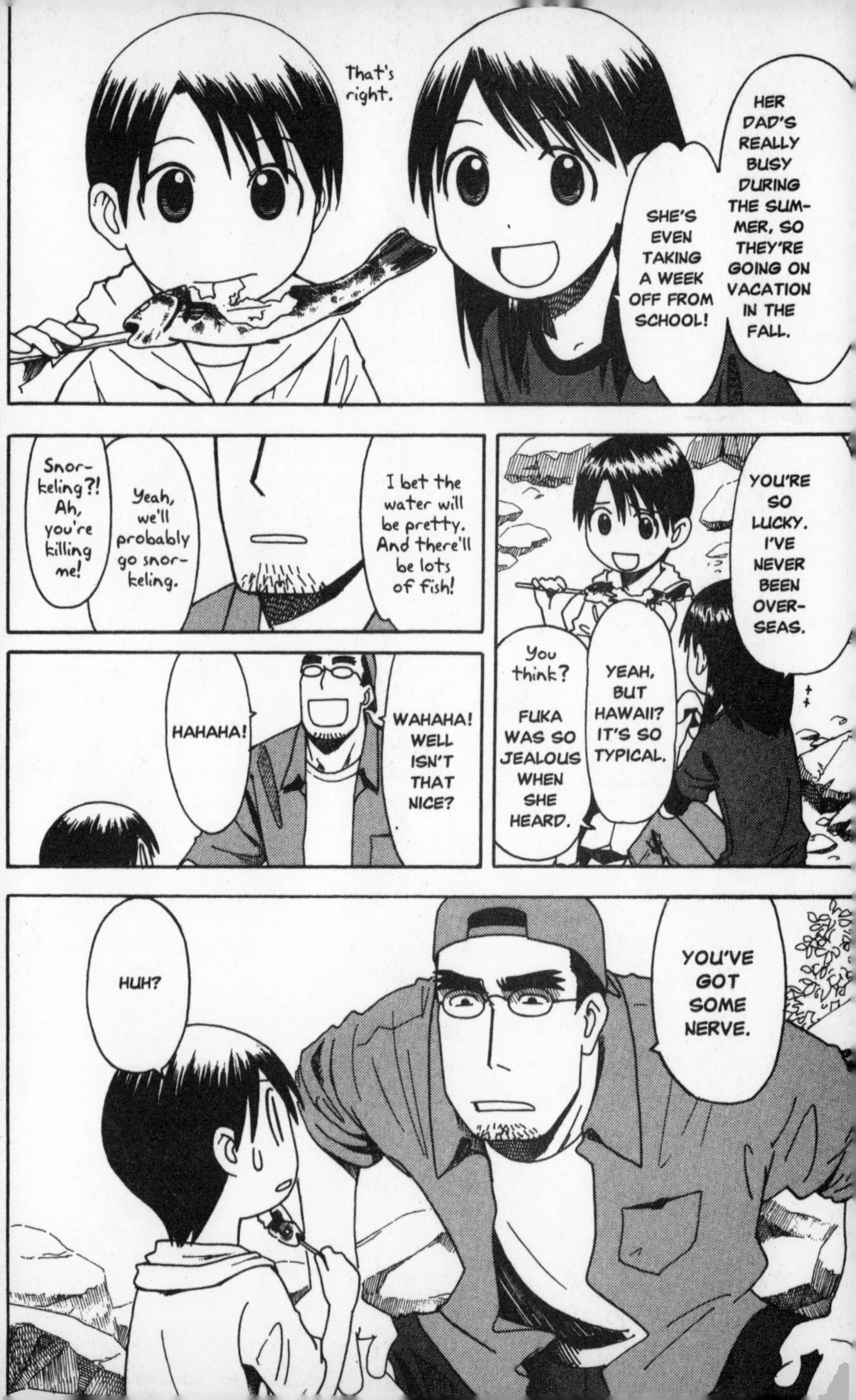
HER DAD'S REALLY BUSY DURING THE SUMMER, SO THEY'RE GOING ON VACATION IN THE FALL.
SHE'S EVEN TAKING A WEEK OFF FROM SCHOOL!
That's right.
YOU'RE SO LUCKY. I'VE NEVER BEEN OVERSEAS.
YEAH, BUT HAWAII? IT'S SO TYPICAL.
You think?
FUKA WAS SO JEALOUS WHEN SHE HEARD.
I bet the water will be pretty. And there'll be lots of fish!
Yeah, we'll probably go snorkeling.
Snorkeling?! Ah, you're killing me!
WAHAHA! WELL ISN'T THAT NICE?
HAHAHA!
YOU'VE GOT SOME NERVE.
HUH?

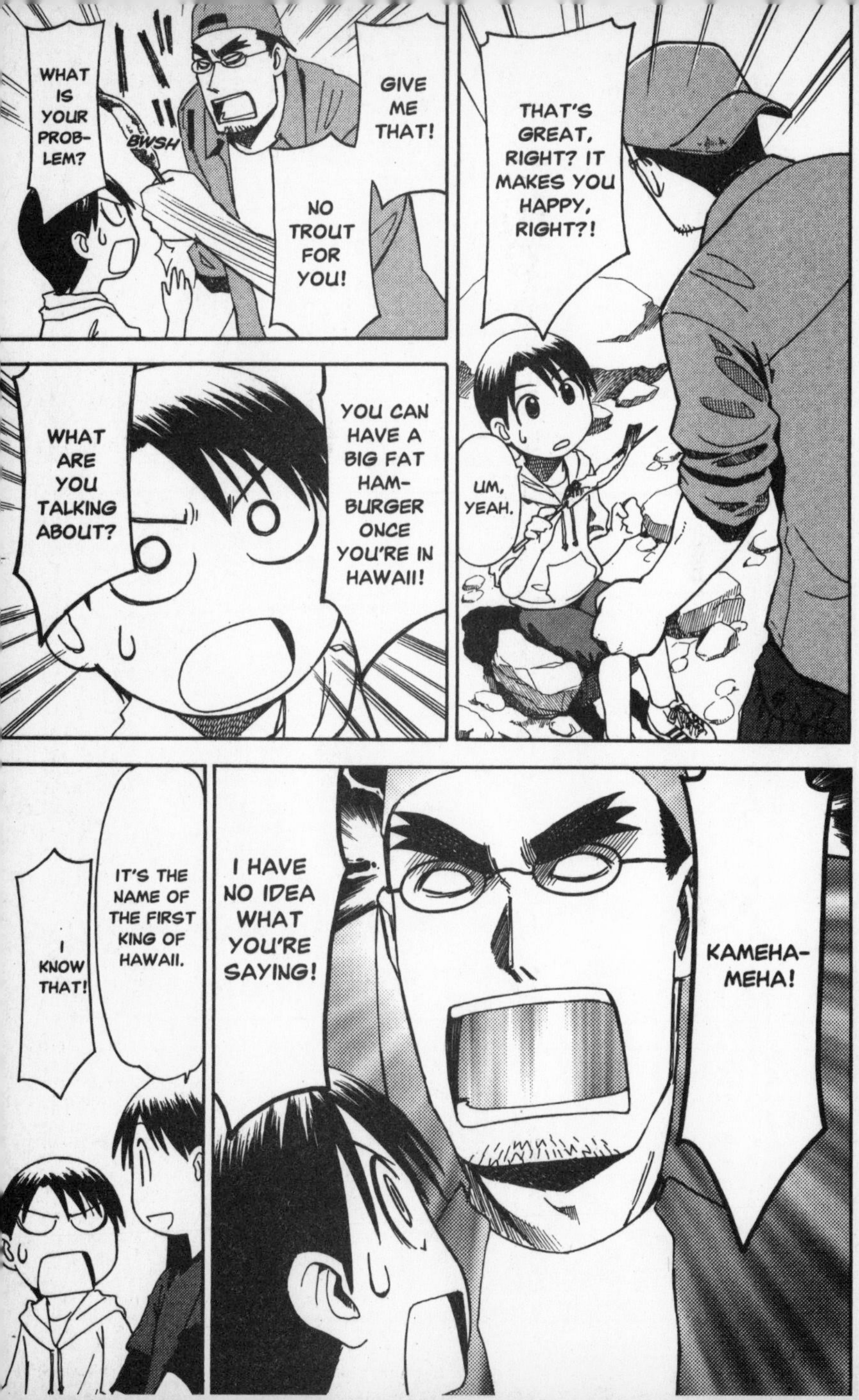
THAT'S GREAT, RIGHT? IT MAKES YOU HAPPY, RIGHT?!
UM, YEAH.
GIVE ME THAT!
NO TROUT FOR YOU!
BWSH
WHAT IS YOUR PROB-LEM?
YOU CAN HAVE A BIG FAT HAM-BURGER ONCE YOU'RE IN HAWAII!
WHAT ARE YOU TALKING ABOUT?
KAMEHA-MEHA!
I HAVE NO IDEA WHAT YOU'RE SAYING!
IT'S THE NAME OF THE FIRST KING OF HAWAII.
I KNOW THAT!

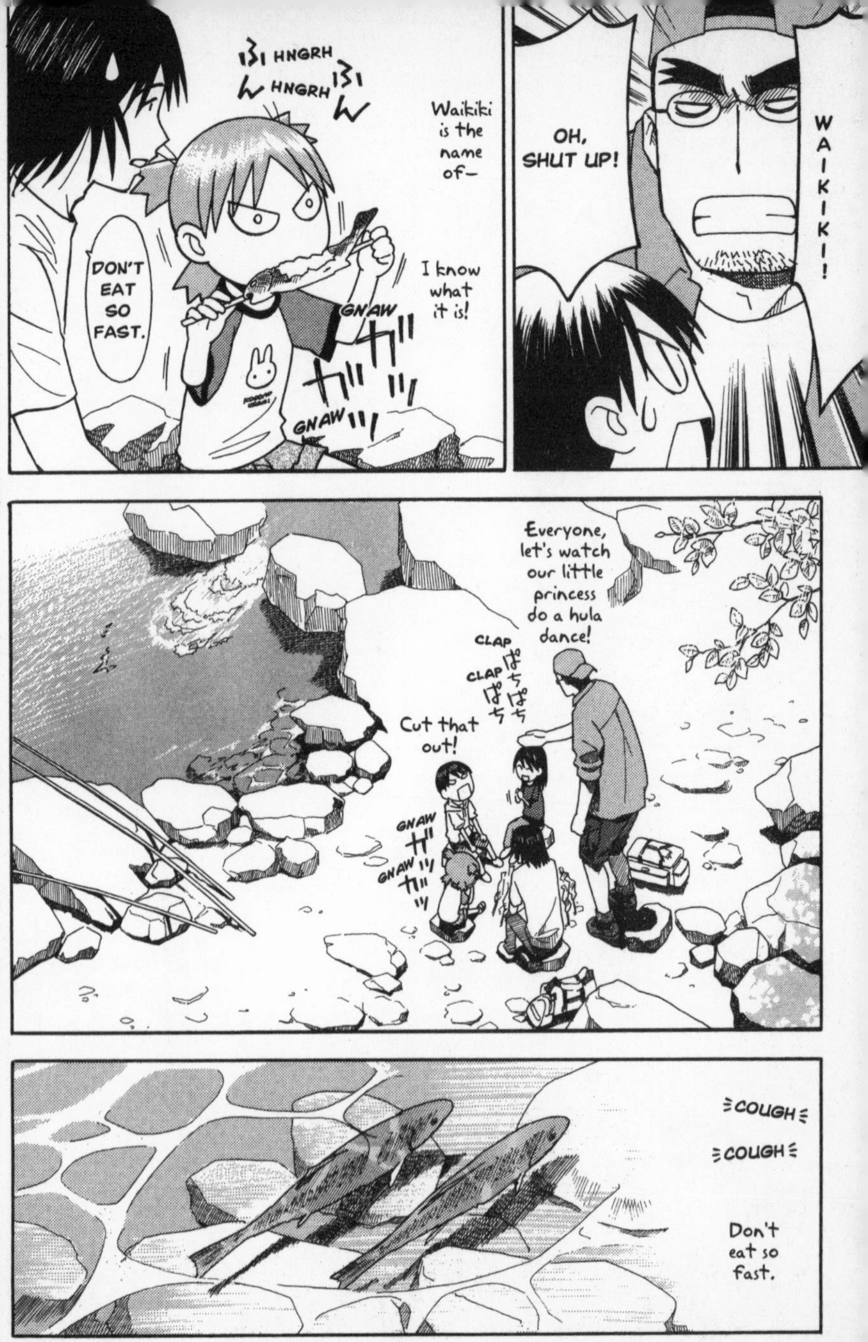
WAIKIKI!
OH, SHUT UP!
Waikiki is the name of–
HNGRH
HNGRH
I know what it is!
GNAW
DON'T EAT SO FAST.
GNAW
Everyone, let's watch our little princess do a hula dance!
CLAP
CLAP
Cut that out!
GNAW
GNAW
COUGH
COUGH
Don't eat so fast.

YOTSUBA&!

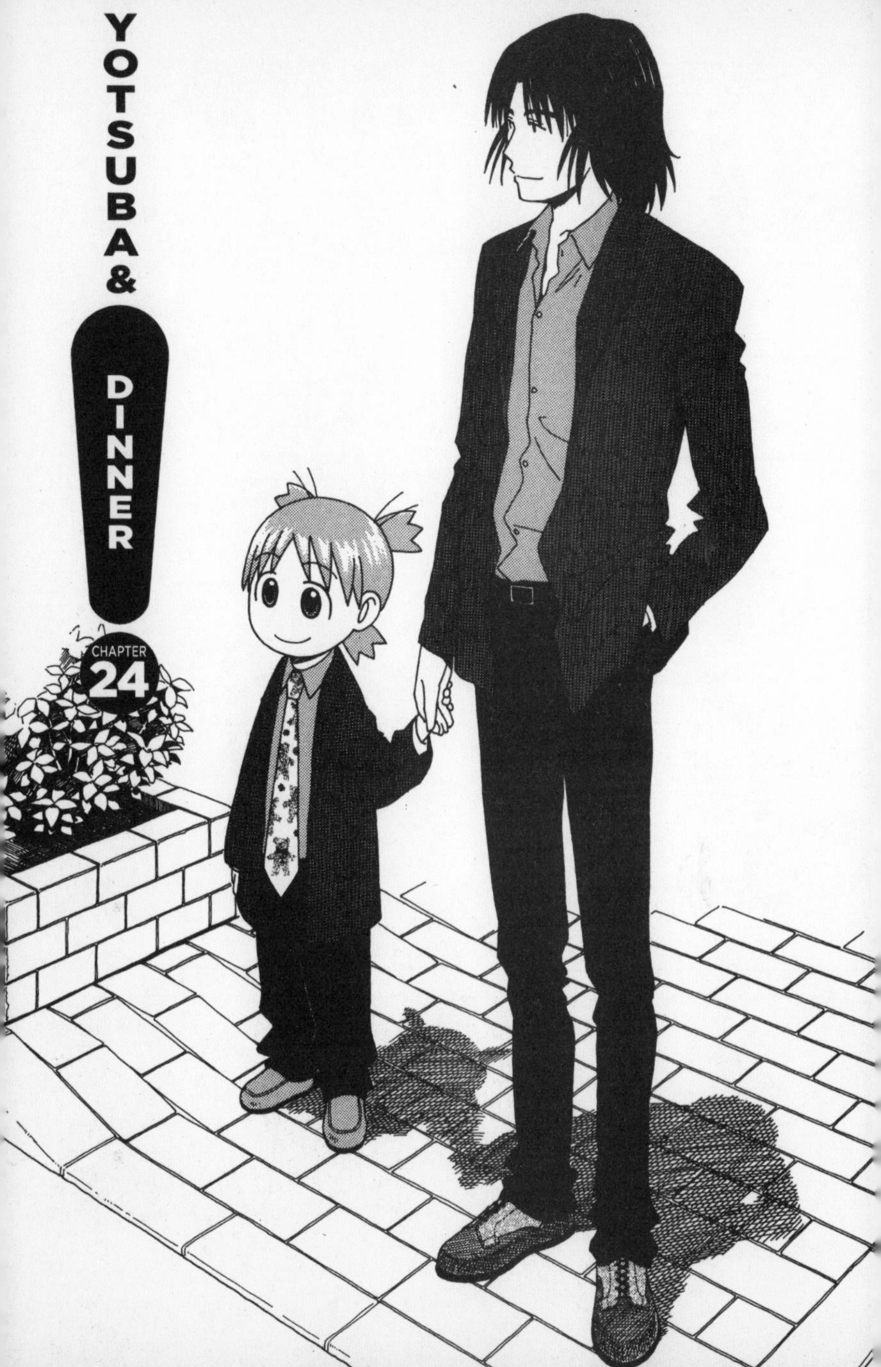
YOTSUBA&!
DINNER
CHAPTER 24

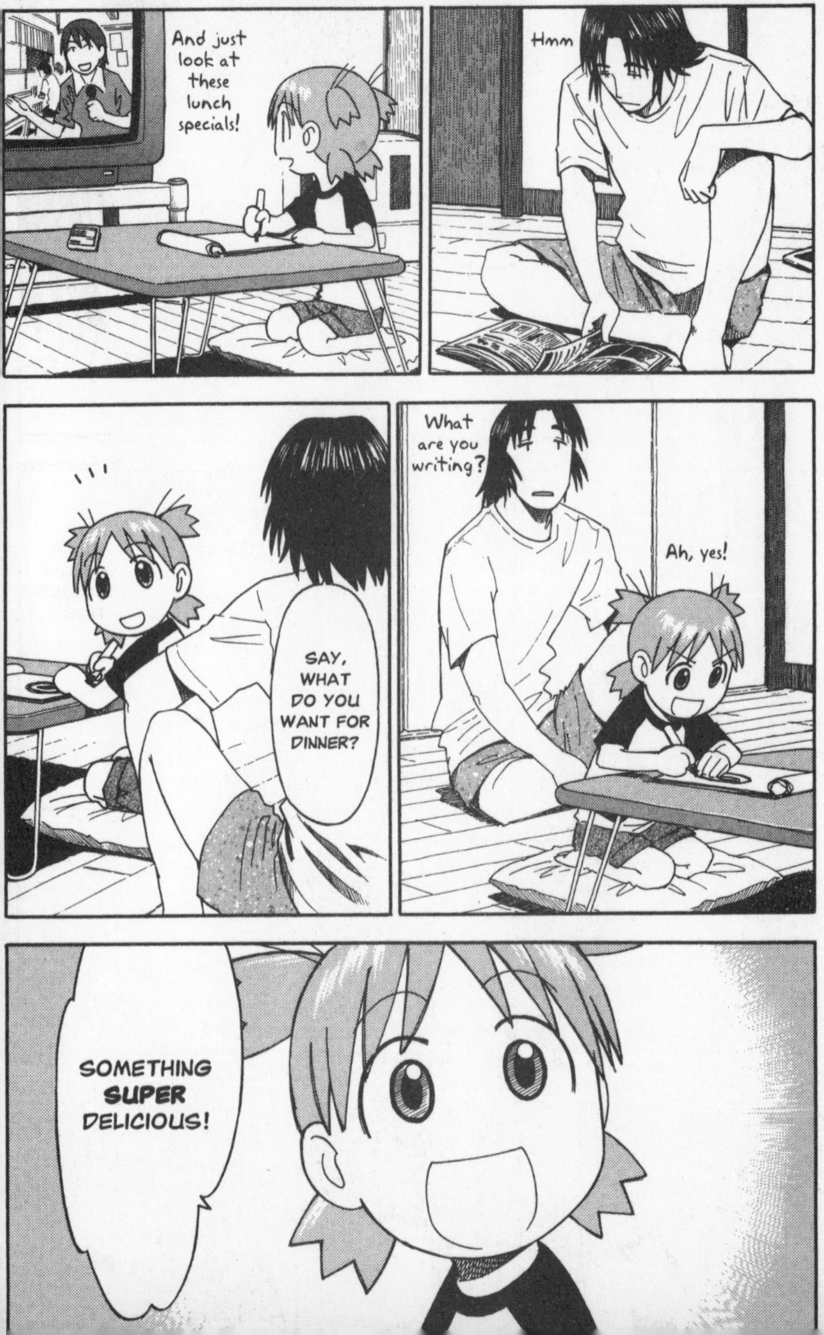
Hmm
And just look at these lunch specials!
What are you writing?
Ah, yes!
SAY, WHAT DO YOU WANT FOR DINNER?
SOMETHING **SUPER** DELICIOUS!

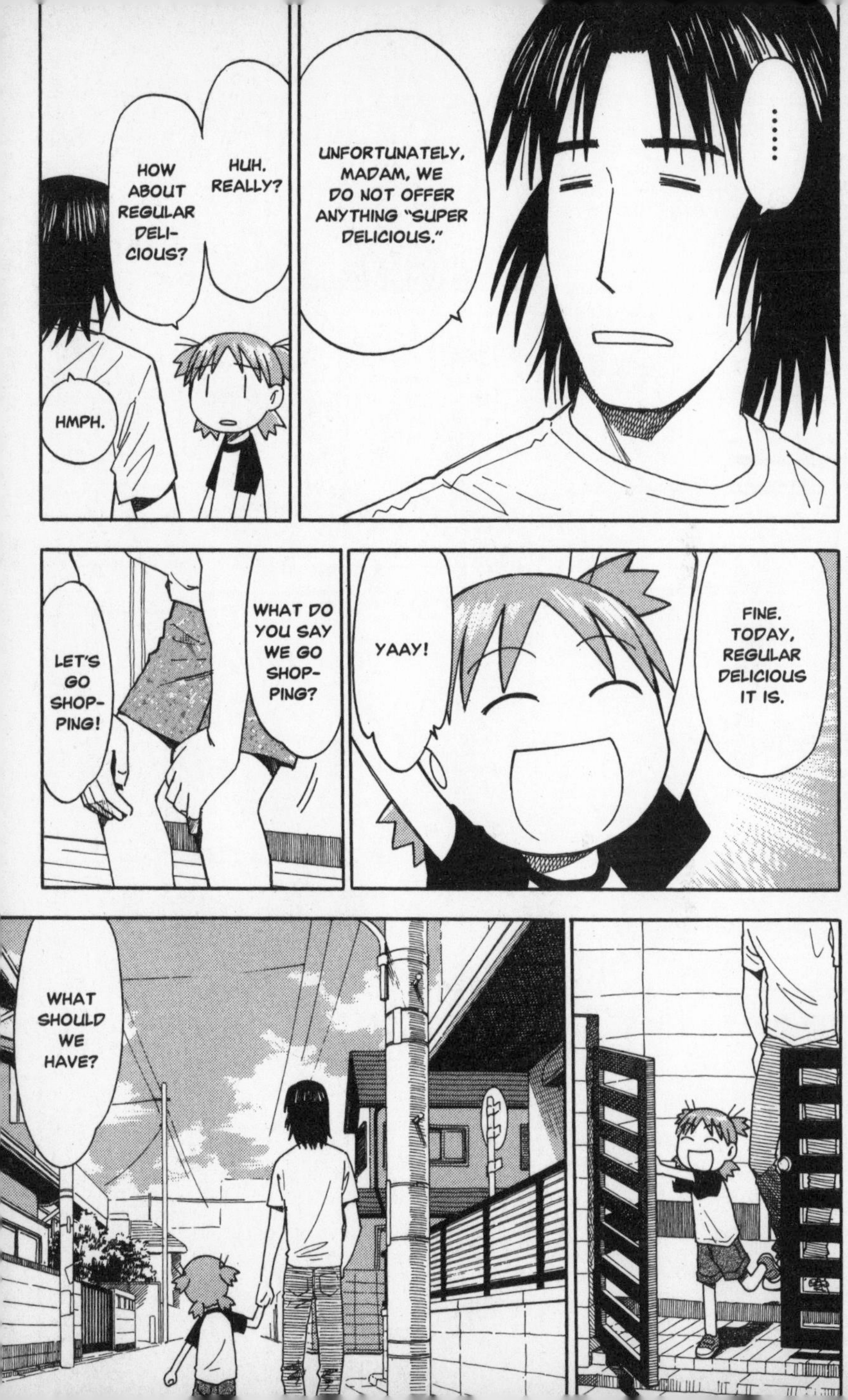
......
UNFORTUNATELY, MADAM, WE DO NOT OFFER ANYTHING "SUPER DELICIOUS."
HUH. REALLY?
HOW ABOUT REGULAR DELI-CIOUS?
HMPH.
FINE. TODAY, REGULAR DELICIOUS IT IS.
YAAY!
WHAT DO YOU SAY WE GO SHOP-PING?
LET'S GO SHOP-PING!
WHAT SHOULD WE HAVE?

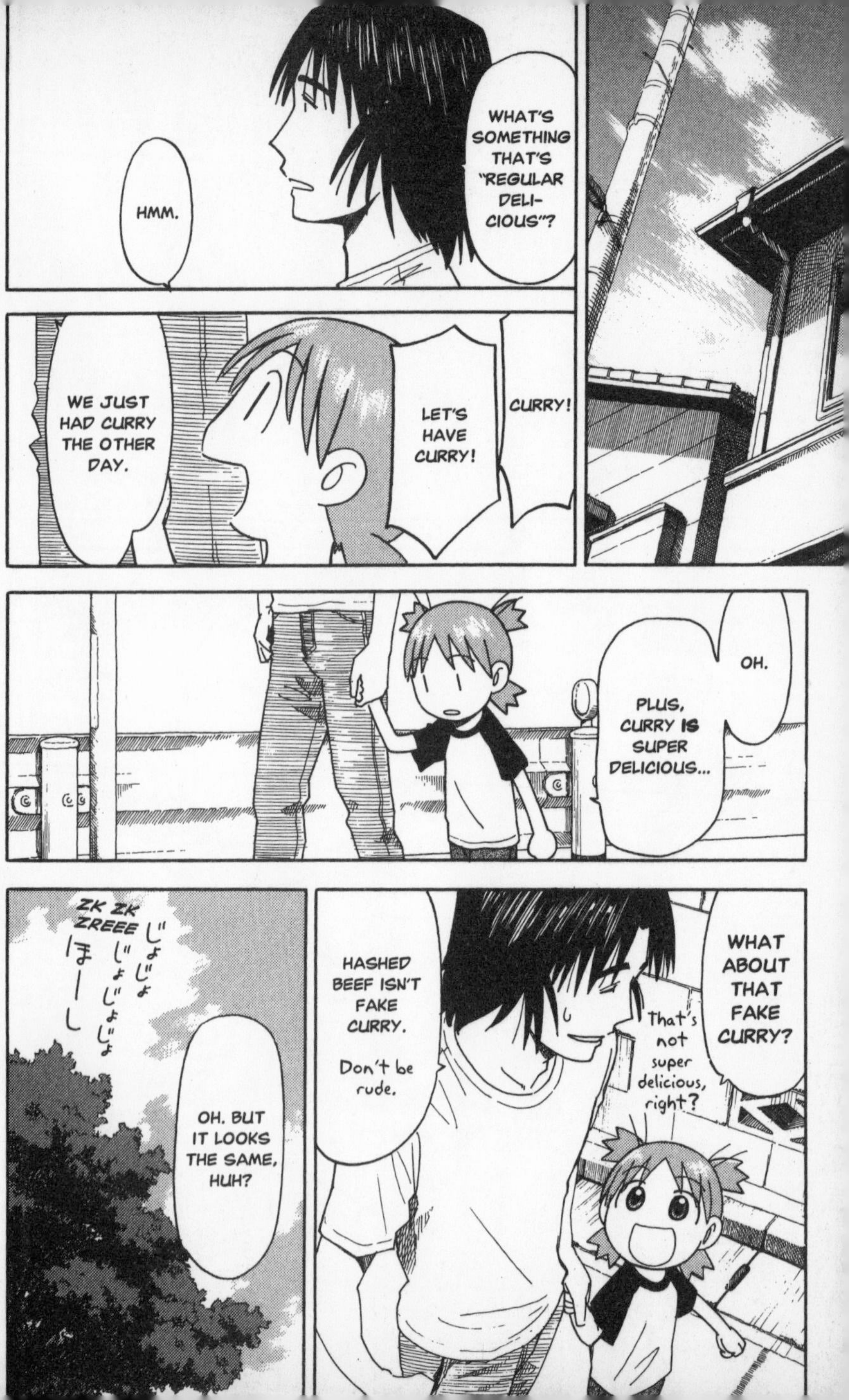
WHAT'S SOMETHING THAT'S "REGULAR DELICIOUS"?
HMM.
CURRY!
LET'S HAVE CURRY!
WE JUST HAD CURRY THE OTHER DAY.
OH.
PLUS, CURRY IS SUPER DELICIOUS...
WHAT ABOUT THAT FAKE CURRY?
That's not super delicious, right?
HASHED BEEF ISN'T FAKE CURRY.
Don't be rude.
じょじょ じょじょじょ ほーし
ZK ZK ZREEE
OH. BUT IT LOOKS THE SAME, HUH?

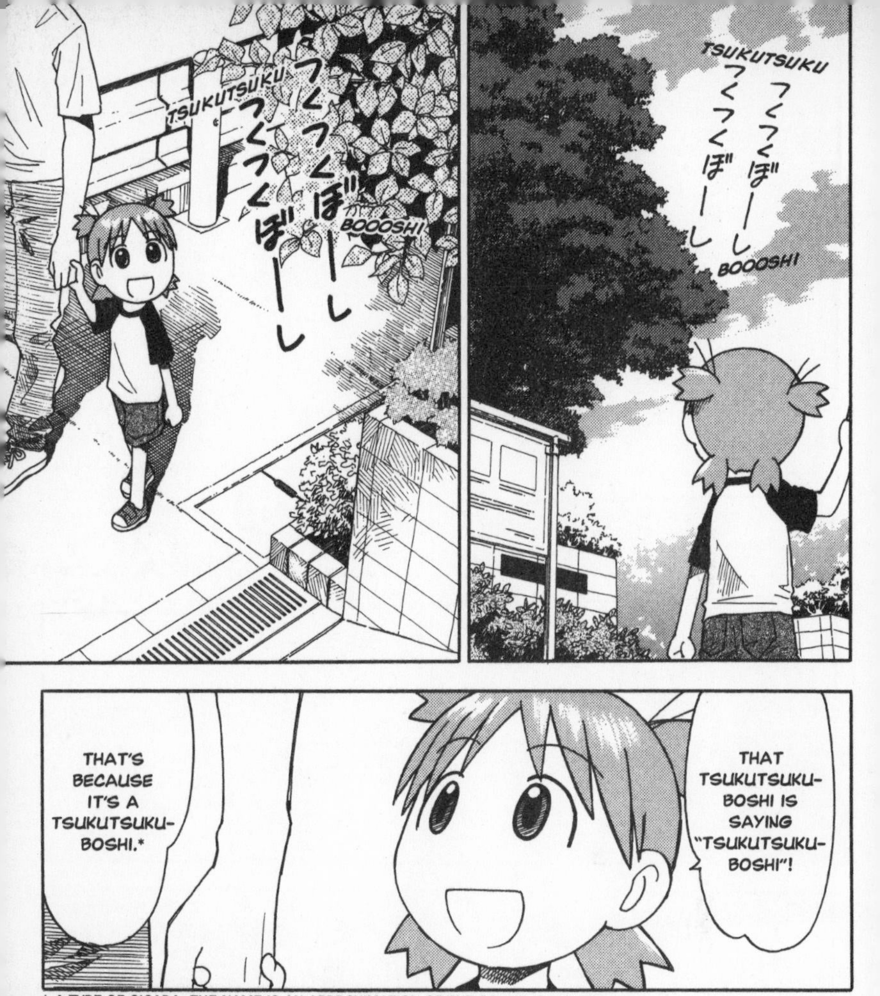
TSUKUTSUKU
つくつくぼーし
BOOOSHI
TSUKUTSUKU
つくつくぼーし
BOOOSHI
THAT TSUKUTSUKU-BOSHI IS SAYING "TSUKUTSUKU-BOSHI"!
THAT'S BECAUSE IT'S A TSUKUTSUKU-BOSHI.*

* A TYPE OF CICADA; THE NAME IS AN APPROXIMATION OF THE SOUND IT MAKES.

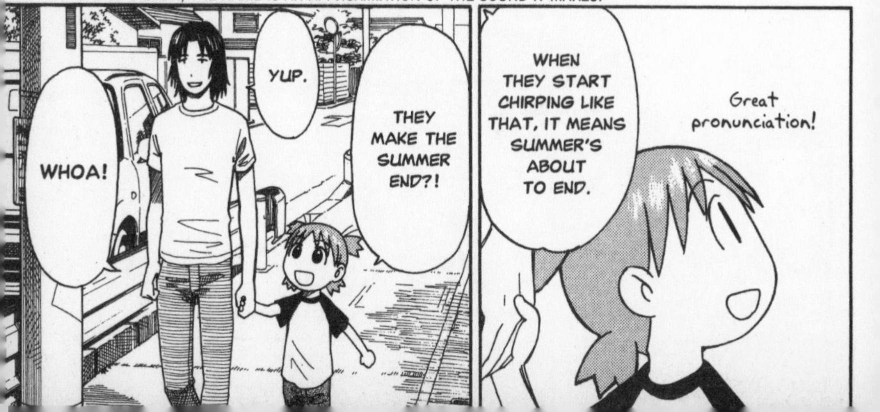
WHEN THEY START CHIRPING LIKE THAT, IT MEANS SUMMER'S ABOUT TO END.
Great pronunciation!
THEY MAKE THE SUMMER END?!
YUP.
WHOA!

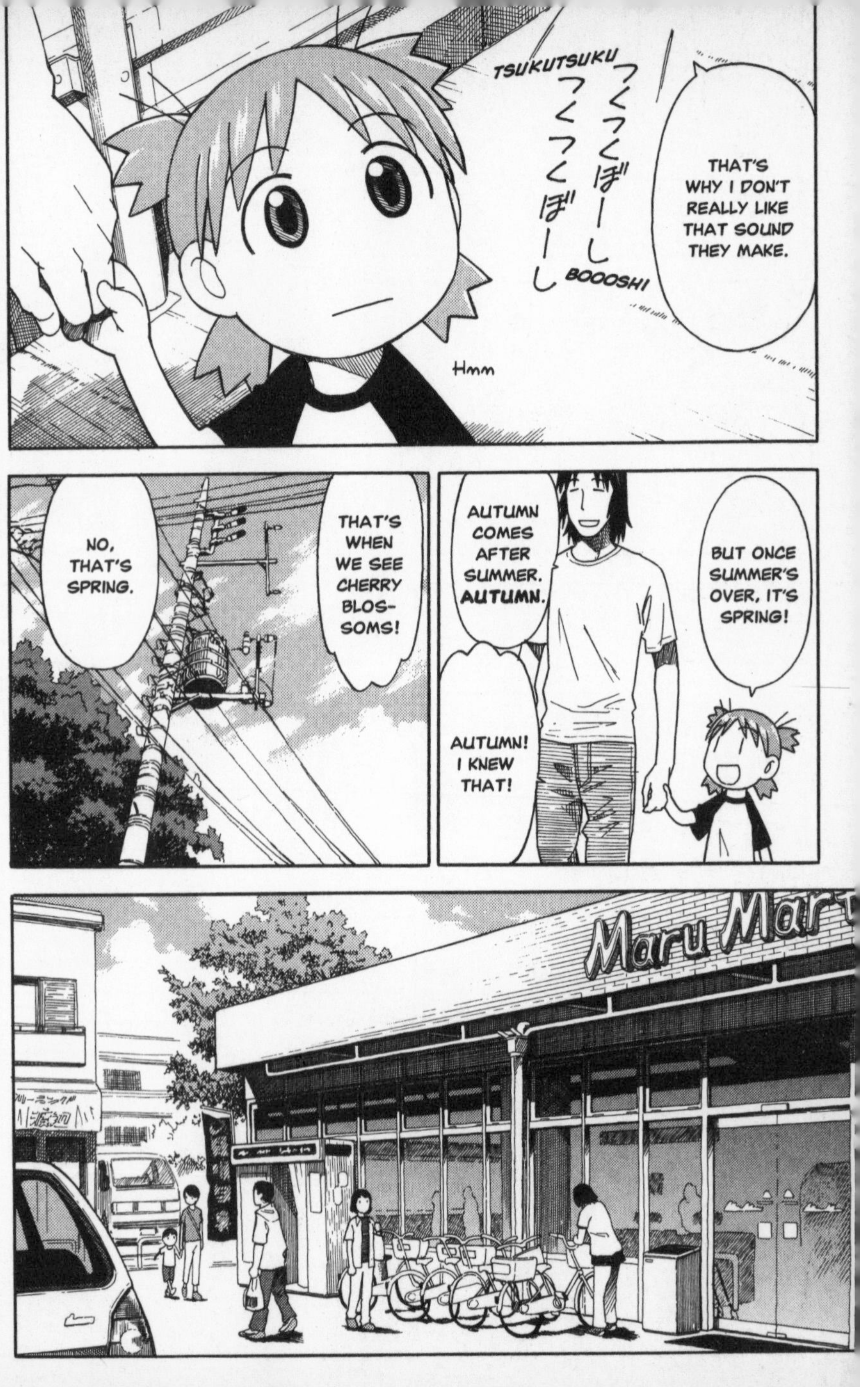
THAT'S WHY I DON'T REALLY LIKE THAT SOUND THEY MAKE.
つくつくぼーし
つくつくぼーし
TSUKUTSUKU
BOOOSHI
Hmm
BUT ONCE SUMMER'S OVER, IT'S SPRING!
AUTUMN COMES AFTER SUMMER. AUTUMN.
AUTUMN! I KNEW THAT!
THAT'S WHEN WE SEE CHERRY BLOS-SOMS!
NO, THAT'S SPRING.
Maru Mar

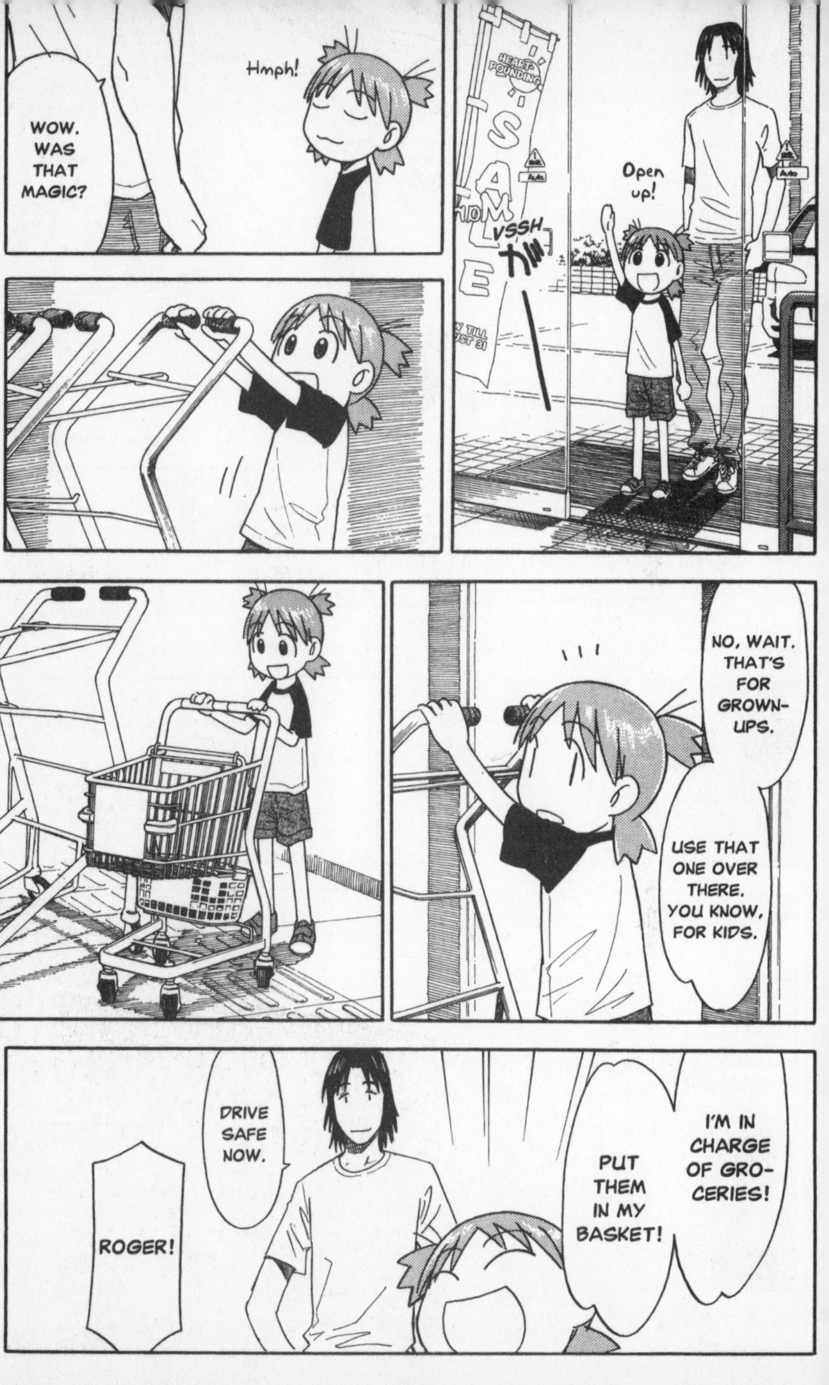
HEART-POUNDING
SALE
Open up!
VSSH
Hmph!
WOW. WAS THAT MAGIC?
NO, WAIT. THAT'S FOR GROWN-UPS.
USE THAT ONE OVER THERE. YOU KNOW, FOR KIDS.
I'M IN CHARGE OF GRO-CERIES!
PUT THEM IN MY BASKET!
DRIVE SAFE NOW.
ROGER!

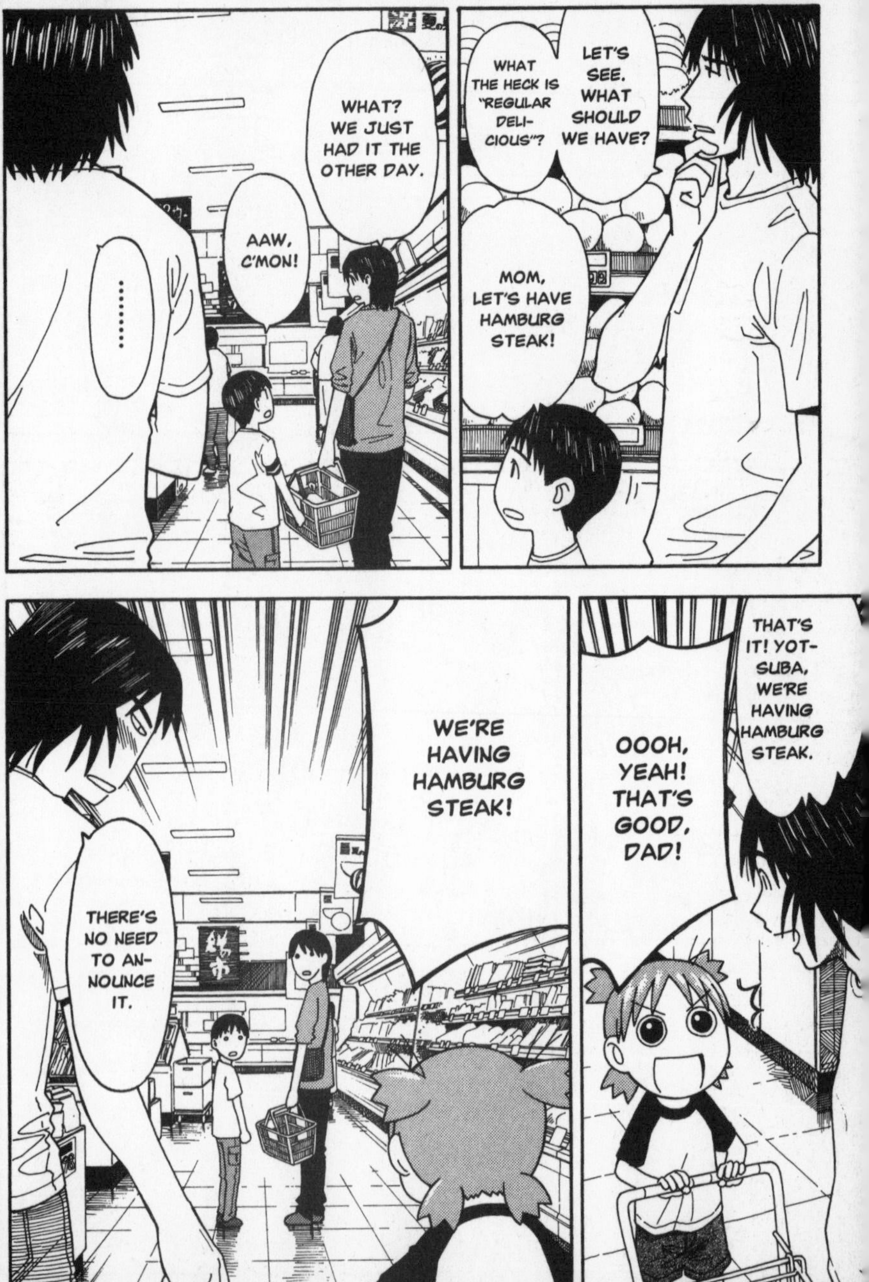
LET'S SEE. WHAT SHOULD WE HAVE?
WHAT THE HECK IS "REGULAR DELICIOUS"?
MOM, LET'S HAVE HAMBURG STEAK!
WHAT? WE JUST HAD IT THE OTHER DAY.
AAW, C'MON!
....
THAT'S IT! YOTSUBA, WE'RE HAVING HAMBURG STEAK.
OOOH, YEAH! THAT'S GOOD, DAD!
WE'RE HAVING HAMBURG STEAK!
THERE'S NO NEED TO ANNOUNCE IT.

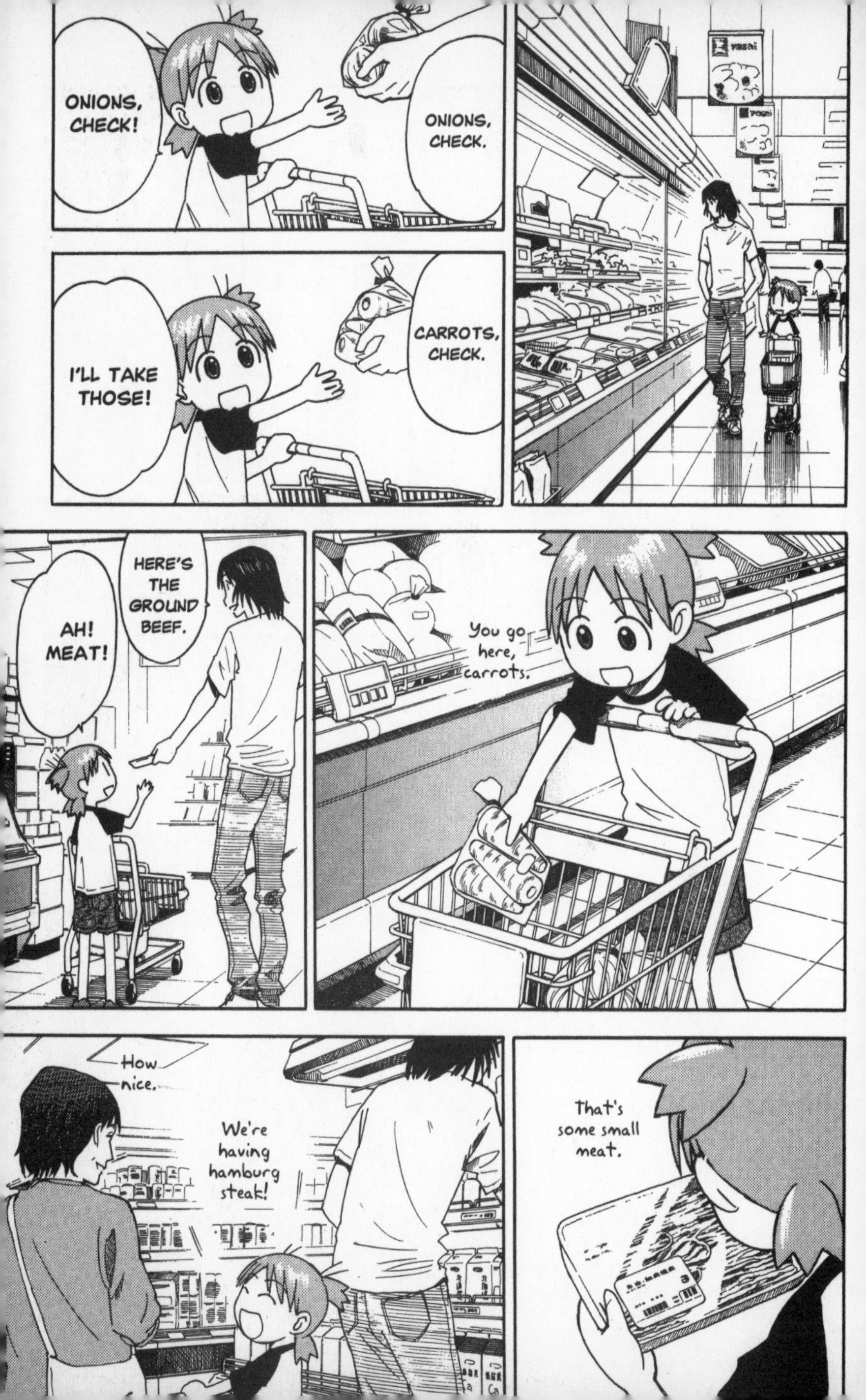
yasai
ONIONS, CHECK.
ONIONS, CHECK!
CARROTS, CHECK.
I'LL TAKE THOSE!
You go here, carrots.
HERE'S THE GROUND BEEF.
AH! MEAT!
That's some small meat.
We're having hamburg steak!
How nice.

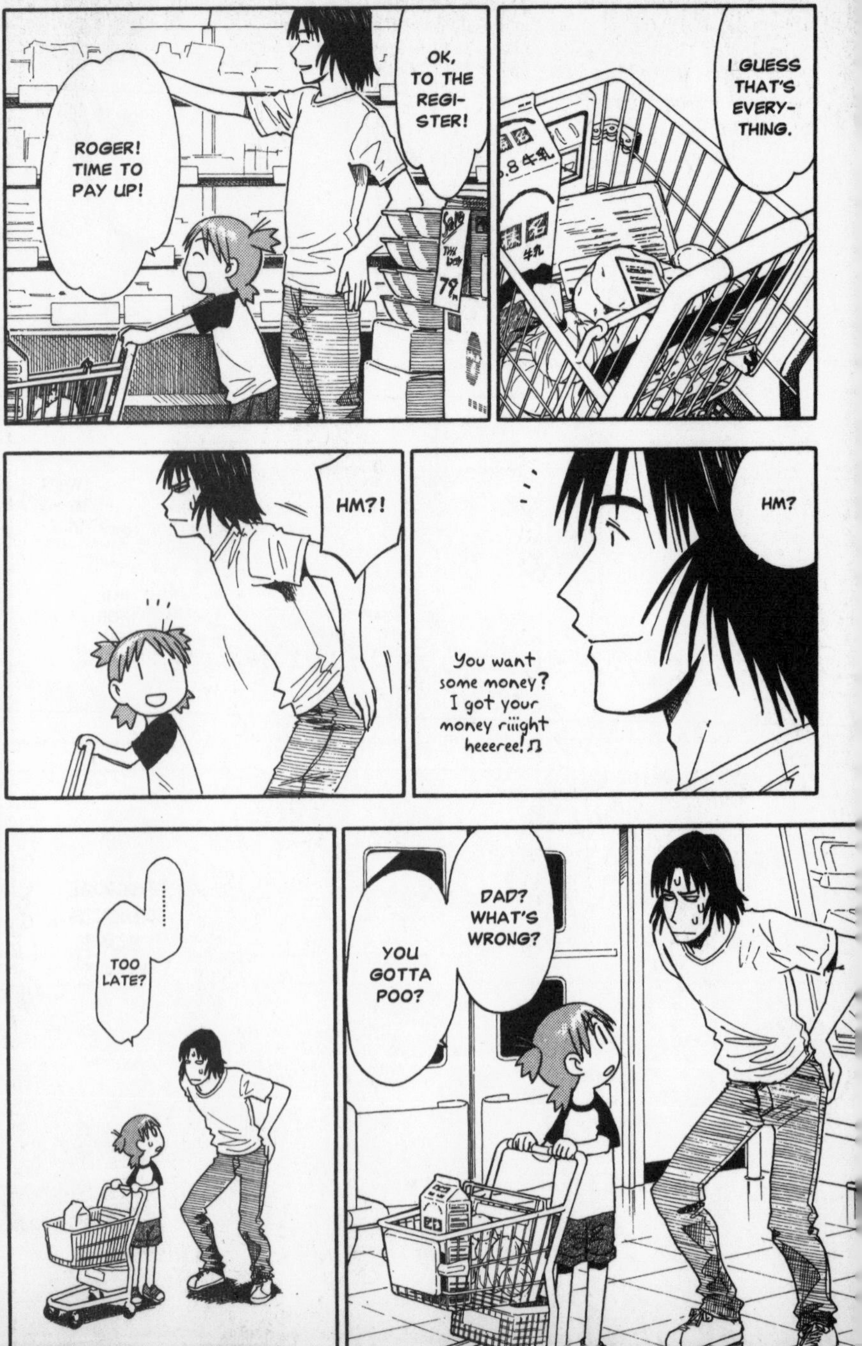
I GUESS THAT'S EVERY-THING.
OK, TO THE REGI-STER!
ROGER! TIME TO PAY UP!
HM?
You want some money? I got your money riiight heeeree! ♫
HM?!
DAD? WHAT'S WRONG?
YOU GOTTA POO?
......
TOO LATE?

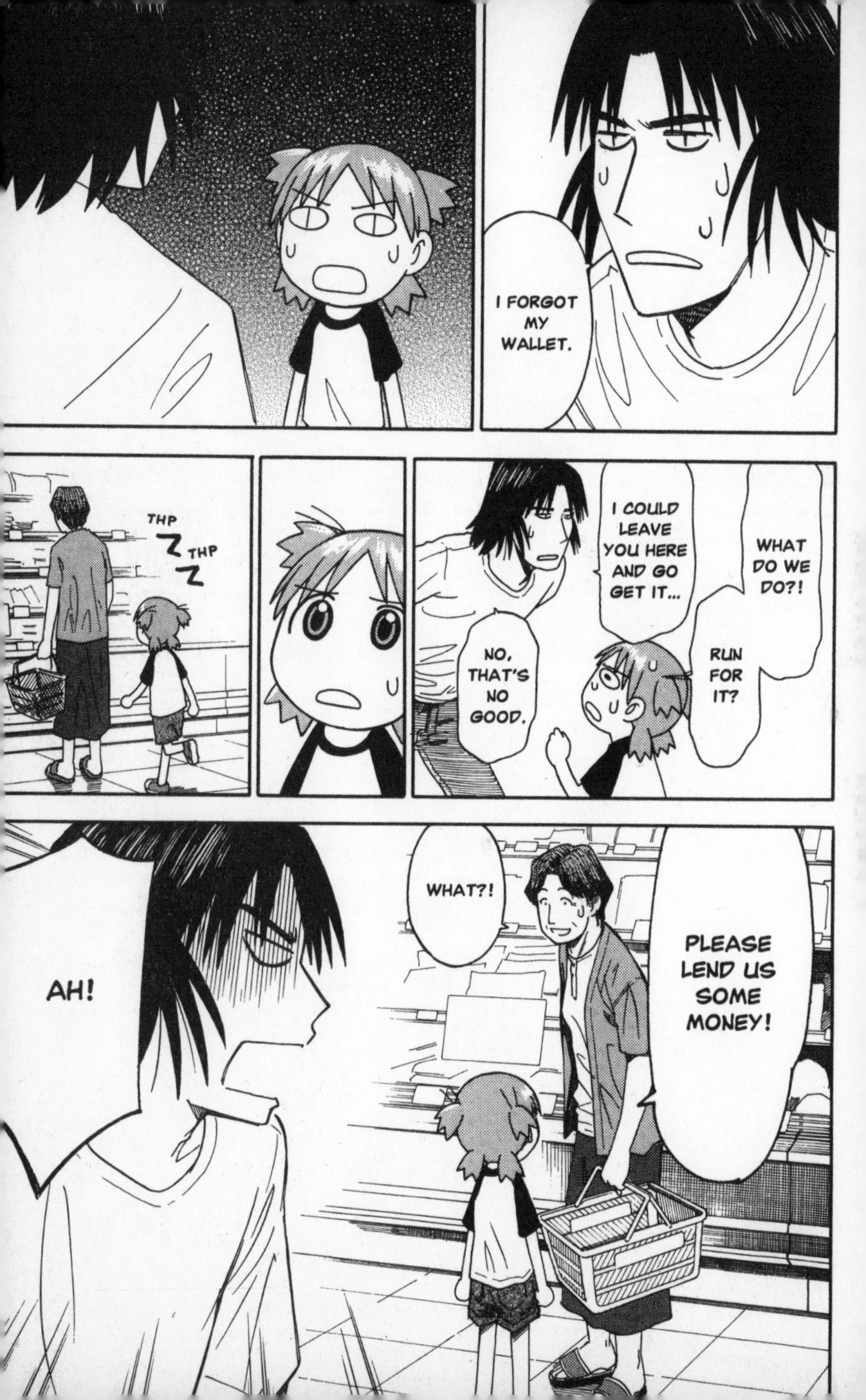
I FORGOT MY WALLET.
WHAT DO WE DO?!
RUN FOR IT?
I COULD LEAVE YOU HERE AND GO GET IT...
NO, THAT'S NO GOOD.
THP THP
PLEASE LEND US SOME MONEY!
WHAT?!
AH!

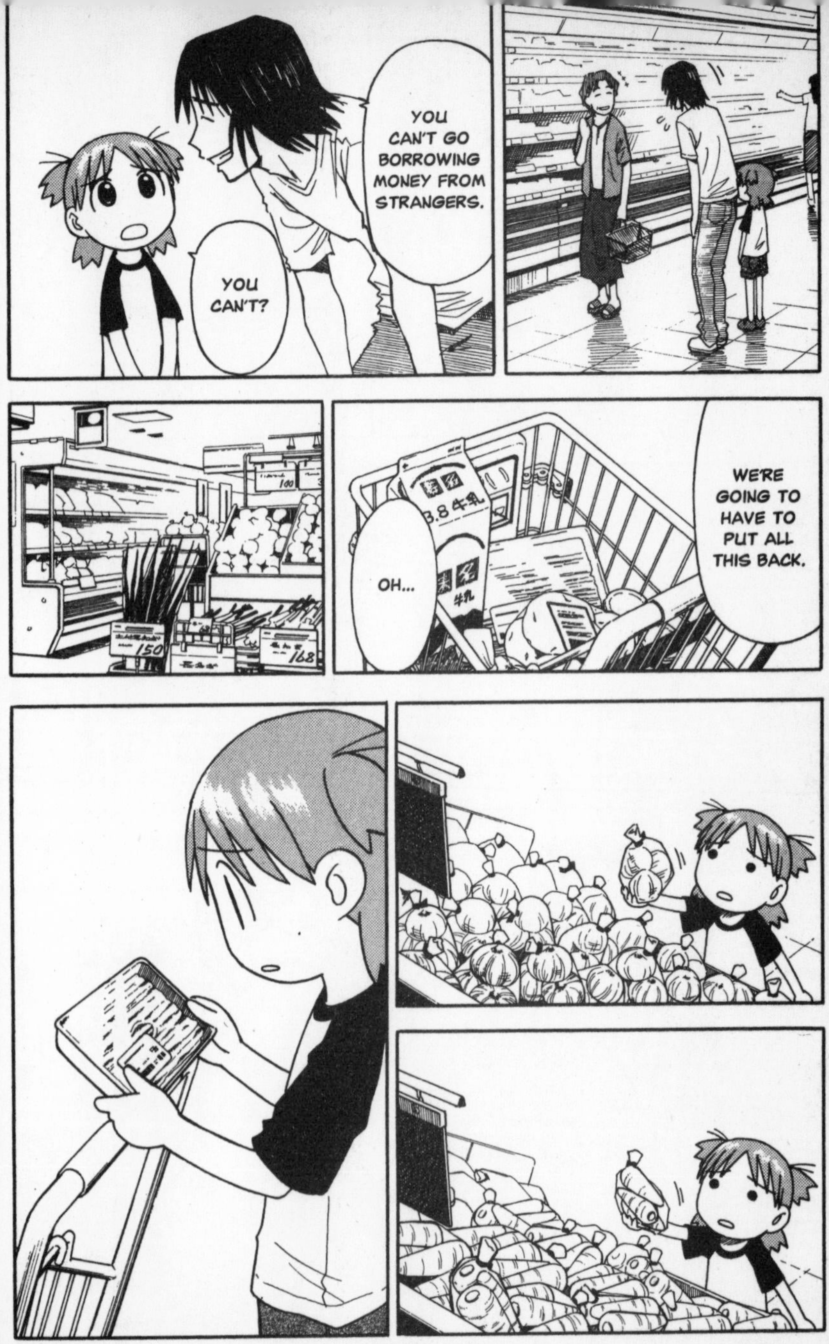
YOU CAN'T GO BORROWING MONEY FROM STRANGERS.
YOU CAN'T?
WE'RE GOING TO HAVE TO PUT ALL THIS BACK.
OH...

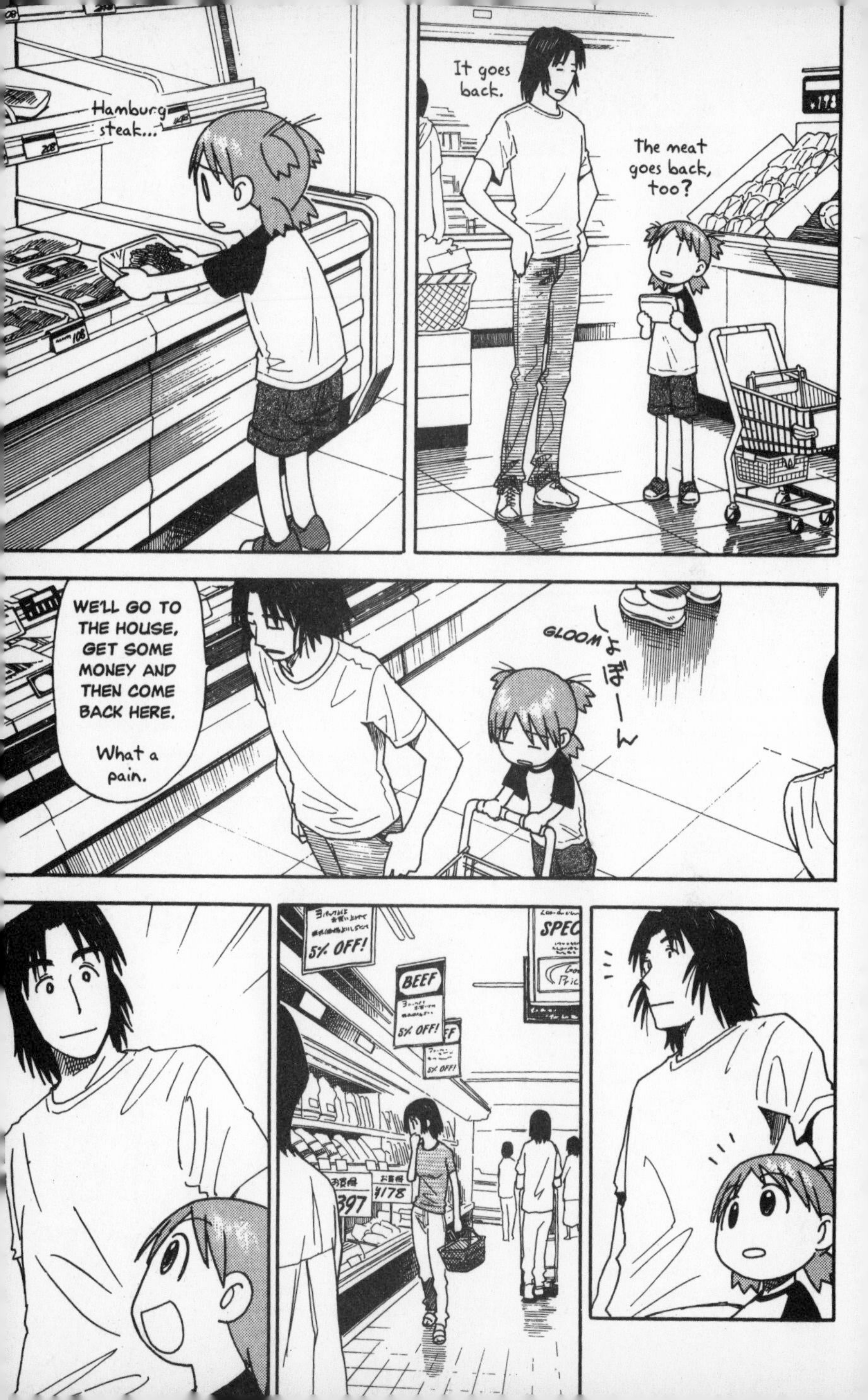
It goes back.
The meat goes back, too?
Hamburg steak...
GLOOM
しょぼーん
WE'LL GO TO THE HOUSE, GET SOME MONEY AND THEN COME BACK HERE.
What a pain.
SPEC
5% OFF!
BEEF
5% OFF!
5% OFF!
お買得
397
¥178

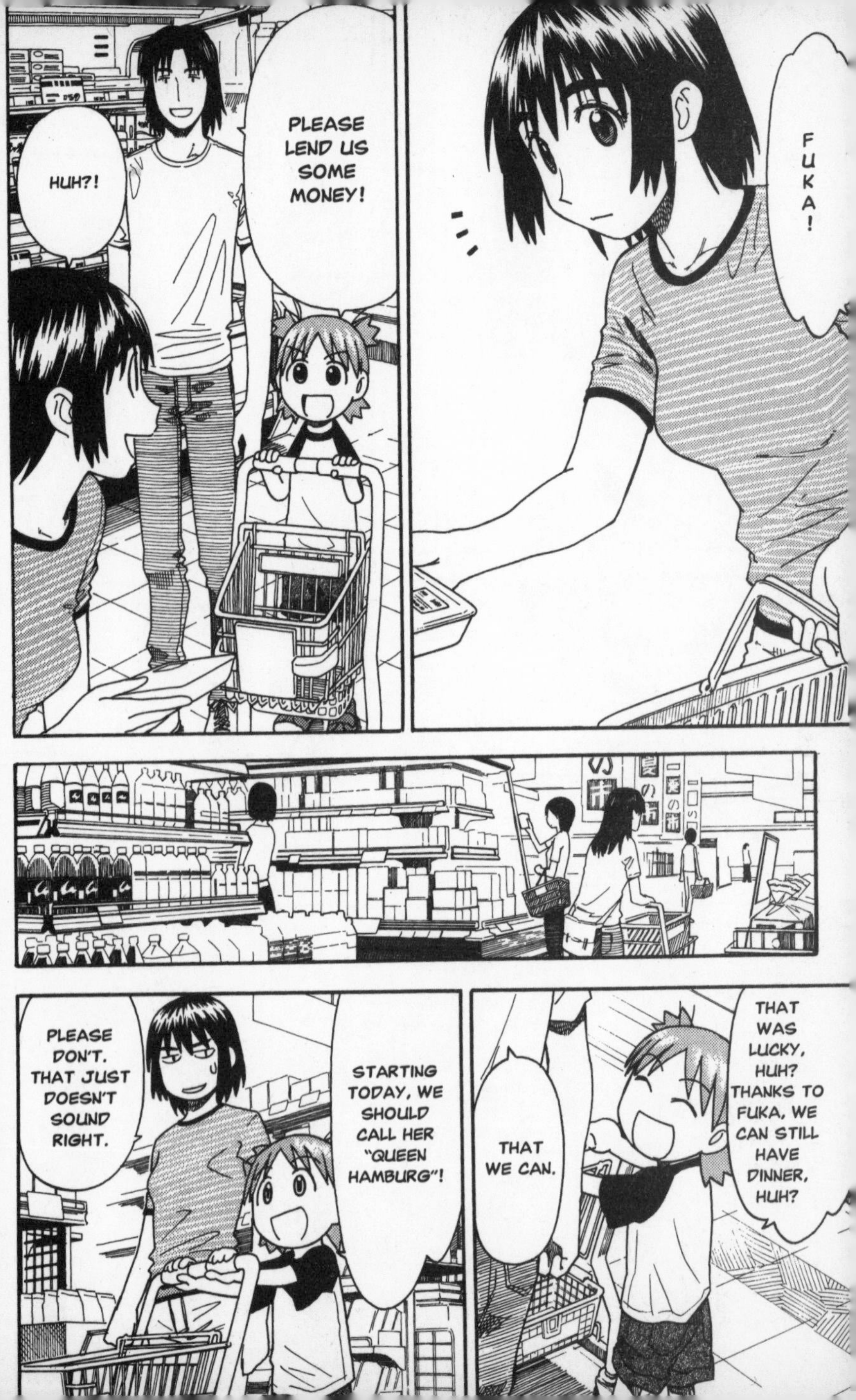
FUKA!
PLEASE LEND US SOME MONEY!
HUH?!
THAT WAS LUCKY, HUH? THANKS TO FUKA, WE CAN STILL HAVE DINNER, HUH?
THAT WE CAN.
STARTING TODAY, WE SHOULD CALL HER "QUEEN HAMBURG"!
PLEASE DON'T. THAT JUST DOESN'T SOUND RIGHT.

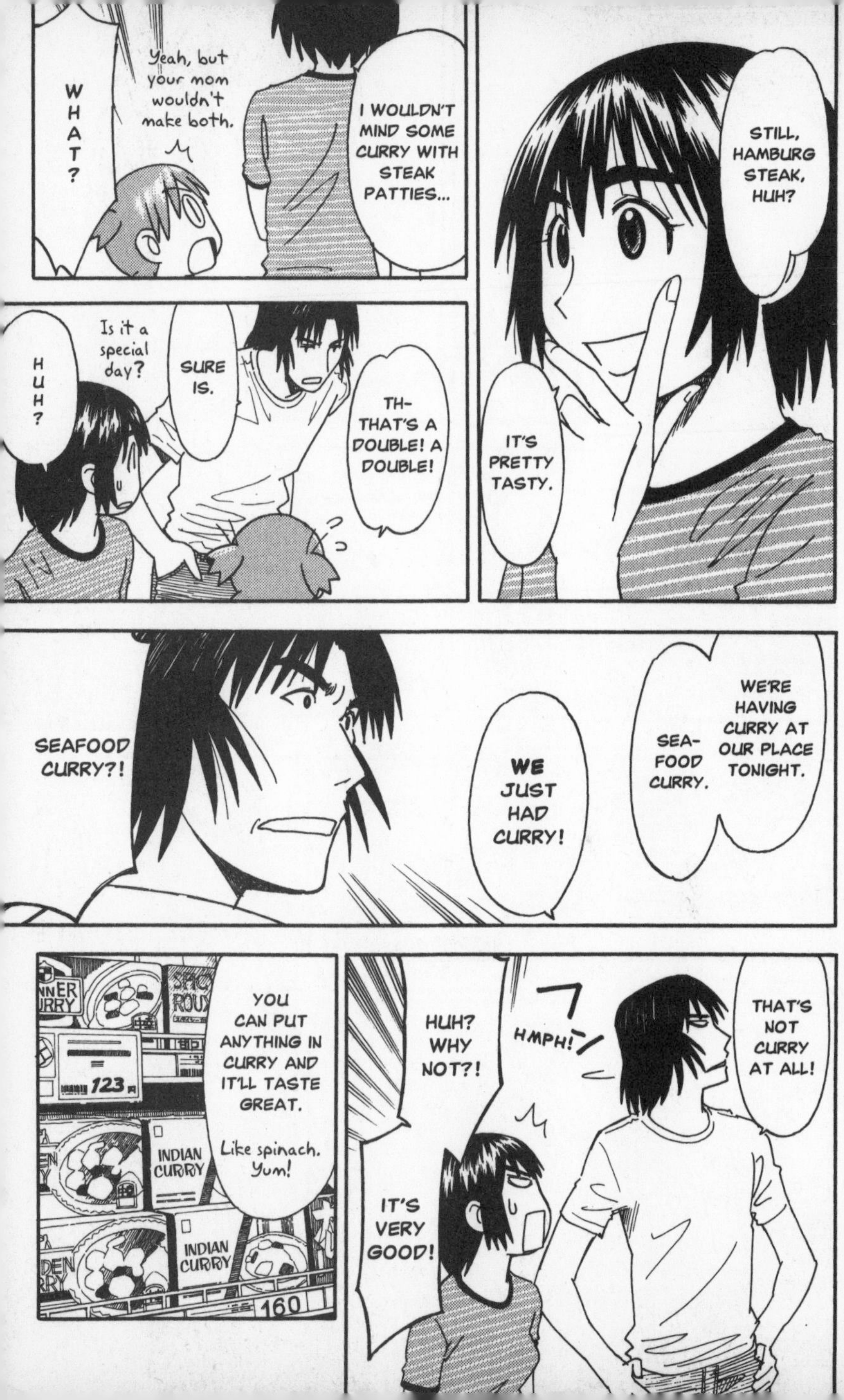

STILL, HAMBURG STEAK, HUH?
IT'S PRETTY TASTY.
I WOULDN'T MIND SOME CURRY WITH STEAK PATTIES...
Yeah, but your mom wouldn't make both.
WHAT?
TH- THAT'S A DOUBLE! A DOUBLE!
SURE IS.
Is it a special day?
HUH?
WE'RE HAVING CURRY AT OUR PLACE TONIGHT.
SEA-FOOD CURRY.
WE JUST HAD CURRY!
SEAFOOD CURRY?!
THAT'S NOT CURRY AT ALL!
HMPH!
HUH? WHY NOT?!
IT'S VERY GOOD!
YOU CAN PUT ANYTHING IN CURRY AND IT'LL TASTE GREAT.
Like spinach. Yum!
123円
INDIAN CURRY
INDIAN CURRY
160

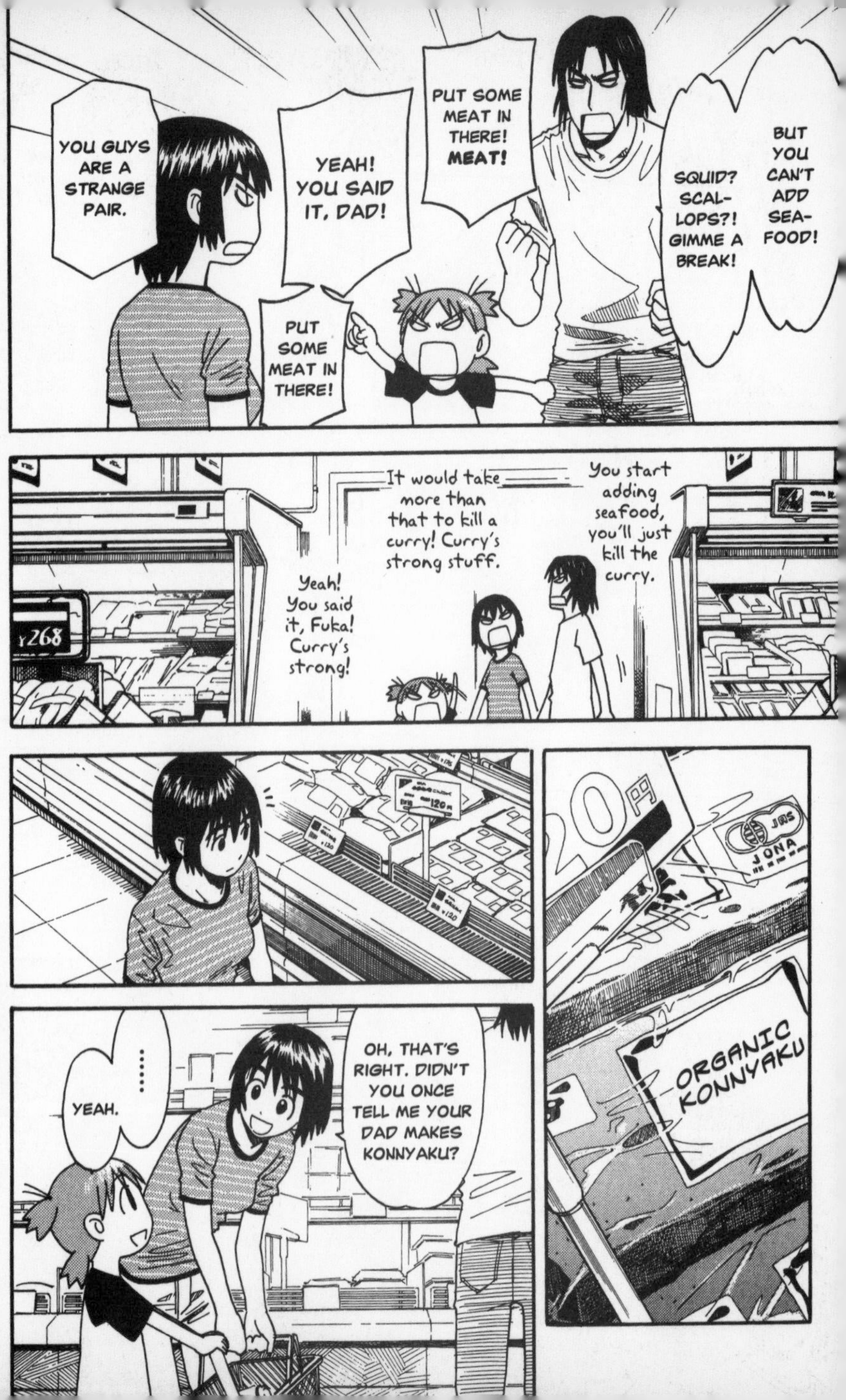
BUT YOU CAN'T ADD SEAFOOD!
SQUID? SCAL-LOPS?! GIMME A BREAK!
PUT SOME MEAT IN THERE! **MEAT!**
YEAH! YOU SAID IT, DAD!
PUT SOME MEAT IN THERE!
YOU GUYS ARE A STRANGE PAIR.
You start adding seafood, you'll just kill the curry.
It would take more than that to kill a curry! Curry's strong stuff.
Yeah! You said it, Fuka! Curry's strong!
¥268
20円
JAS
JONA
ORGANIC KONNYAKU
OH, THAT'S RIGHT. DIDN'T YOU ONCE TELL ME YOUR DAD MAKES KONNYAKU?
......
YEAH.

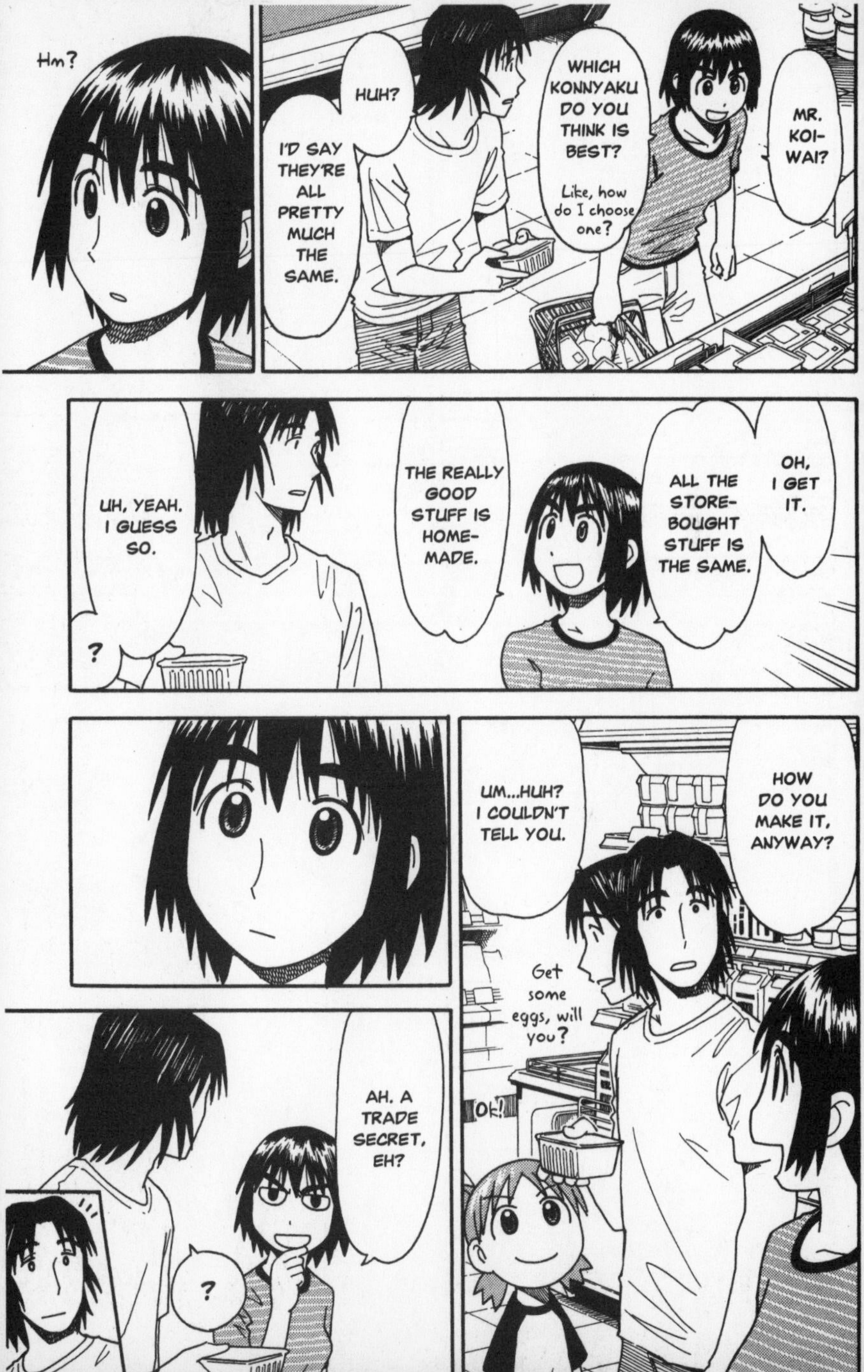
MR. KOI-WAI?
WHICH KONNYAKU DO YOU THINK IS BEST?
Like, how do I choose one?
HUH?
I'D SAY THEY'RE ALL PRETTY MUCH THE SAME.
Hm?
OH, I GET IT.
ALL THE STORE-BOUGHT STUFF IS THE SAME.
THE REALLY GOOD STUFF IS HOME-MADE.
UH, YEAH. I GUESS SO.
?
HOW DO YOU MAKE IT, ANYWAY?
UM...HUH? I COULDN'T TELL YOU.
Get some eggs, will you?
Ok!
AH. A TRADE SECRET, EH?
?

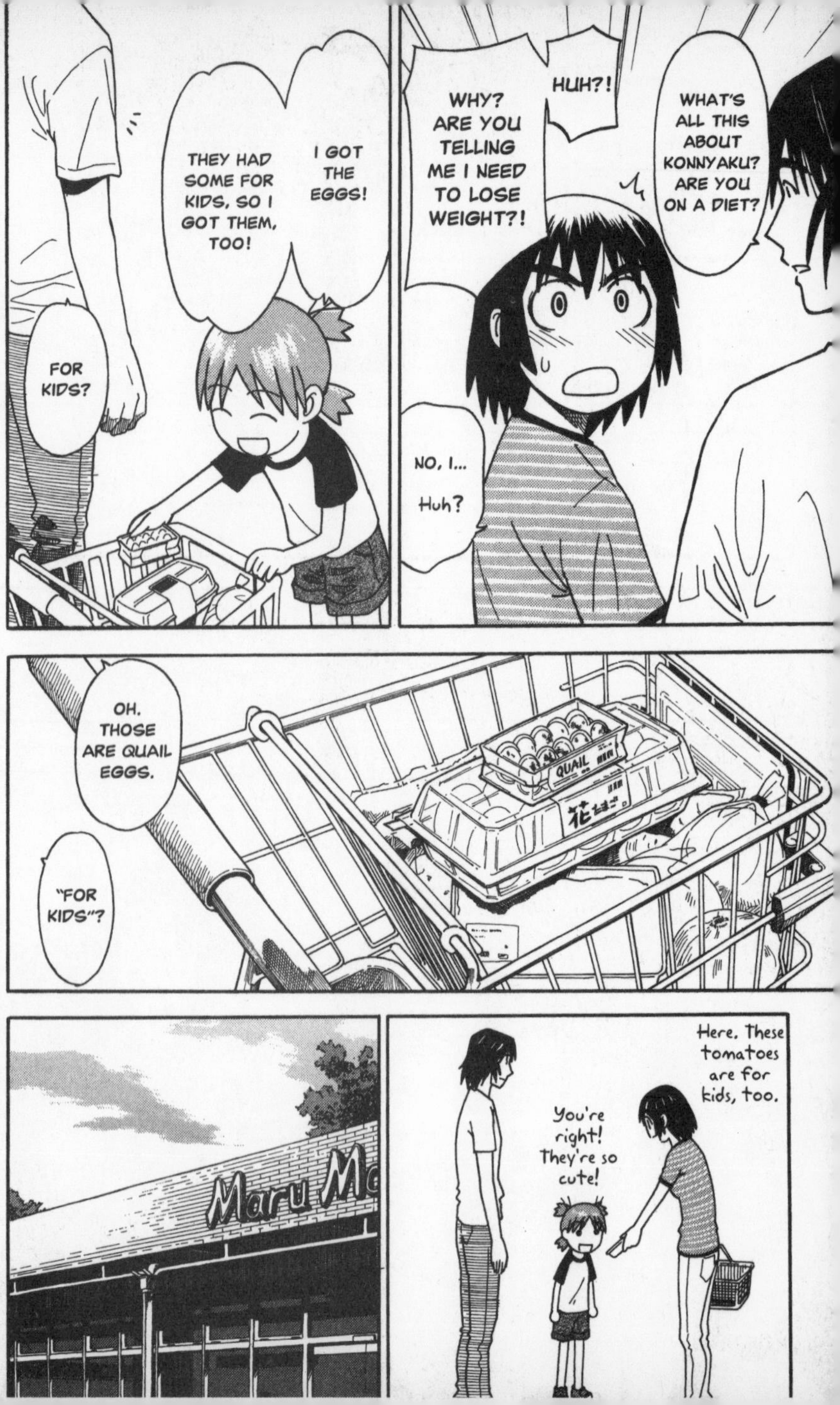
WHAT'S ALL THIS ABOUT KONNYAKU? ARE YOU ON A DIET?
HUH?!
WHY? ARE YOU TELLING ME I NEED TO LOSE WEIGHT?!
NO, I...
Huh?
I GOT THE EGGS!
THEY HAD SOME FOR KIDS, SO I GOT THEM, TOO!
FOR KIDS?
OH. THOSE ARE QUAIL EGGS.
QUAIL
"FOR KIDS"?
Here. These tomatoes are for kids, too.
You're right! They're so cute!

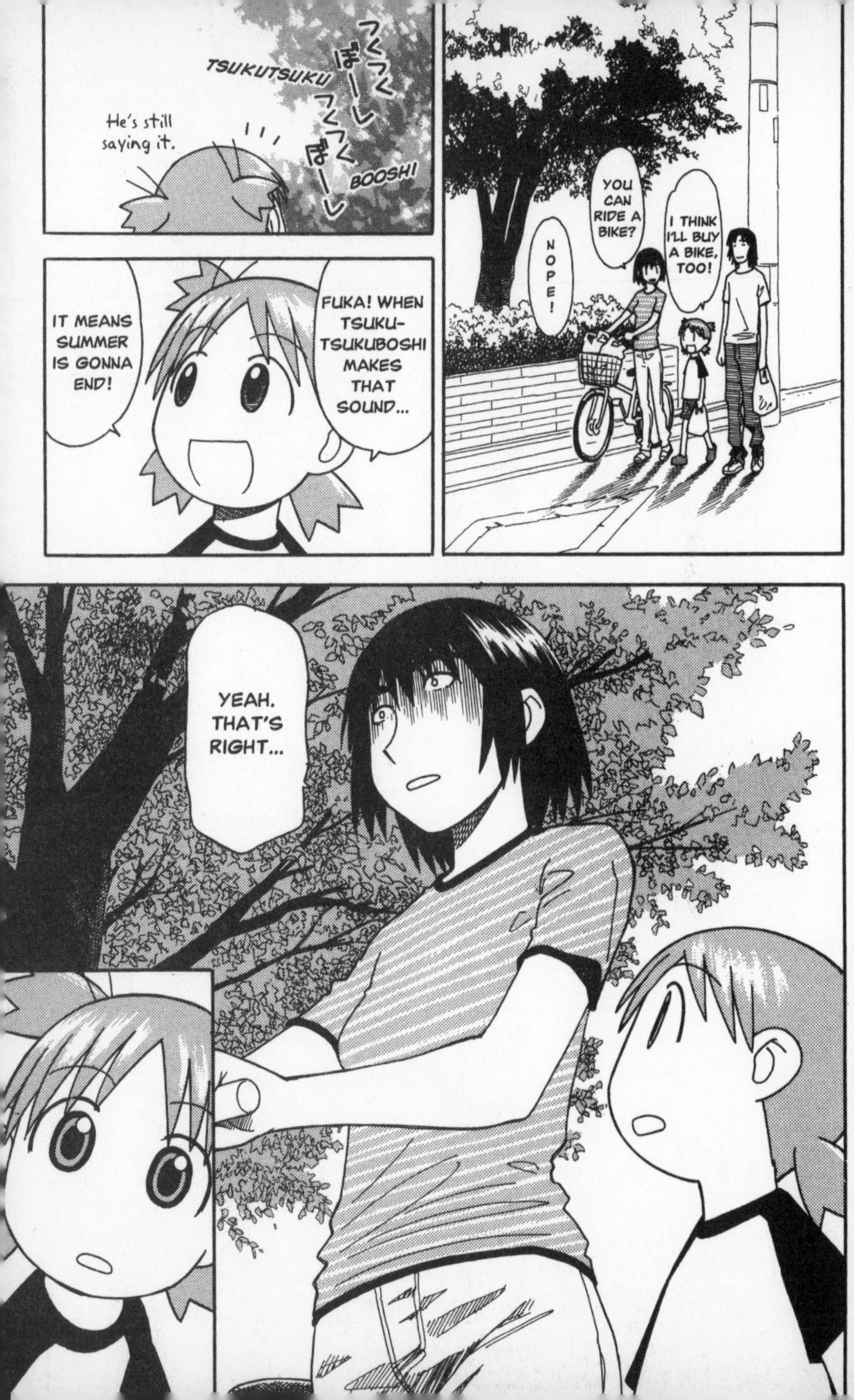
I THINK I'LL BUY A BIKE, TOO!
YOU CAN RIDE A BIKE?
NOPE!
つくつくぼーし
つくつくぼーし
TSUKUTSUKU
BOOSHI
He's still saying it.
FUKA! WHEN TSUKU-TSUKUBOSHI MAKES THAT SOUND...
IT MEANS SUMMER IS GONNA END!
YEAH. THAT'S RIGHT...

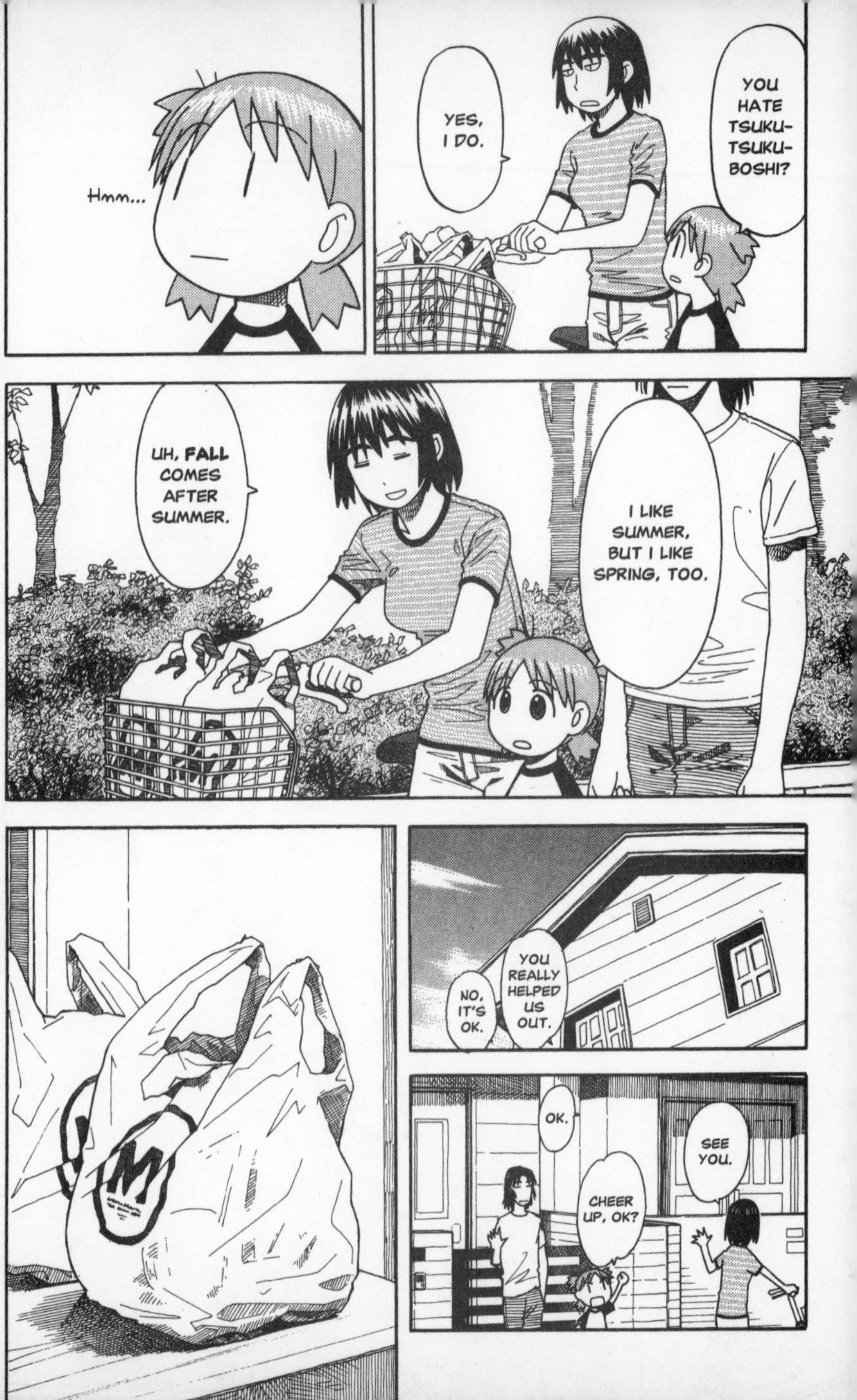
YOU HATE TSUKU-TSUKU-BOSHI?
YES, I DO.
Hmm...
I LIKE SUMMER, BUT I LIKE SPRING, TOO.
UH, FALL COMES AFTER SUMMER.
YOU REALLY HELPED US OUT.
NO, IT'S OK.
SEE YOU.
CHEER UP, OK?
OK.

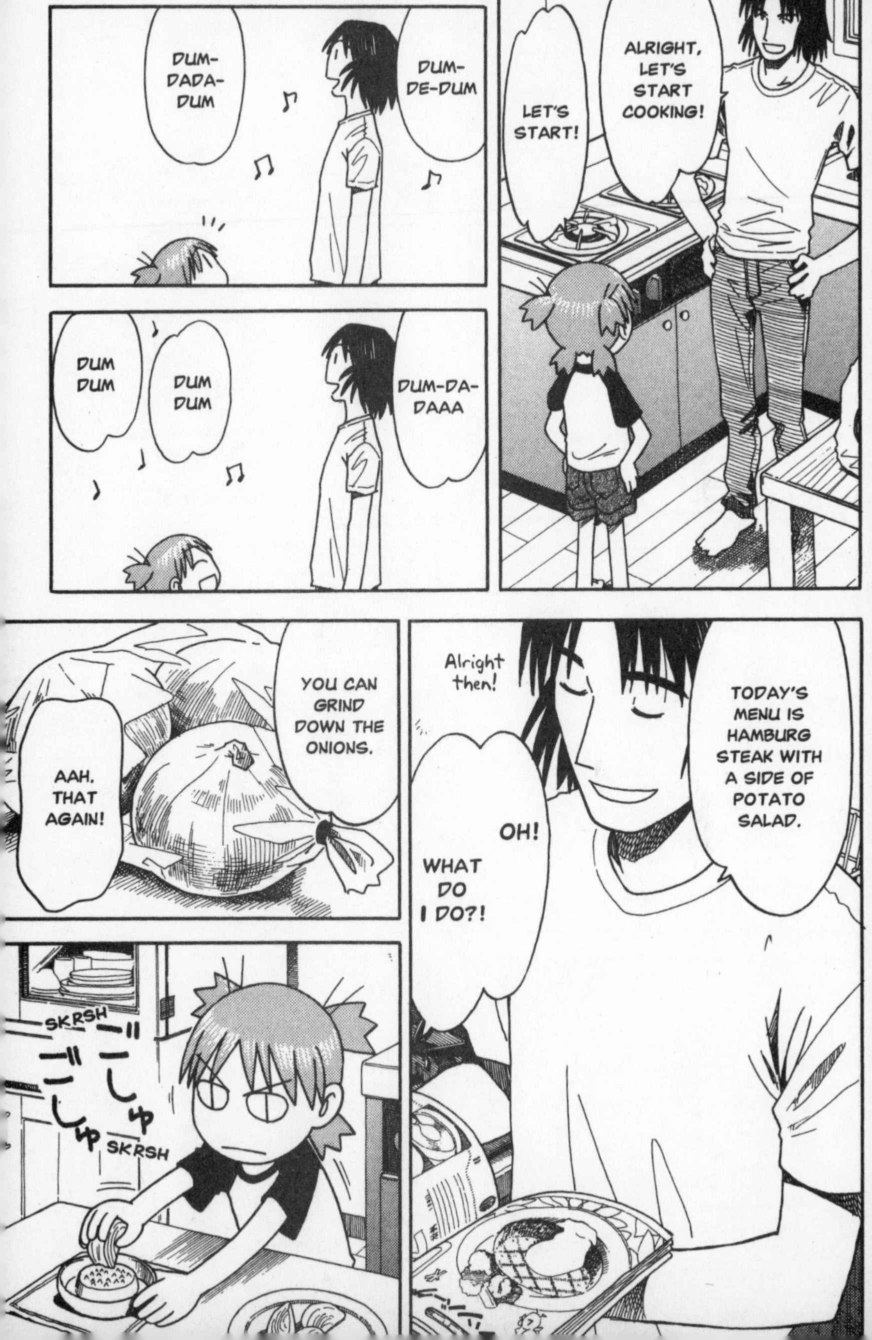

ALRIGHT, LET'S START COOKING!
LET'S START!
DUM-DE-DUM
DUM-DADA-DUM
DUM-DA-DAAA
DUM DUM
DUM DUM
Alright then!
TODAY'S MENU IS HAMBURG STEAK WITH A SIDE OF POTATO SALAD.
OH!
WHAT DO I DO?!
YOU CAN GRIND DOWN THE ONIONS.
AAH. THAT AGAIN!
SKRSH
SKRSH

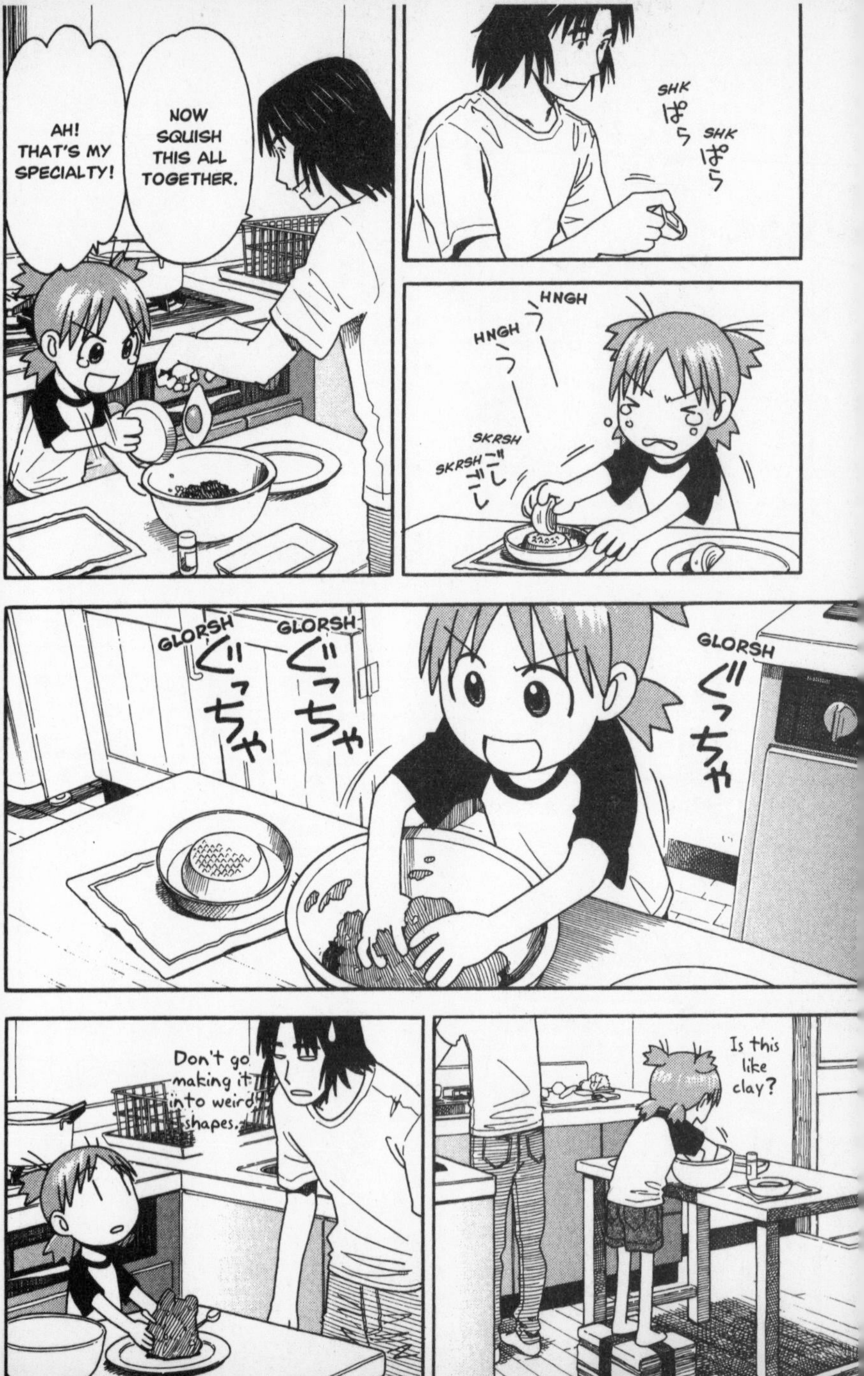
SHK
ぱら
SHK
ぱら
HNGH
う
HNGH
う
SKRSH
ごし
SKRSH
ごし
NOW SQUISH THIS ALL TOGETHER.
AH! THAT'S MY SPECIALTY!
GLORSH
ぐっちゃ
GLORSH
ぐっちゃ
GLORSH
ぐっちゃ
Is this like clay?
Don't go making it into weird shapes.

TIME TO FRY THEM UP.

USE MEDIUM HEAT! MEDIUM!

DON'T BURN 'EM!

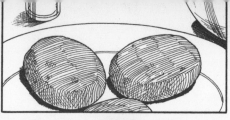

FWP
FWP
FWP

OK!

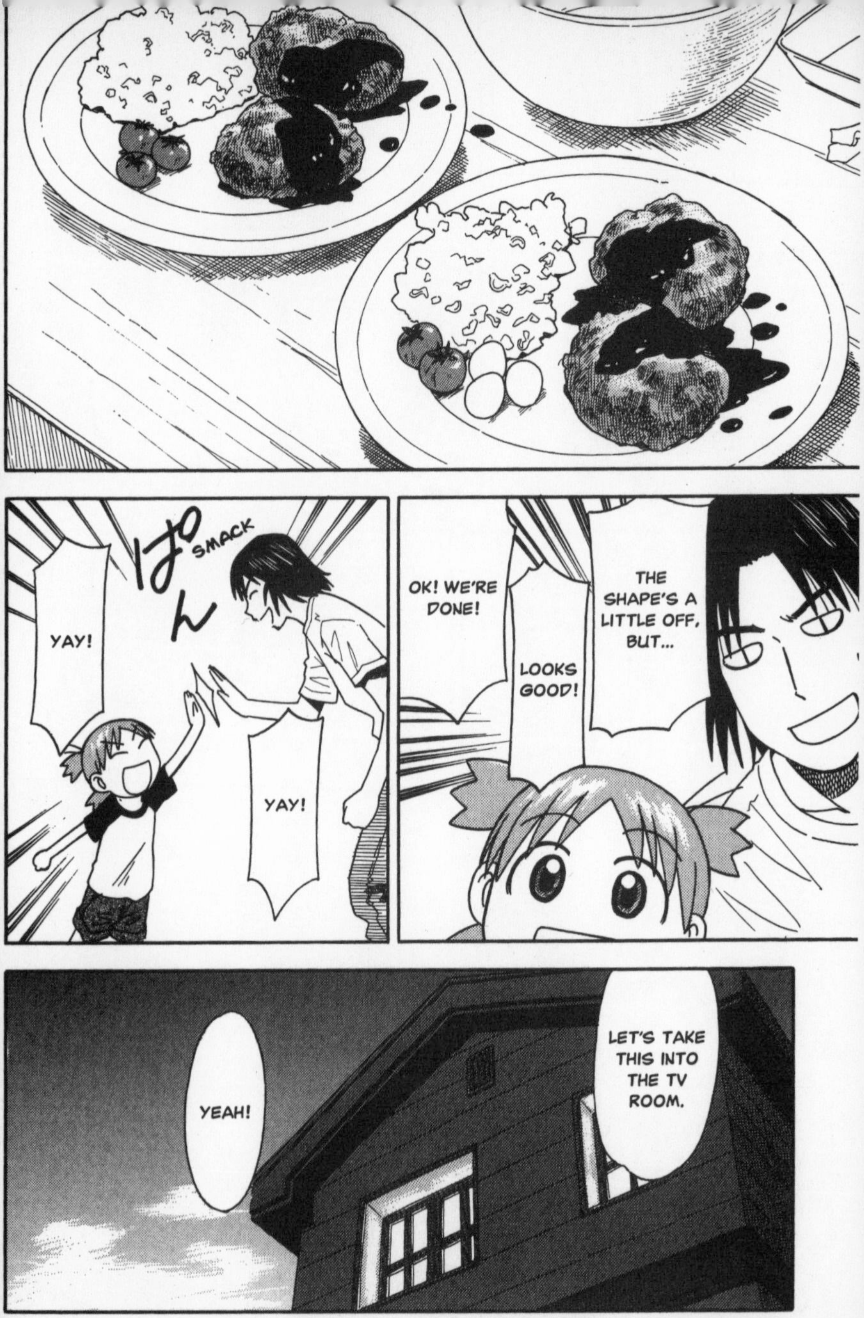
THE SHAPE'S A LITTLE OFF, BUT...
LOOKS GOOD!
OK! WE'RE DONE!
ぱん SMACK
YAY!
YAY!
LET'S TAKE THIS INTO THE TV ROOM.
YEAH!

YOTSUBA&!

YOTSUBA&

FOUR-PANEL MANGA

INTERMISSION

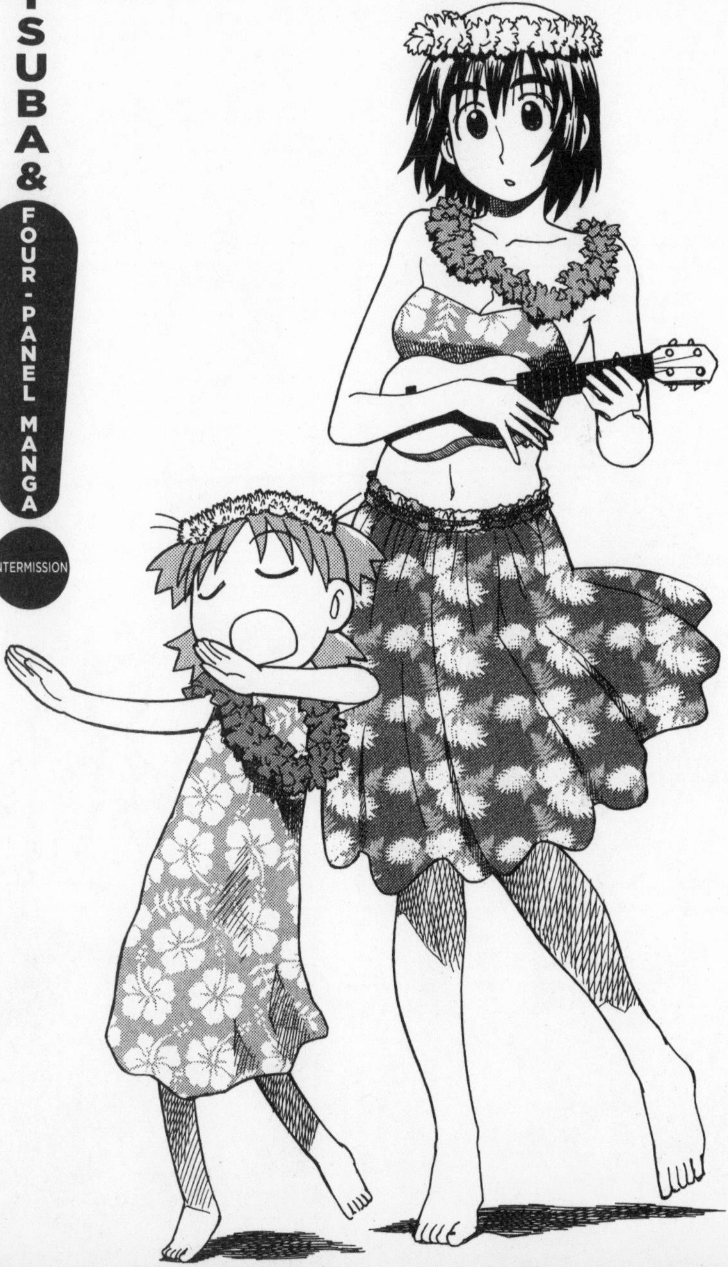

TRUE IDENTITY

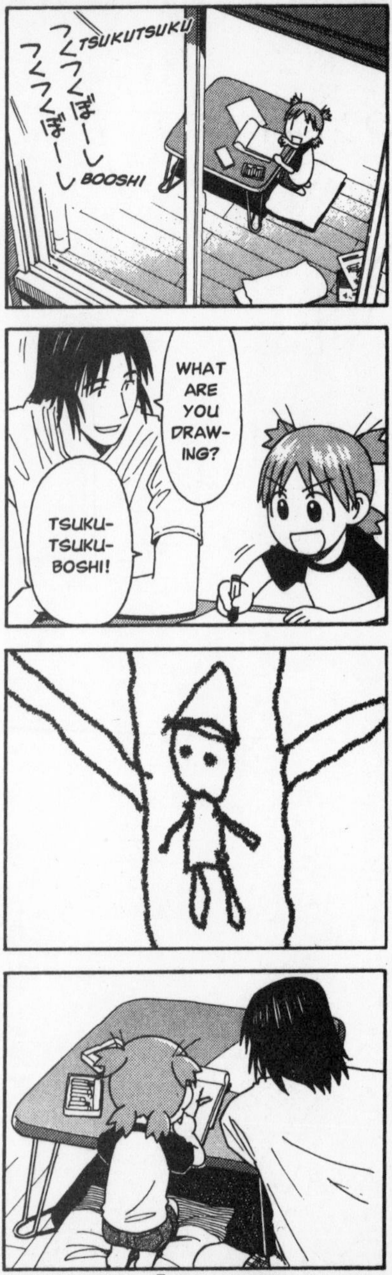
つくつくぼーし
つくつくぼーし
TSUKUTSUKU
BOOSHI
WHAT ARE YOU DRAWING?
TSUKU-TSUKU-BOSHI!

NOTE: IN JAPANESE, *BŌSHI* IS A HOMONYM FOR "CAP."

FLYING

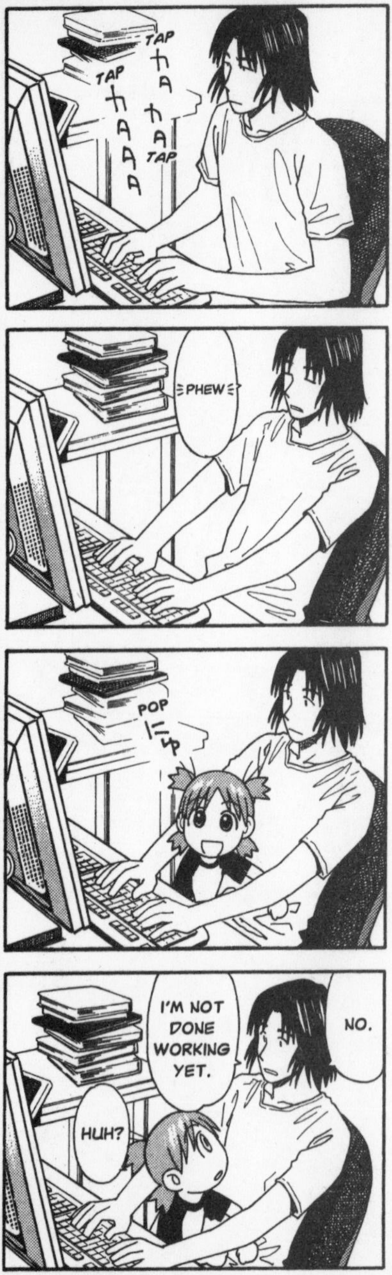
TAP
カタ
TAP
カタ
カタ
TAP
カタ
PHEW
POP
にゅ
NO.
I'M NOT DONE WORKING YET.
HUH?

READY, SET...

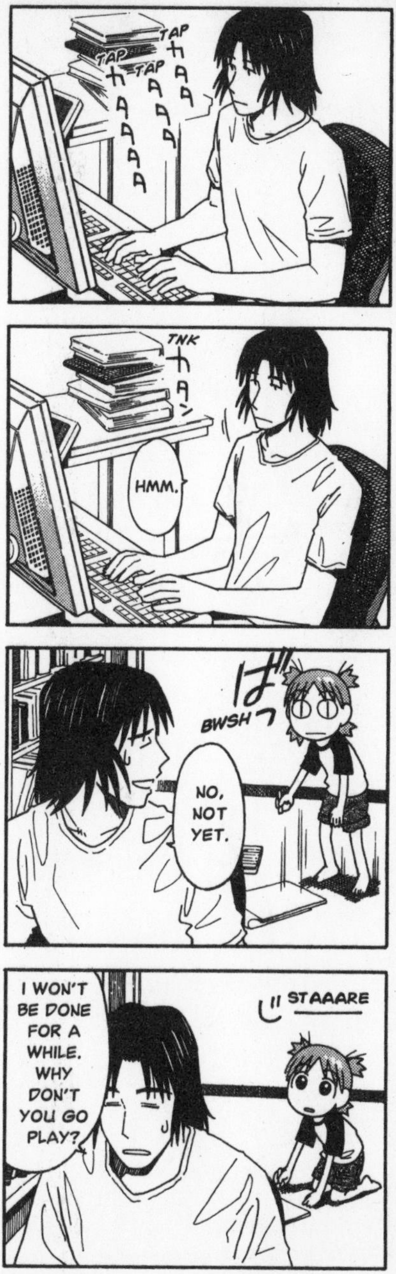
TAP
TAP
TAP
TNK
HMM.
BWSH
NO, NOT YET.
STAAARE
I WON'T BE DONE FOR A WHILE. WHY DON'T YOU GO PLAY?

THE KICKOFF

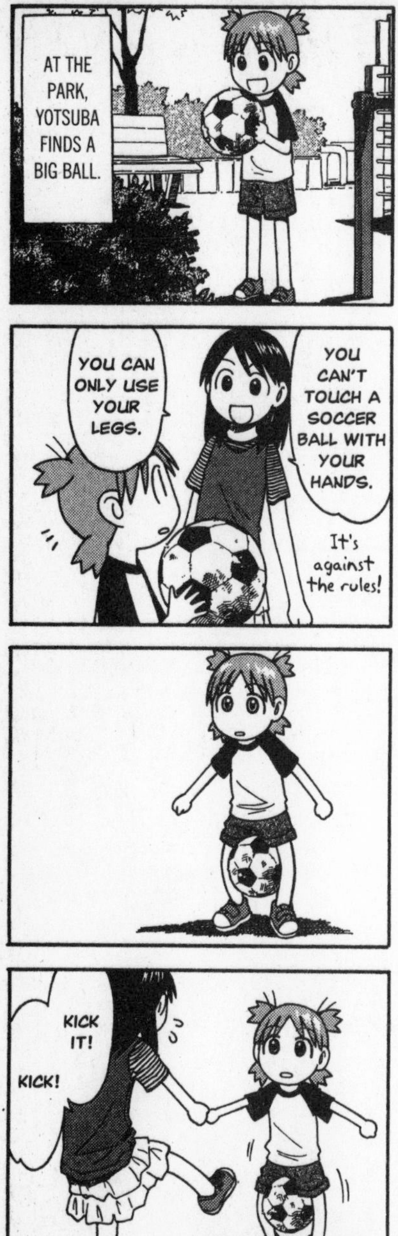
AT THE PARK, YOTSUBA FINDS A BIG BALL.
YOU CAN'T TOUCH A SOCCER BALL WITH YOUR HANDS.
It's against the rules!
YOU CAN ONLY USE YOUR LEGS.
KICK IT!
KICK!

GOAL

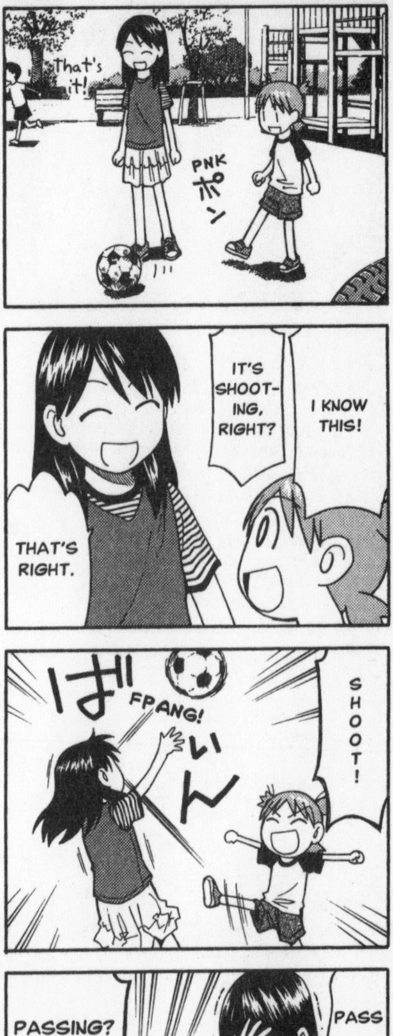
That's it!
PNK
ポン
I KNOW THIS!
IT'S SHOOTING, RIGHT?
THAT'S RIGHT.
SHOOT!
FPANG!
ばいん
PASS...
I PASS...
PASSING? OH, I'VE HEARD OF THAT!

PLAYING BY THE RULES

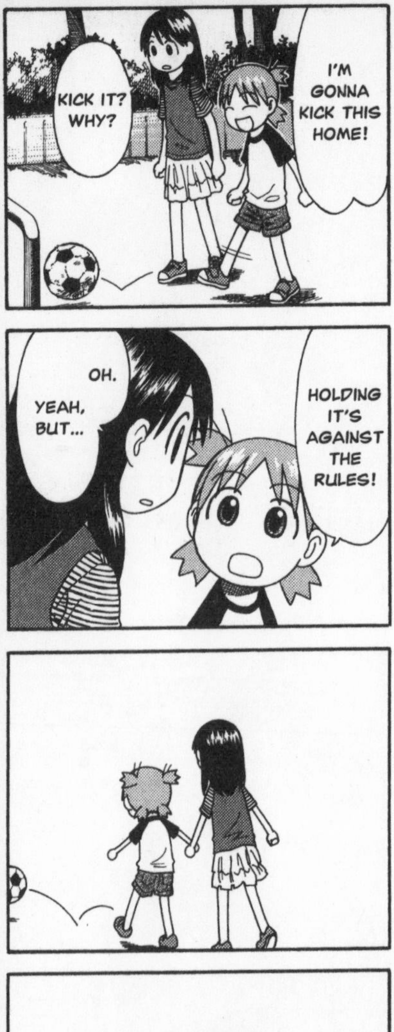
I'M GONNA KICK THIS HOME!
KICK IT? WHY?
HOLDING IT'S AGAINST THE RULES!
OH.
YEAH, BUT...

THE HAND OF GOD

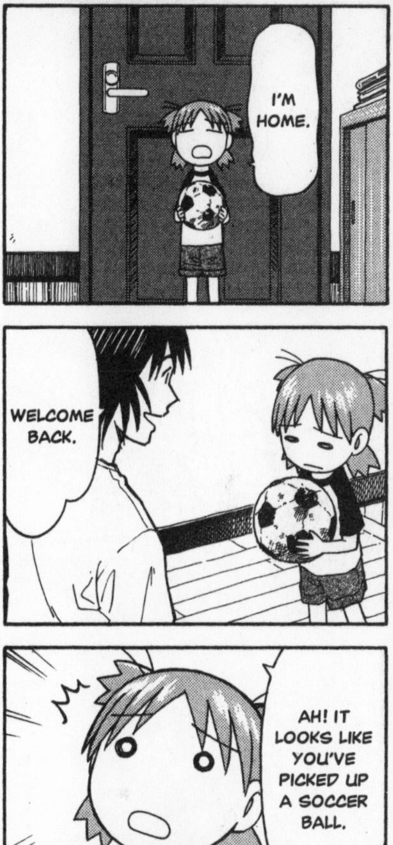
I'M HOME.
WELCOME BACK.
AH! IT LOOKS LIKE YOU'VE PICKED UP A SOCCER BALL.
I HAD TO, OR I'D NEVER HAVE MADE IT HOME!
I'D NEVER HAVE MADE IT HOME!

CRUEL

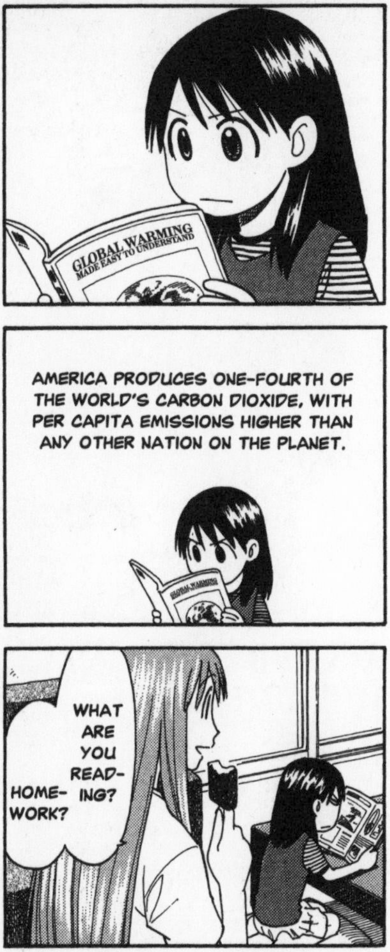
GLOBAL WARMING MADE EASY TO UNDERSTAND
AMERICA PRODUCES ONE-FOURTH OF THE WORLD'S CARBON DIOXIDE, WITH PER CAPITA EMISSIONS HIGHER THAN ANY OTHER NATION ON THE PLANET.
WHAT ARE YOU READING?
HOMEWORK?
SIS! HOW CAN AMERICA BE SO CRUEL?!
HUH?
AMERICA?
GLOBAL WARMING

ACTUALLY, IT'S BROWN

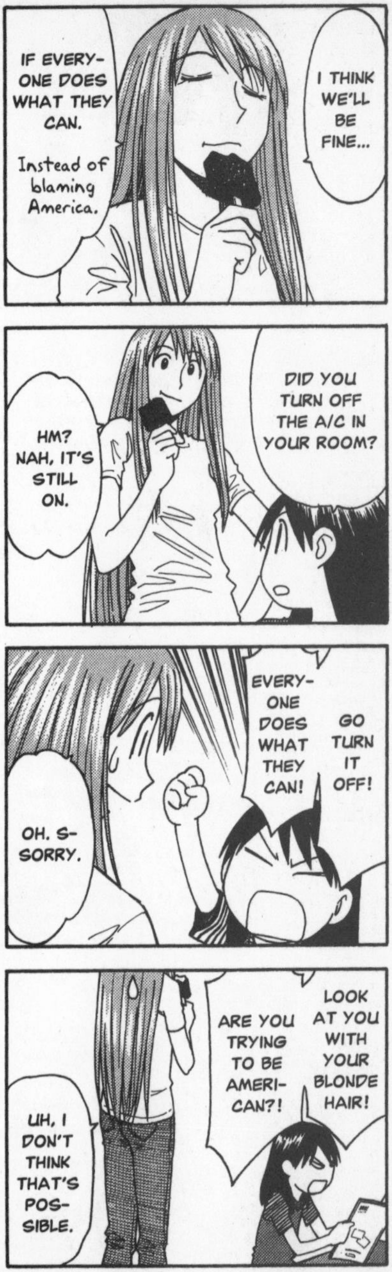
I THINK WE'LL BE FINE...
IF EVERYONE DOES WHAT THEY CAN.
Instead of blaming America.
DID YOU TURN OFF THE A/C IN YOUR ROOM?
HM? NAH, IT'S STILL ON.
GO TURN IT OFF!
EVERYONE DOES WHAT THEY CAN!
OH. S-SORRY.
LOOK AT YOU WITH YOUR BLONDE HAIR!
ARE YOU TRYING TO BE AMERICAN?!
UH, I DON'T THINK THAT'S POSSIBLE.

A TOUGH ONE

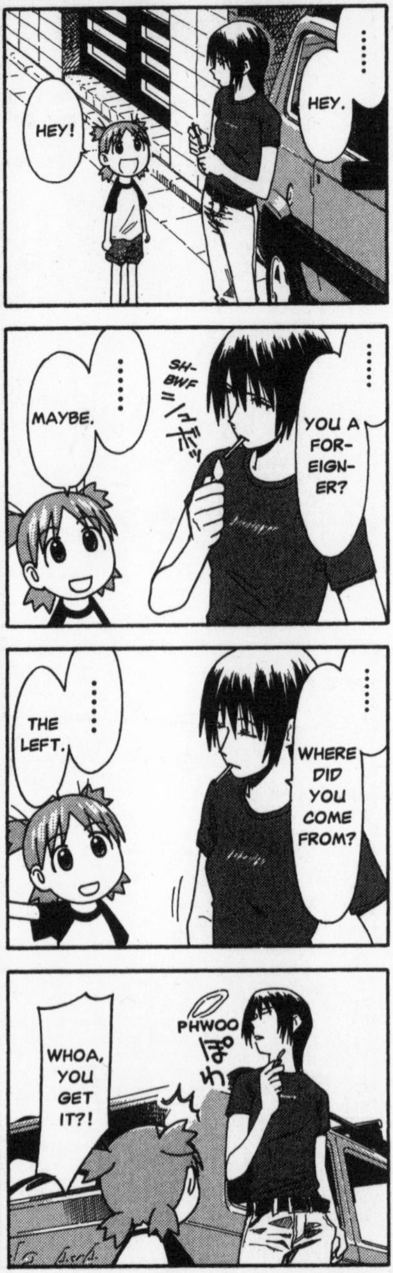
......
HEY.
HEY!
......
YOU A FOREIGNER?
SH-BWF
......
MAYBE.
......
WHERE DID YOU COME FROM?
......
THE LEFT.
PHWOO
WHOA, YOU GET IT?!

NOT GETTING IT

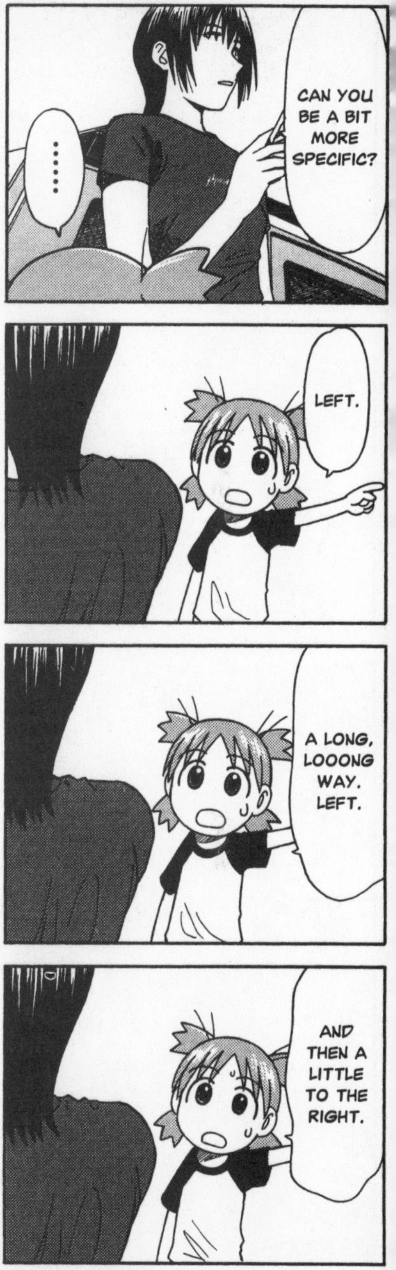
CAN YOU BE A BIT MORE SPECIFIC?
......
LEFT.
A LONG, LOOONG WAY. LEFT.
AND THEN A LITTLE TO THE RIGHT.

WHERE'S SHE GOING?

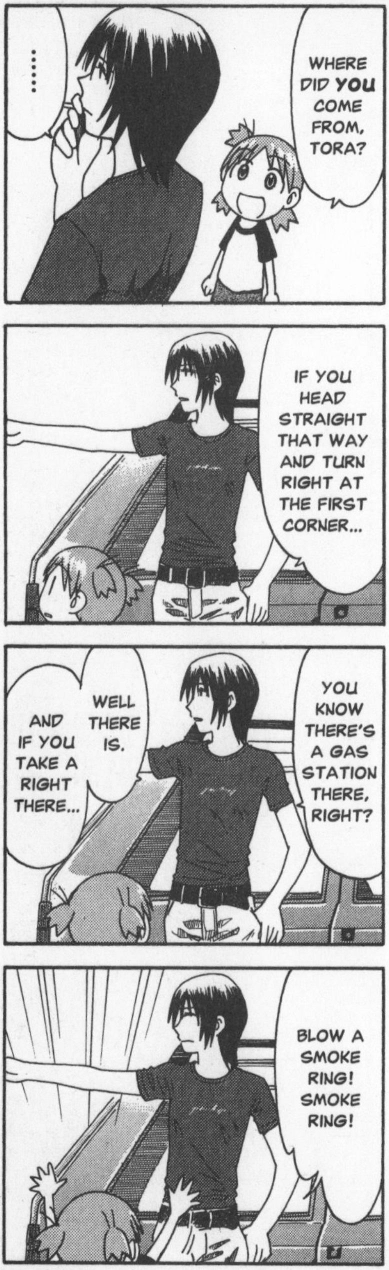
WHERE DID **YOU** COME FROM, TORA?
......
IF YOU HEAD STRAIGHT THAT WAY AND TURN RIGHT AT THE FIRST CORNER...
YOU KNOW THERE'S A GAS STATION THERE, RIGHT?
WELL THERE IS.
AND IF YOU TAKE A RIGHT THERE...
BLOW A SMOKE RING! SMOKE RING!

THE SPANKING

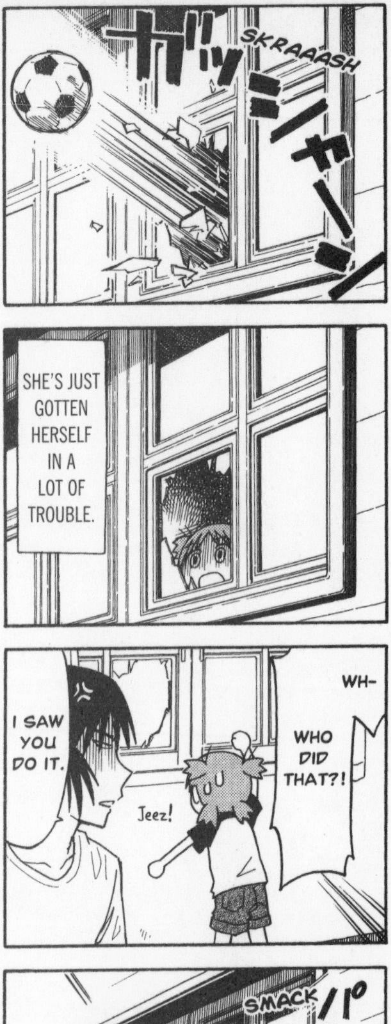
SKRAAASH
SHE'S JUST GOTTEN HERSELF IN A LOT OF TROUBLE.
WH-
WHO DID THAT?!
Jeez!
I SAW YOU DO IT.
SMACK
Ow! I'm sorry!
SMACK

DONE A BAD THING

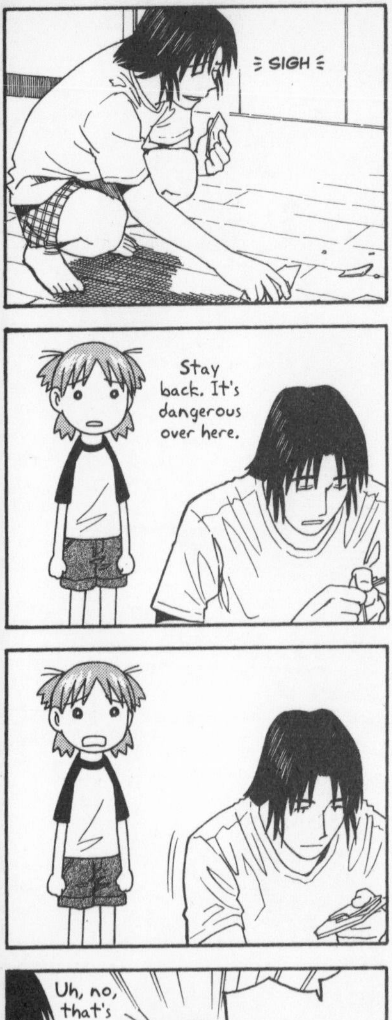
SIGH
Stay back. It's dangerous over here.
I'LL PAY THE DAMAGES!
WHEN I'M GROWN UP, I'LL PAY THE DAMAGES!
Uh, no, that's fine.

YOTSUBA&!

YOTSUBA & THE BLOOM OF YOUTH

CHAPTER 25

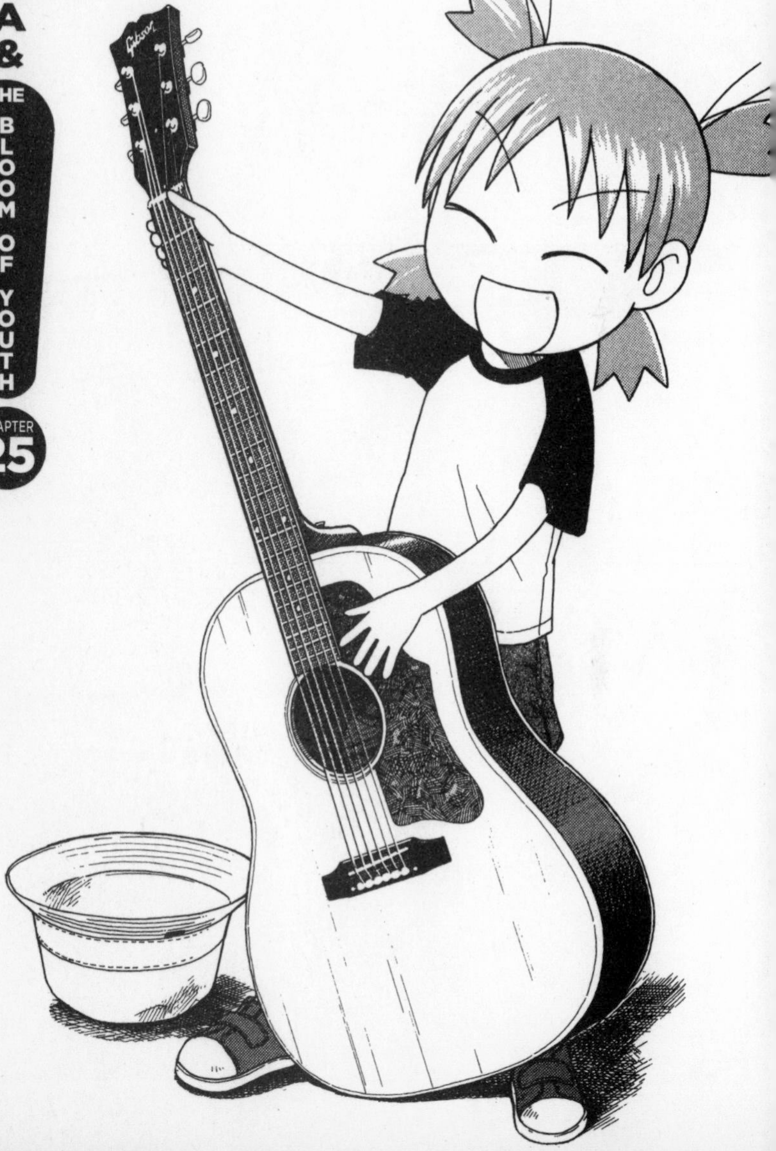

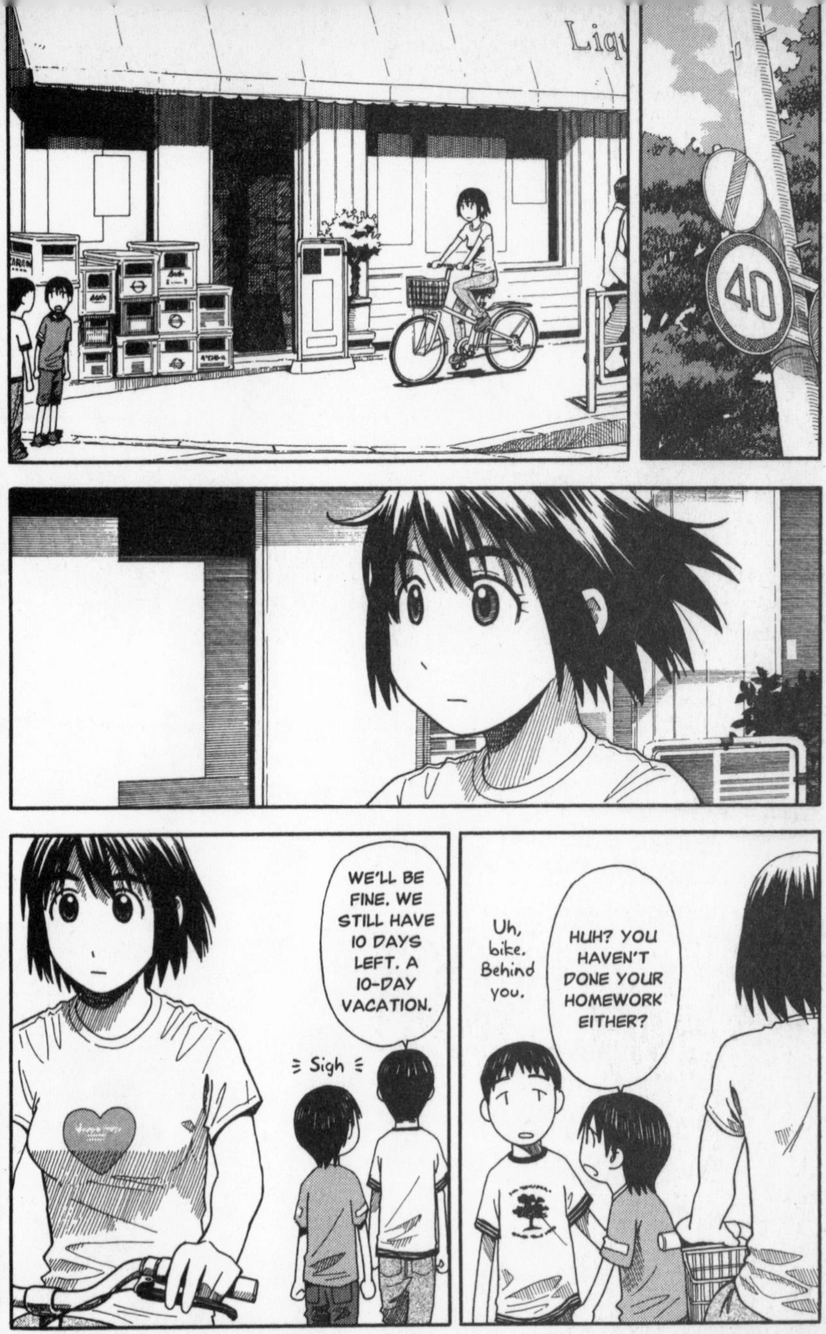
40
Liqu
HUH? YOU HAVEN'T DONE YOUR HOMEWORK EITHER?
Uh, bike. Behind you.
WE'LL BE FINE. WE STILL HAVE 10 DAYS LEFT. A 10-DAY VACATION.
Sigh

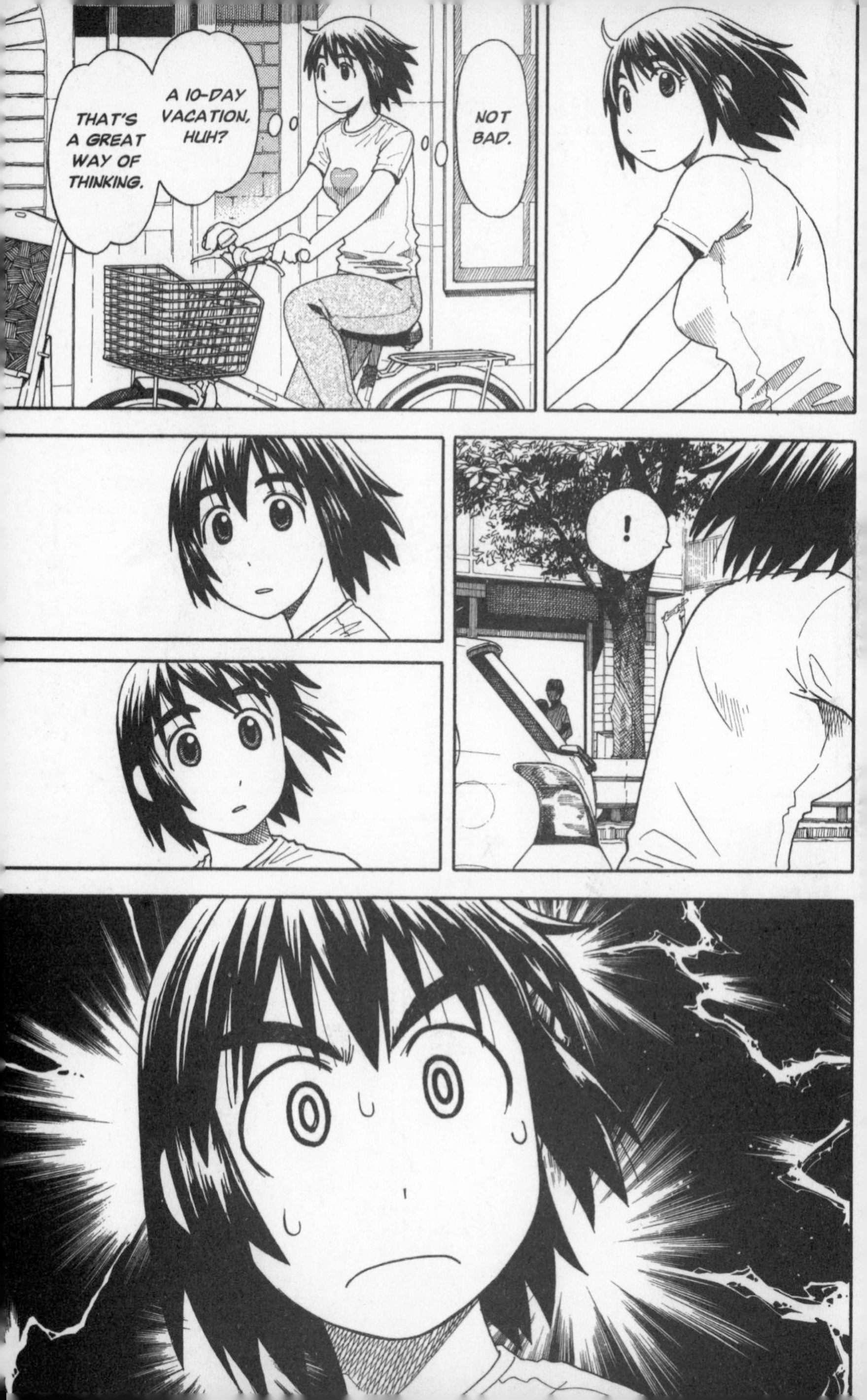
NOT BAD.
A 10-DAY VACATION, HUH?
THAT'S A GREAT WAY OF THINKING.
!

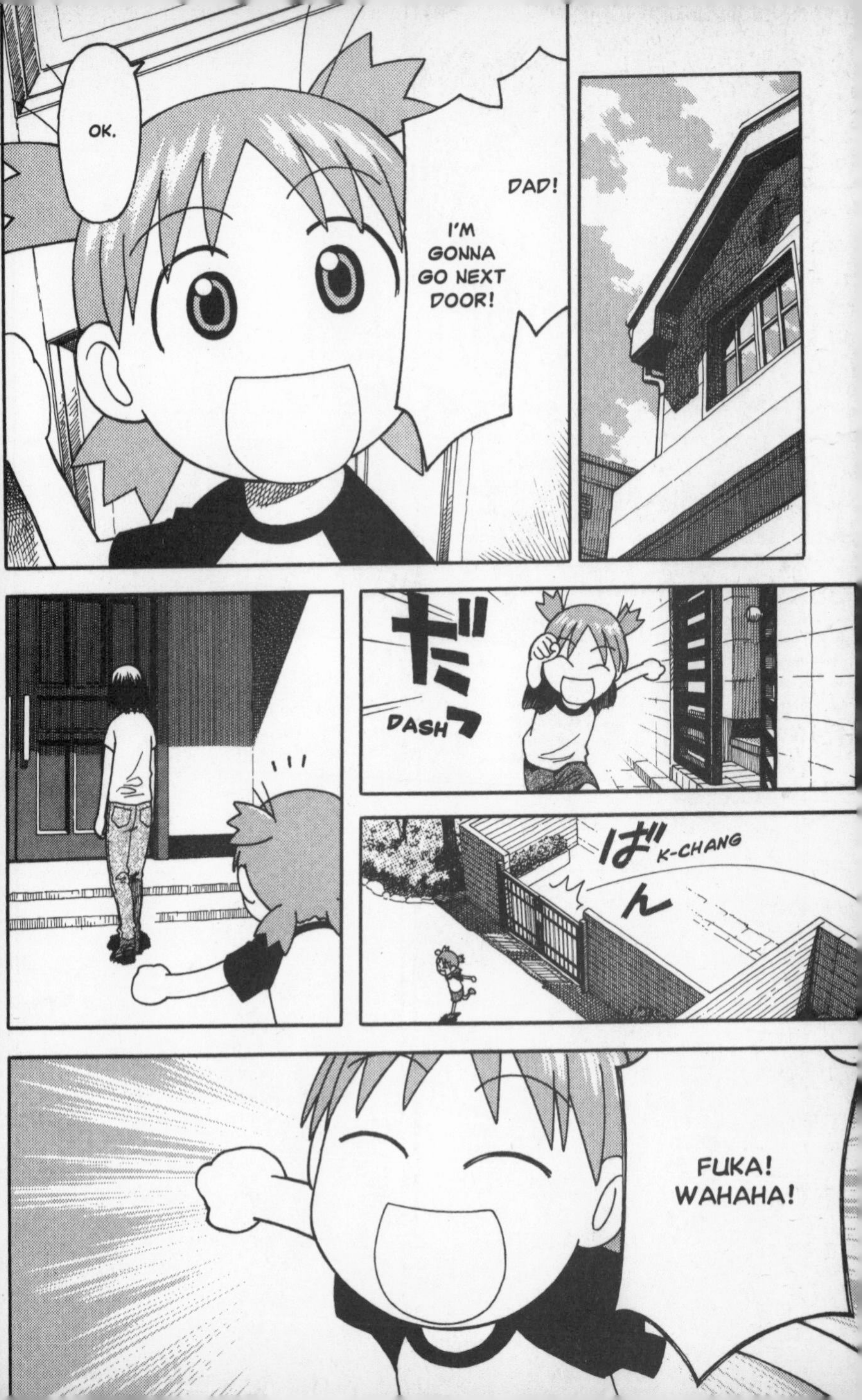
DAD!
I'M GONNA GO NEXT DOOR!
OK.
だっ
DASH
ばん
K-CHANG
FUKA! WAHAHA!

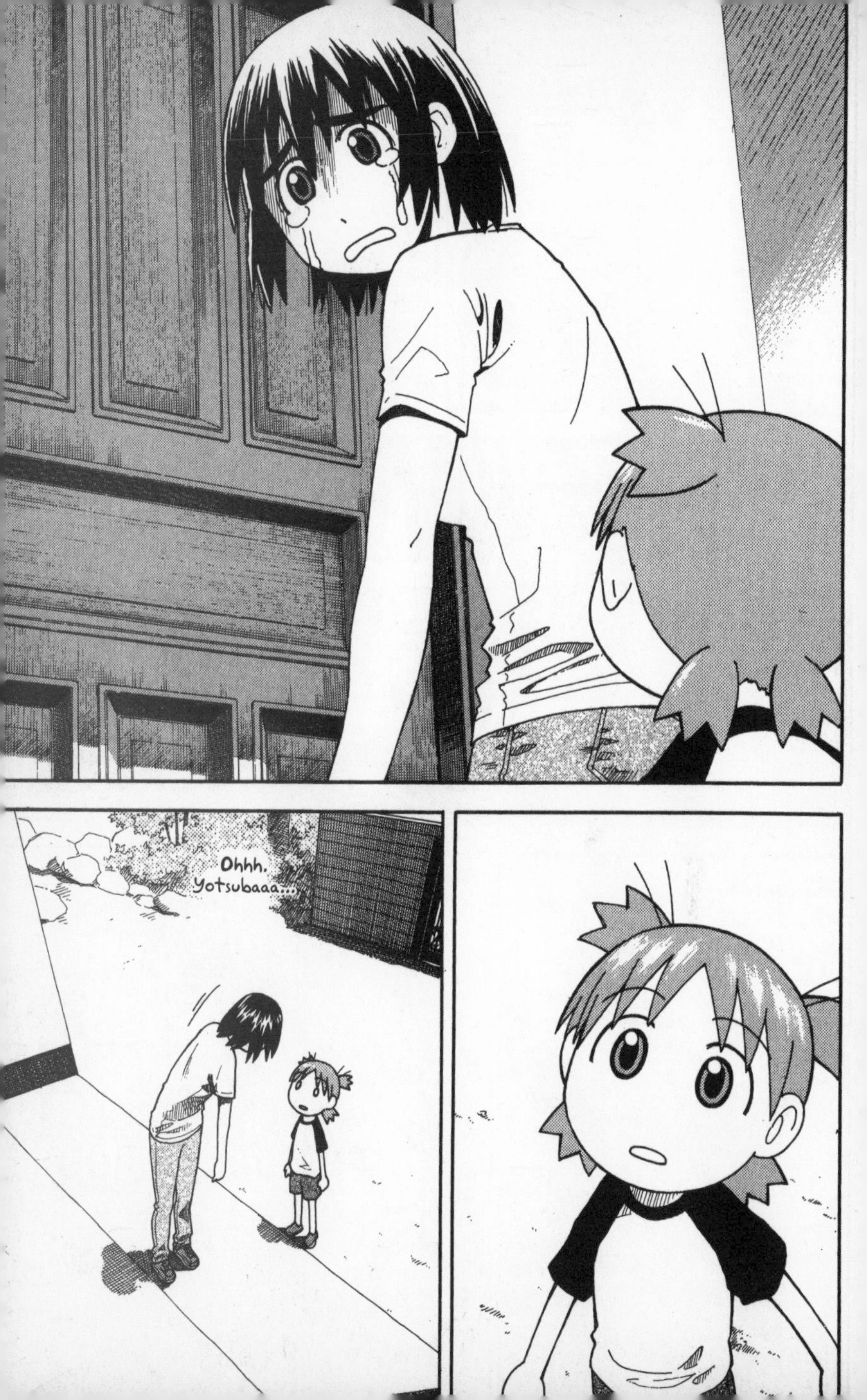
Ohhh.
Yotsubaaa...

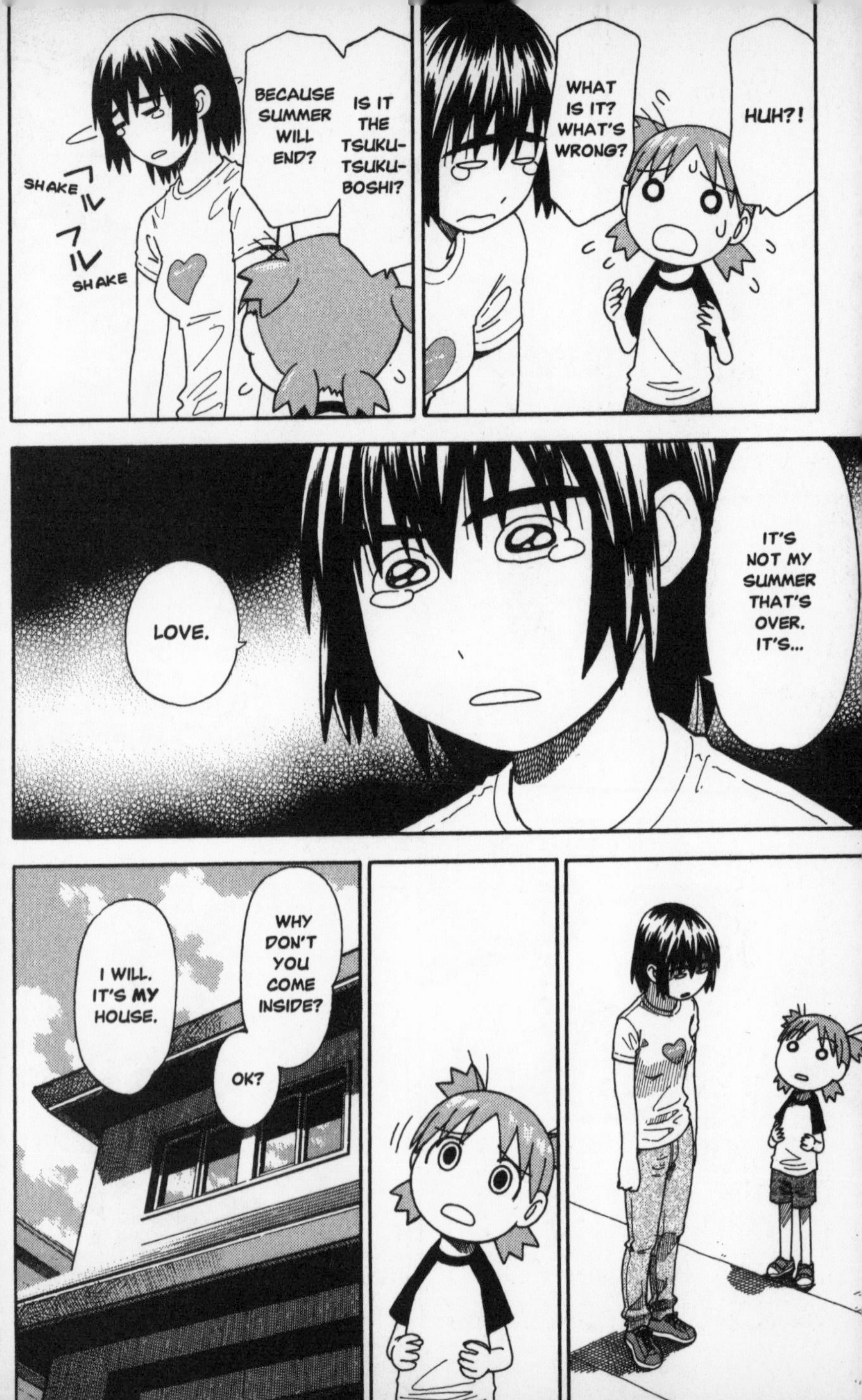
HUH?!
WHAT IS IT? WHAT'S WRONG?
IS IT THE TSUKU-TSUKU-BOSHI?
BECAUSE SUMMER WILL END?
SHAKE
SHAKE
IT'S NOT MY SUMMER THAT'S OVER. IT'S...
LOVE.
WHY DON'T YOU COME INSIDE?
OK?
I WILL. IT'S MY HOUSE.

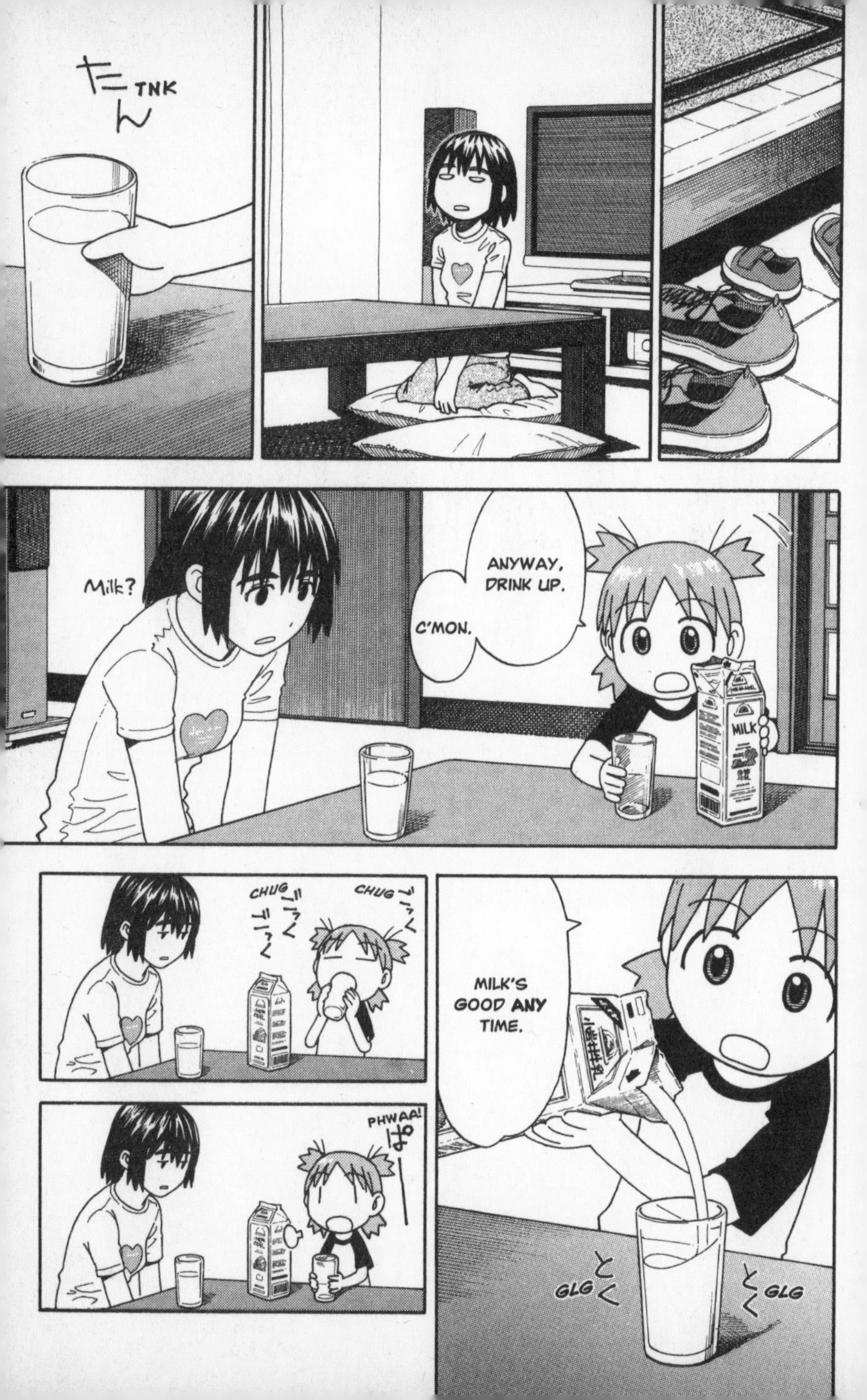
たん
TNK
Milk?
ANYWAY, DRINK UP.
C'MON.
MILK
MILK'S GOOD ANY TIME.
とく GLG
とく GLG
ごっく CHUG
ごっく ごっく CHUG
ぱー PHWAA!

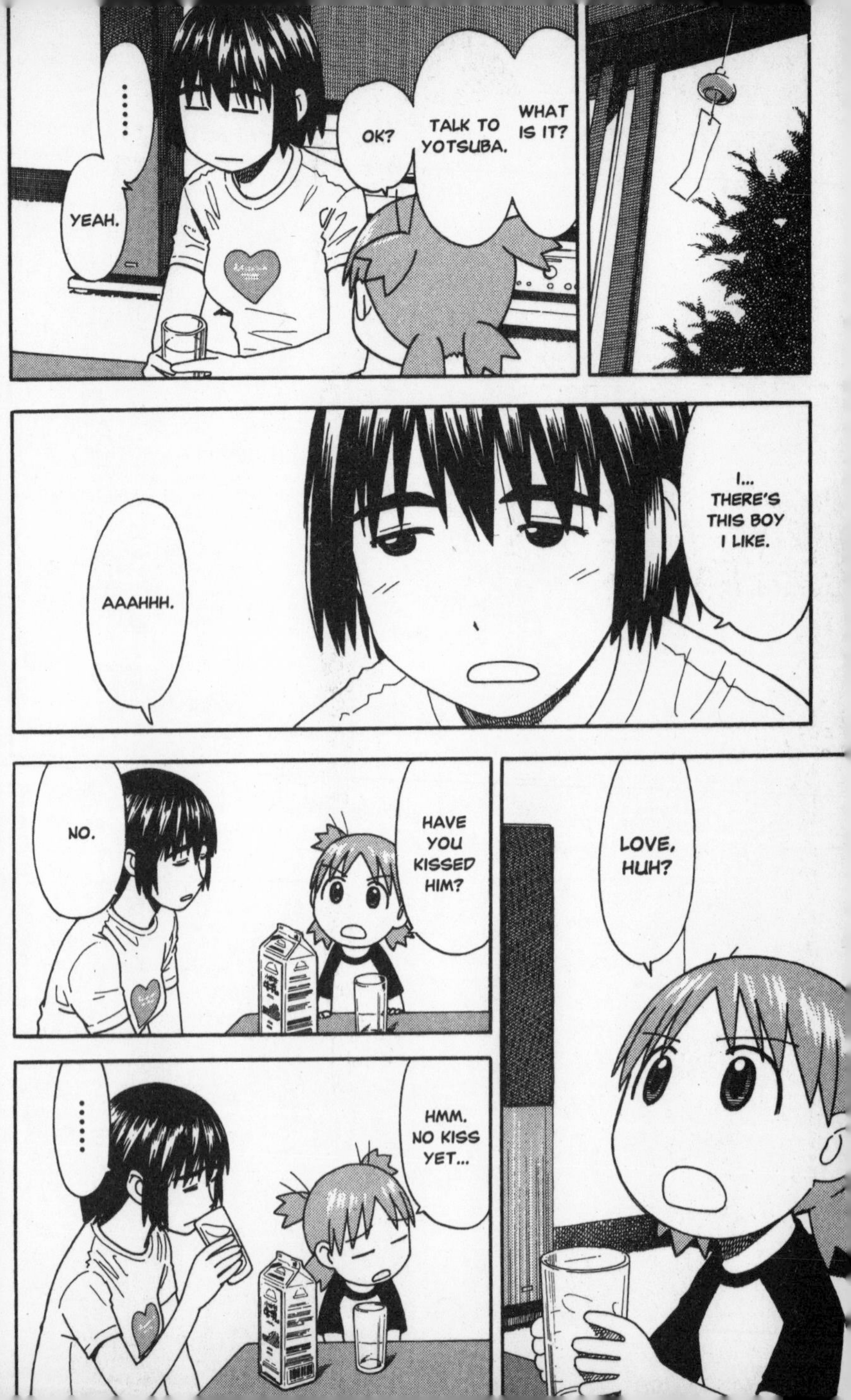
WHAT IS IT?
TALK TO YOTSUBA.
OK?
......
YEAH.
I... THERE'S THIS BOY I LIKE.
AAAHHH.
LOVE, HUH?
HAVE YOU KISSED HIM?
NO.
HMM. NO KISS YET...
......

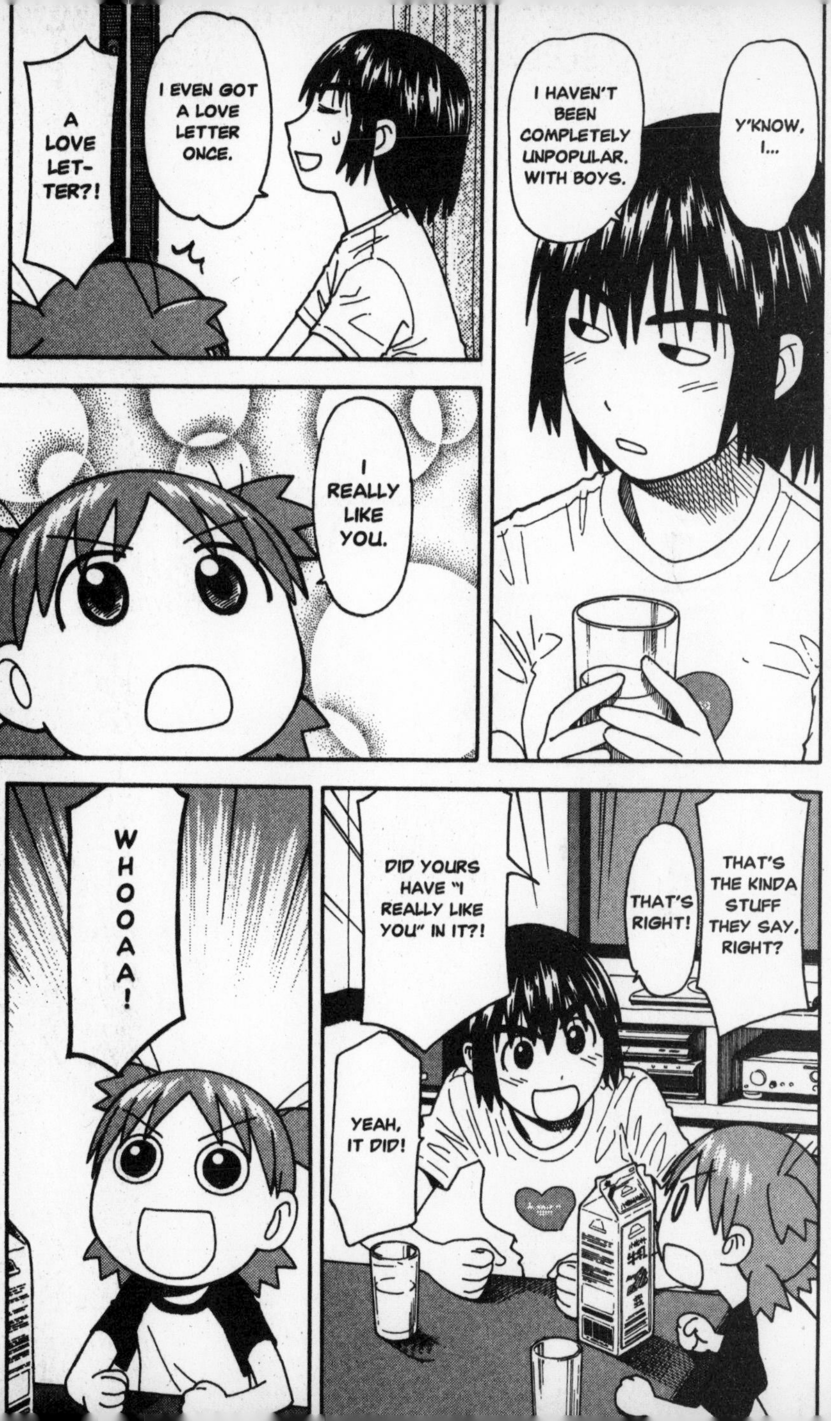
Y'KNOW, I...
I HAVEN'T BEEN COMPLETELY UNPOPULAR. WITH BOYS.
I EVEN GOT A LOVE LETTER ONCE.
A LOVE LET-TER?!
I REALLY LIKE YOU.
THAT'S THE KINDA STUFF THEY SAY, RIGHT?
THAT'S RIGHT!
DID YOURS HAVE "I REALLY LIKE YOU" IN IT?!
YEAH, IT DID!
WHOOAA!

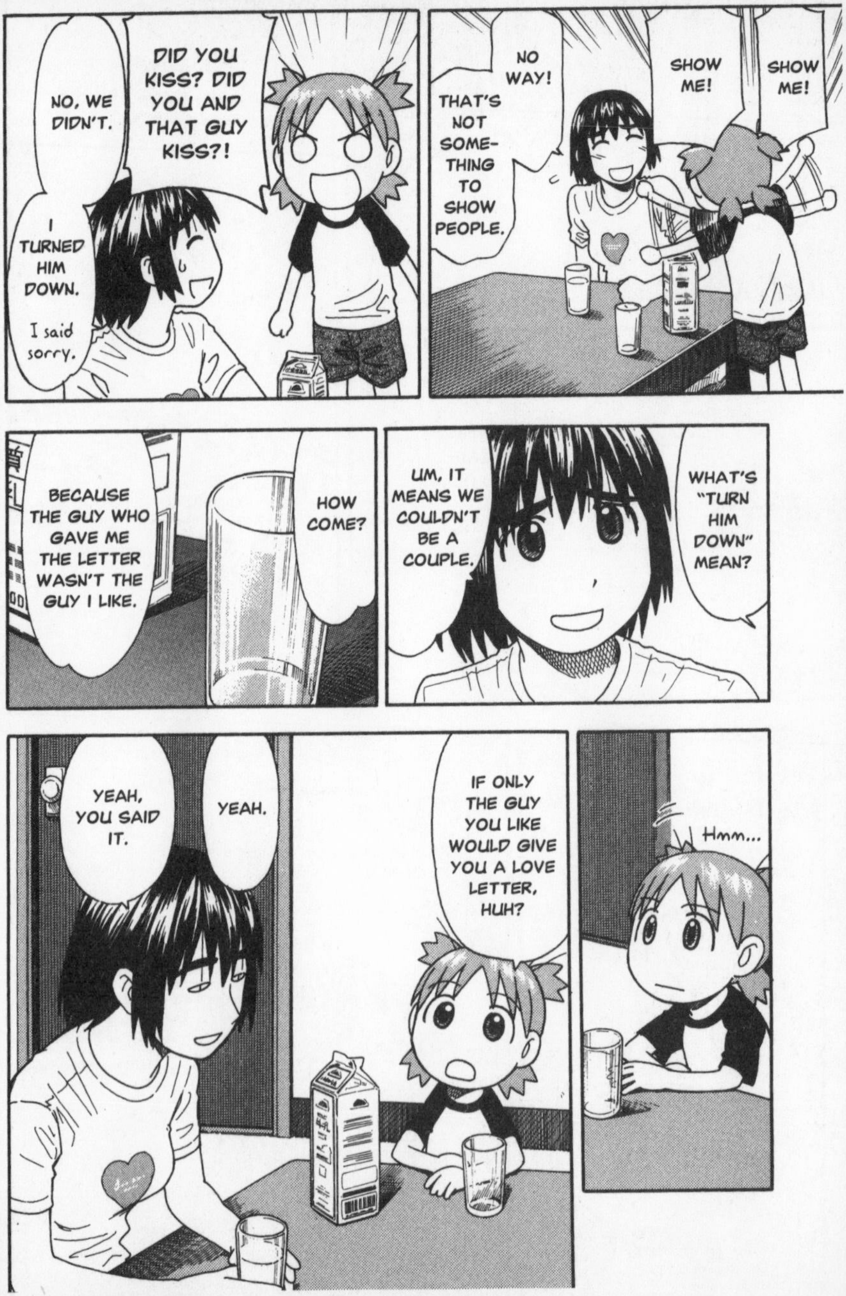
SHOW ME!
SHOW ME!
NO WAY!
THAT'S NOT SOME-THING TO SHOW PEOPLE.
DID YOU KISS? DID YOU AND THAT GUY KISS?!
NO, WE DIDN'T.
I TURNED HIM DOWN.
I said sorry.
WHAT'S "TURN HIM DOWN" MEAN?
UM, IT MEANS WE COULDN'T BE A COUPLE.
HOW COME?
BECAUSE THE GUY WHO GAVE ME THE LETTER WASN'T THE GUY I LIKE.
Hmm...
IF ONLY THE GUY YOU LIKE WOULD GIVE YOU A LOVE LETTER, HUH?
YEAH.
YEAH, YOU SAID IT.

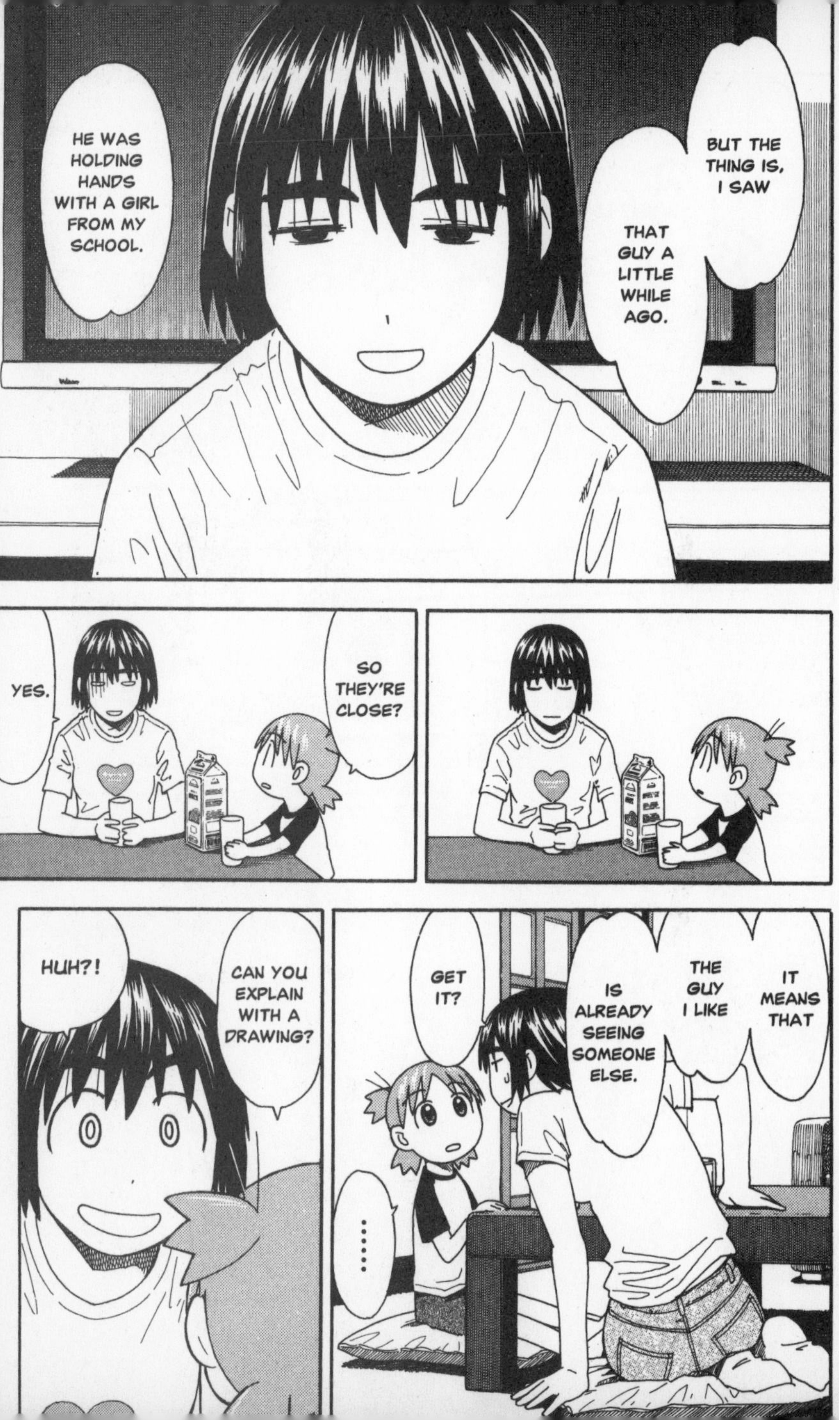
BUT THE THING IS, I SAW
THAT GUY A LITTLE WHILE AGO.
HE WAS HOLDING HANDS WITH A GIRL FROM MY SCHOOL.
SO THEY'RE CLOSE?
YES.
IT MEANS THAT
THE GUY I LIKE
IS ALREADY SEEING SOMEONE ELSE.
GET IT?
……
CAN YOU EXPLAIN WITH A DRAWING?
HUH?!

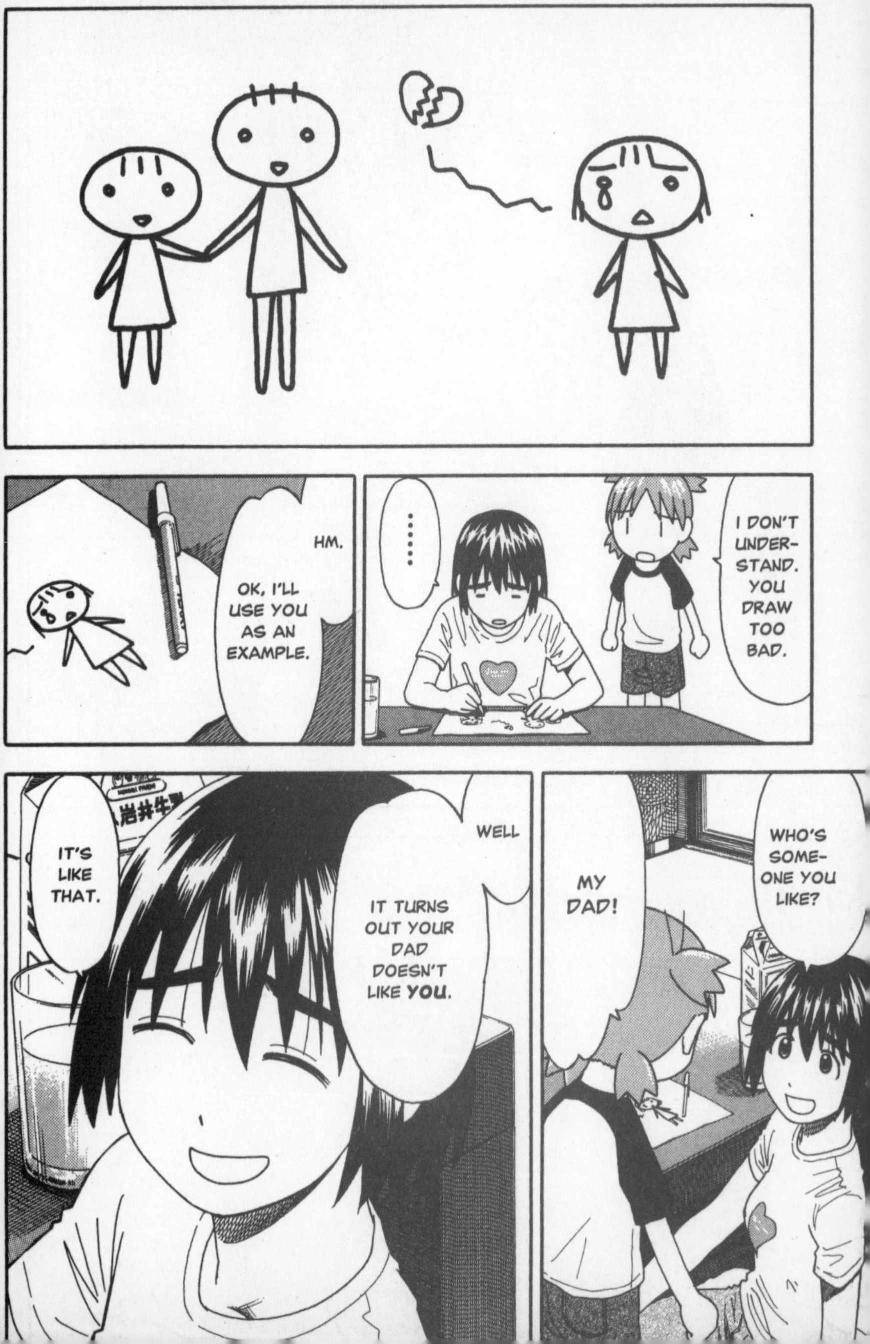
I DON'T UNDER-STAND. YOU DRAW TOO BAD.
......
HM.
OK, I'LL USE YOU AS AN EXAMPLE.
WHO'S SOME-ONE YOU LIKE?
MY DAD!
WELL
IT TURNS OUT YOUR DAD DOESN'T LIKE **YOU**.
IT'S LIKE THAT.

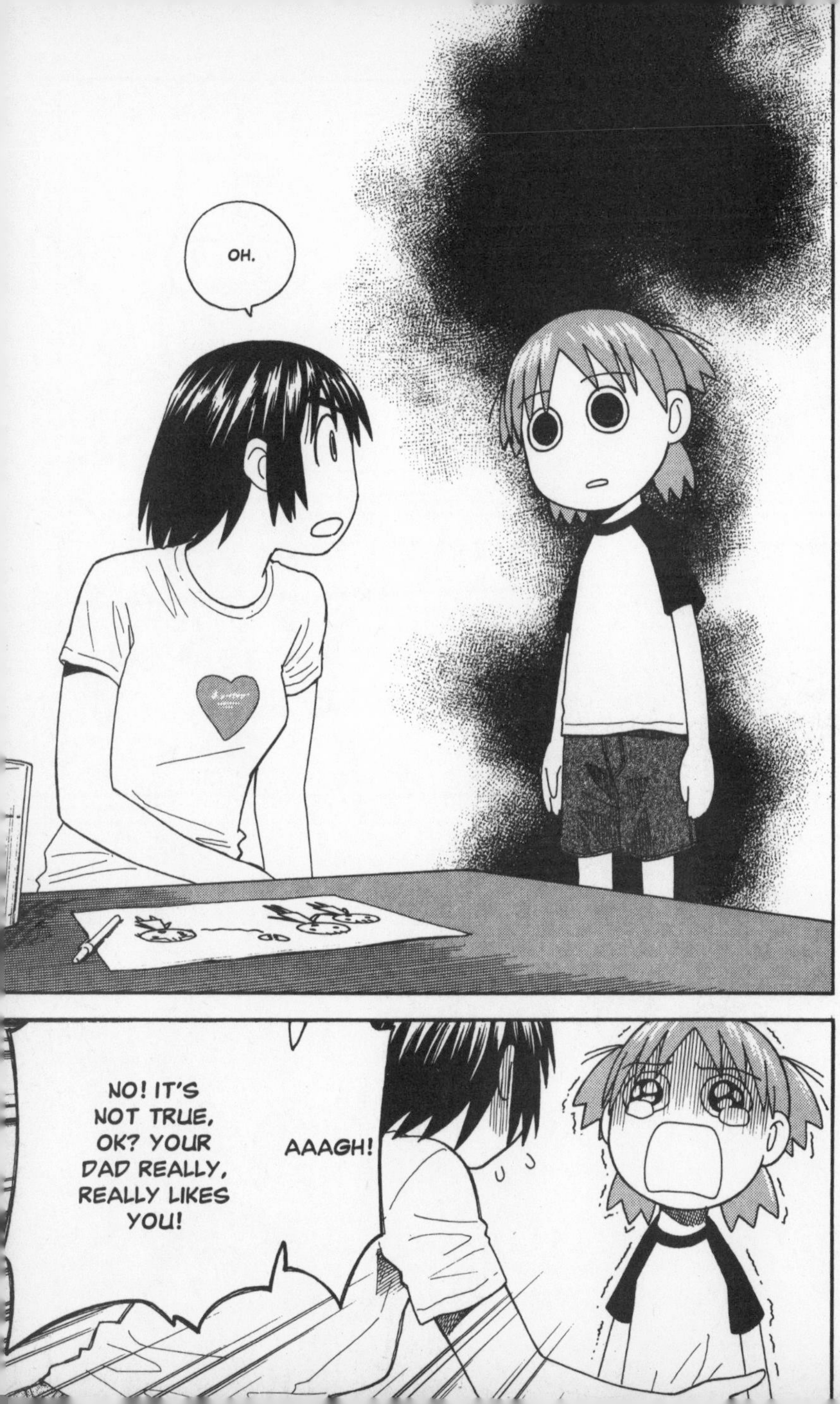
OH.
AAAGH!
NO! IT'S NOT TRUE, OK? YOUR DAD REALLY, REALLY LIKES YOU!

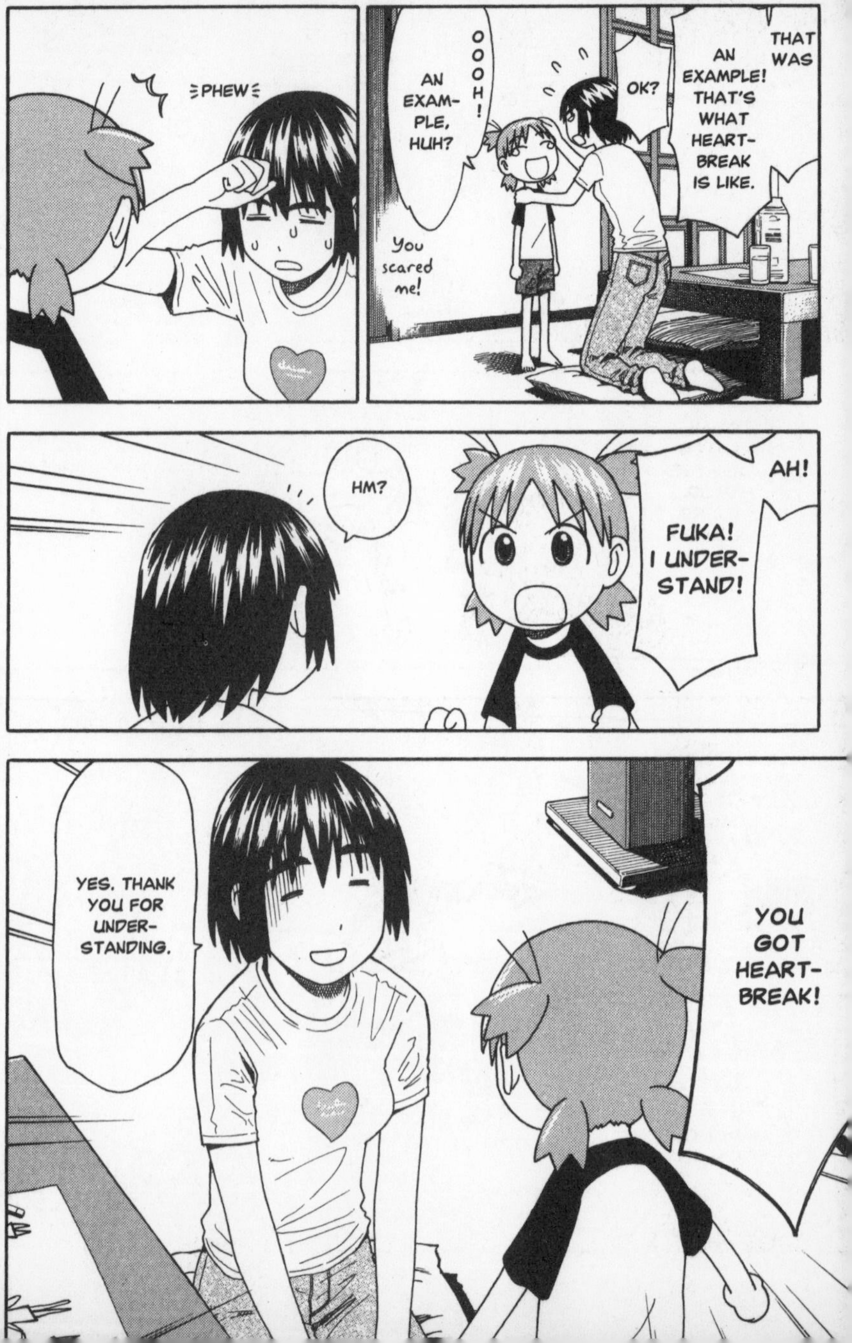
THAT WAS
AN EXAMPLE! THAT'S WHAT HEART-BREAK IS LIKE.
OK?
OOOH!
AN EXAMPLE, HUH?
You scared me!
PHEW
AH!
FUKA! I UNDERSTAND!
HM?
YOU GOT HEART-BREAK!
YES. THANK YOU FOR UNDER-STANDING.

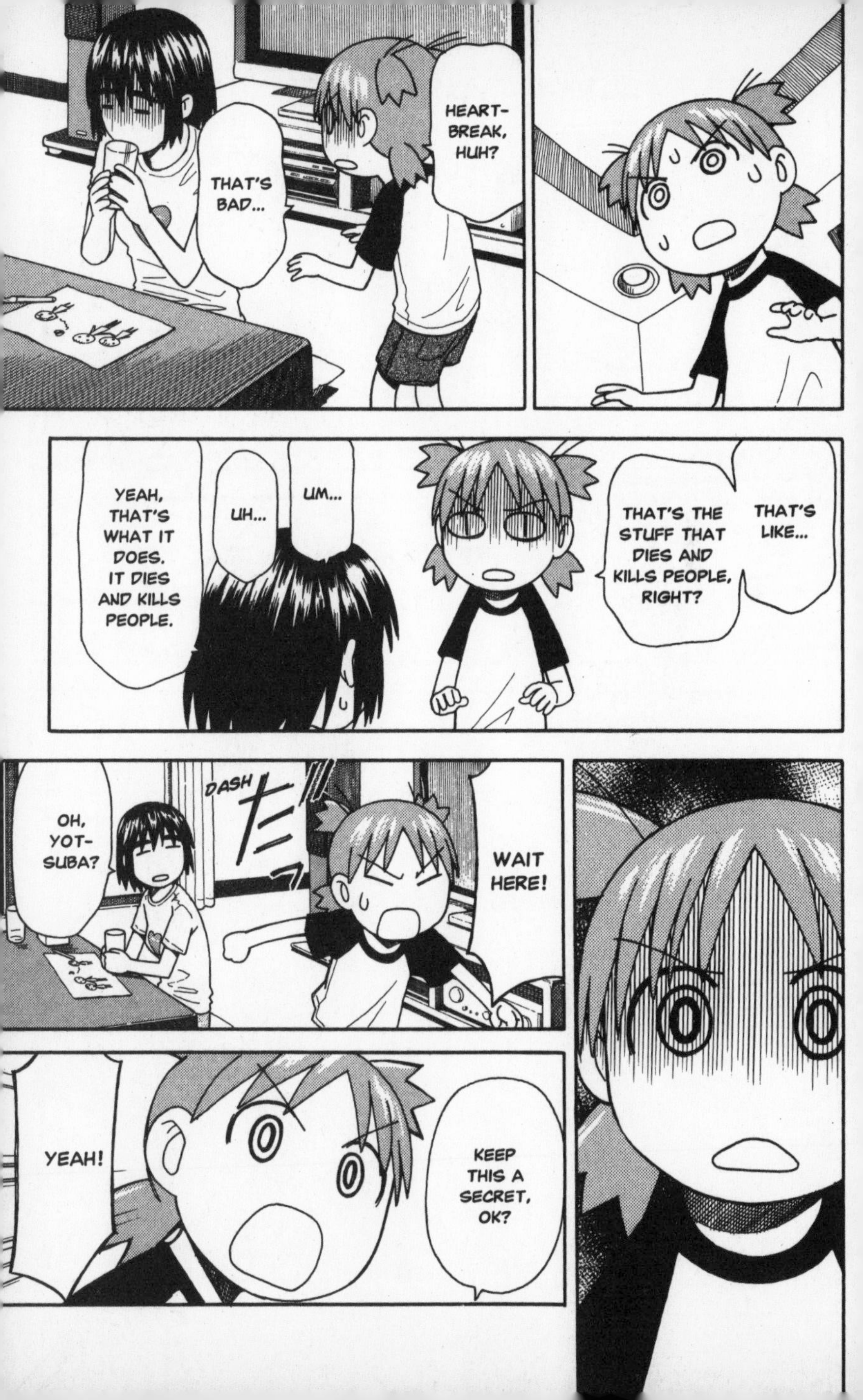
HEART-BREAK, HUH?
THAT'S BAD...
THAT'S LIKE...
THAT'S THE STUFF THAT DIES AND KILLS PEOPLE, RIGHT?
UM...
UH...
YEAH, THAT'S WHAT IT DOES. IT DIES AND KILLS PEOPLE.
WAIT HERE!
DASH
OH, YOT-SUBA?
KEEP THIS A SECRET, OK?
YEAH!

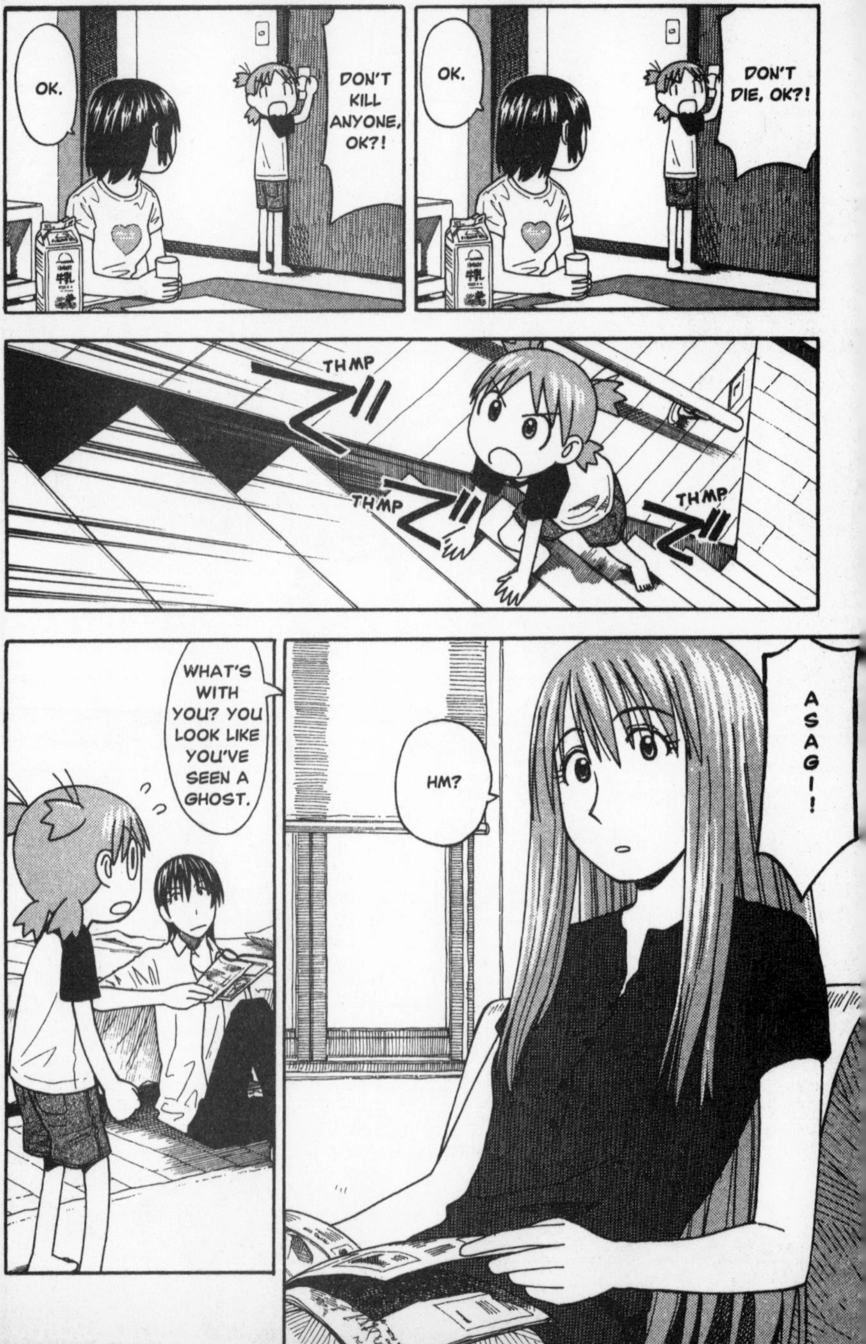
DON'T DIE, OK?!
OK.
DON'T KILL ANYONE, OK?!
OK.
THMP
THMP
THMP
ASAGI!
HM?
WHAT'S WITH YOU? YOU LOOK LIKE YOU'VE SEEN A GHOST.

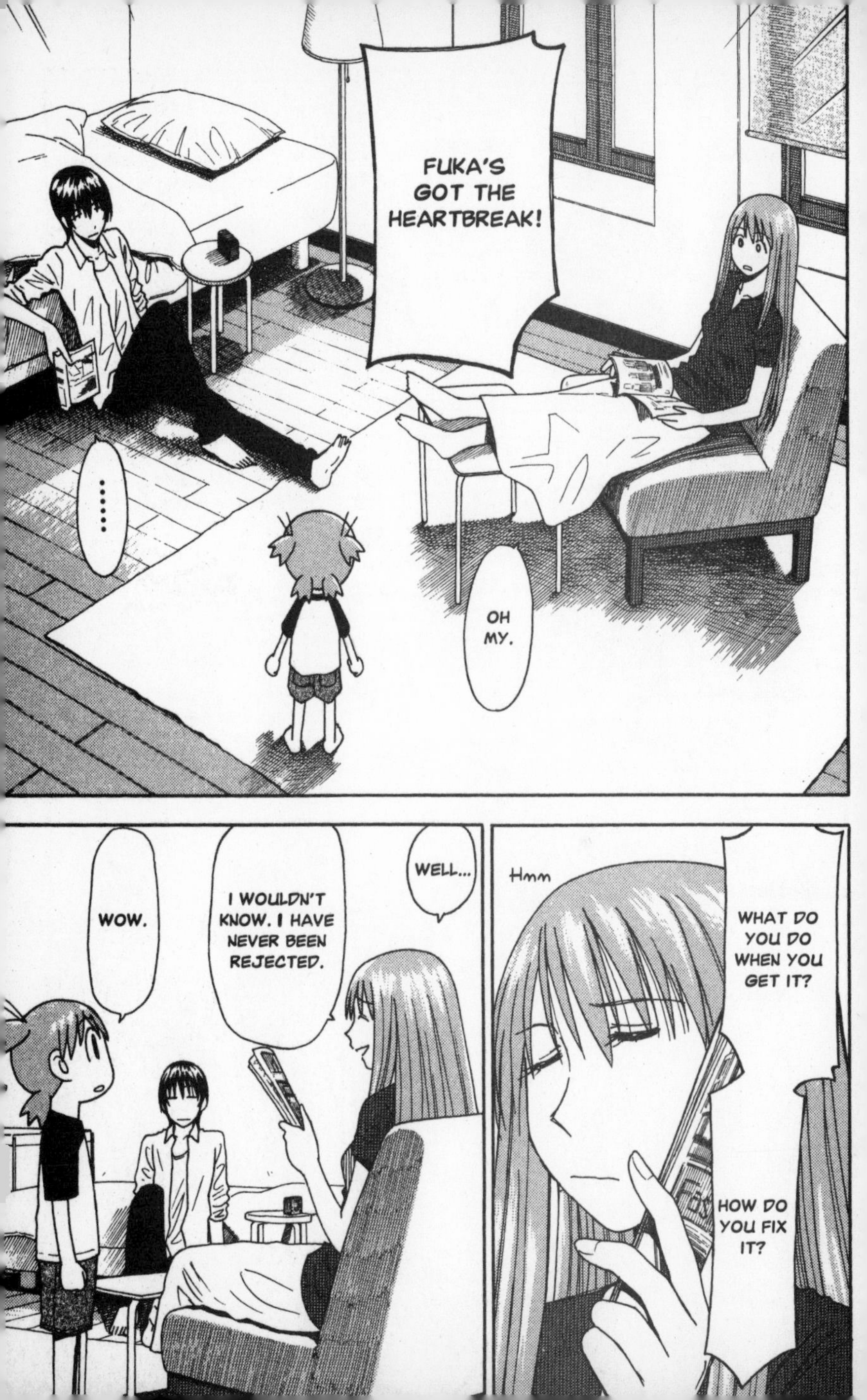
FUKA'S GOT THE HEARTBREAK!
OH MY.
......
WHAT DO YOU DO WHEN YOU GET IT?
Hmm
HOW DO YOU FIX IT?
WELL...
I WOULDN'T KNOW. I HAVE NEVER BEEN REJECTED.
WOW.

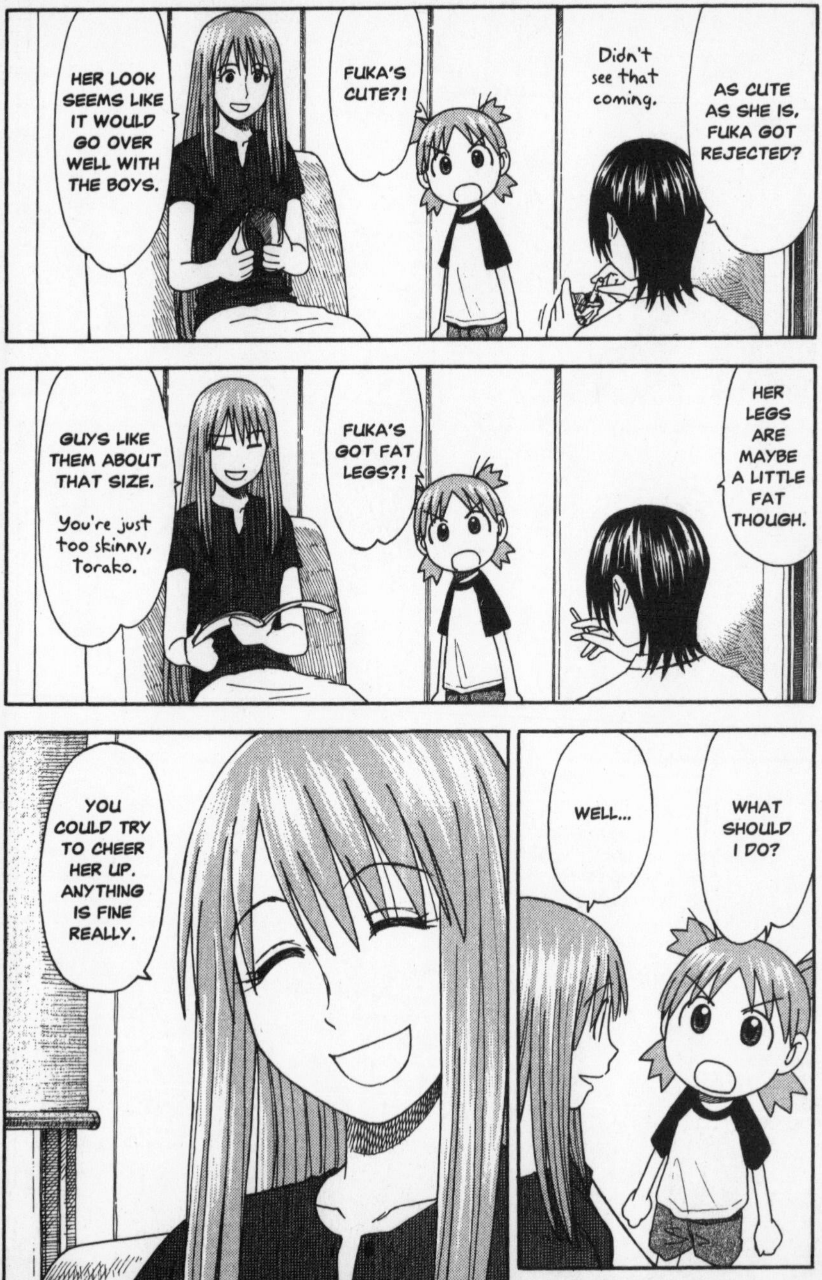
AS CUTE AS SHE IS, FUKA GOT REJECTED?
Didn't see that coming.
FUKA'S CUTE?!
HER LOOK SEEMS LIKE IT WOULD GO OVER WELL WITH THE BOYS.
HER LEGS ARE MAYBE A LITTLE FAT THOUGH.
FUKA'S GOT FAT LEGS?!
GUYS LIKE THEM ABOUT THAT SIZE.
You're just too skinny, Torako.
WHAT SHOULD I DO?
WELL...
YOU COULD TRY TO CHEER HER UP. ANYTHING IS FINE REALLY.

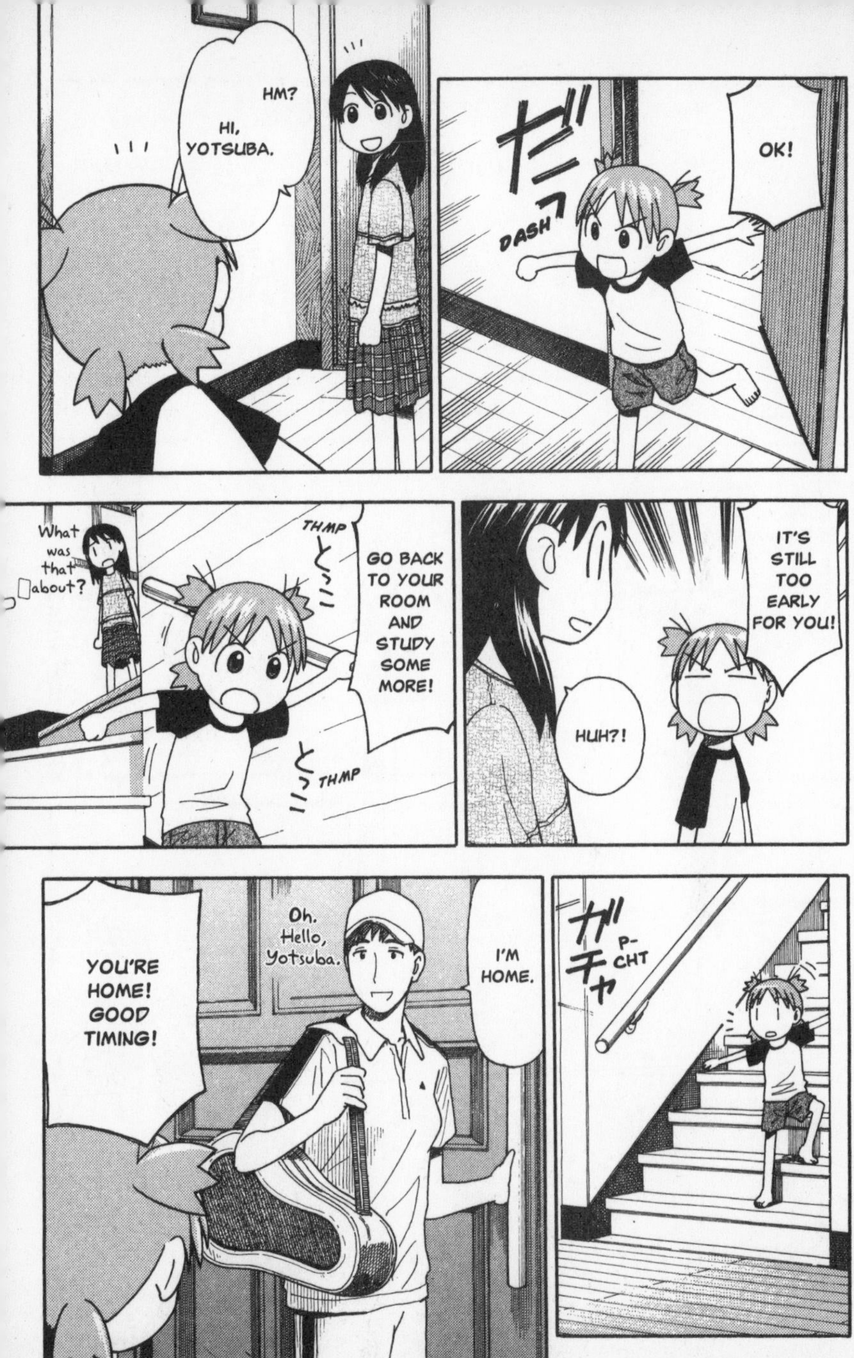
OK!
だっ
DASH
HM?
HI, YOTSUBA.
IT'S STILL TOO EARLY FOR YOU!
HUH?!
THMP
GO BACK TO YOUR ROOM AND STUDY SOME MORE!
THMP
What was that about?
ガチャ
P-CHT
I'M HOME.
Oh. Hello, Yotsuba.
YOU'RE HOME! GOOD TIMING!

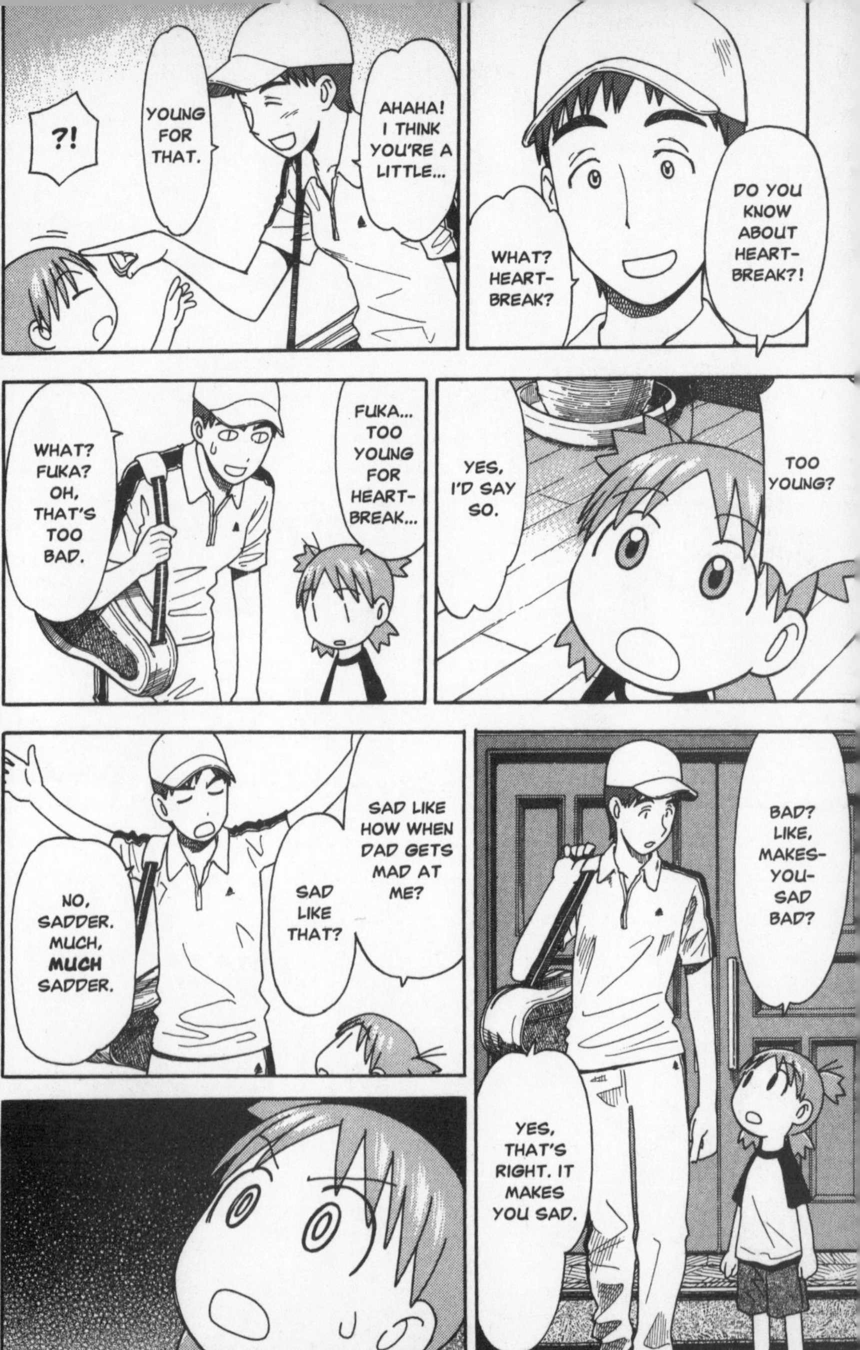
DO YOU KNOW ABOUT HEART-BREAK?!
WHAT? HEART-BREAK?
AHAHA! I THINK YOU'RE A LITTLE...
YOUNG FOR THAT.
?!
TOO YOUNG?
YES, I'D SAY SO.
FUKA... TOO YOUNG FOR HEART-BREAK...
WHAT? FUKA? OH, THAT'S TOO BAD.
BAD? LIKE, MAKES-YOU-SAD BAD?
YES, THAT'S RIGHT. IT MAKES YOU SAD.
SAD LIKE HOW WHEN DAD GETS MAD AT ME?
SAD LIKE THAT?
NO, SADDER. MUCH, **MUCH** SADDER.

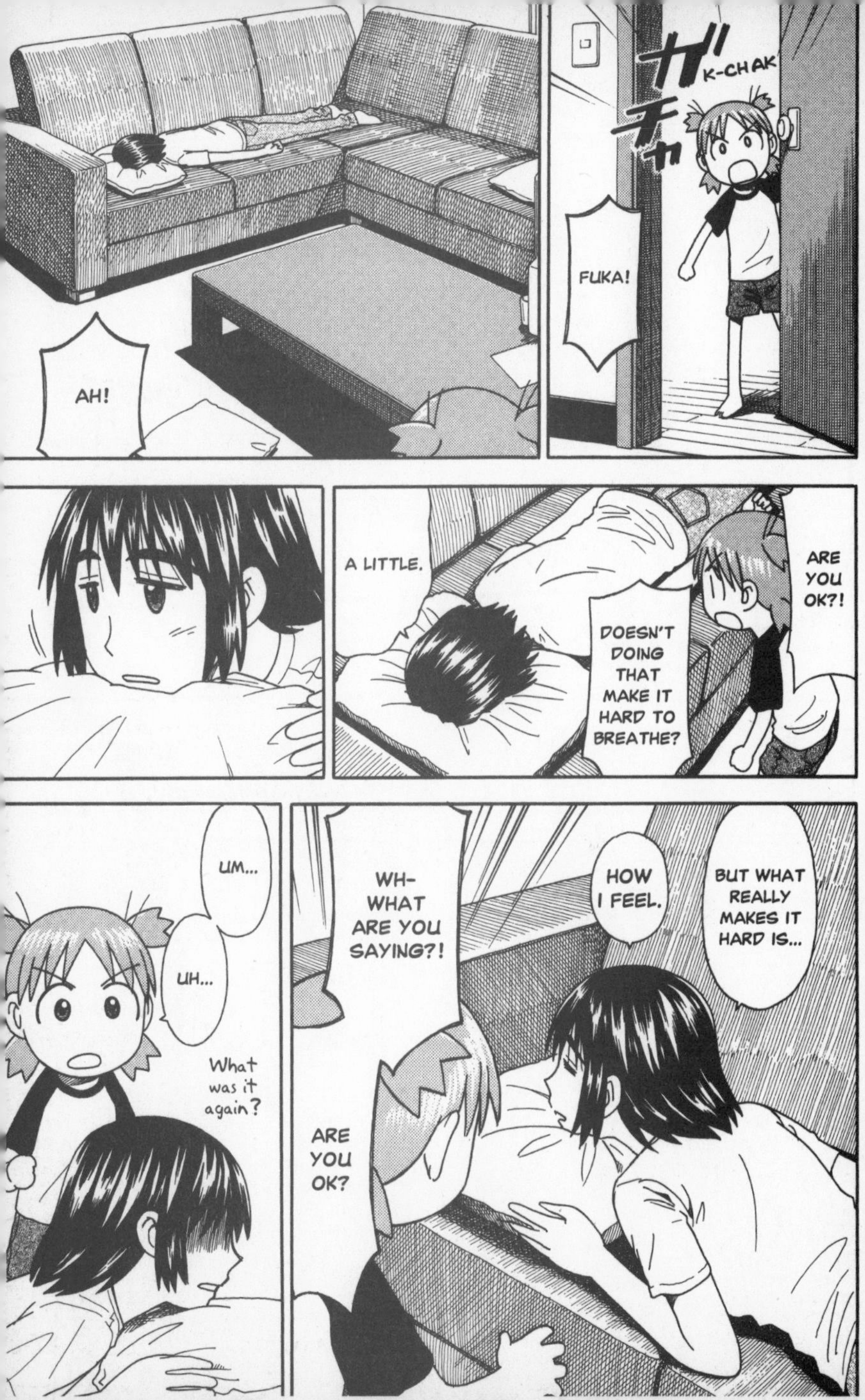
ガチャ
K-CHAK
FUKA!
AH!
ARE YOU OK?!
DOESN'T DOING THAT MAKE IT HARD TO BREATHE?
A LITTLE.
BUT WHAT REALLY MAKES IT HARD IS...
HOW I FEEL.
WH- WHAT ARE YOU SAYING?!
ARE YOU OK?
UM...
UH...
What was it again?

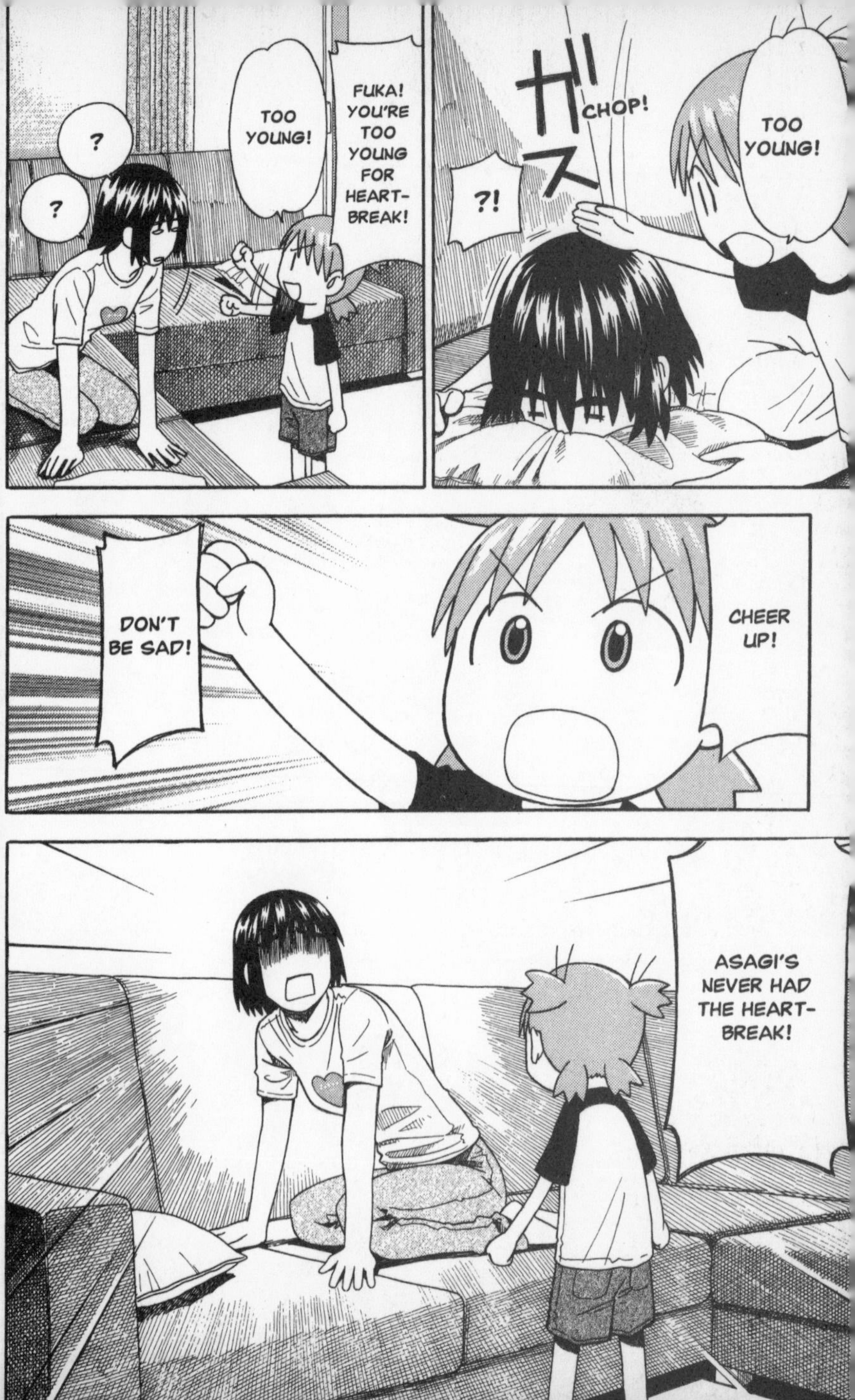
TOO YOUNG!
ガス
CHOP!
?!
FUKA! YOU'RE TOO YOUNG FOR HEART-BREAK!
TOO YOUNG!
?
?
CHEER UP!
DON'T BE SAD!
ASAGI'S NEVER HAD THE HEART-BREAK!

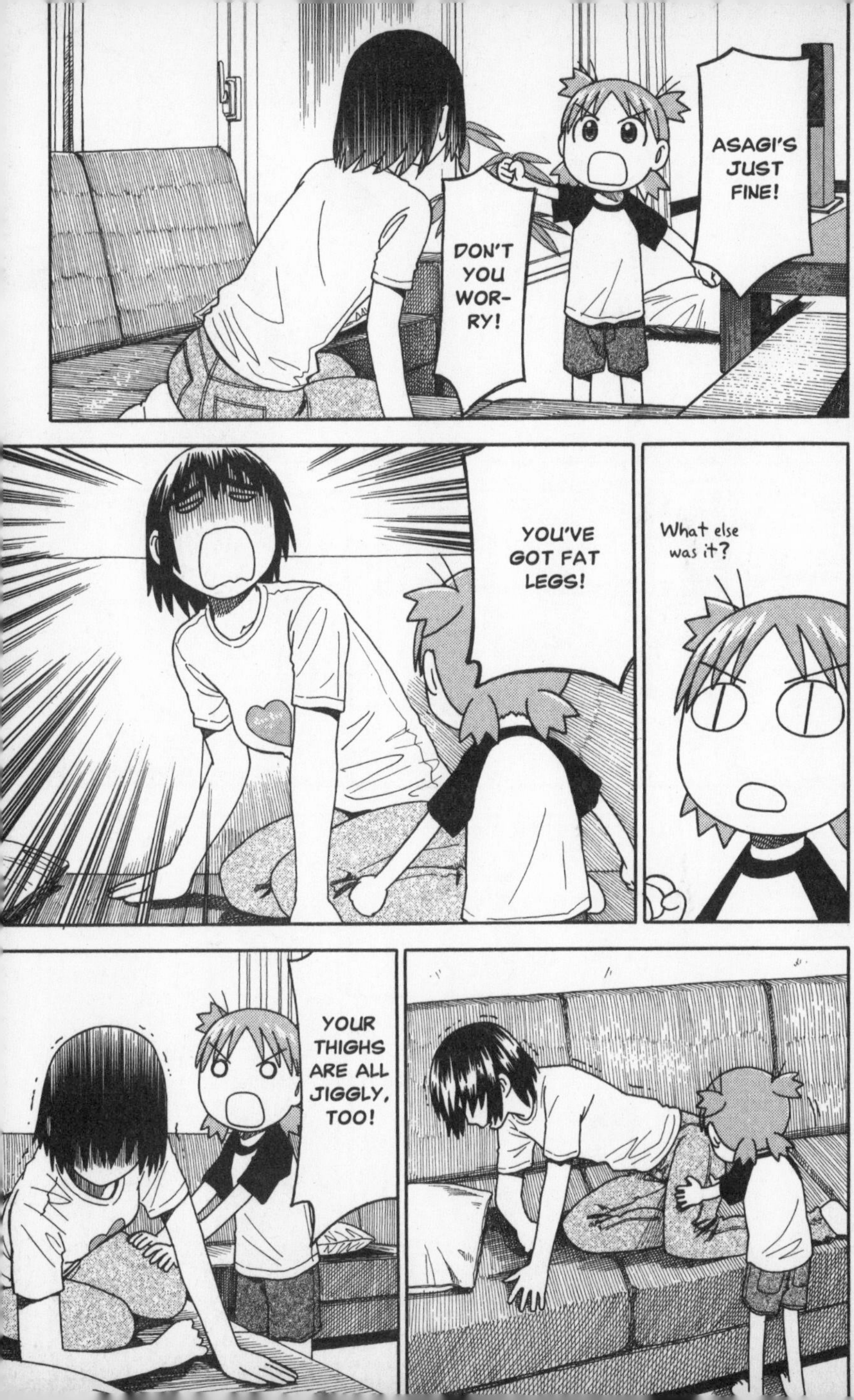
ASAGI'S JUST FINE!
DON'T YOU WORRY!
What else was it?
YOU'VE GOT FAT LEGS!
YOUR THIGHS ARE ALL JIGGLY, TOO!

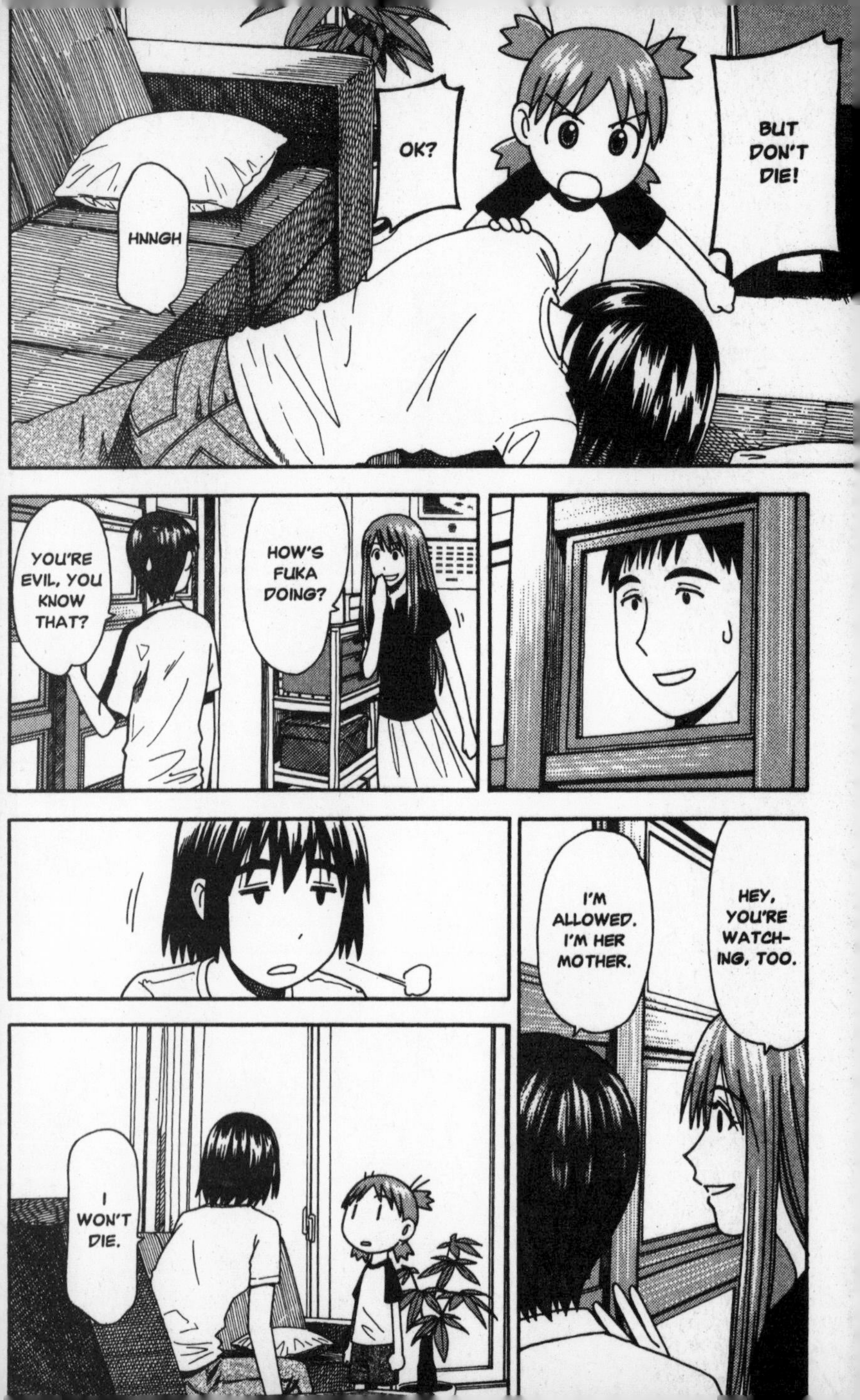
BUT DON'T DIE!
OK?
HNNGH
HOW'S FUKA DOING?
YOU'RE EVIL, YOU KNOW THAT?
HEY, YOU'RE WATCHING, TOO.
I'M ALLOWED. I'M HER MOTHER.
I WON'T DIE.

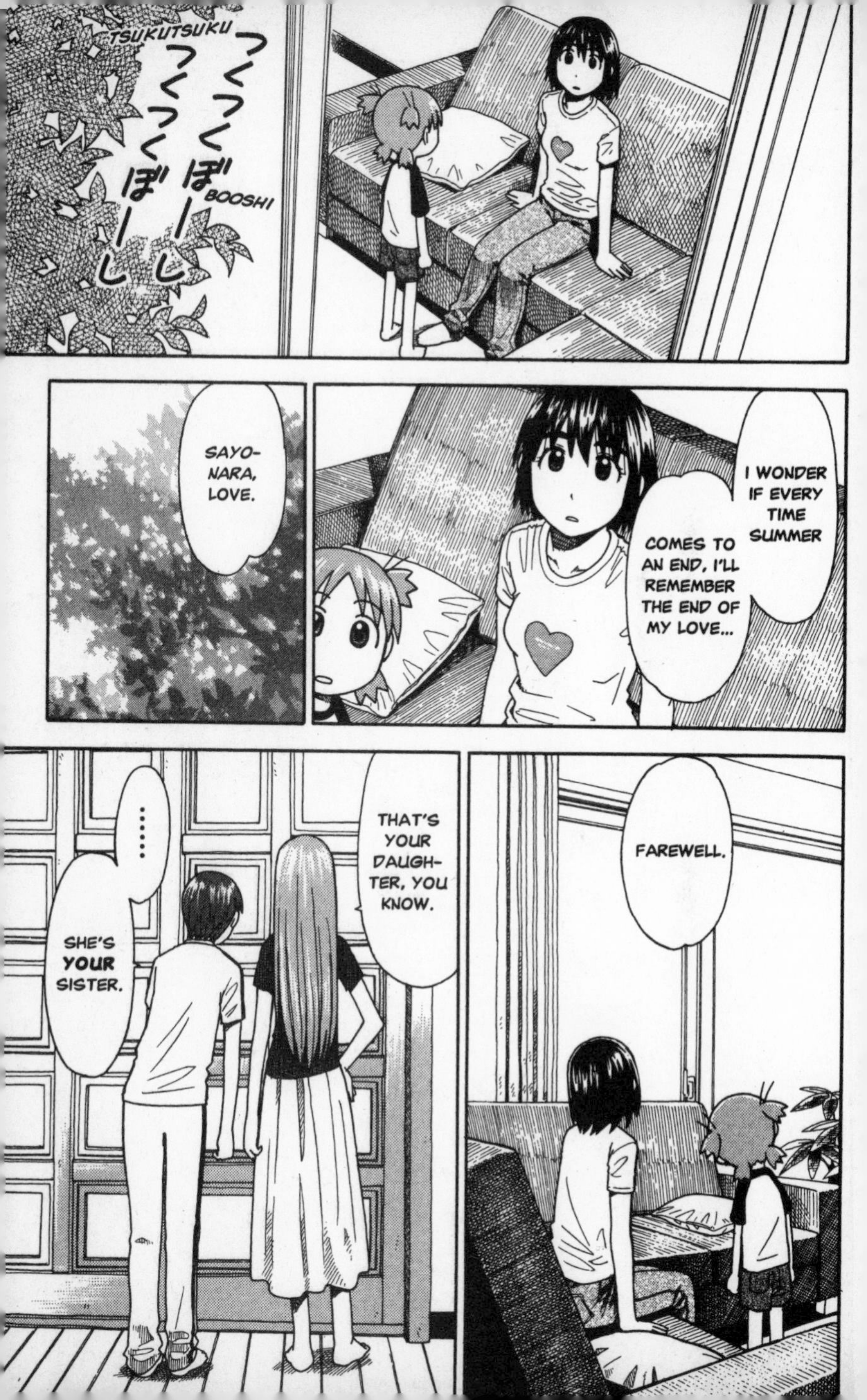

TSUKUTSUKU
つくつくぼーし
つくつくぼーし
BOOSHI
I WONDER IF EVERY TIME SUMMER
COMES TO AN END, I'LL REMEMBER THE END OF MY LOVE...
SAYO-NARA, LOVE.
FAREWELL.
THAT'S YOUR DAUGH-TER, YOU KNOW.
......
SHE'S **YOUR** SISTER.

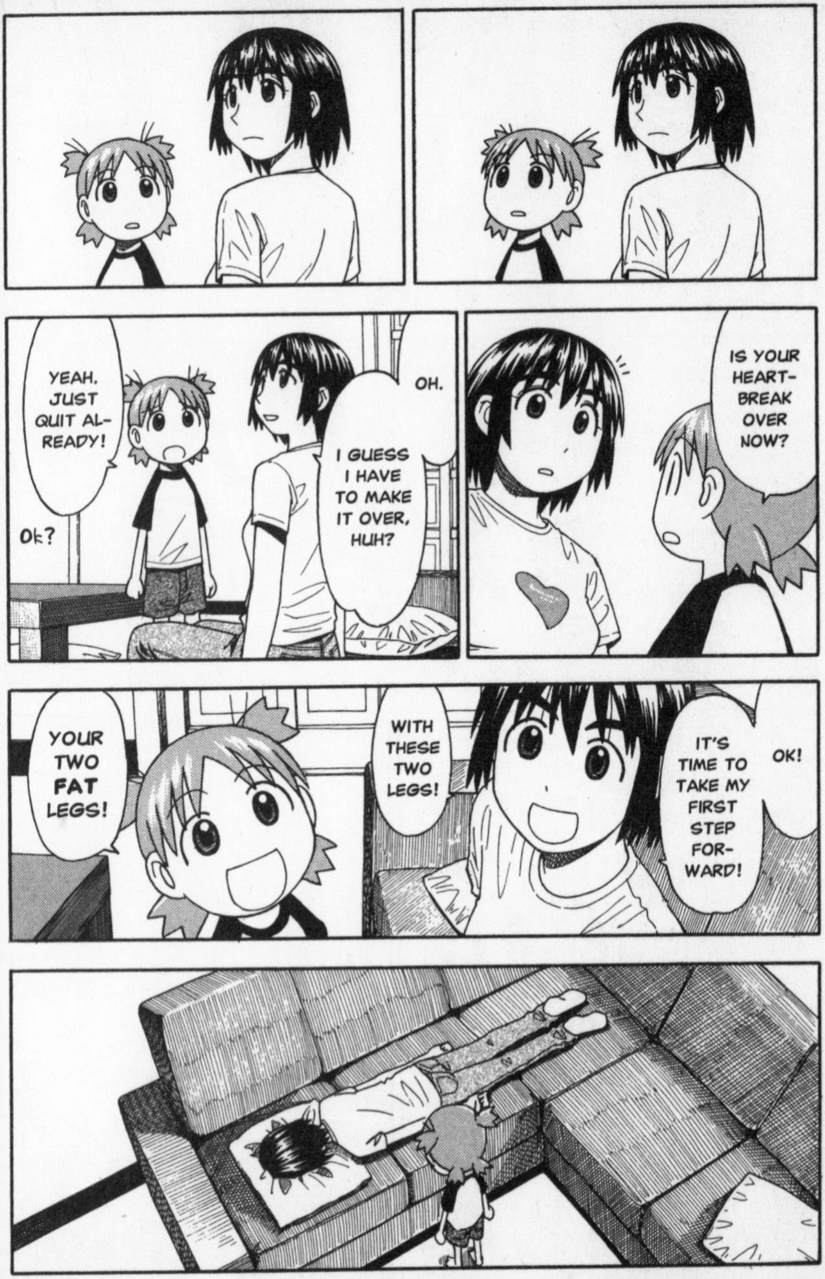
IS YOUR HEART-BREAK OVER NOW?
OH.
I GUESS I HAVE TO MAKE IT OVER, HUH?
YEAH. JUST QUIT AL-READY!
Ok?
OK!
IT'S TIME TO TAKE MY FIRST STEP FOR-WARD!
WITH THESE TWO LEGS!
YOUR TWO **FAT** LEGS!

YOTSUBA&!

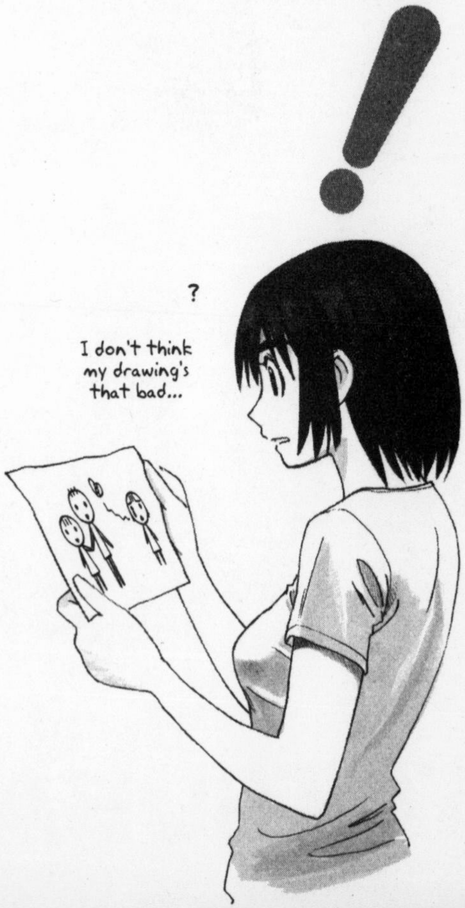

?
I don't think my drawing's that bad...

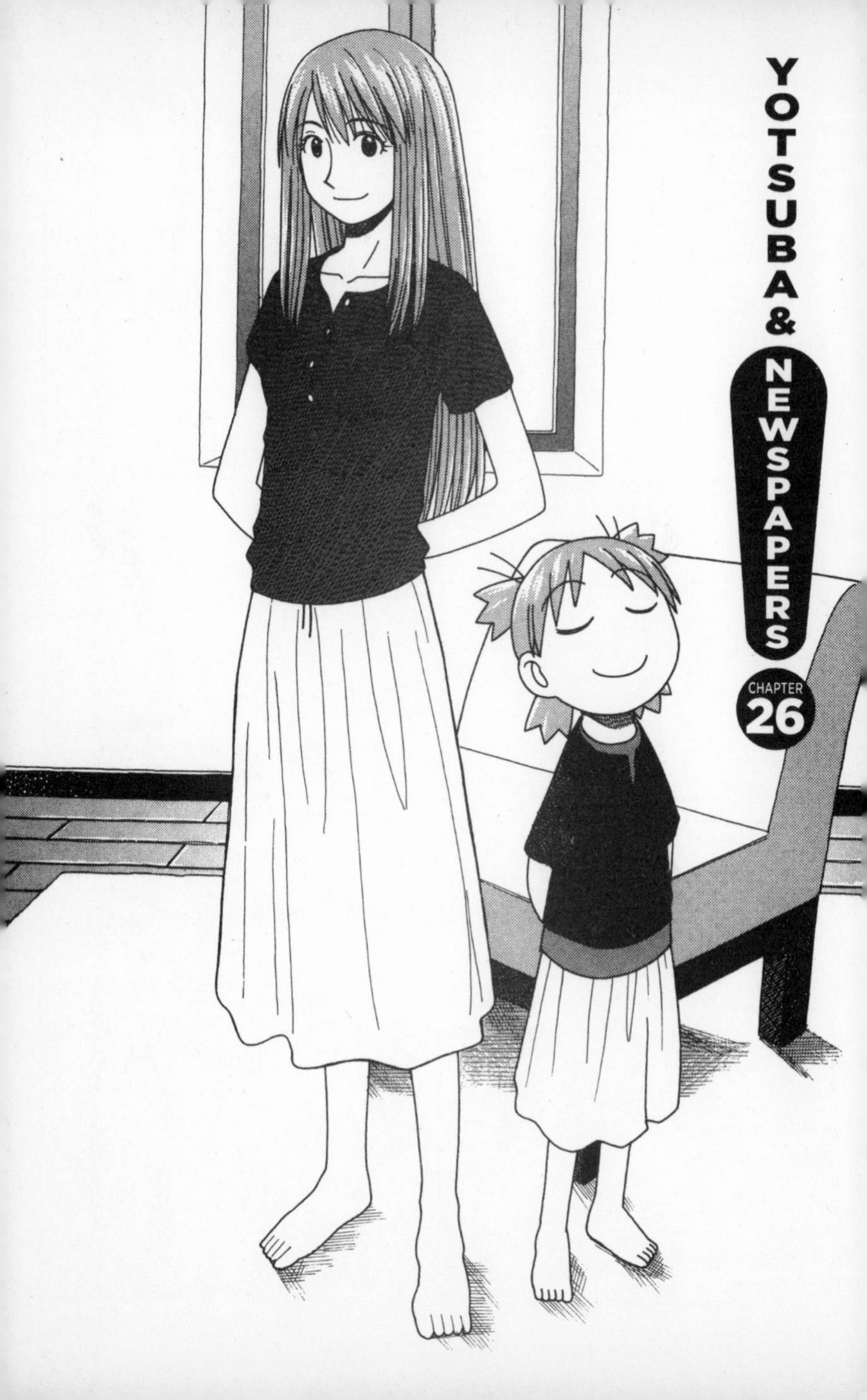
YOTSUBA & NEWSPAPERS
CHAPTER 26

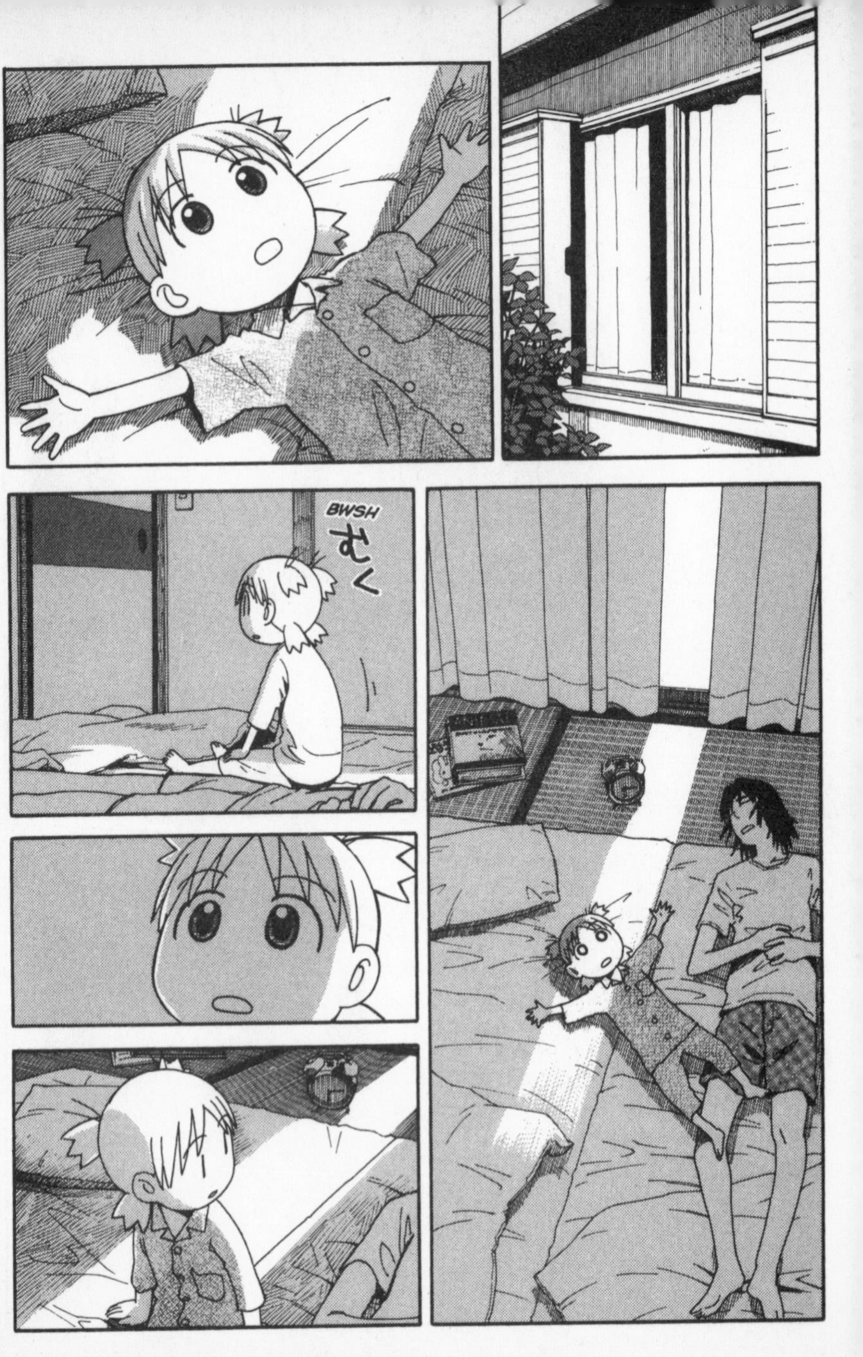
BWSH
むく

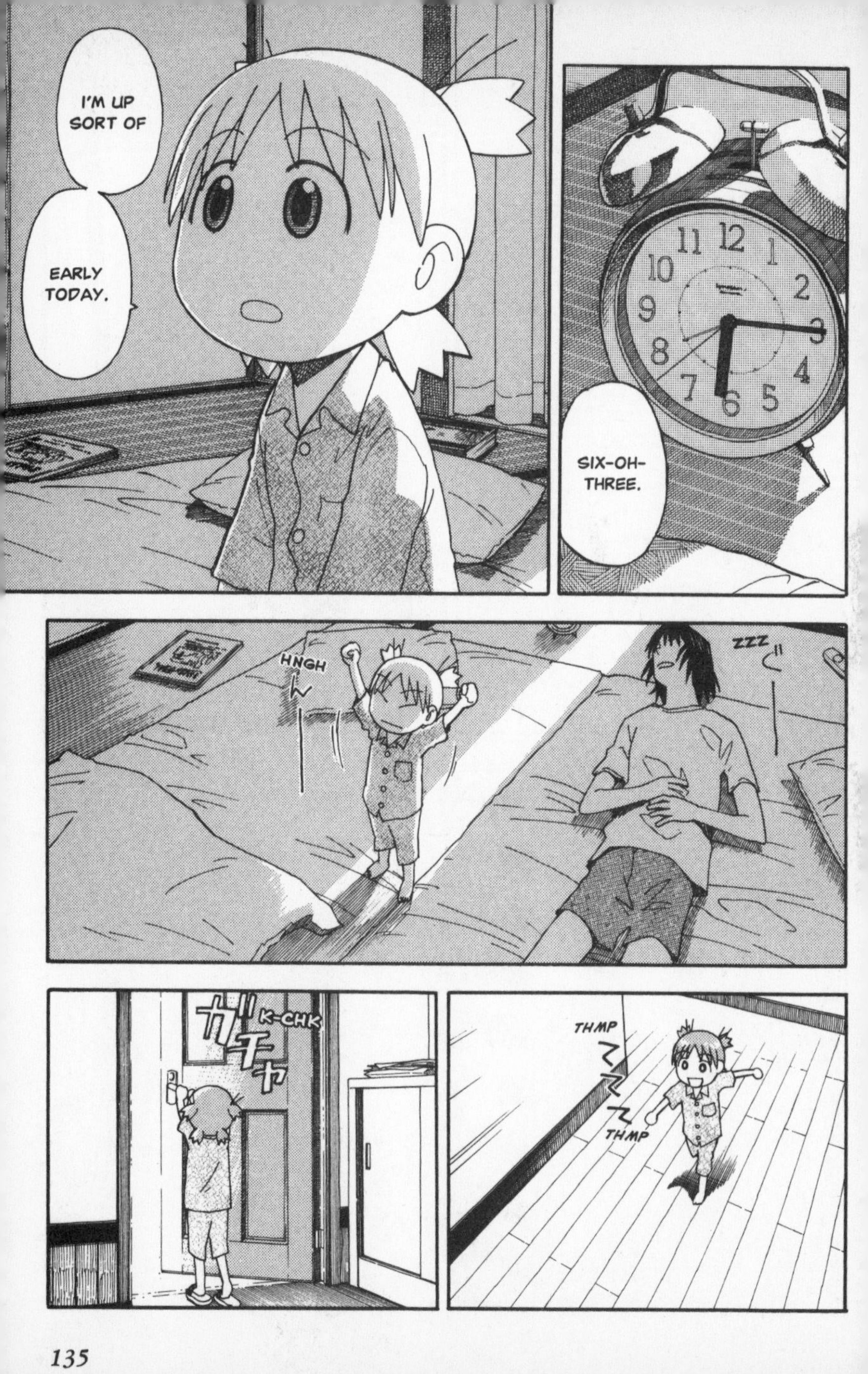
SIX-OH-THREE.
I'M UP SORT OF
EARLY TODAY.
ZZZ
ぐ
HNGH
ん
THMP
THMP
ガチャ
K-CHK

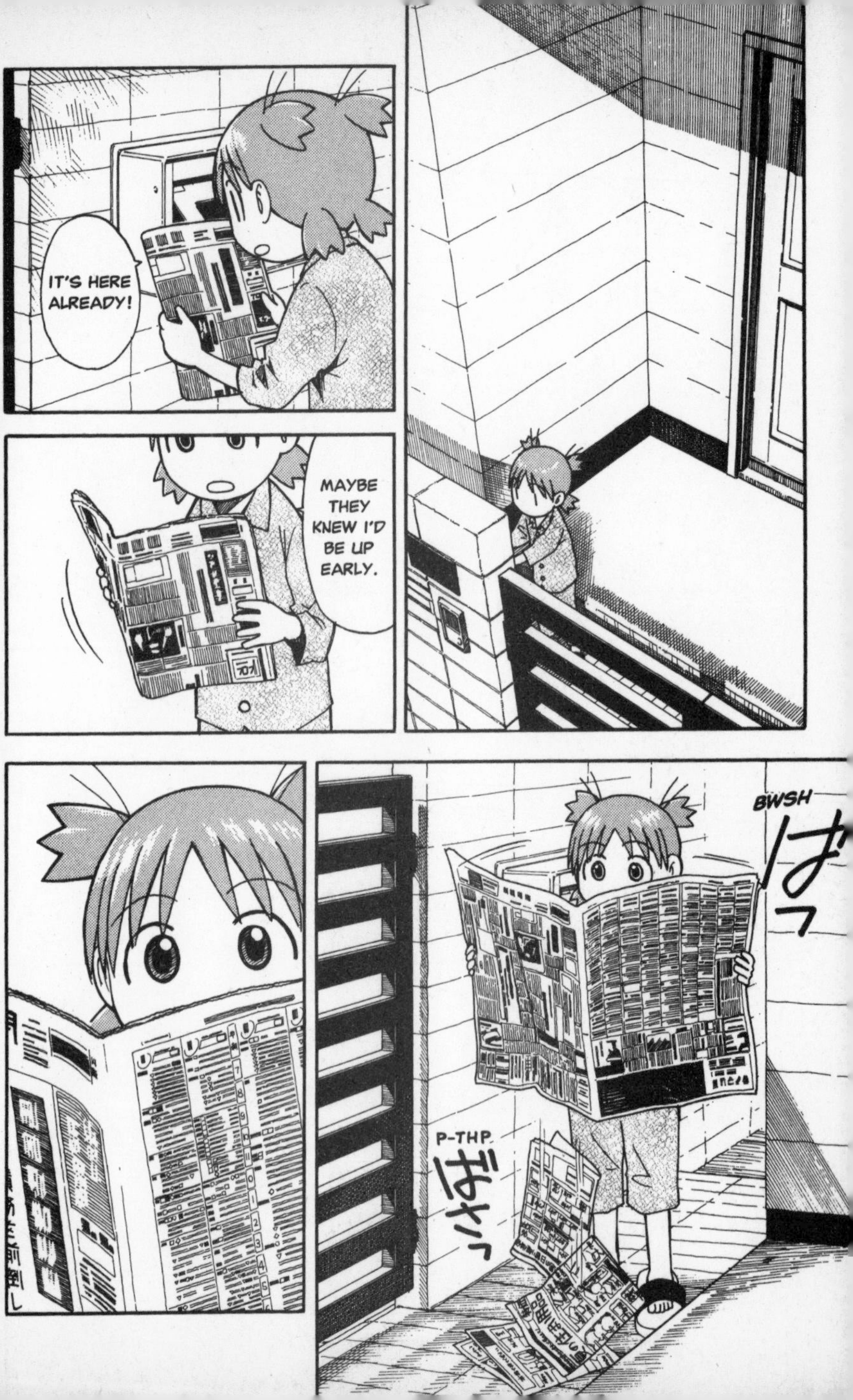
IT'S HERE ALREADY!
MAYBE THEY KNEW I'D BE UP EARLY.
BWSH
ぱっ
P-THP
ばさっ

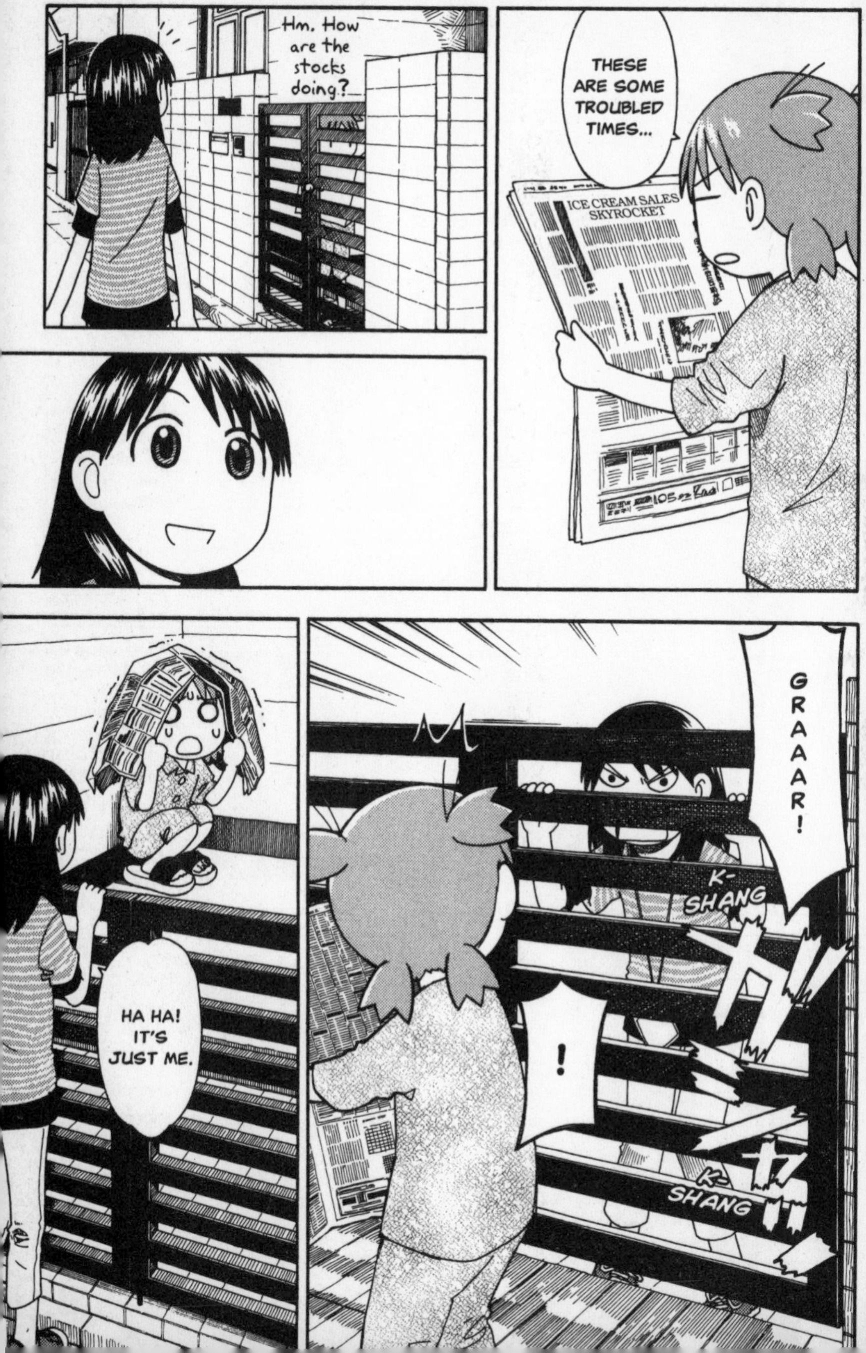
THESE ARE SOME TROUBLED TIMES...
ICE CREAM SALES SKYROCKET
Hm. How are the stocks doing?
GRAAAR!
K-SHANG
!
K-SHANG
HA HA! IT'S JUST ME.

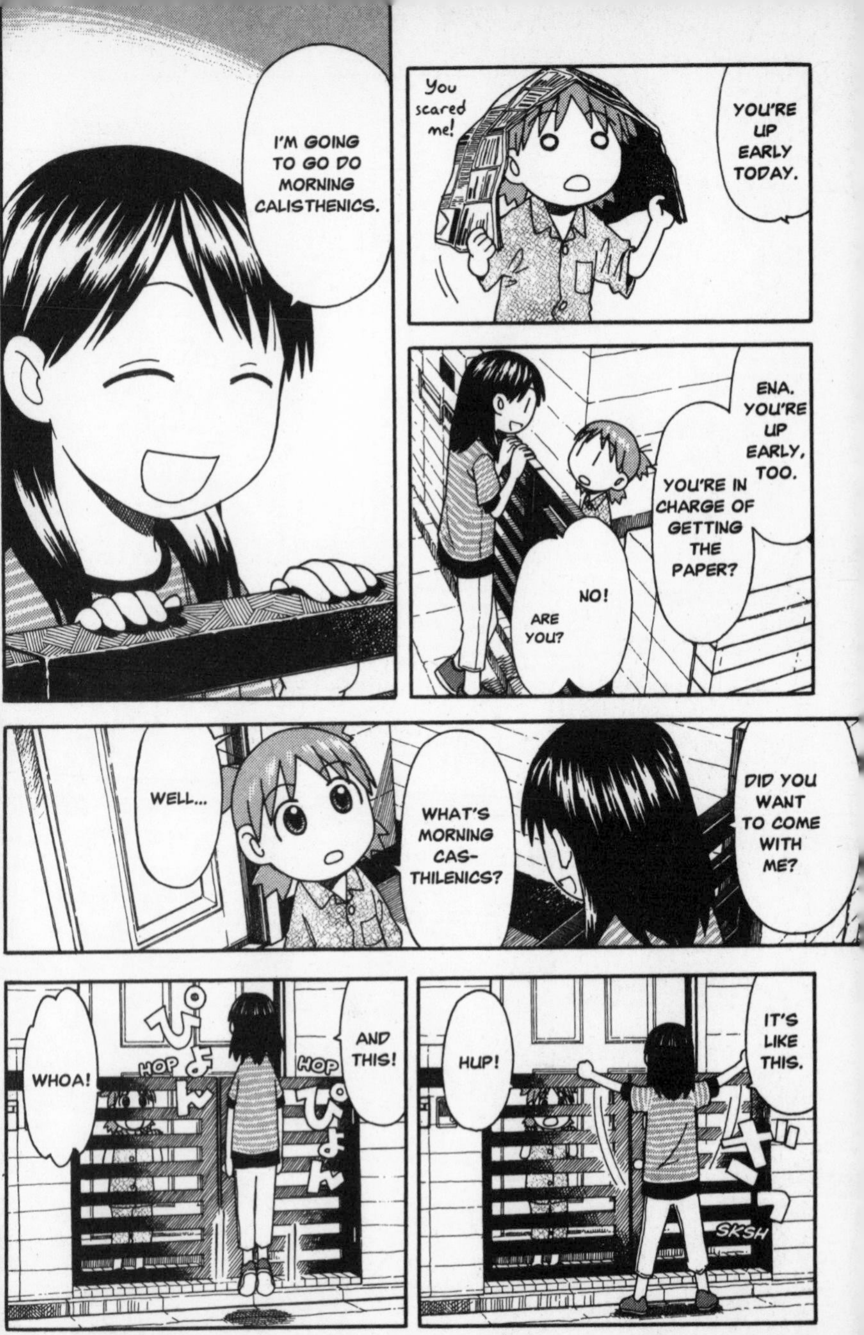
YOU'RE UP EARLY TODAY.
You scared me!
ENA. YOU'RE UP EARLY, TOO.
YOU'RE IN CHARGE OF GETTING THE PAPER?
NO!
ARE YOU?
I'M GOING TO GO DO MORNING CALISTHENICS.
DID YOU WANT TO COME WITH ME?
WHAT'S MORNING CAS-THILENICS?
WELL...
IT'S LIKE THIS.
SKSH
HUP!
AND THIS!
ぴょん
HOP
ぴょん
HOP
WHOA!

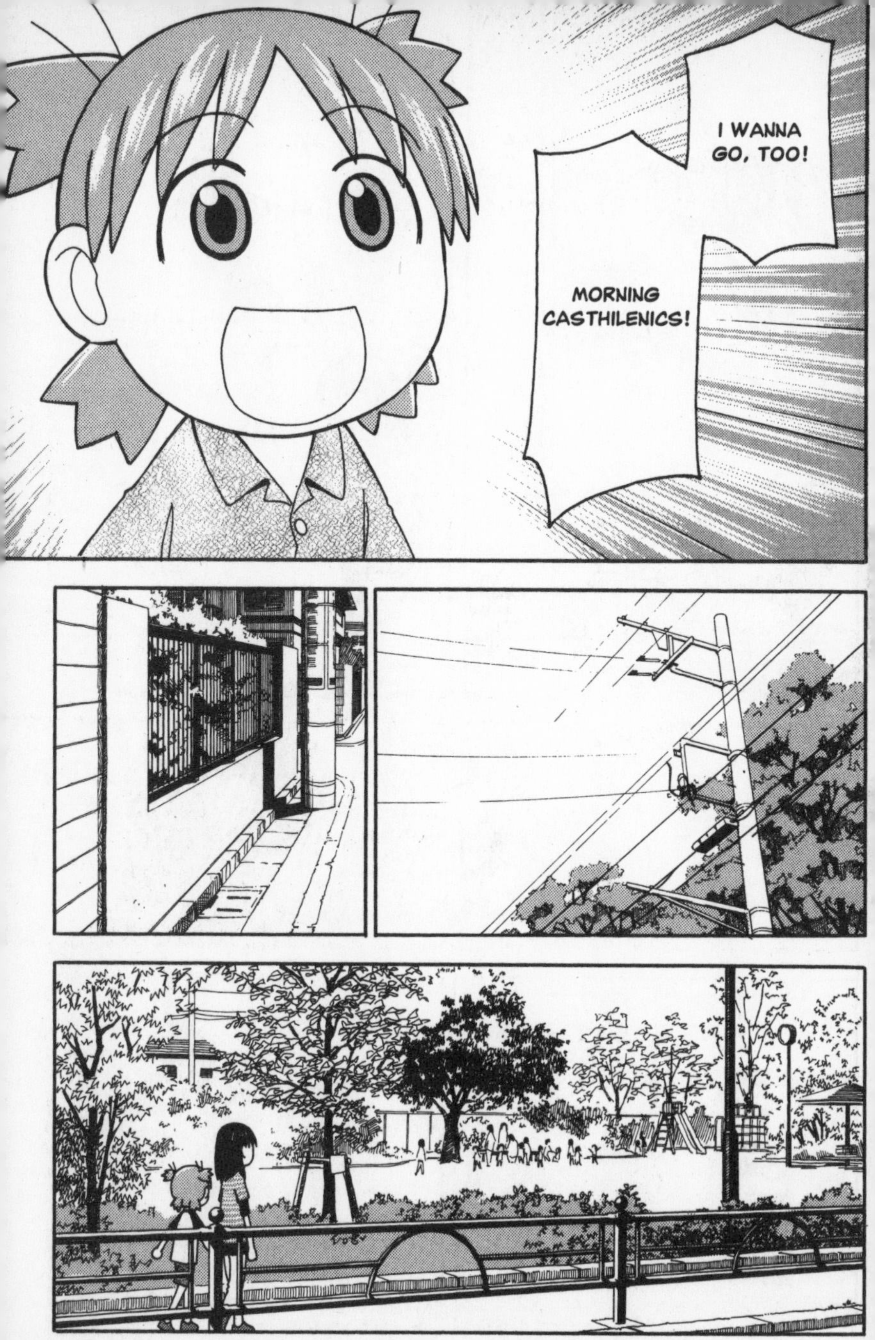
I WANNA GO, TOO!
MORNING CASTHILENICS!

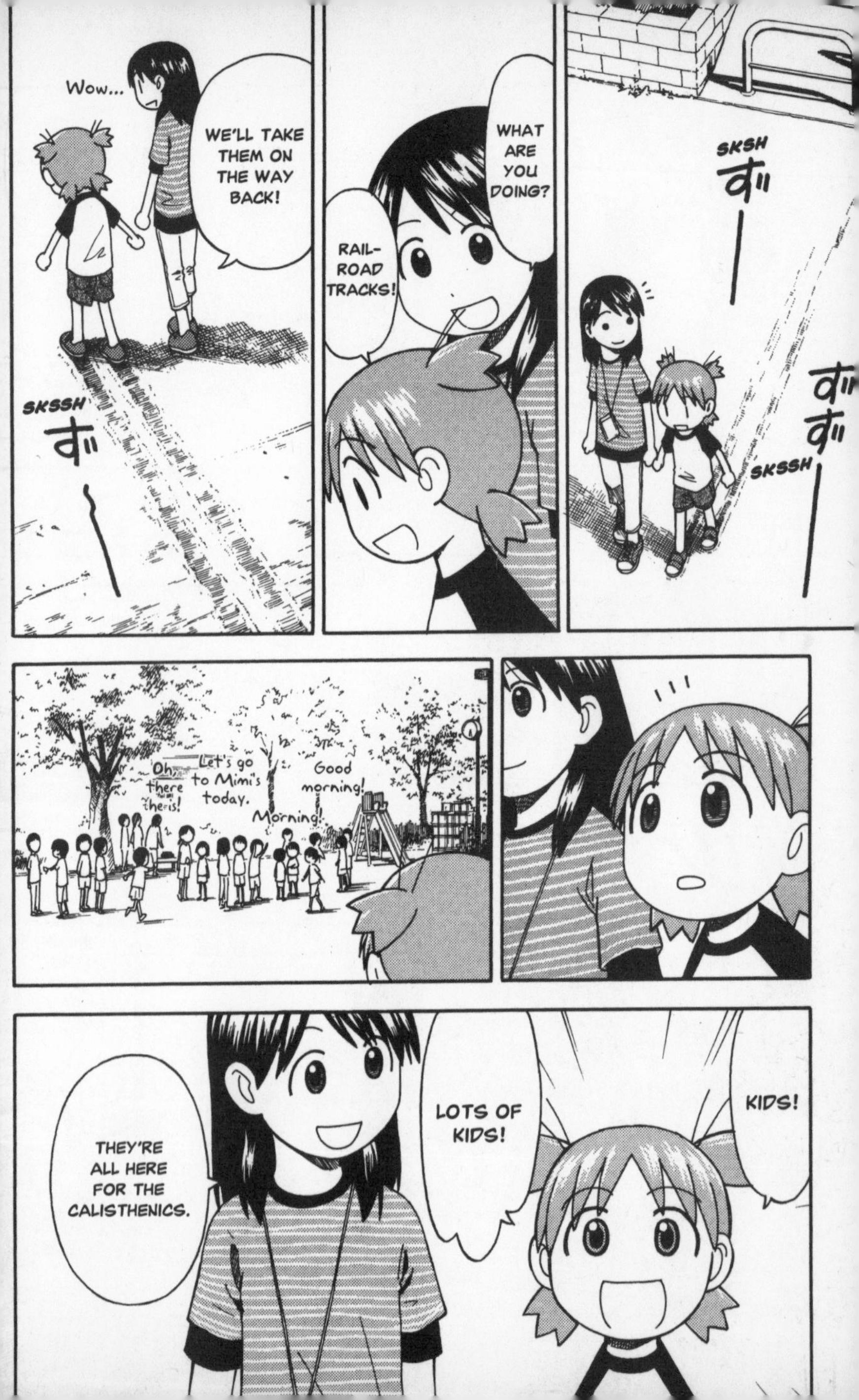
SKSH
ず
ずず
SKSSH
WHAT ARE YOU DOING?
RAIL-ROAD TRACKS!
WE'LL TAKE THEM ON THE WAY BACK!
Wow...
SKSSH
ず
Good morning!
Let's go to Mimi's today.
Oh, there she is!
Morning!
KIDS!
LOTS OF KIDS!
THEY'RE ALL HERE FOR THE CALISTHENICS.

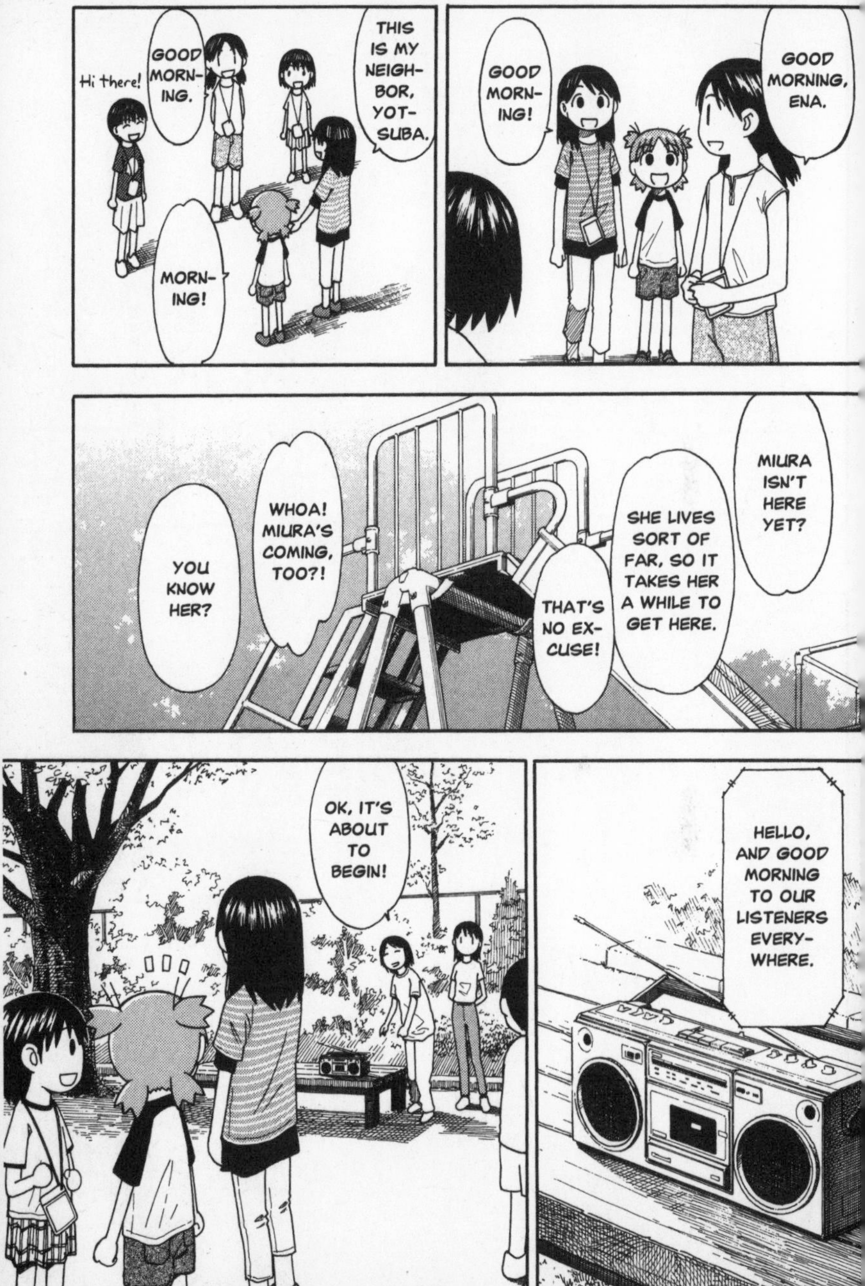
GOOD MORNING, ENA.
GOOD MORNING!
THIS IS MY NEIGHBOR, YOTSUBA.
GOOD MORNING.
Hi there!
MORNING!
MIURA ISN'T HERE YET?
SHE LIVES SORT OF FAR, SO IT TAKES HER A WHILE TO GET HERE.
THAT'S NO EXCUSE!
WHOA! MIURA'S COMING, TOO?!
YOU KNOW HER?
HELLO, AND GOOD MORNING TO OUR LISTENERS EVERYWHERE.
OK, IT'S ABOUT TO BEGIN!

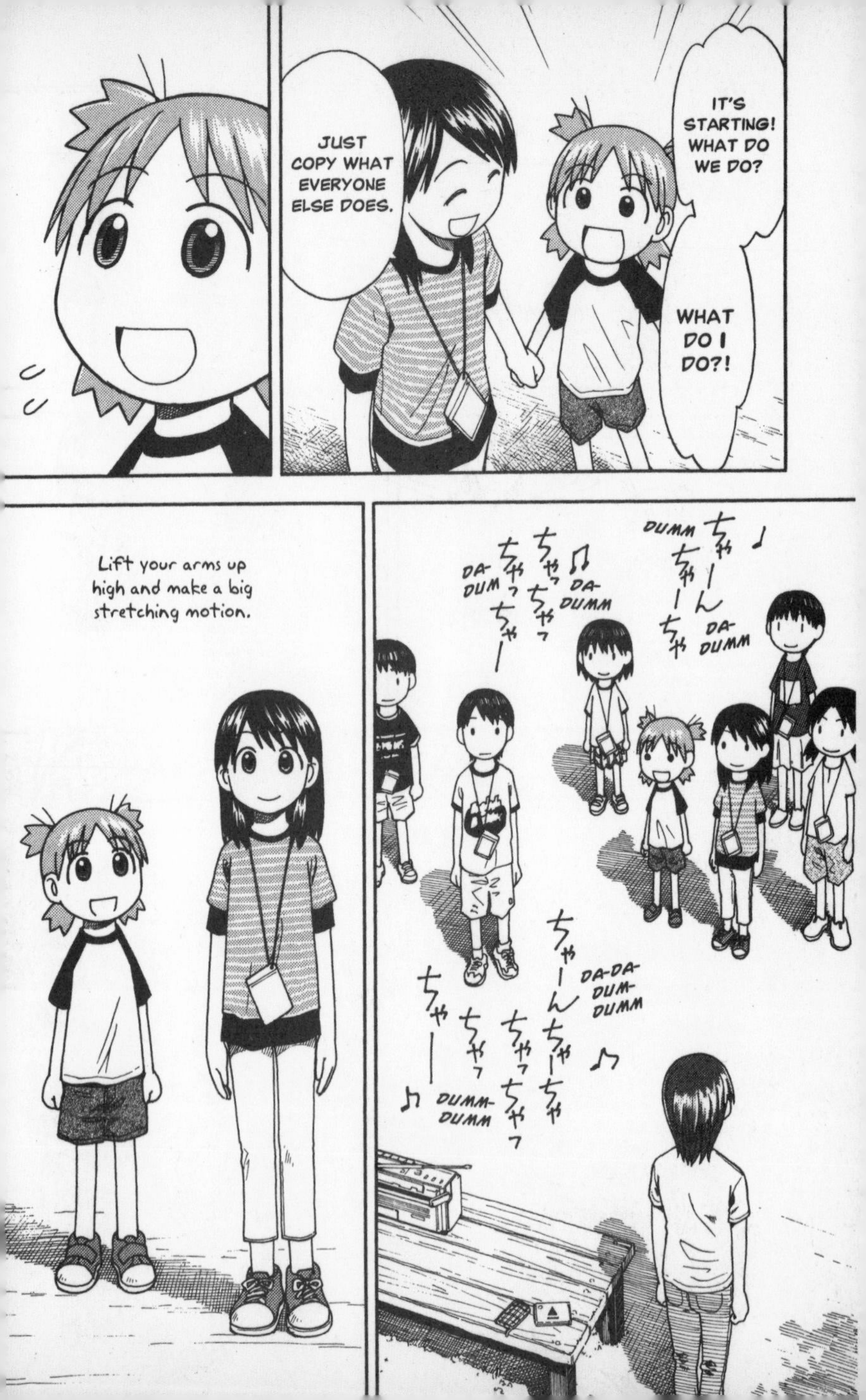
IT'S STARTING! WHAT DO WE DO?
WHAT DO I DO?!
JUST COPY WHAT EVERYONE ELSE DOES.
DUMM
ちゃーんちゃーんちゃ
DA-DUMM
DA-DUMM
ちゃっちゃっちゃー
DA-DUM
DA-DA-DUM-DUMM
ちゃーんちゃーちゃ
ちゃっちゃっ
ちゃっ
ちゃー
DUMM-DUMM
Lift your arms up high and make a big stretching motion.

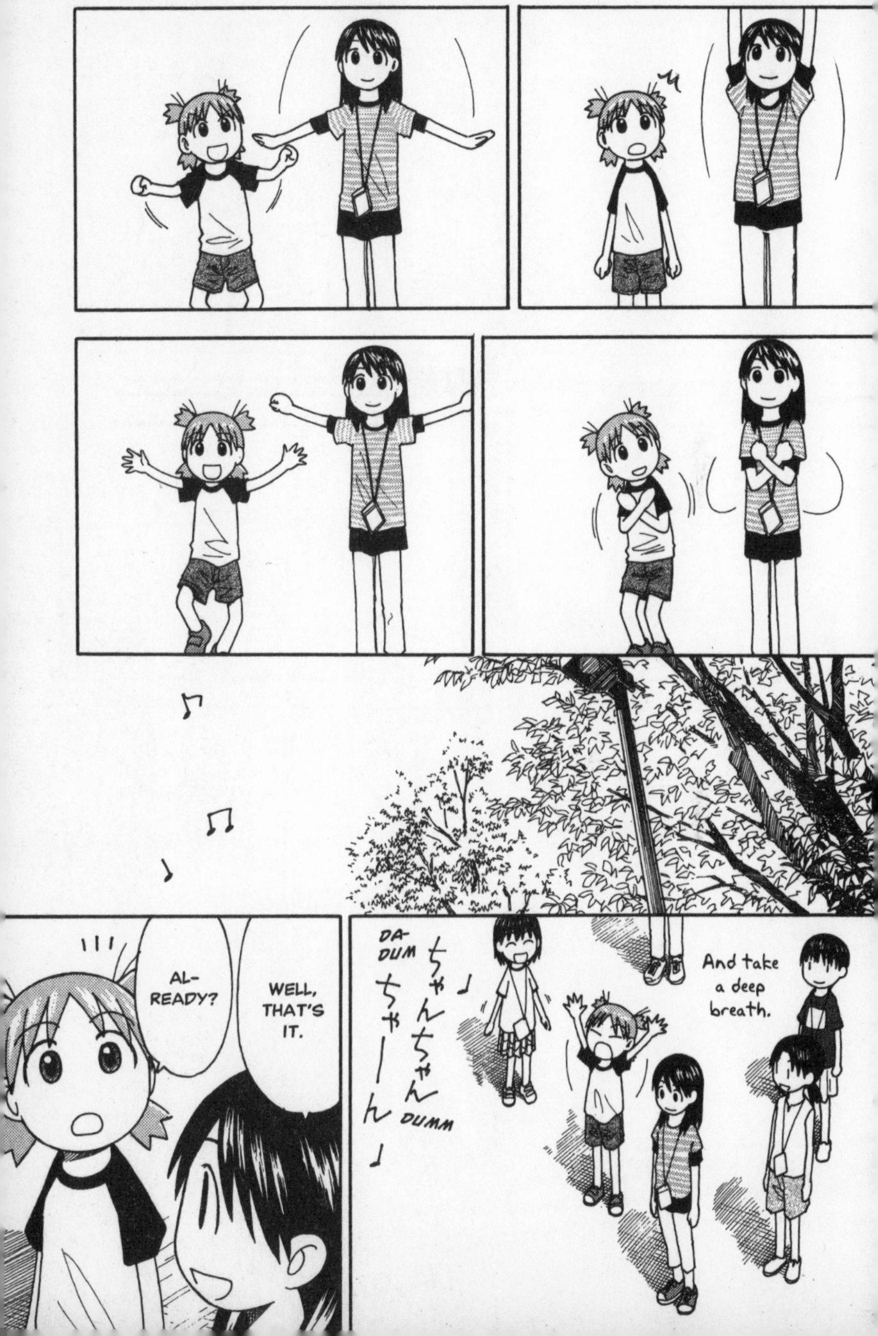
And take a deep breath.
DA-DUM
ちゃんちゃんちゃーん
DUMM
WELL, THAT'S IT.
AL-READY?

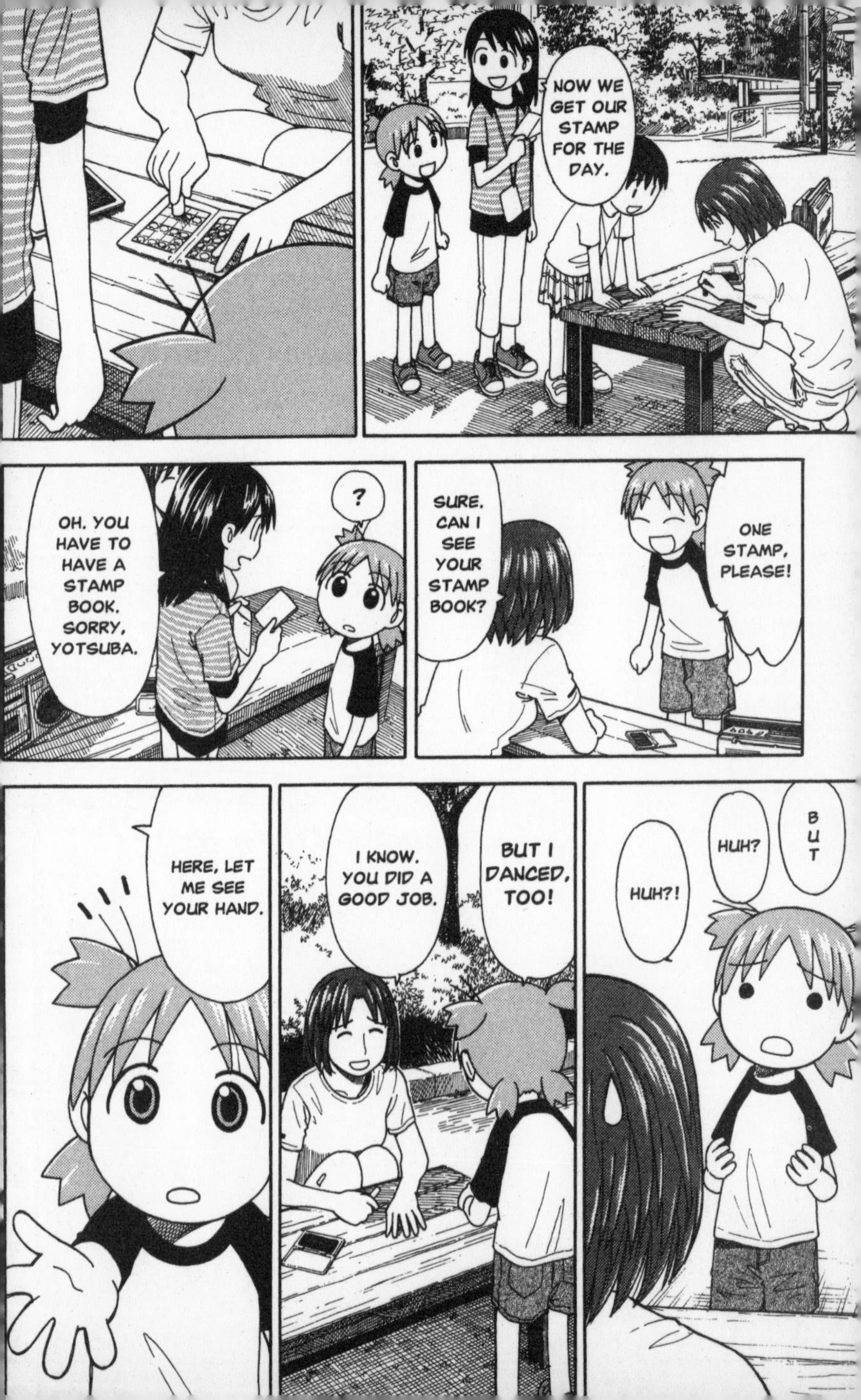
NOW WE GET OUR STAMP FOR THE DAY.
ONE STAMP, PLEASE!
SURE. CAN I SEE YOUR STAMP BOOK?
?
OH. YOU HAVE TO HAVE A STAMP BOOK. SORRY, YOTSUBA.
BUT
HUH?
HUH?!
BUT I DANCED, TOO!
I KNOW. YOU DID A GOOD JOB.
HERE, LET ME SEE YOUR HAND.

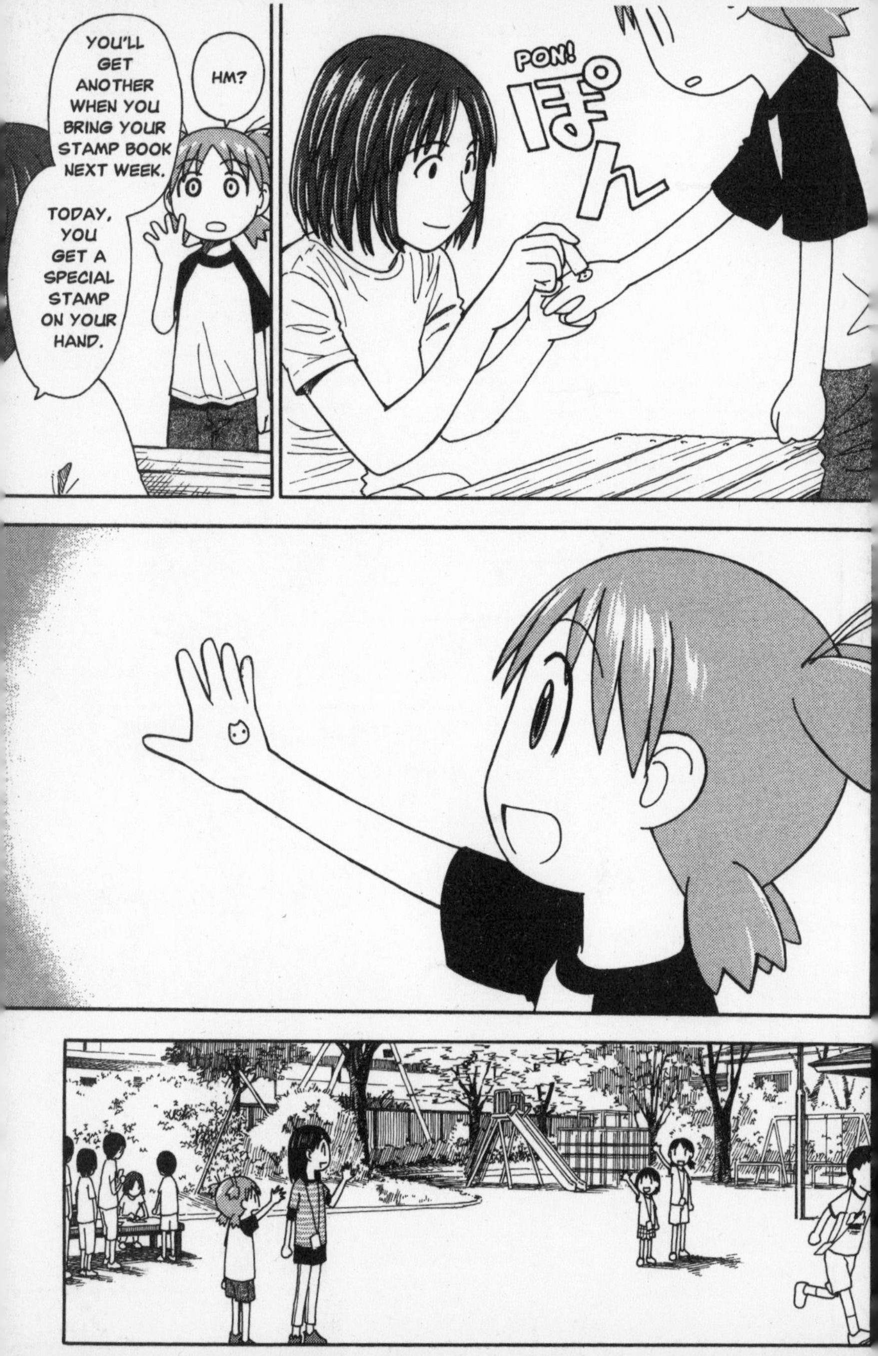
PON!
ぽん
HM?
YOU'LL GET ANOTHER WHEN YOU BRING YOUR STAMP BOOK NEXT WEEK.
TODAY, YOU GET A SPECIAL STAMP ON YOUR HAND.

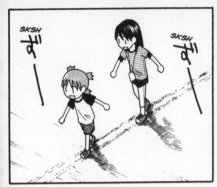

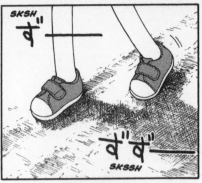

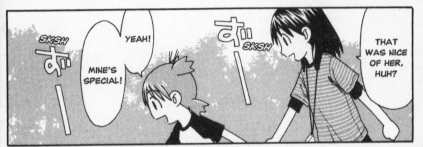

SKSH
ずー
ずずー
SKSSH
SKSH
ずー
SKSH
ずー
THAT WAS NICE OF HER, HUH?
SKSH
ずー
YEAH!
MINE'S SPECIAL!
SKSH
ずー
VRRMM
ブルルルル

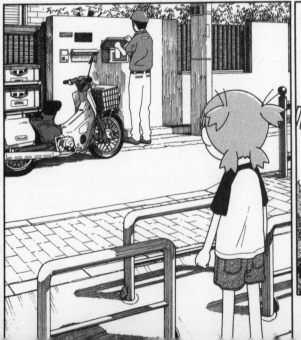

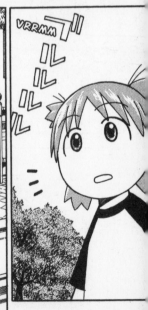

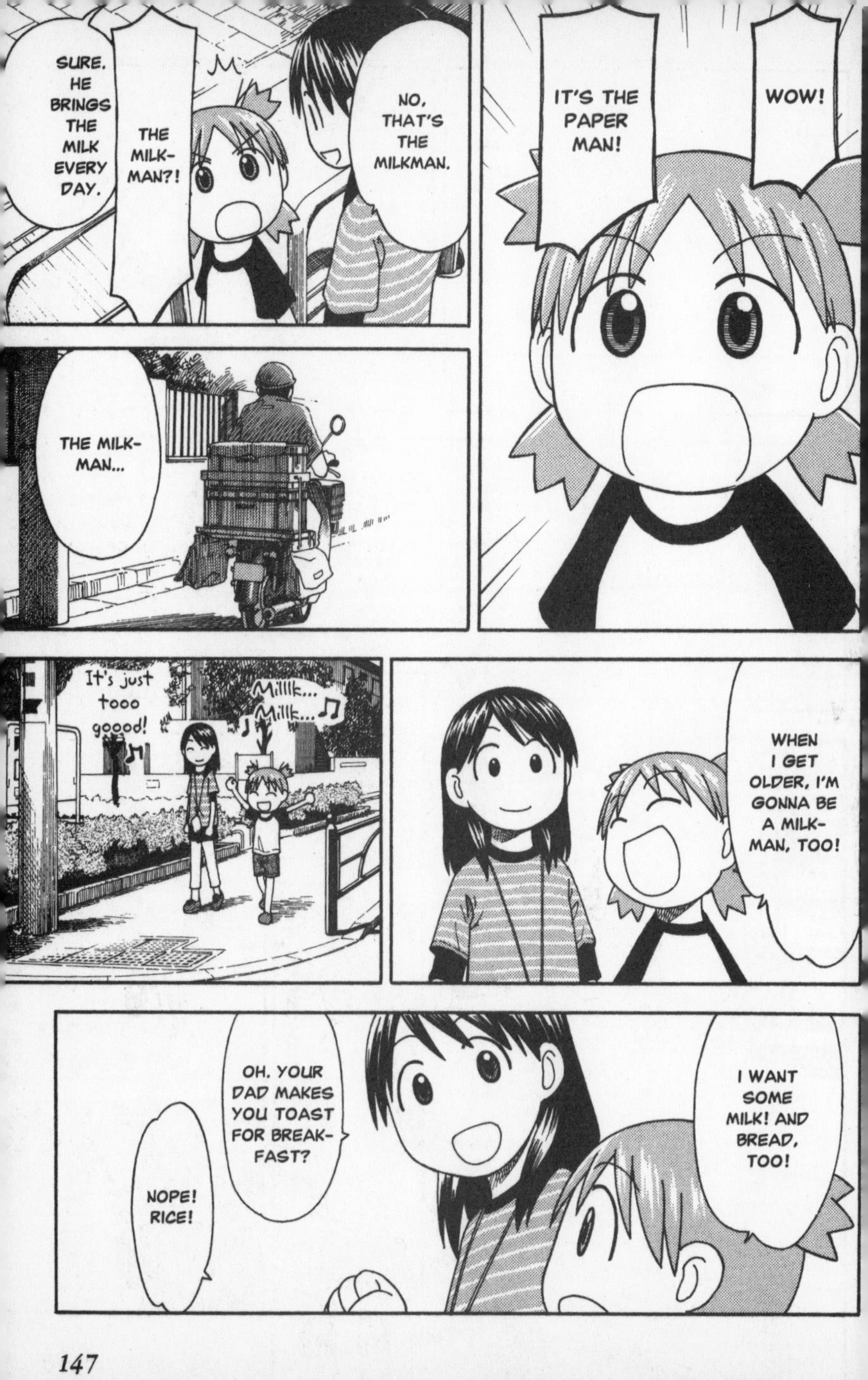
WOW!
IT'S THE PAPER MAN!
NO, THAT'S THE MILKMAN.
THE MILK-MAN?!
SURE. HE BRINGS THE MILK EVERY DAY.
THE MILK-MAN...
WHEN I GET OLDER, I'M GONNA BE A MILK-MAN, TOO!
Millk... Millk...
It's just tooo goood!
I WANT SOME MILK! AND BREAD, TOO!
OH. YOUR DAD MAKES YOU TOAST FOR BREAK-FAST?
NOPE! RICE!

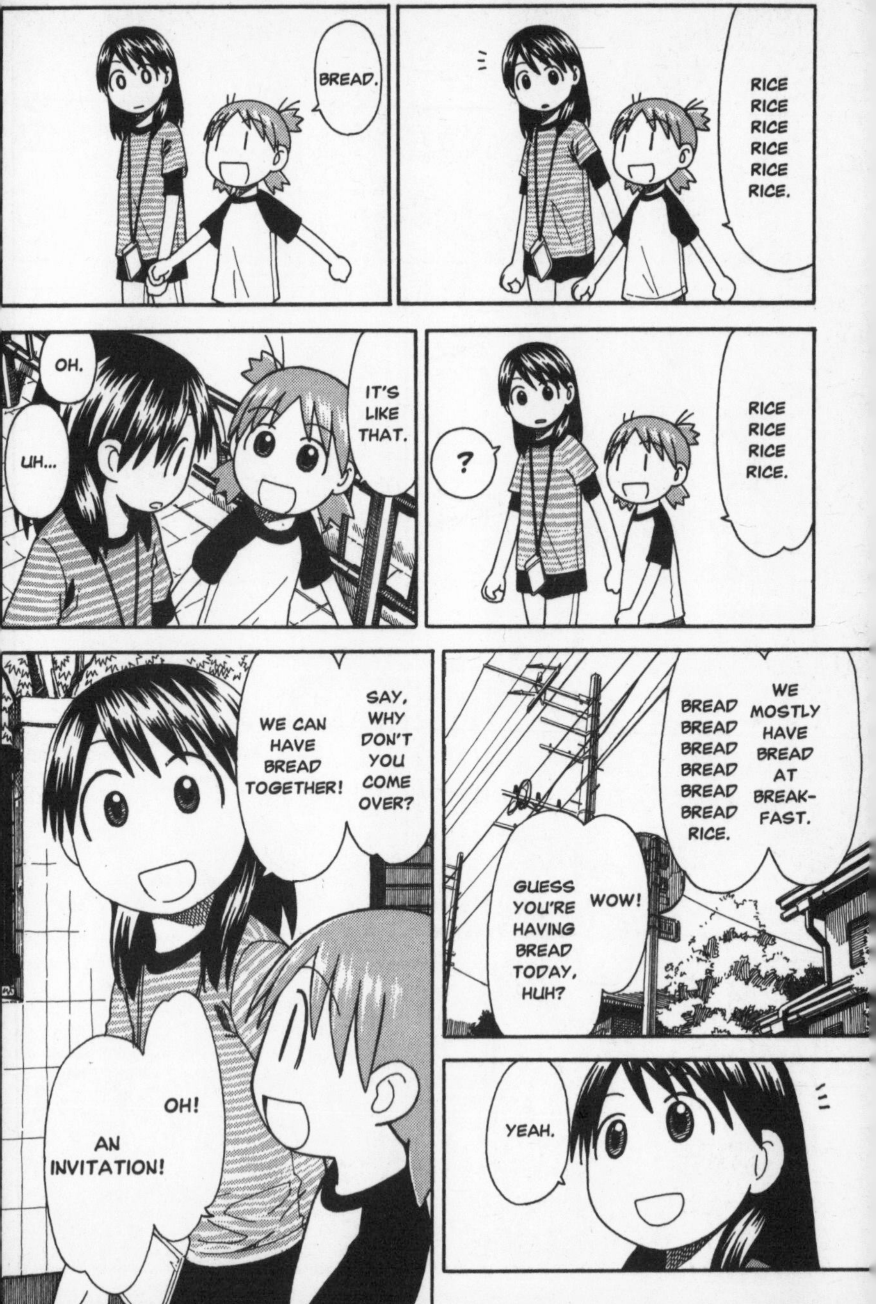
RICE RICE RICE RICE RICE RICE.
BREAD.
RICE RICE RICE RICE.
?
IT'S LIKE THAT.
OH.
UH...
WE MOSTLY HAVE BREAD AT BREAK-FAST.
BREAD BREAD BREAD BREAD BREAD BREAD RICE.
WOW!
GUESS YOU'RE HAVING BREAD TODAY, HUH?
YEAH.
SAY, WHY DON'T YOU COME OVER?
WE CAN HAVE BREAD TOGETHER!
OH!
AN INVITATION!

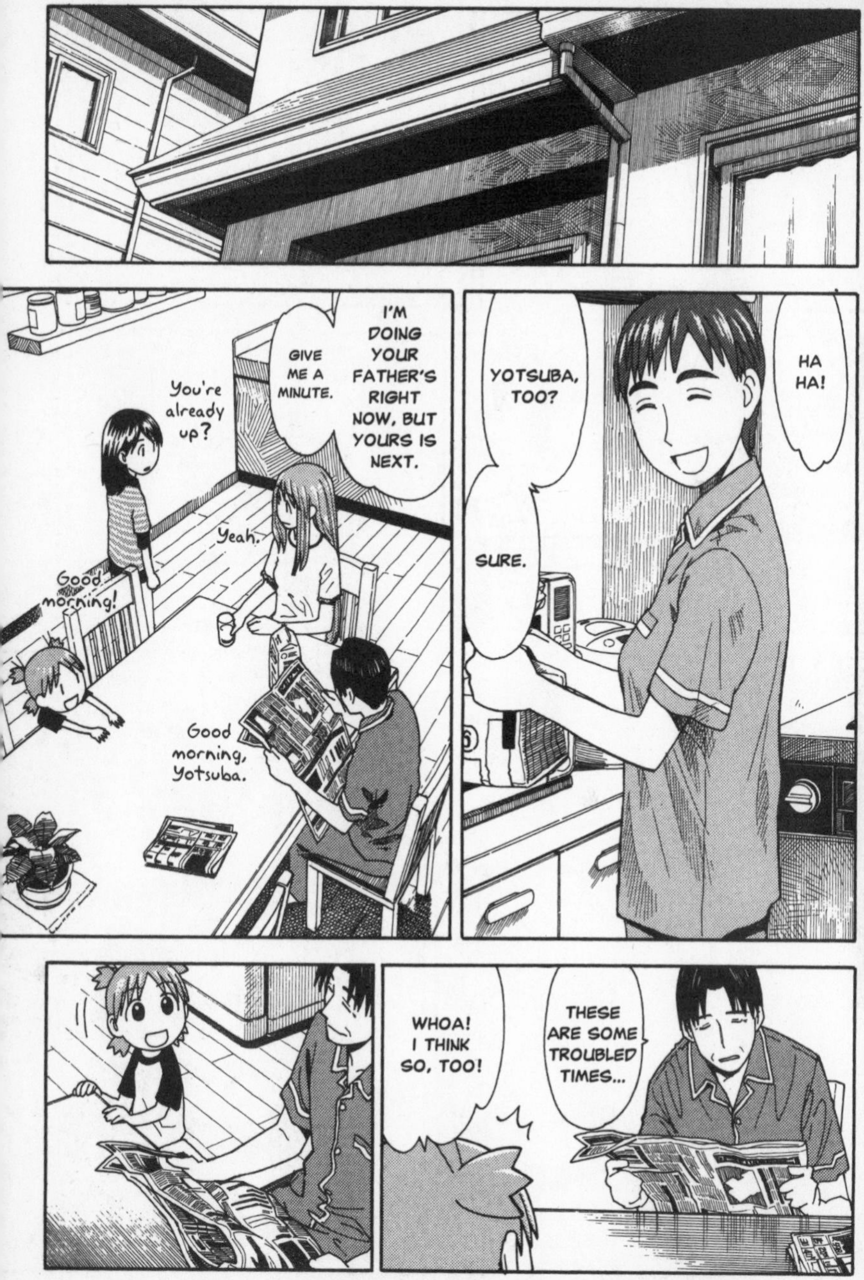
HA HA!
YOTSUBA, TOO?
SURE.
I'M DOING YOUR FATHER'S RIGHT NOW, BUT YOURS IS NEXT.
GIVE ME A MINUTE.
You're already up?
Yeah.
Good morning!
Good morning, Yotsuba.
THESE ARE SOME TROUBLED TIMES...
WHOA! I THINK SO, TOO!

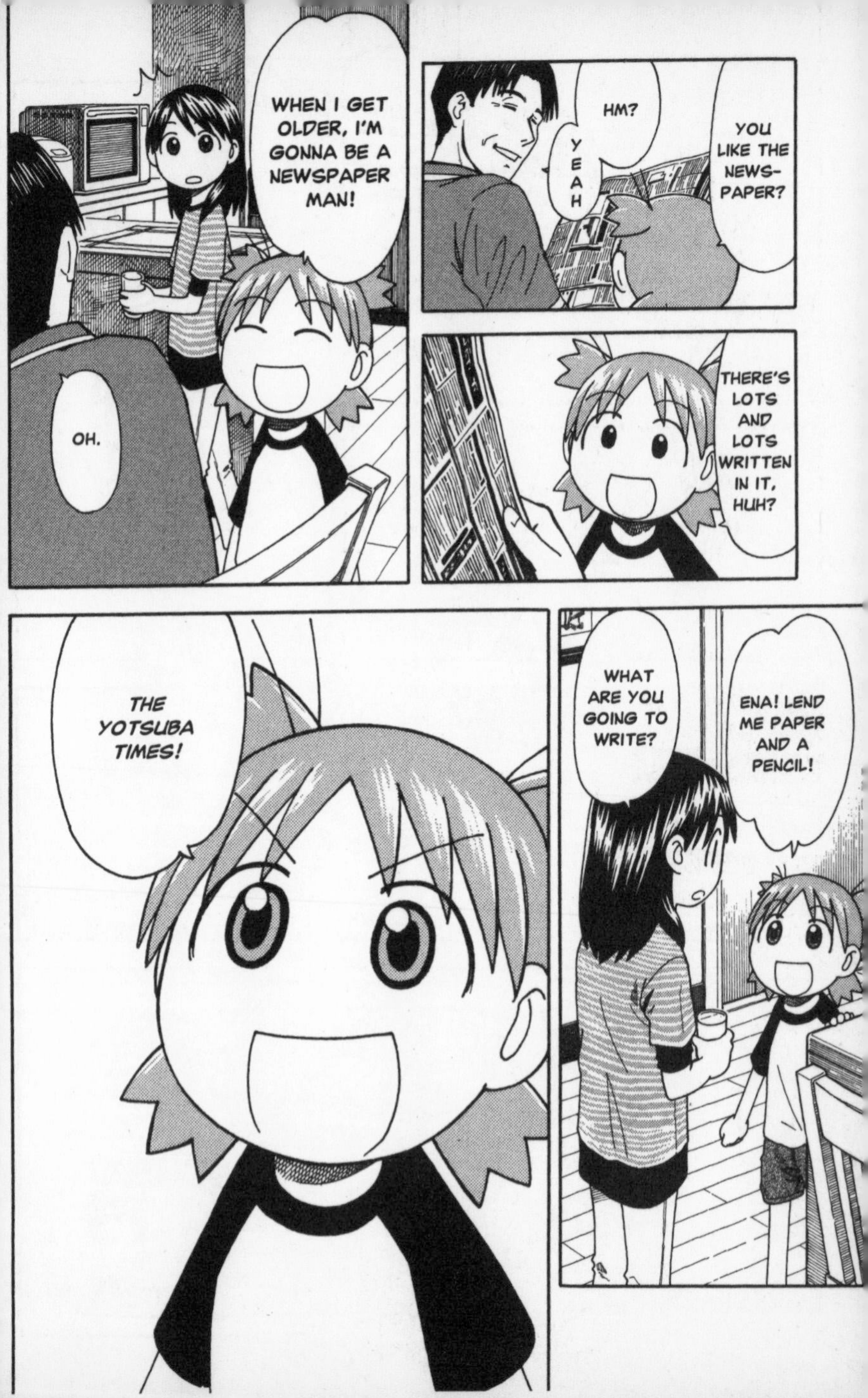
YOU LIKE THE NEWS-PAPER?
HM?
YEAH
THERE'S LOTS AND LOTS WRITTEN IN IT, HUH?
WHEN I GET OLDER, I'M GONNA BE A NEWSPAPER MAN!
OH.
ENA! LEND ME PAPER AND A PENCIL!
WHAT ARE YOU GOING TO WRITE?
THE YOTSUBA TIMES!

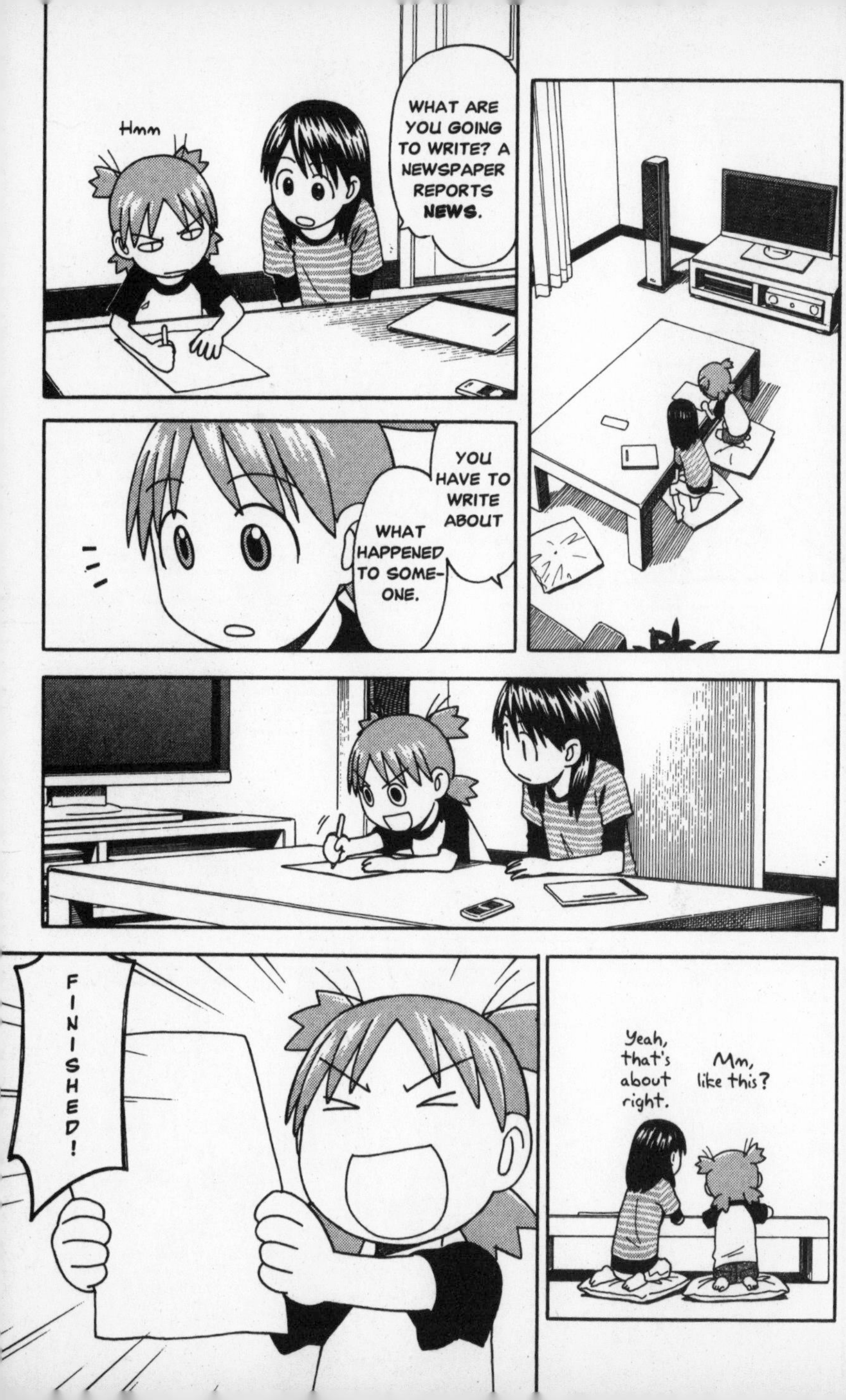
WHAT ARE YOU GOING TO WRITE? A NEWSPAPER REPORTS **NEWS.**
Hmm
YOU HAVE TO WRITE ABOUT
WHAT HAPPENED TO SOME-ONE.
Mm, like this?
Yeah, that's about right.
FINISHED!

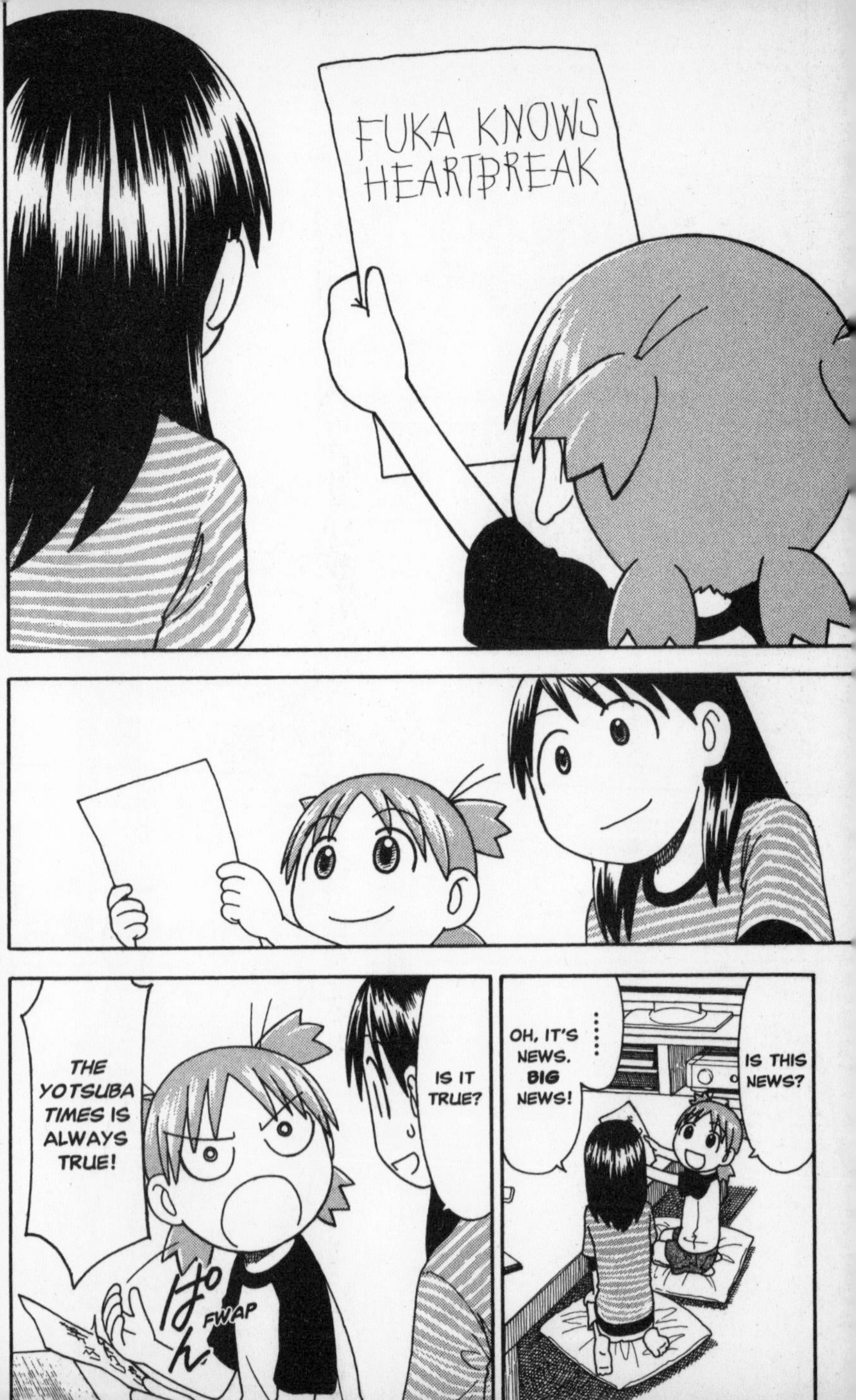
FUKA KNOWS HEARTBREAK
IS THIS NEWS?
......
OH, IT'S NEWS. BIG NEWS!
IS IT TRUE?
THE YOTSUBA TIMES IS ALWAYS TRUE!
ぱん
FWAP

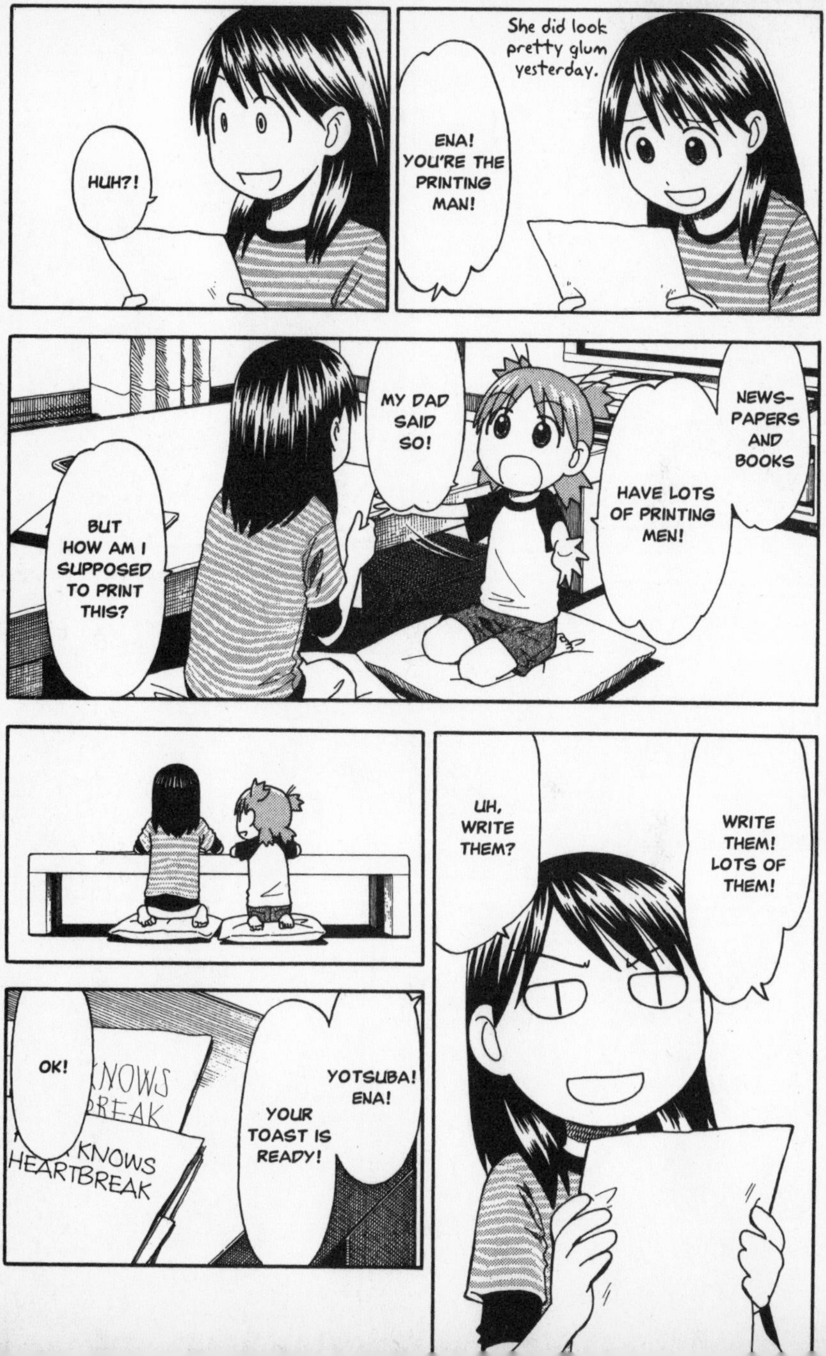
She did look pretty glum yesterday.
ENA! YOU'RE THE PRINTING MAN!
HUH?!
NEWS-PAPERS AND BOOKS
HAVE LOTS OF PRINTING MEN!
MY DAD SAID SO!
BUT HOW AM I SUPPOSED TO PRINT THIS?
WRITE THEM! LOTS OF THEM!
UH, WRITE THEM?
YOTSUBA! ENA!
YOUR TOAST IS READY!
OK!
KNOWS HEARTBREAK

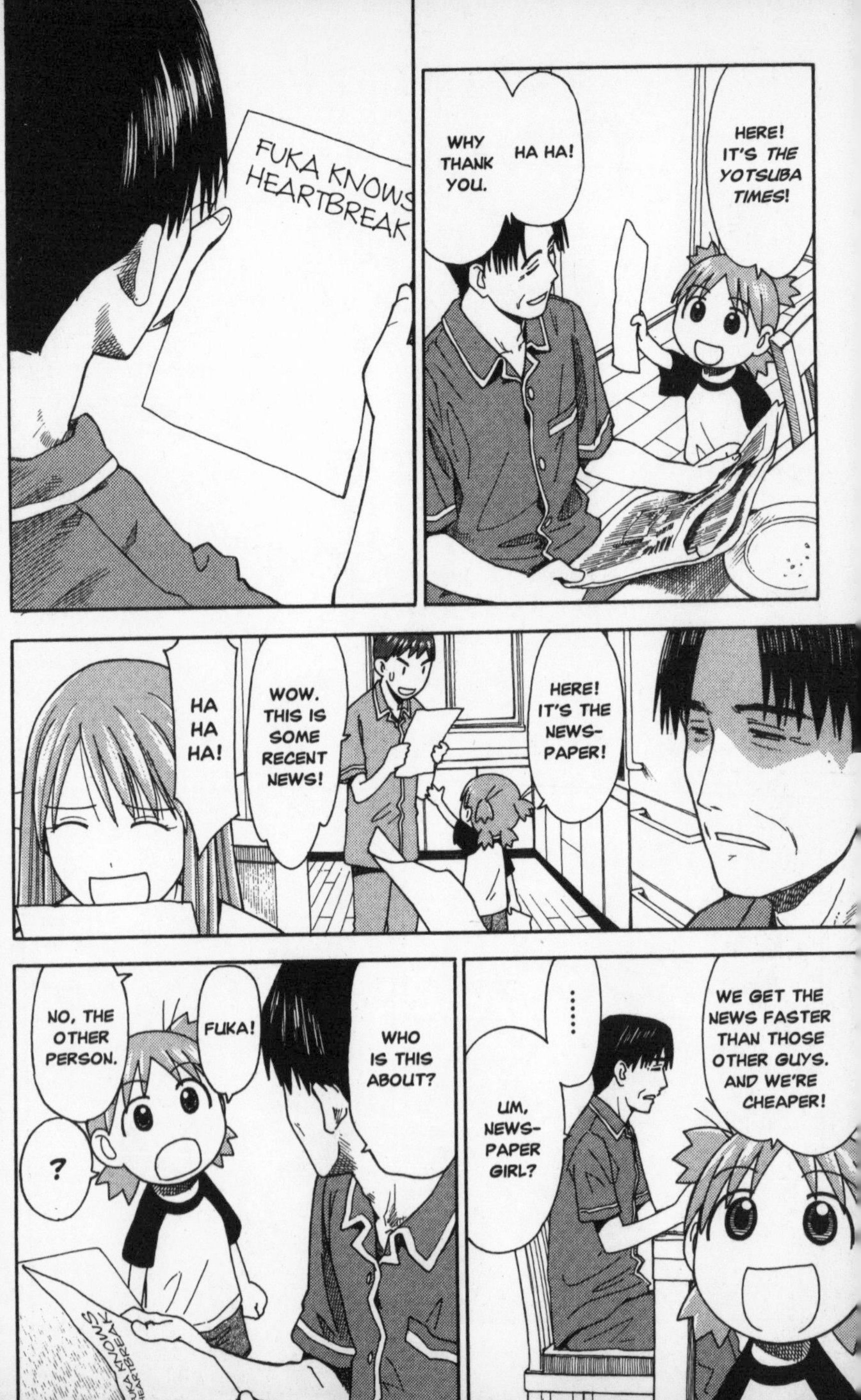
HERE! IT'S THE YOTSUBA TIMES!
HA HA!
WHY THANK YOU.
FUKA KNOWS HEARTBREAK
HERE! IT'S THE NEWS-PAPER!
WOW. THIS IS SOME RECENT NEWS!
HA HA HA!
WE GET THE NEWS FASTER THAN THOSE OTHER GUYS. AND WE'RE CHEAPER!
......
UM, NEWS-PAPER GIRL?
WHO IS THIS ABOUT?
FUKA!
NO, THE OTHER PERSON.
?
FUKA KNOWS HEARTBREAK

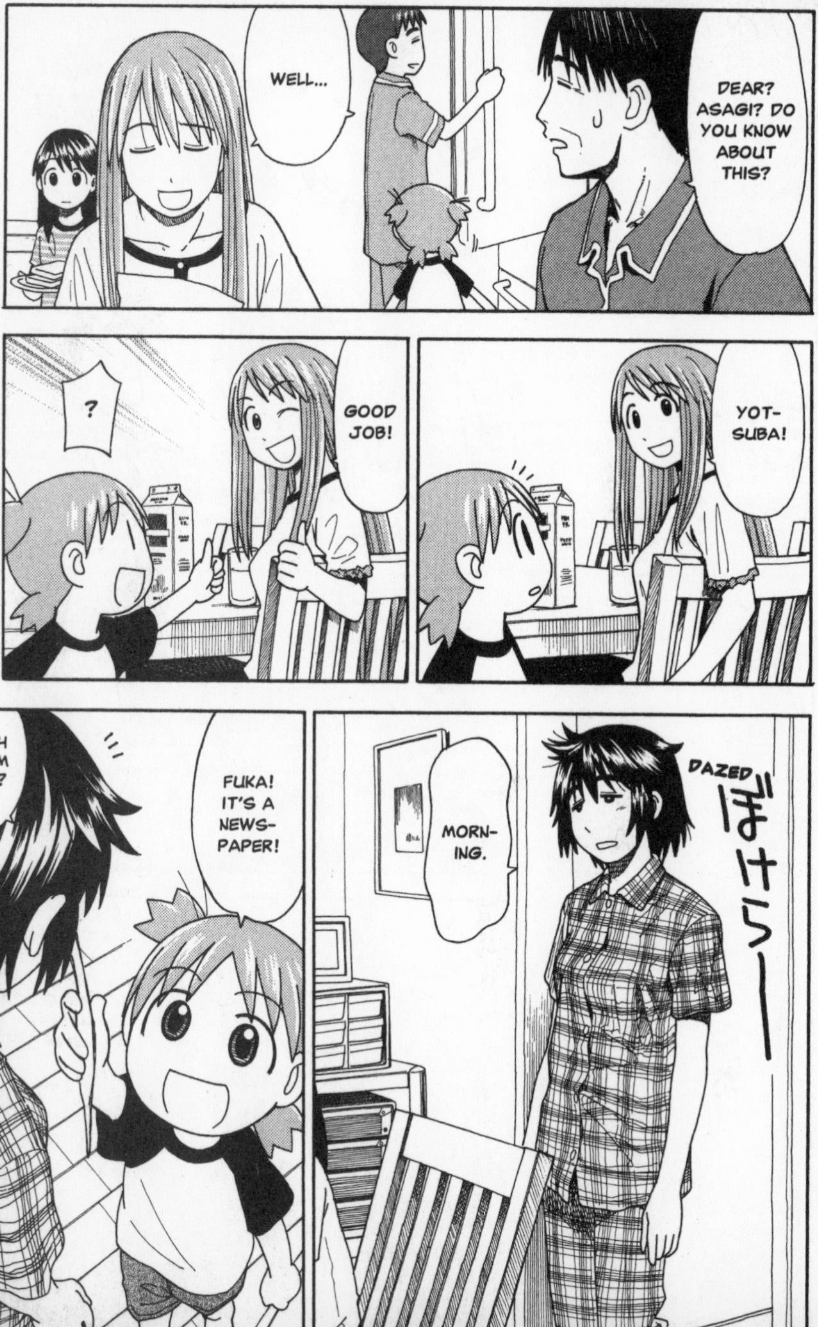
DEAR? ASAGI? DO YOU KNOW ABOUT THIS?
WELL...
YOT-SUBA!
GOOD JOB!
?
DAZED
ぼけらー
MORN-ING.
FUKA! IT'S A NEWS-PAPER!
HM?

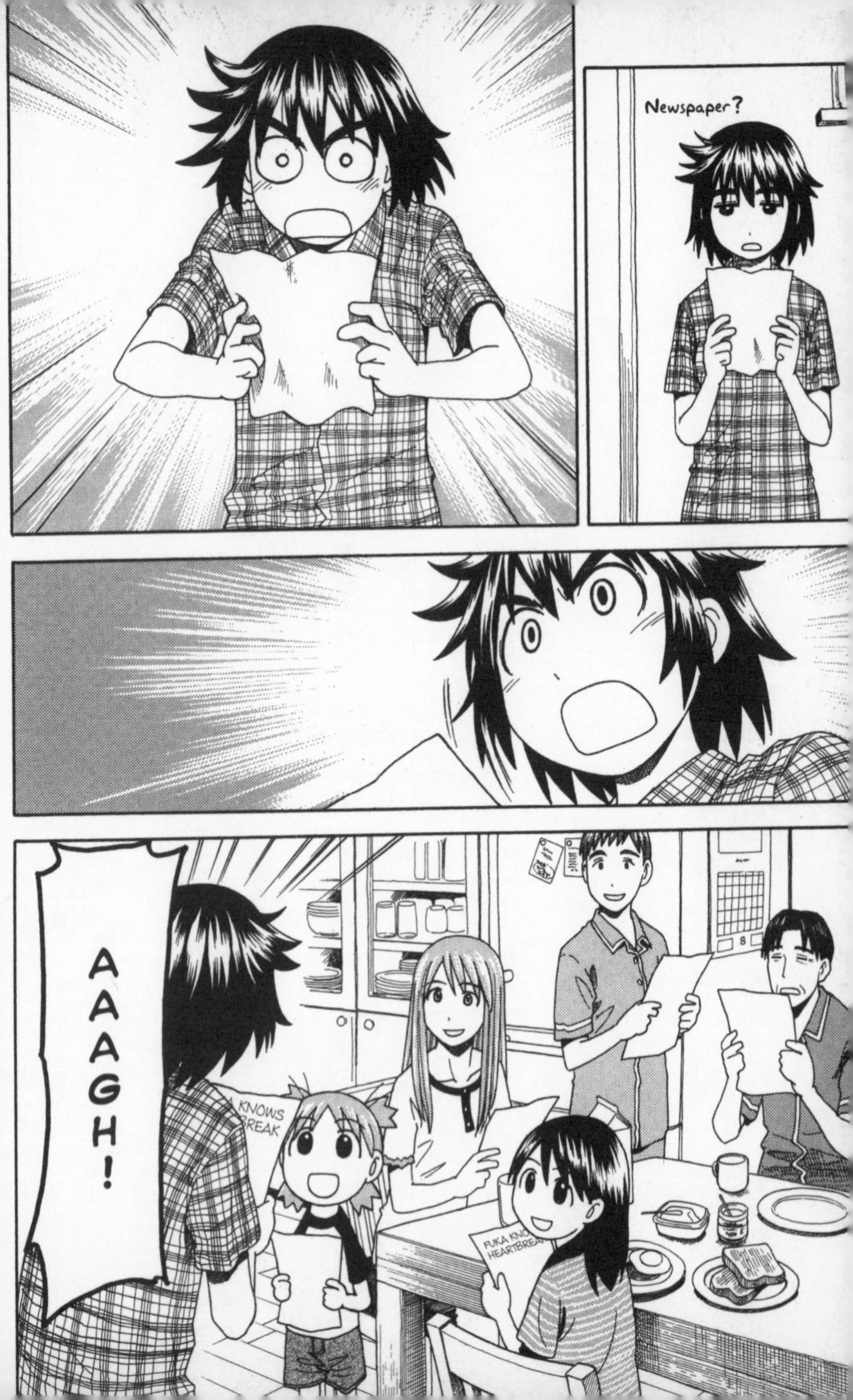

Newspaper?
AAAGH!

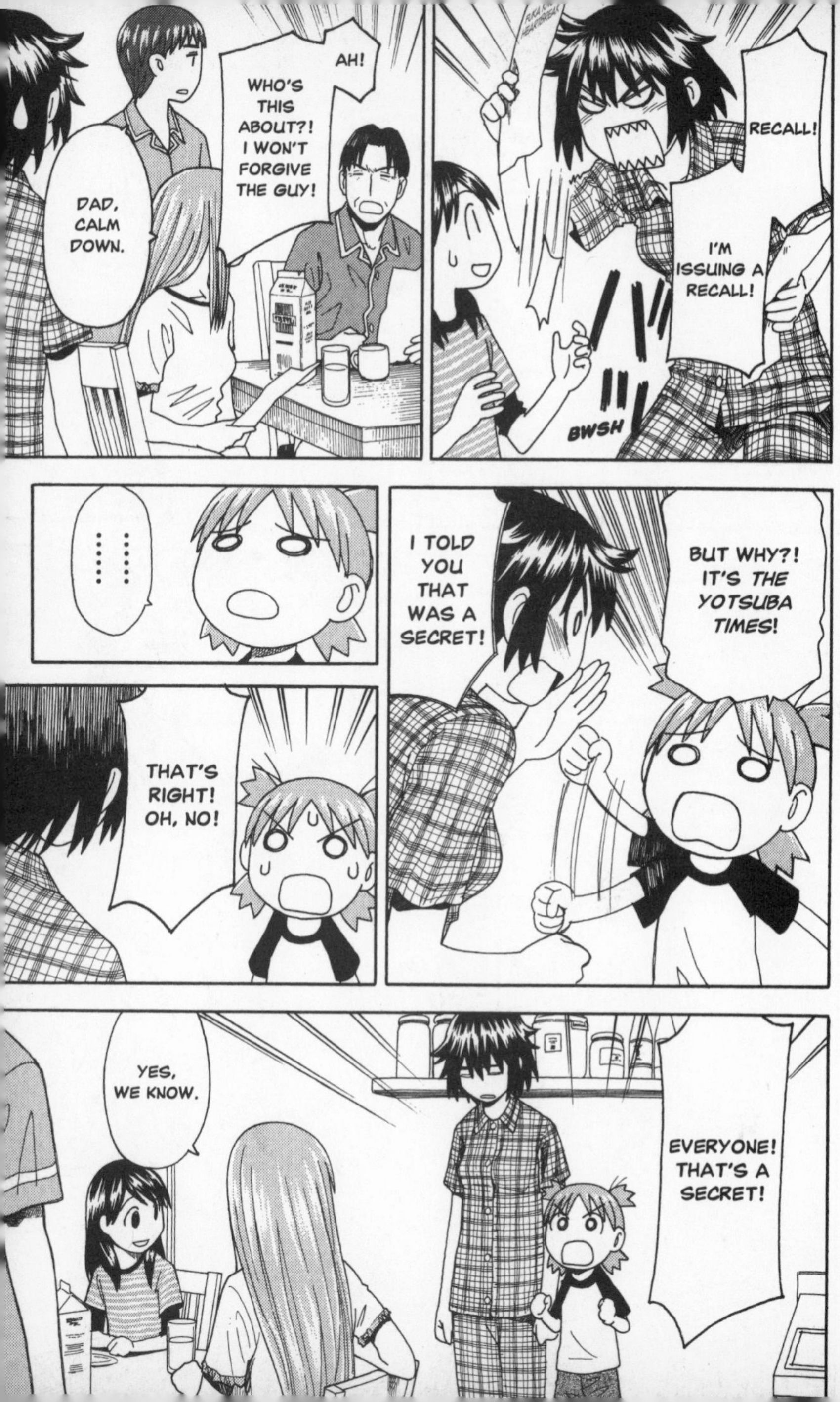
RECALL!
I'M ISSUING A RECALL!
BWSH
AH! WHO'S THIS ABOUT?! I WON'T FORGIVE THE GUY!
DAD, CALM DOWN.
BUT WHY?! IT'S THE YOTSUBA TIMES!
I TOLD YOU THAT WAS A SECRET!
......
THAT'S RIGHT! OH, NO!
EVERYONE! THAT'S A SECRET!
YES, WE KNOW.

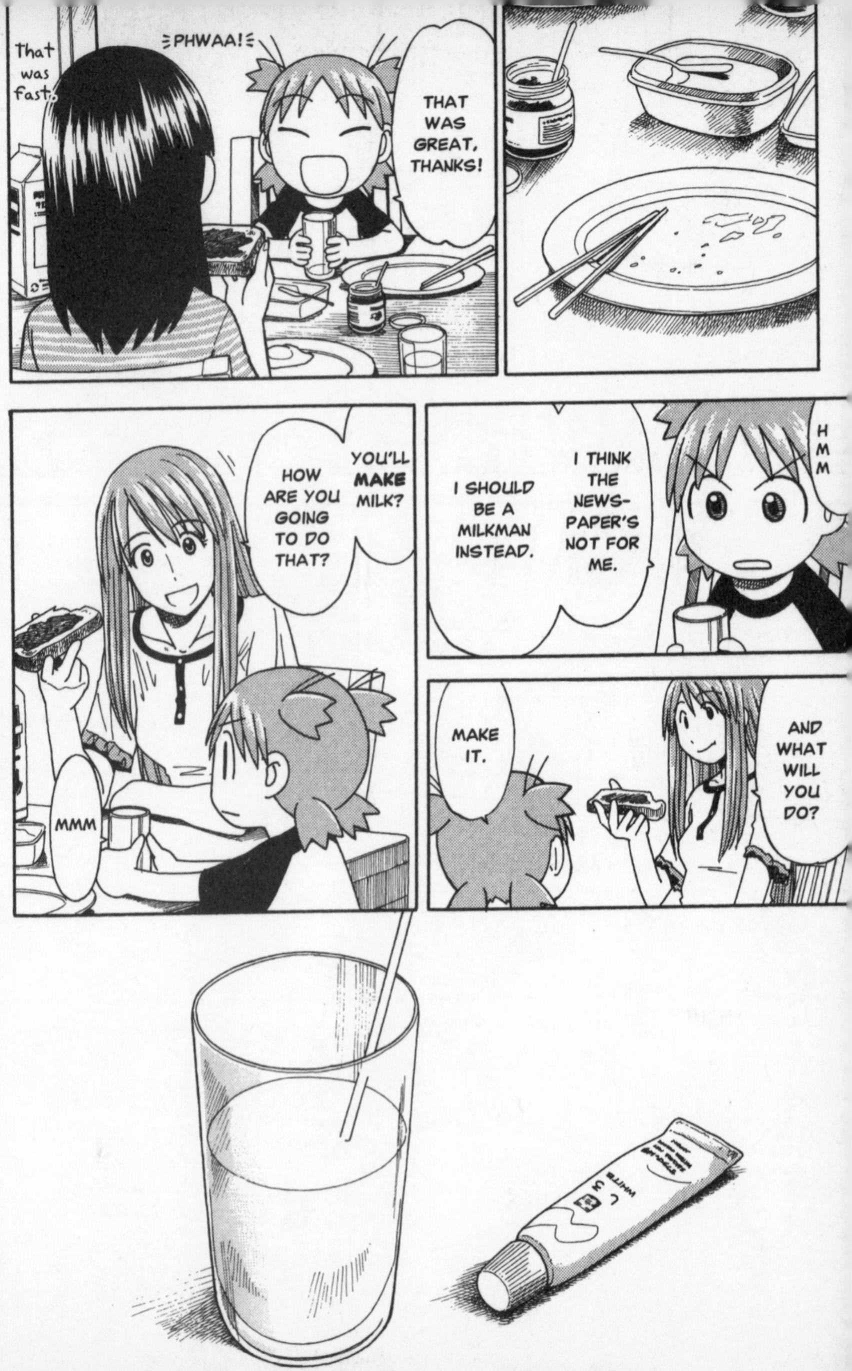
THAT WAS GREAT, THANKS!
PHWAA!
That was fast.
HMM
I THINK THE NEWS-PAPER'S NOT FOR ME.
I SHOULD BE A MILKMAN INSTEAD.
AND WHAT WILL YOU DO?
MAKE IT.
YOU'LL MAKE MILK?
HOW ARE YOU GOING TO DO THAT?
MMM
WHITE

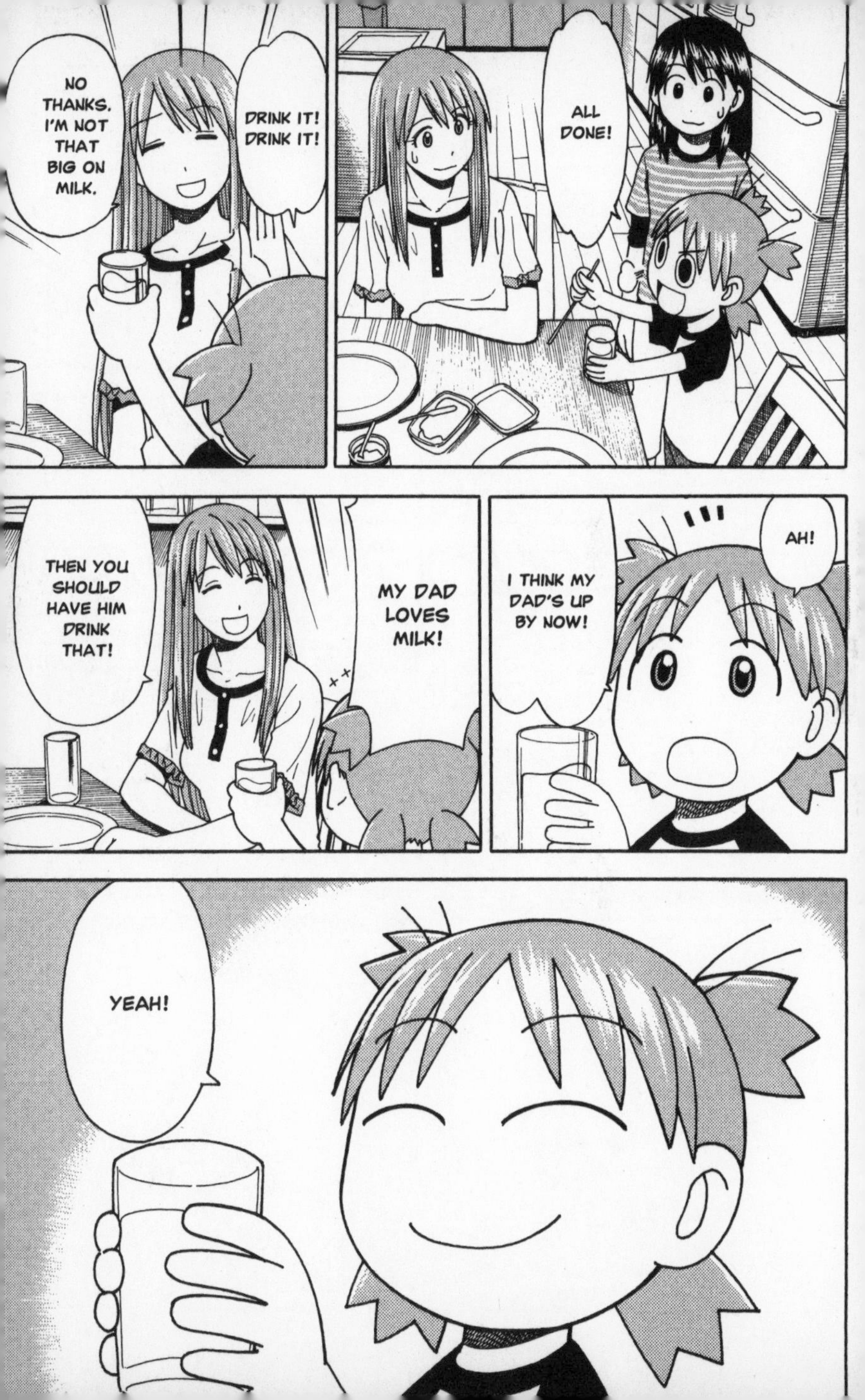
ALL DONE!
DRINK IT! DRINK IT!
NO THANKS. I'M NOT THAT BIG ON MILK.
AH!
I THINK MY DAD'S UP BY NOW!
MY DAD LOVES MILK!
THEN YOU SHOULD HAVE HIM DRINK THAT!
YEAH!

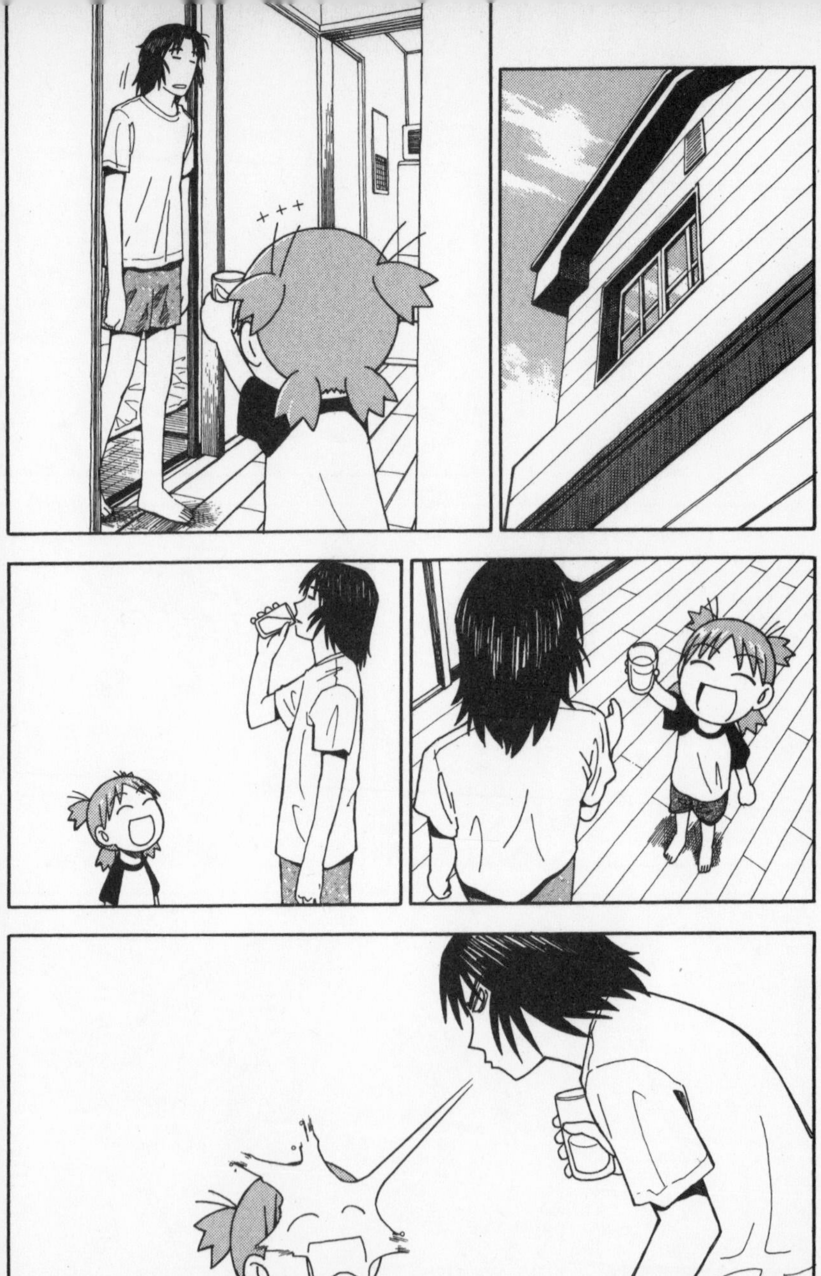

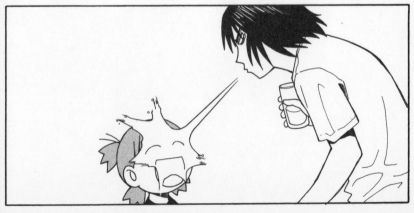

YOTSUBA&!

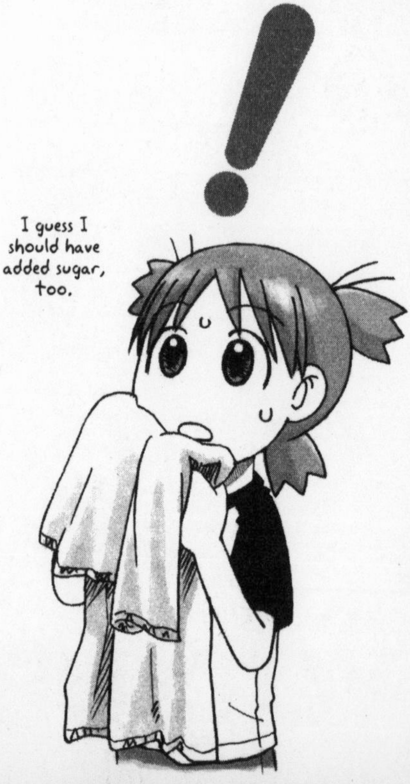
I guess I should have added sugar, too.

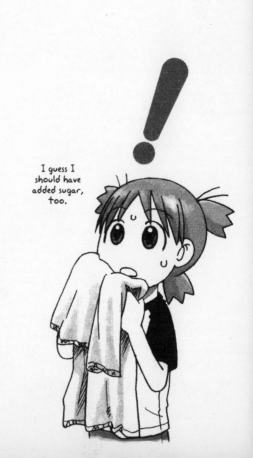

YOTSUBA & TSUKUTSUKUBOSHI

CHAPTER 27

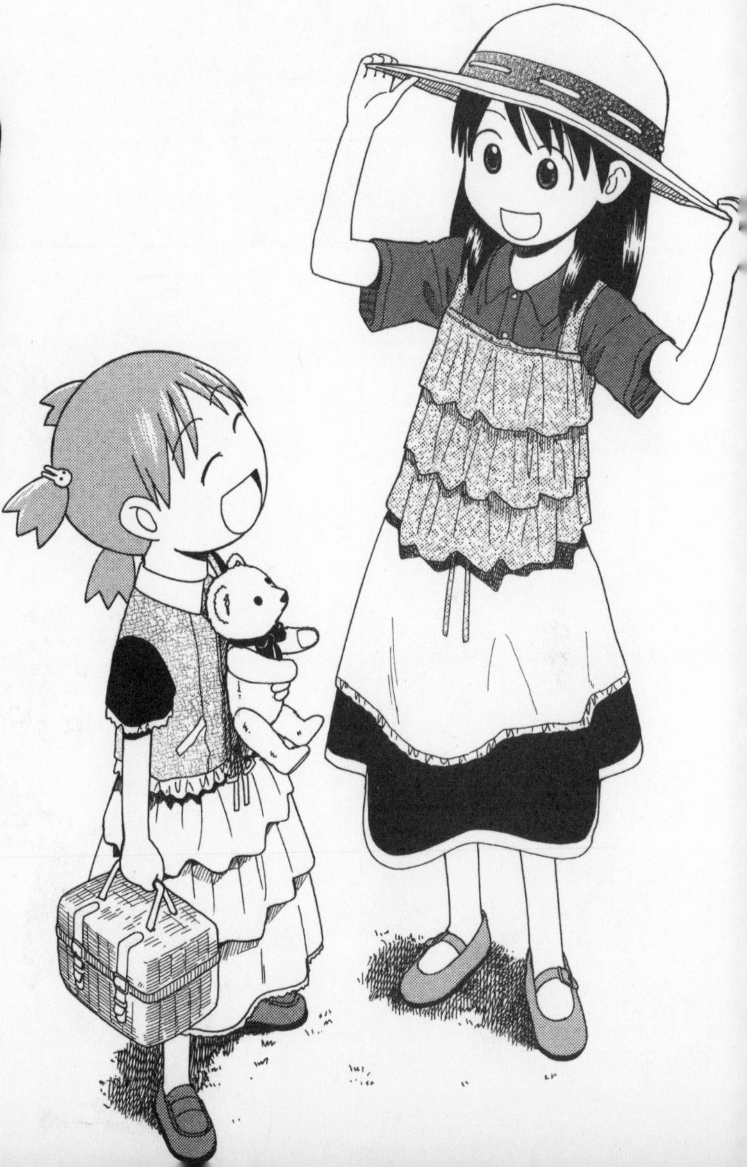

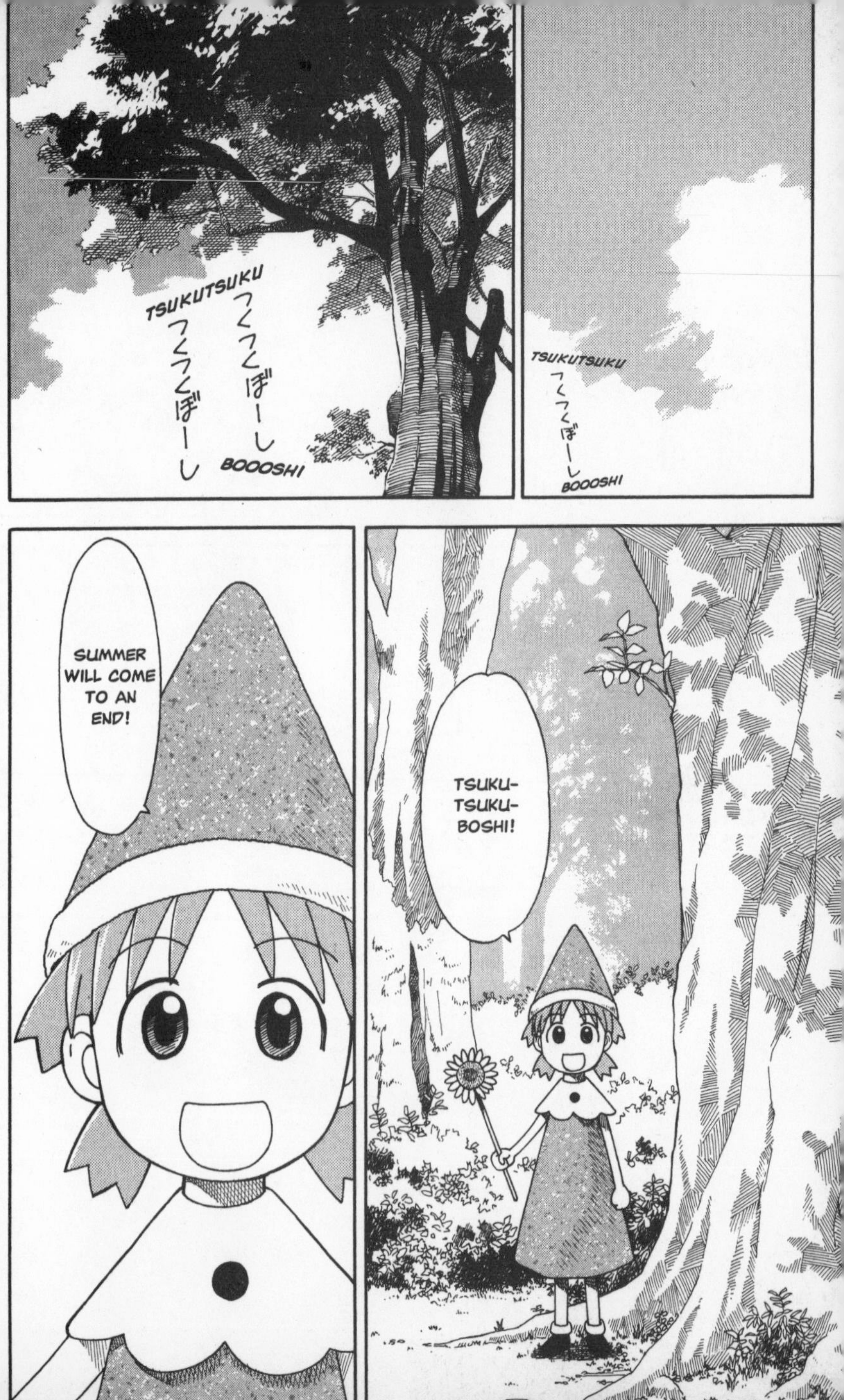
TSUKUTSUKU
つくつくぼーし
BOOOSHI
TSUKUTSUKU
つくつくぼーし
つくつくぼーし
BOOOSHI
TSUKU-TSUKU-BOSHI!
SUMMER WILL COME TO AN END!

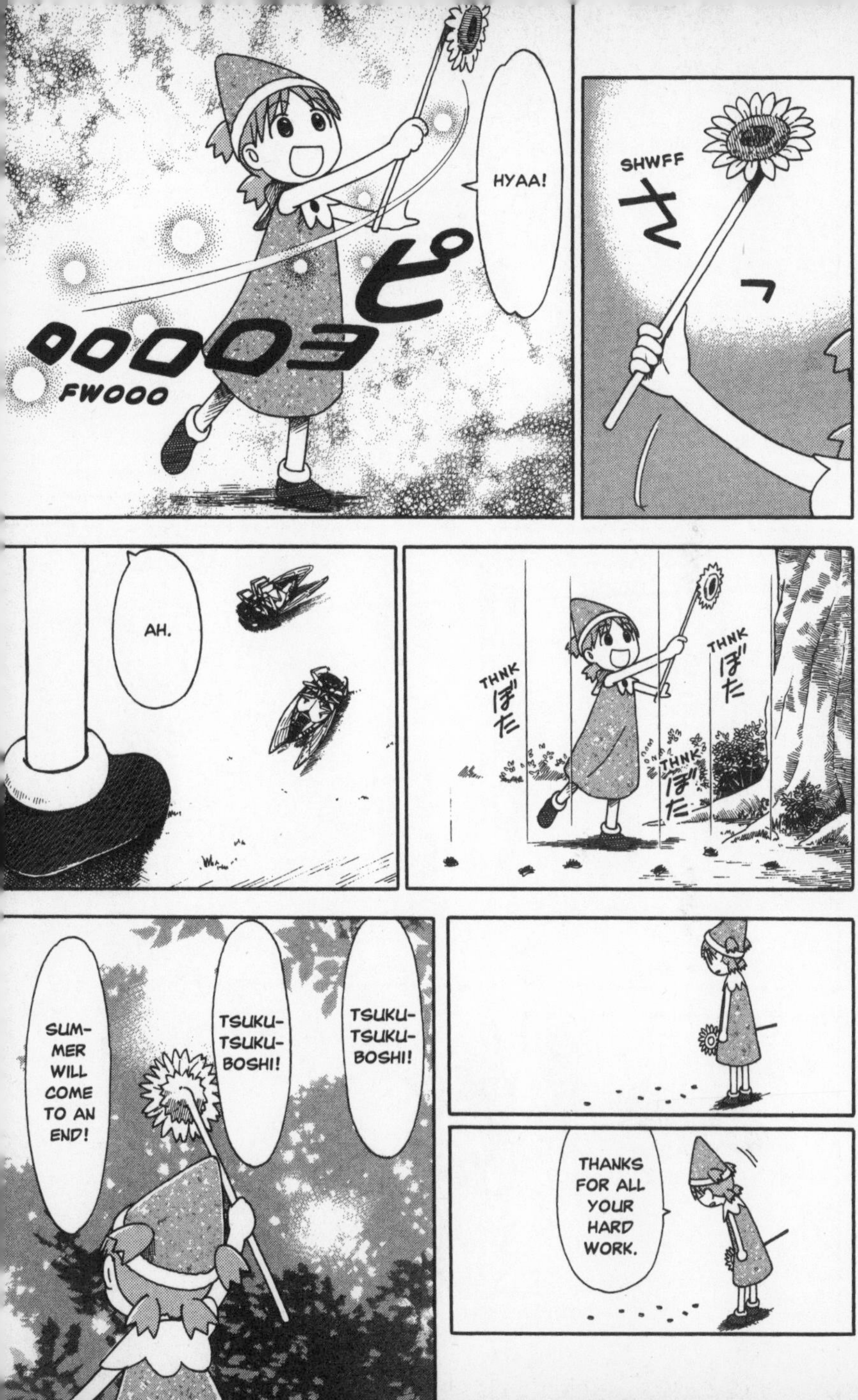
SHWFF
さっ
HYAA!
FWOOO
THNK
ぼた
THNK
ぼた
THNK
ぼた
AH.
THANKS FOR ALL YOUR HARD WORK.
TSUKU-TSUKU-BOSHI!
TSUKU-TSUKU-BOSHI!
SUM-MER WILL COME TO AN END!

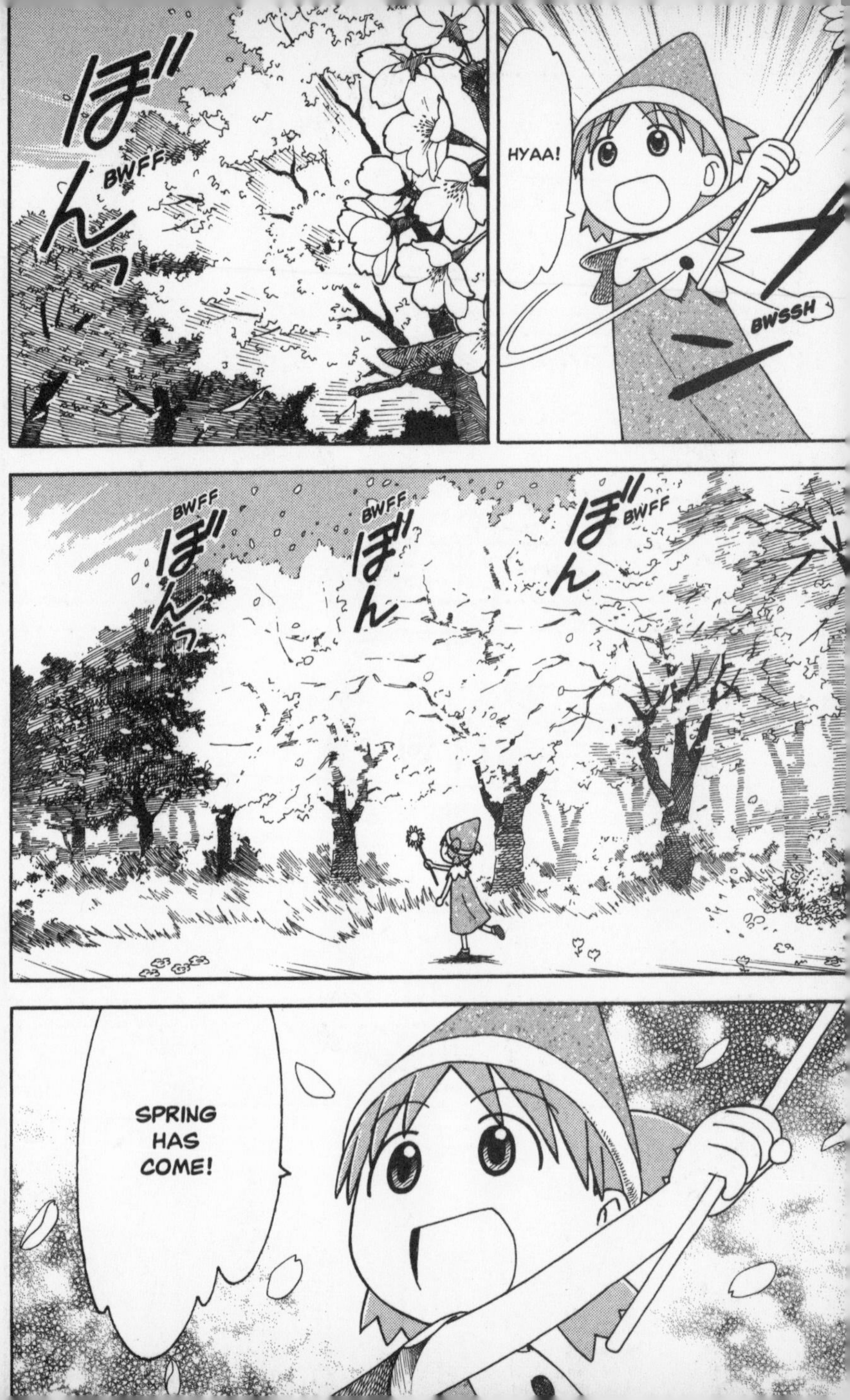
HYAA!
BWSSH
ぼんっ
BWFF
ぼん
BWFF
ぼん
BWFF
ぼんっ
BWFF
SPRING HAS COME!

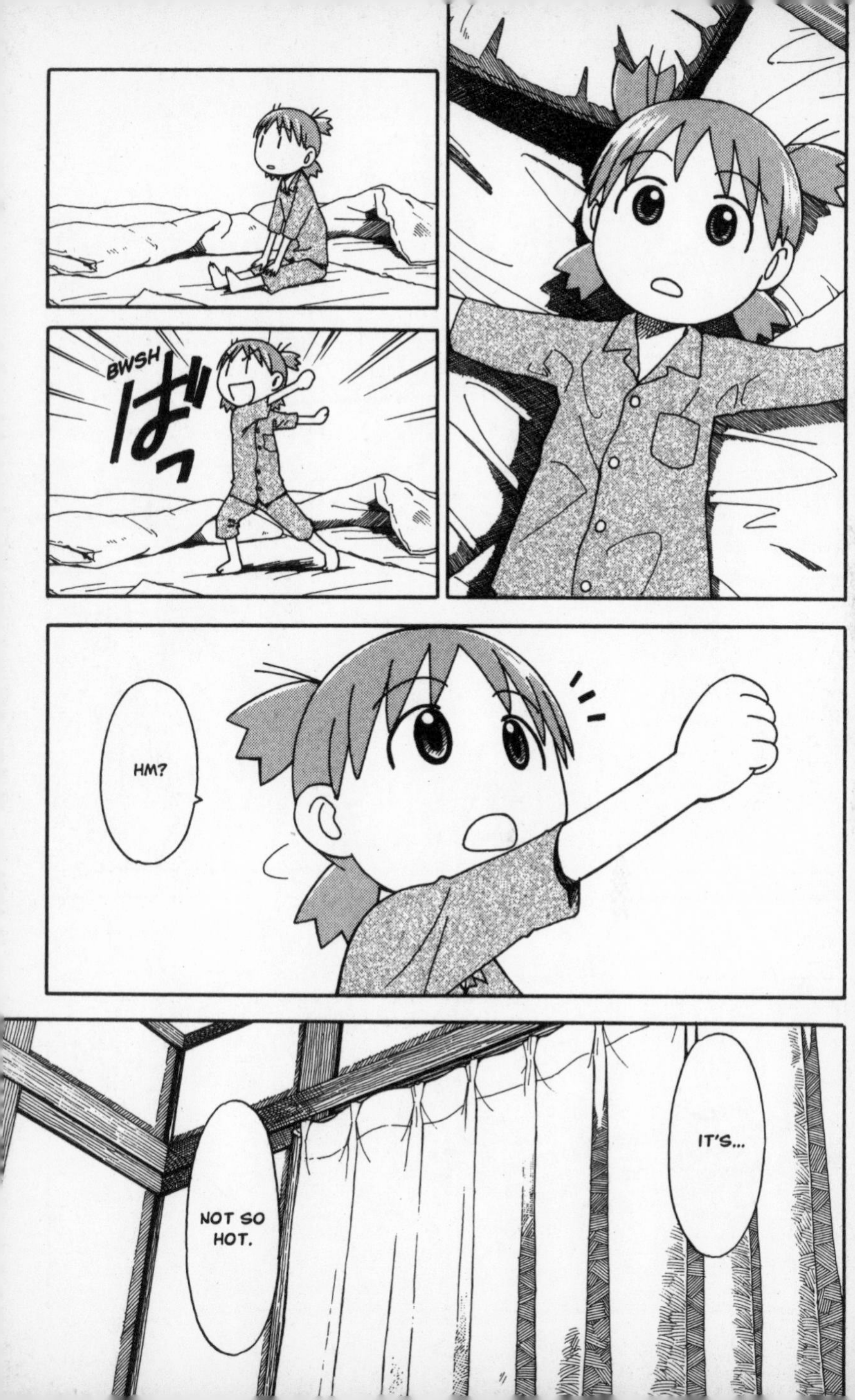
BWSH
ばっ
HM?
IT'S...
NOT SO HOT.

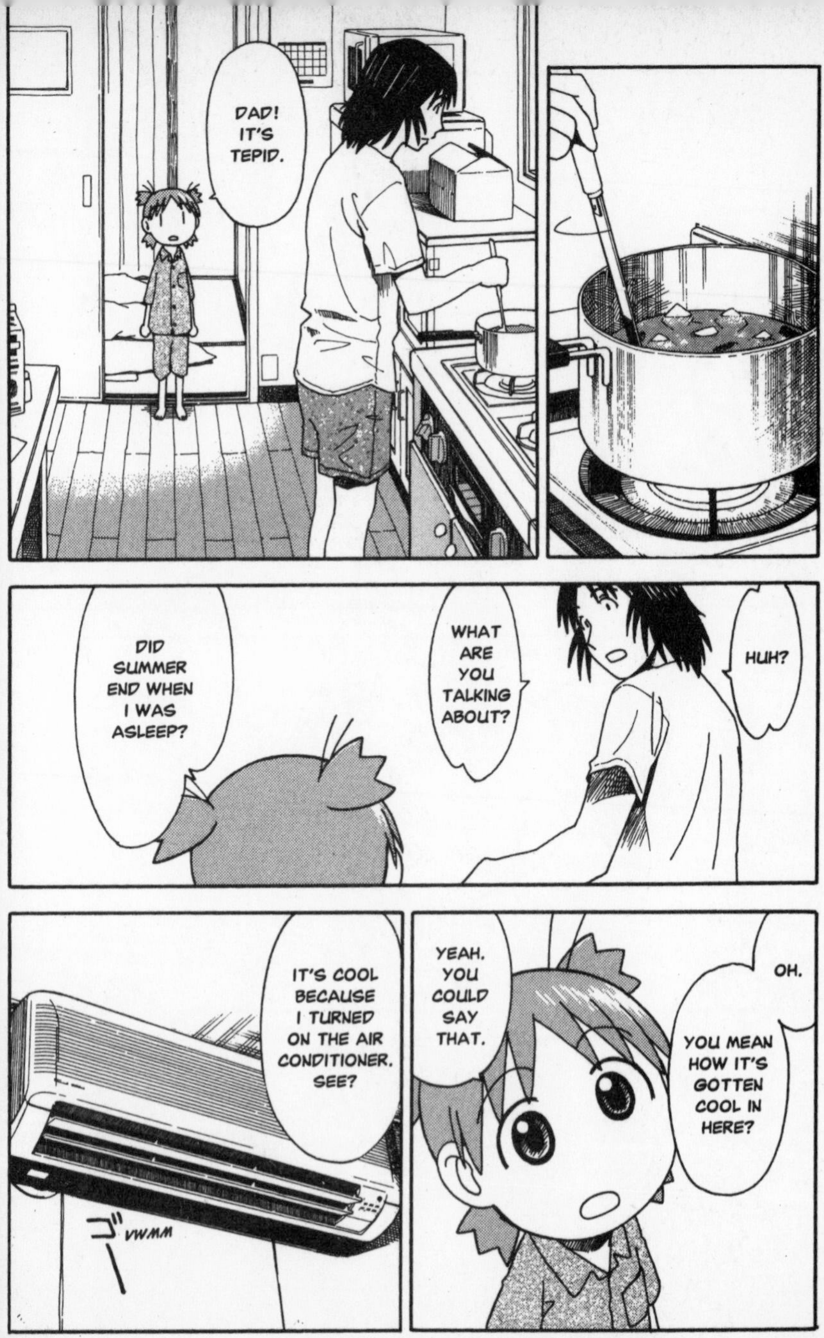

DAD! IT'S TEPID.
HUH?
WHAT ARE YOU TALKING ABOUT?
DID SUMMER END WHEN I WAS ASLEEP?
OH.
YOU MEAN HOW IT'S GOTTEN COOL IN HERE?
YEAH. YOU COULD SAY THAT.
IT'S COOL BECAUSE I TURNED ON THE AIR CONDITIONER. SEE?
ゴー VWMM

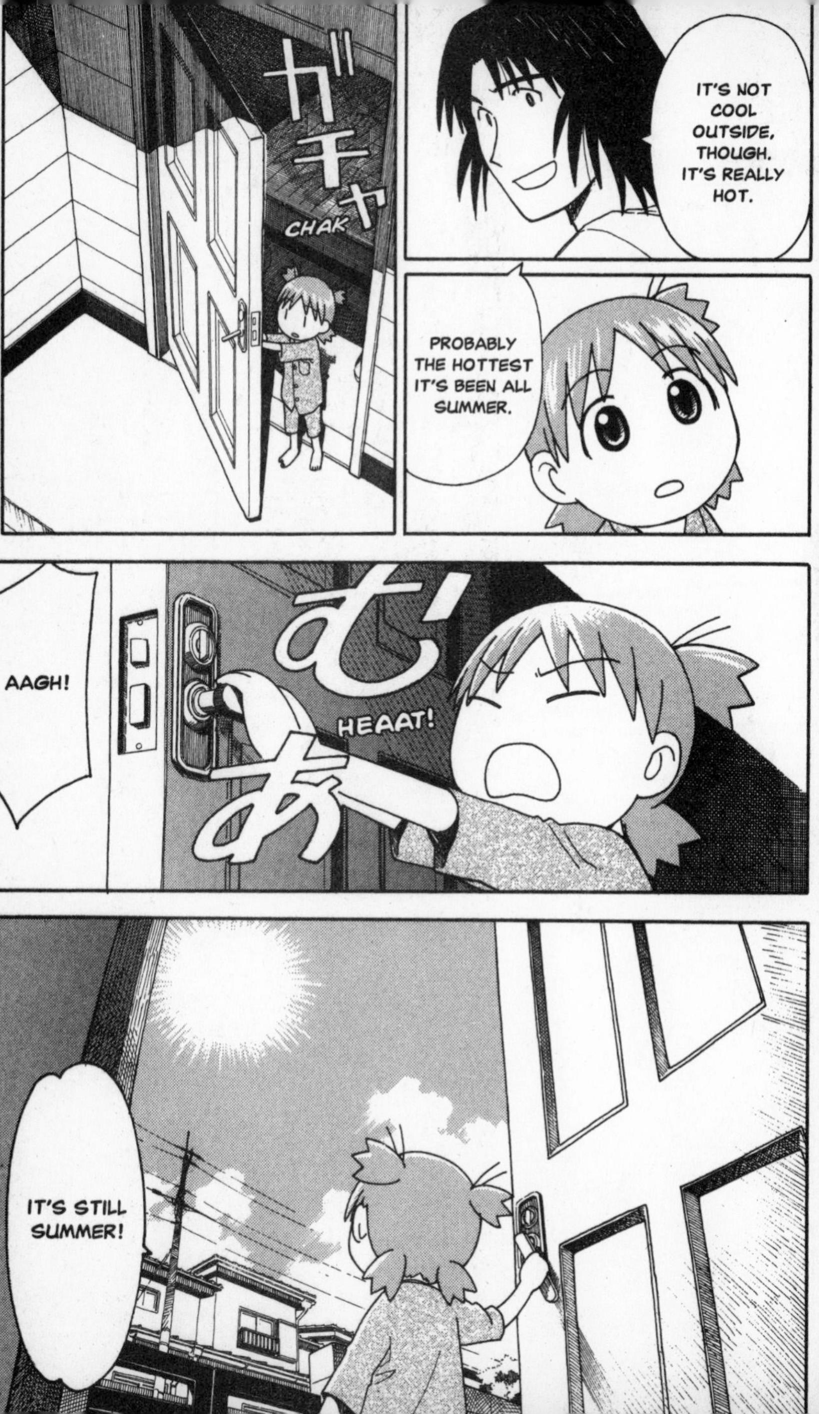
IT'S NOT COOL OUTSIDE, THOUGH. IT'S REALLY HOT.
PROBABLY THE HOTTEST IT'S BEEN ALL SUMMER.
ガチャ
CHAK
むあ
HEAAT!
AAGH!
IT'S STILL SUMMER!

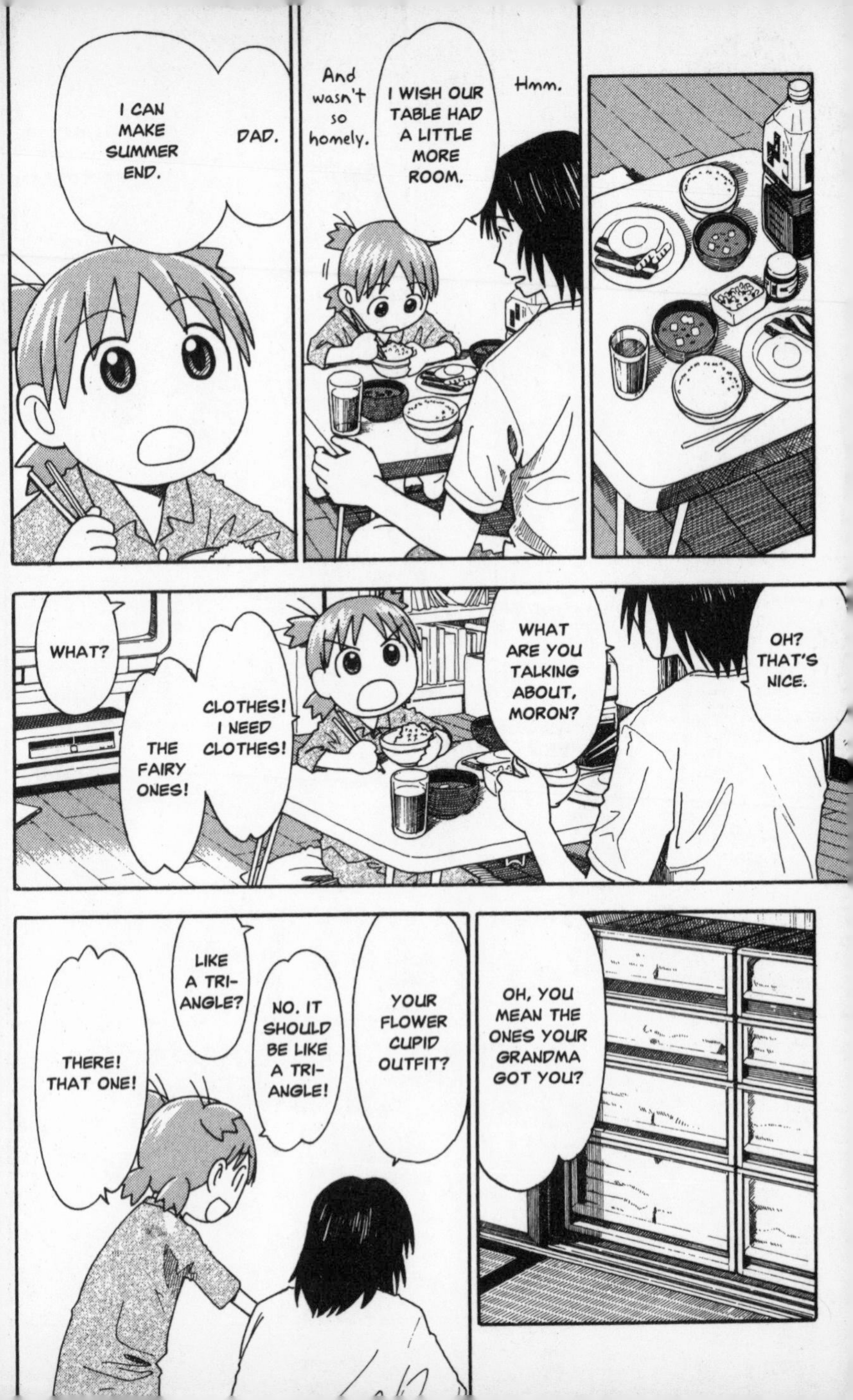
Hmm.
I WISH OUR TABLE HAD A LITTLE MORE ROOM.
And wasn't so homely.
DAD.
I CAN MAKE SUMMER END.
OH? THAT'S NICE.
WHAT ARE YOU TALKING ABOUT, MORON?
CLOTHES! I NEED CLOTHES!
THE FAIRY ONES!
WHAT?
OH, YOU MEAN THE ONES YOUR GRANDMA GOT YOU?
YOUR FLOWER CUPID OUTFIT?
NO. IT SHOULD BE LIKE A TRI-ANGLE!
LIKE A TRI-ANGLE?
THERE! THAT ONE!

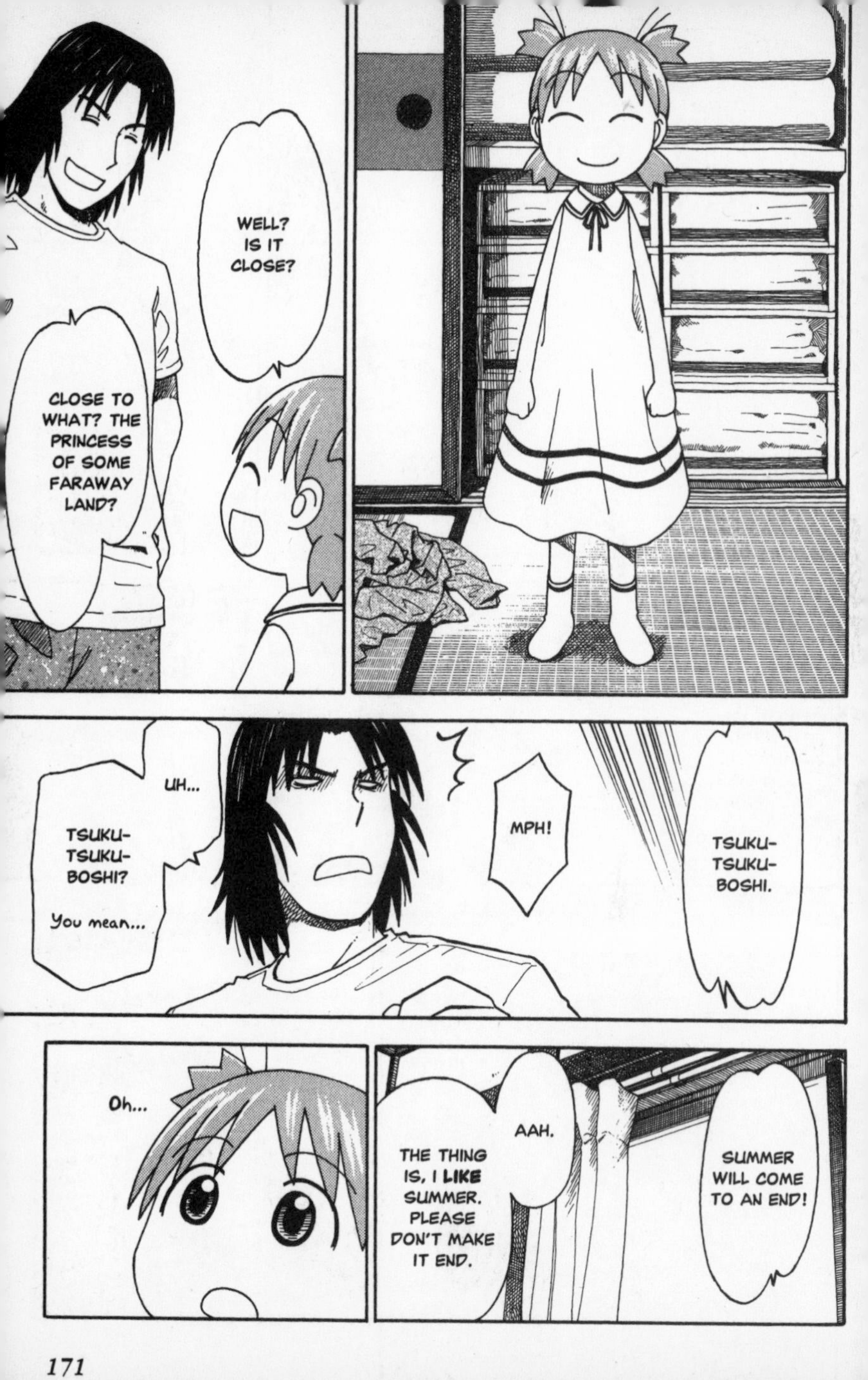
WELL? IS IT CLOSE?
CLOSE TO WHAT? THE PRINCESS OF SOME FARAWAY LAND?
TSUKU-TSUKU-BOSHI.
MPH!
UH...
TSUKU-TSUKU-BOSHI?
You mean...
SUMMER WILL COME TO AN END!
AAH.
THE THING IS, I **LIKE** SUMMER. PLEASE DON'T MAKE IT END.
Oh...

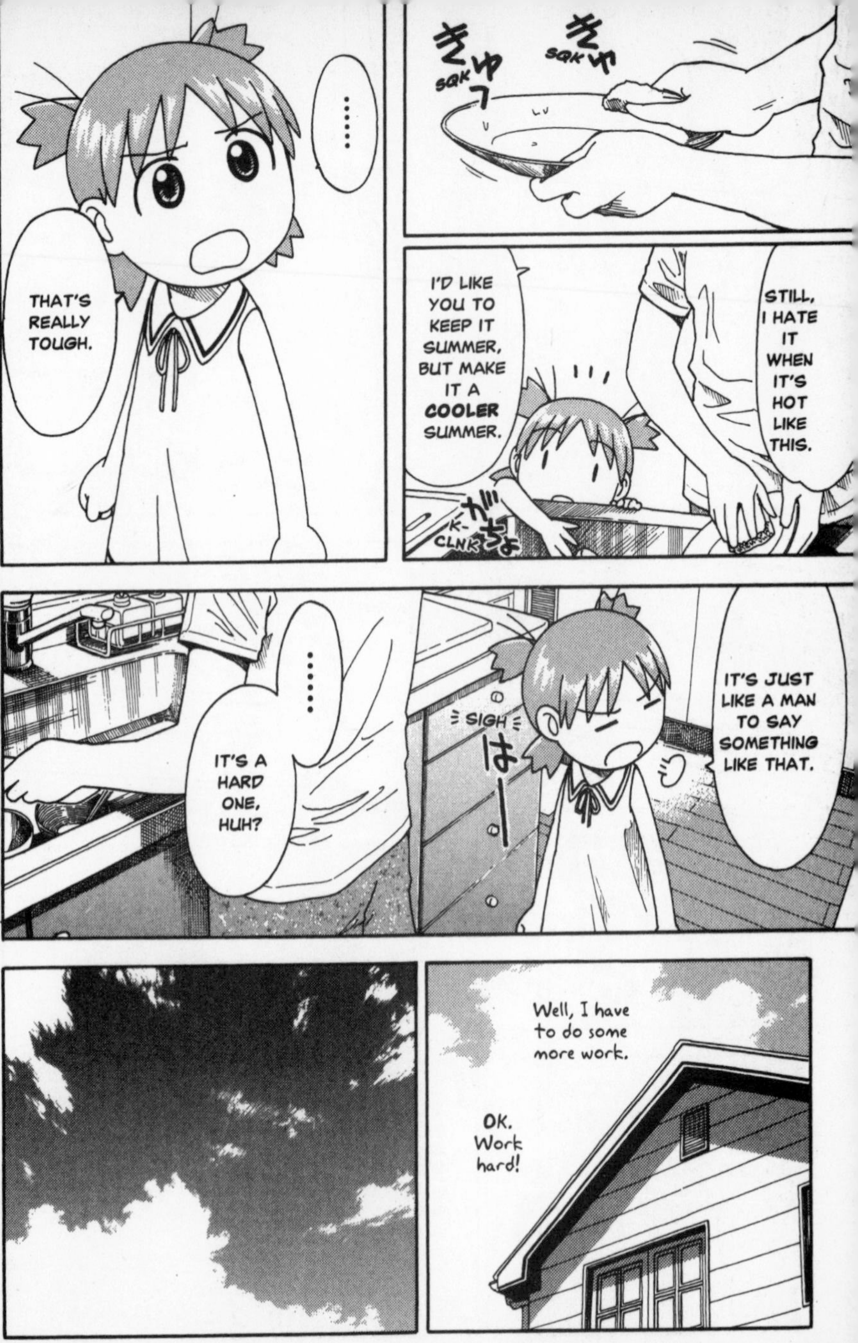
きゅ SQK
きゅっ SQK
STILL, I HATE IT WHEN IT'S HOT LIKE THIS.
I'D LIKE YOU TO KEEP IT SUMMER, BUT MAKE IT A **COOLER** SUMMER.
がちょ K-CLNK
......
THAT'S REALLY TOUGH.
IT'S JUST LIKE A MAN TO SAY SOMETHING LIKE THAT.
はー SIGH
......
IT'S A HARD ONE, HUH?
Well, I have to do some more work.
OK. Work hard!

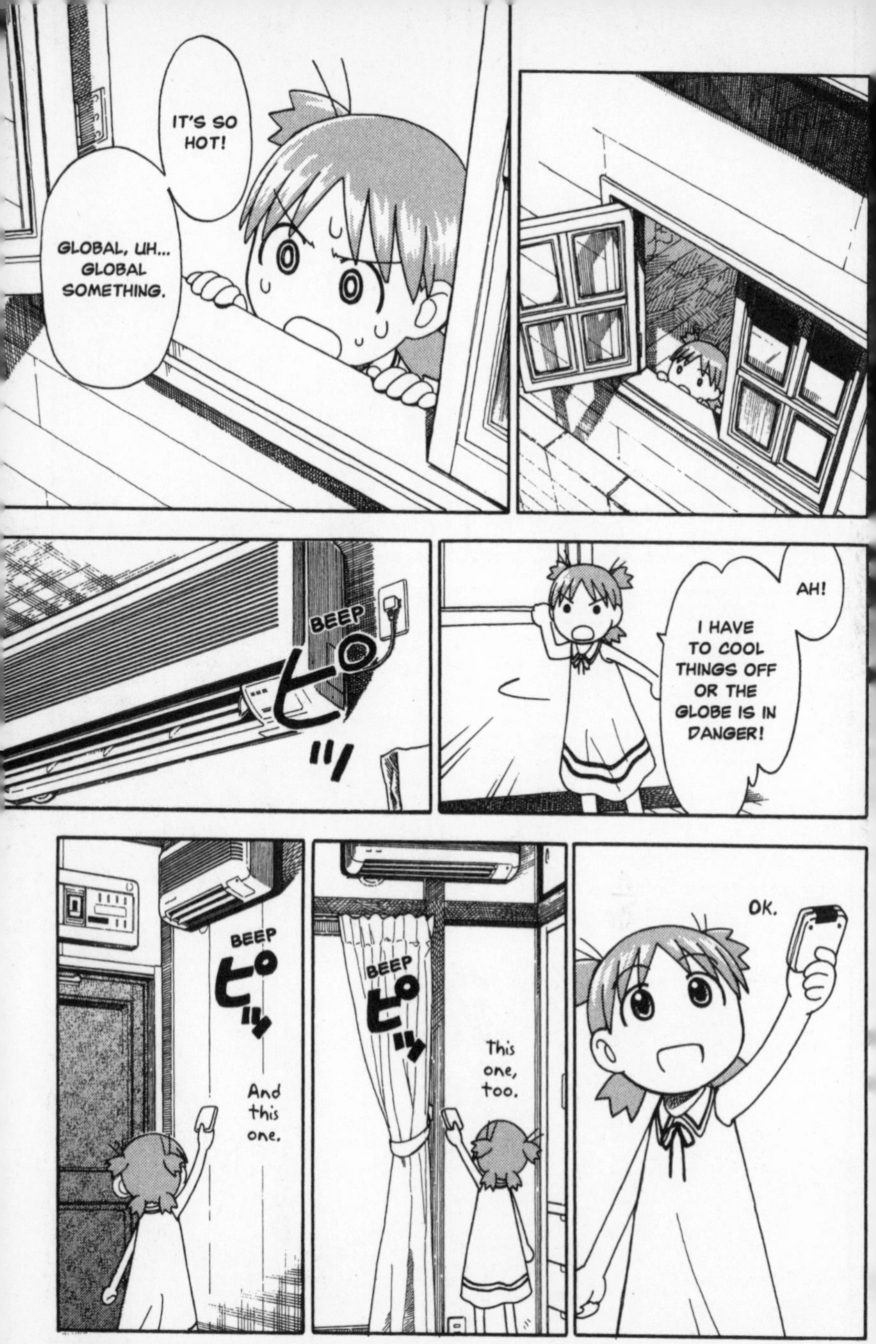
IT'S SO HOT!
GLOBAL, UH... GLOBAL SOMETHING.
AH!
I HAVE TO COOL THINGS OFF OR THE GLOBE IS IN DANGER!
BEEP
OK.
BEEP
This one, too.
BEEP
And this one.

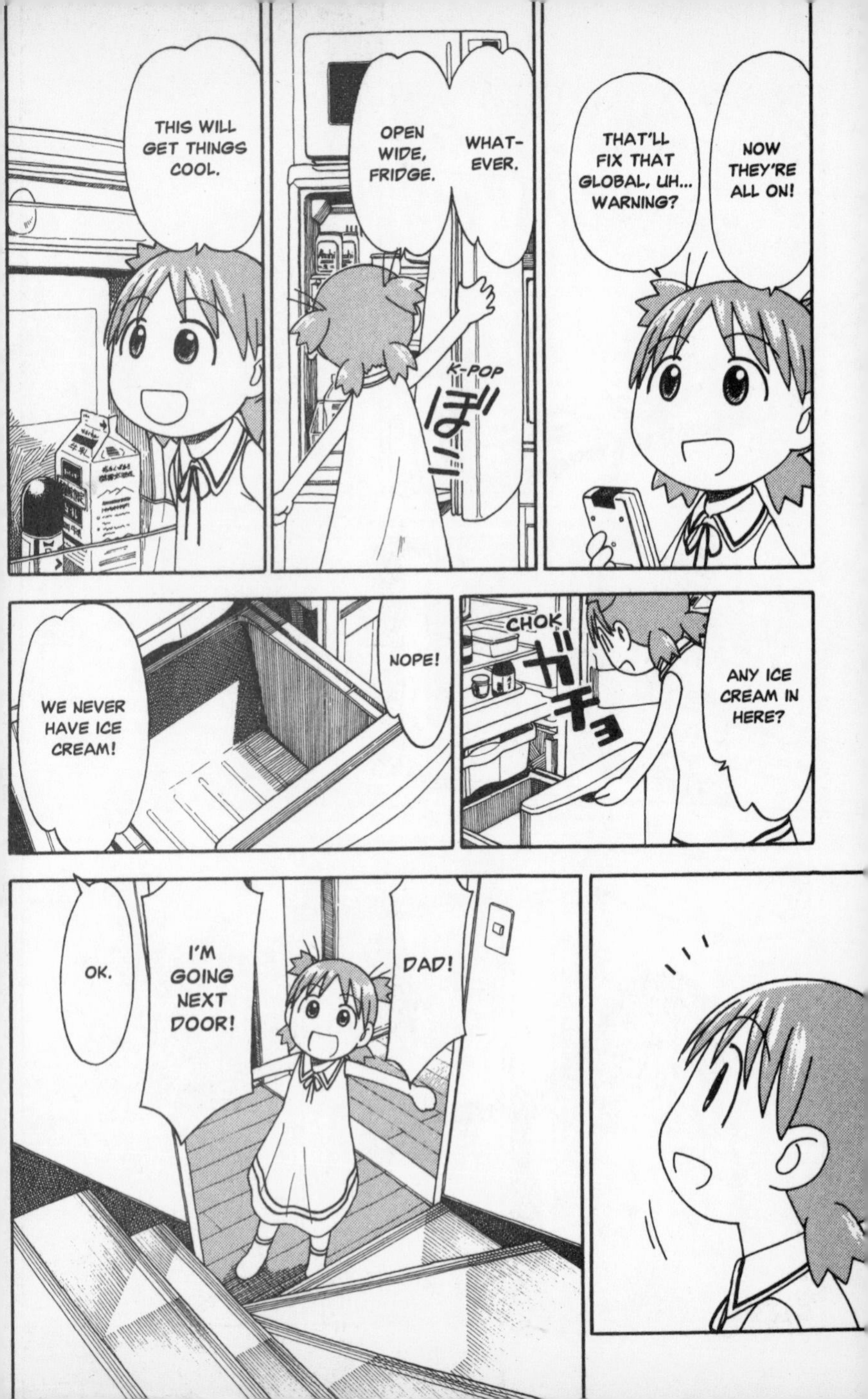
NOW THEY'RE ALL ON!
THAT'LL FIX THAT GLOBAL, UH... WARNING?
WHAT-EVER.
OPEN WIDE, FRIDGE.
K-POP
ぼこ
THIS WILL GET THINGS COOL.
ANY ICE CREAM IN HERE?
CHOK
ガチョ
NOPE!
WE NEVER HAVE ICE CREAM!
DAD!
I'M GOING NEXT DOOR!
OK.

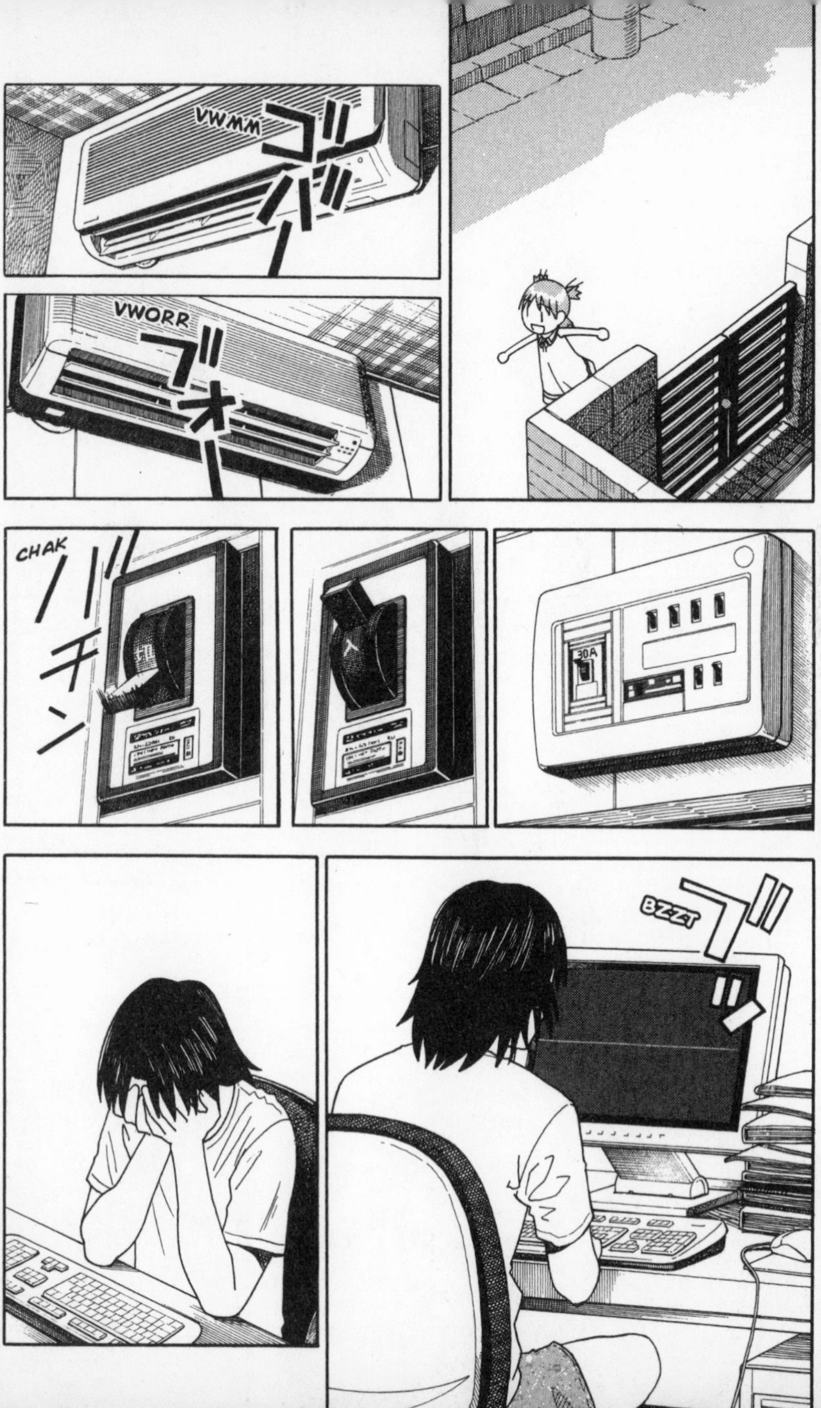
VWMM
ゴバー
VWORR
ブオー
30A
CHAK
バチン
BZZT
ブツッ

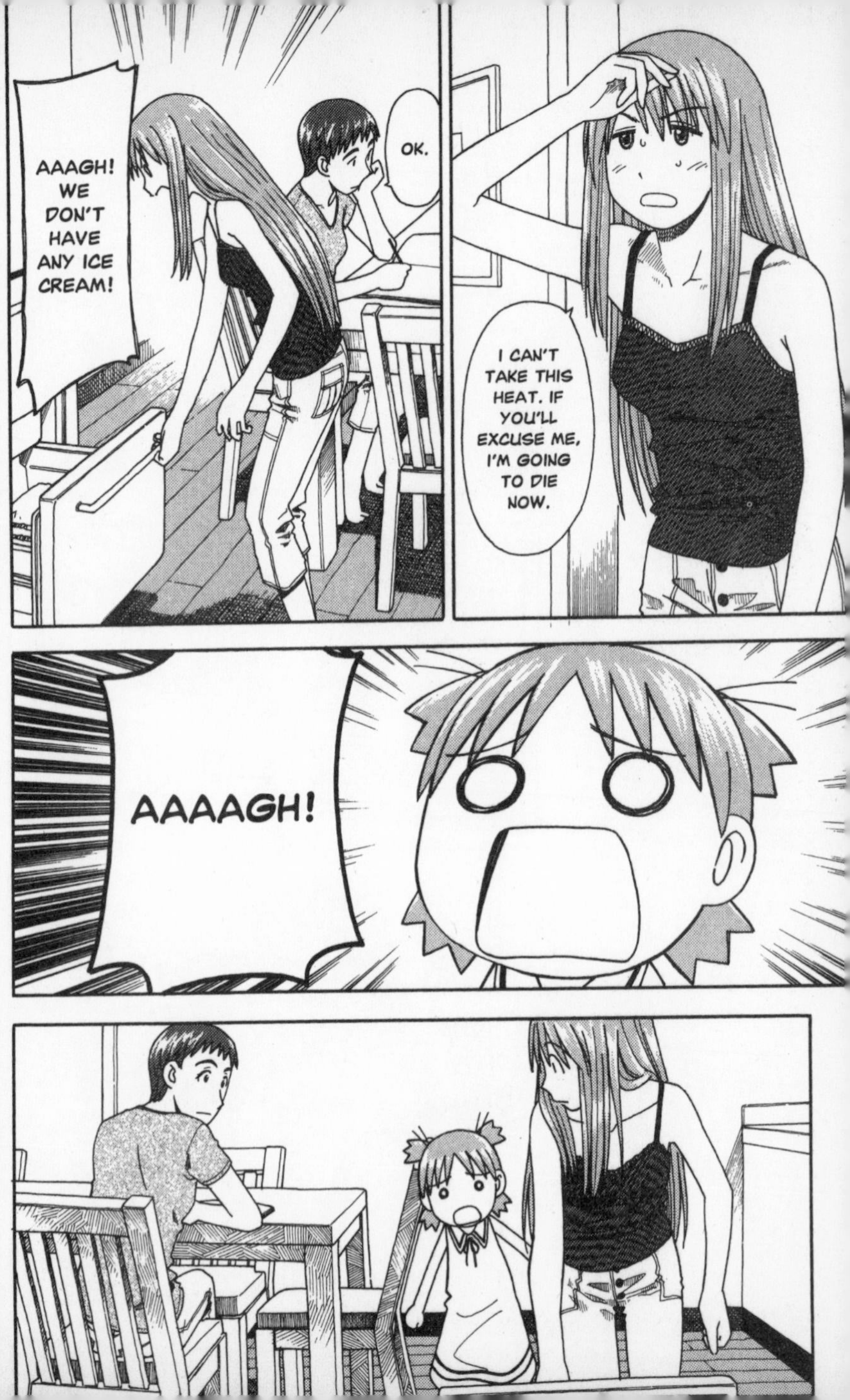

I CAN'T TAKE THIS HEAT. IF YOU'LL EXCUSE ME, I'M GOING TO DIE NOW.
OK.
AAAGH! WE DON'T HAVE ANY ICE CREAM!
AAAAGH!

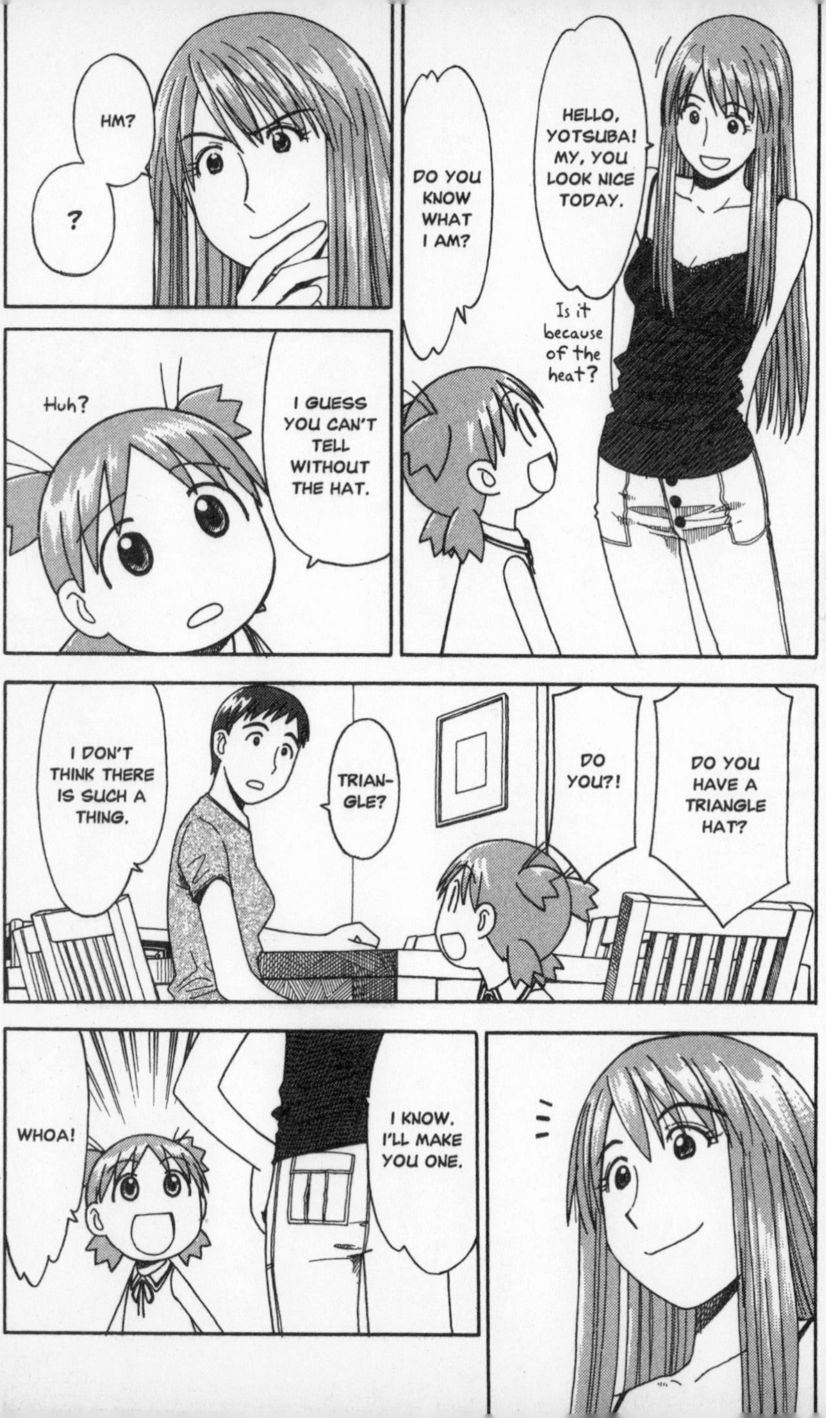
HELLO, YOTSUBA! MY, YOU LOOK NICE TODAY.
Is it because of the heat?
DO YOU KNOW WHAT I AM?
HM?
?
I GUESS YOU CAN'T TELL WITHOUT THE HAT.
Huh?
DO YOU HAVE A TRIANGLE HAT?
DO YOU?!
TRIAN-GLE?
I DON'T THINK THERE IS SUCH A THING.
I KNOW. I'LL MAKE YOU ONE.
WHOA!

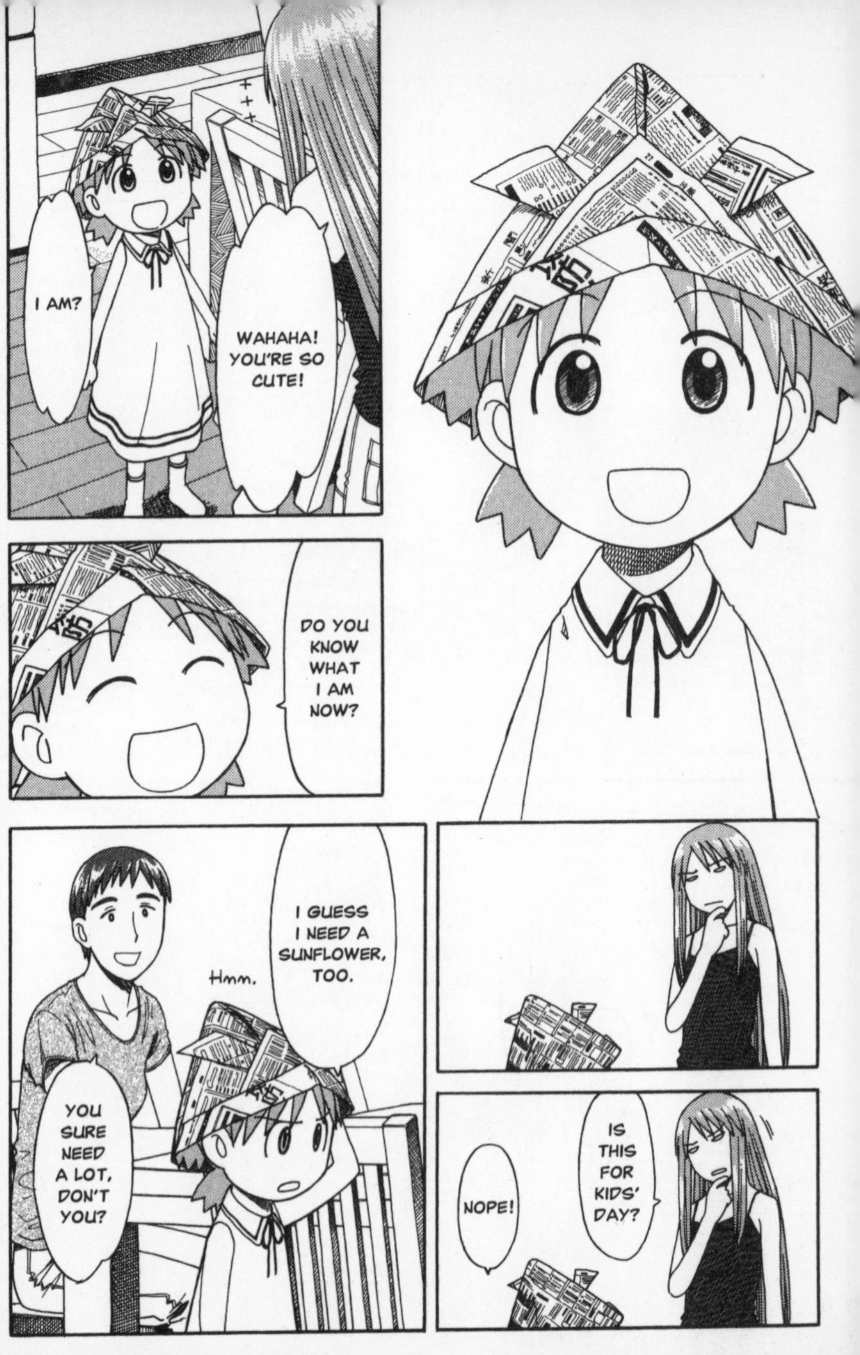
WAHAHA! YOU'RE SO CUTE!
I AM?
DO YOU KNOW WHAT I AM NOW?
IS THIS FOR KIDS' DAY?
NOPE!
I GUESS I NEED A SUNFLOWER, TOO.
Hmm.
YOU SURE NEED A LOT, DON'T YOU?

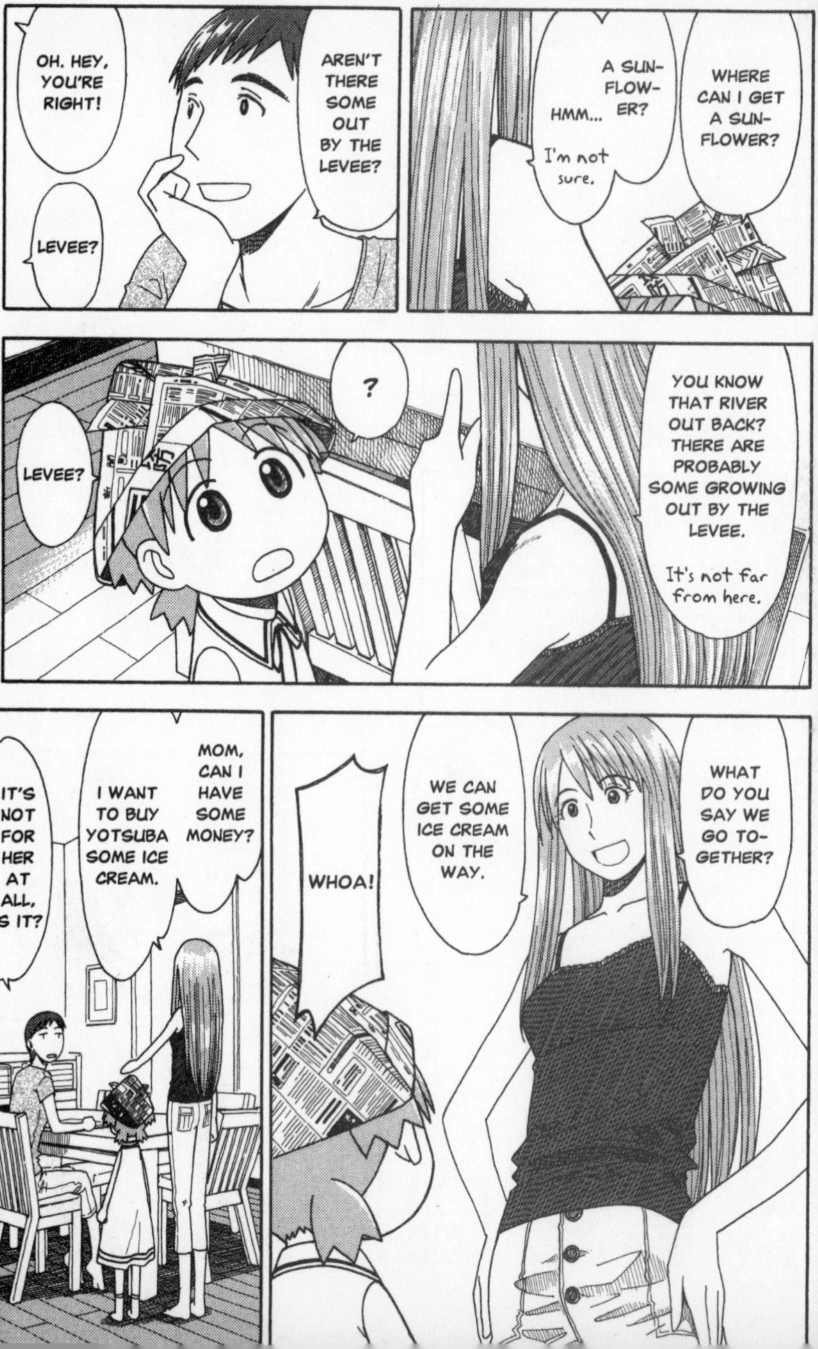
WHERE CAN I GET A SUNFLOWER?
A SUNFLOWER?
HMM... I'm not sure.
AREN'T THERE SOME OUT BY THE LEVEE?
OH. HEY, YOU'RE RIGHT!
LEVEE?
YOU KNOW THAT RIVER OUT BACK? THERE ARE PROBABLY SOME GROWING OUT BY THE LEVEE.
It's not far from here.
?
LEVEE?
WHAT DO YOU SAY WE GO TOGETHER?
WE CAN GET SOME ICE CREAM ON THE WAY.
WHOA!
MOM, CAN I HAVE SOME MONEY?
I WANT TO BUY YOTSUBA SOME ICE CREAM.
IT'S NOT FOR HER AT ALL, IS IT?

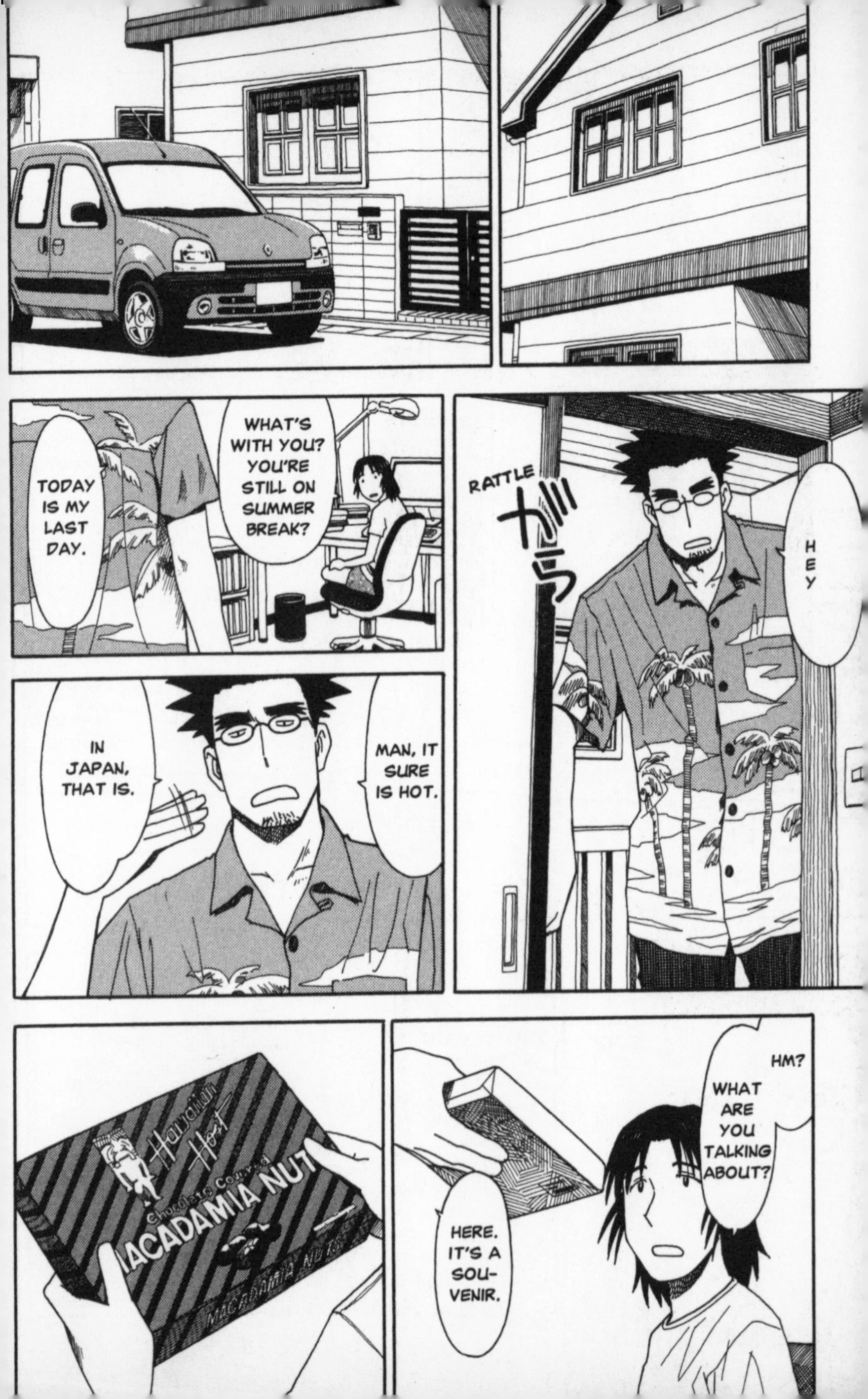
HEY
RATTLE
ガラ
WHAT'S WITH YOU? YOU'RE STILL ON SUMMER BREAK?
TODAY IS MY LAST DAY.
MAN, IT SURE IS HOT.
IN JAPAN, THAT IS.
HM? WHAT ARE YOU TALKING ABOUT?
HERE. IT'S A SOU-VENIR.
Hawaiian Host
Chocolate Covered
MACADAMIA NUT

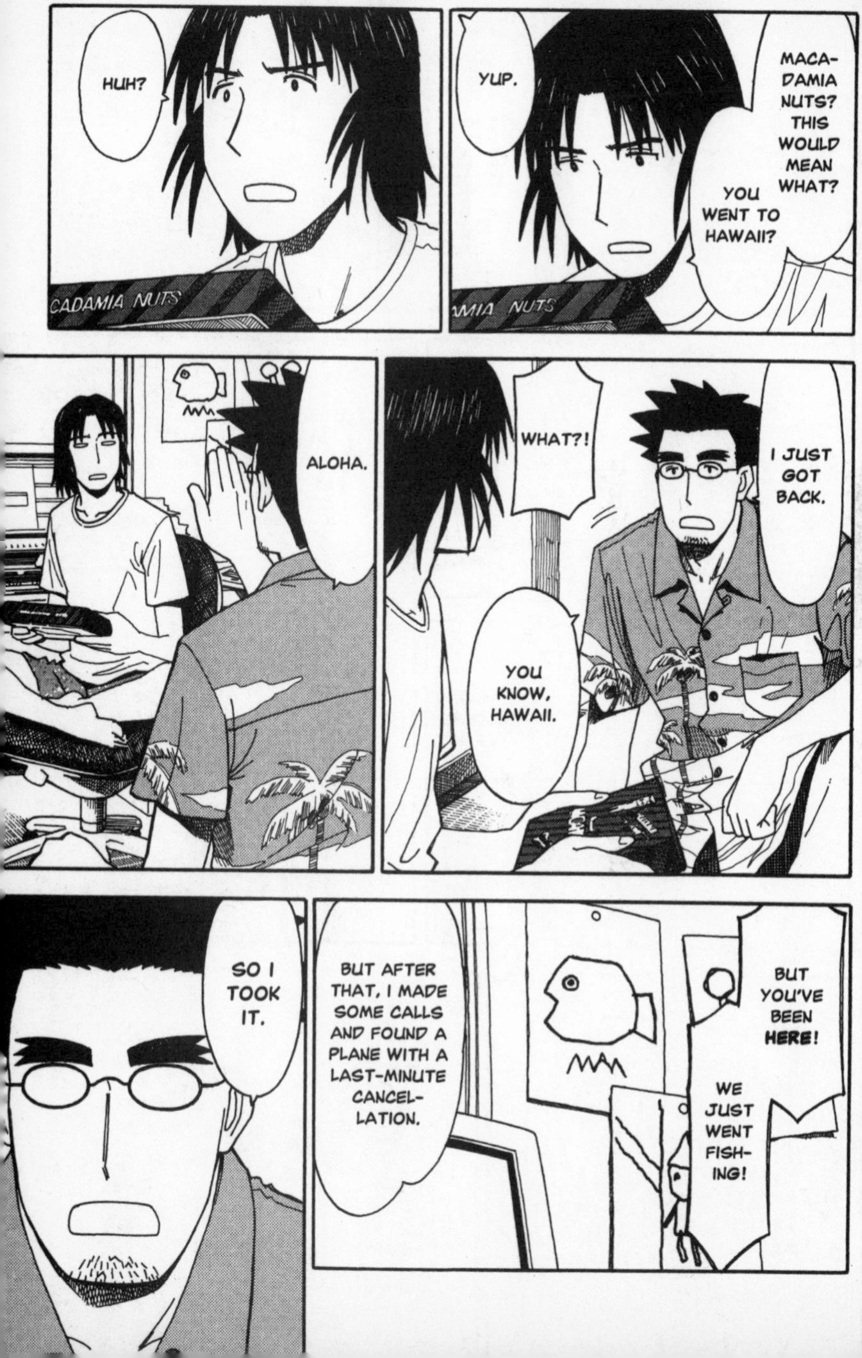
MACA-DAMIA NUTS? THIS WOULD MEAN WHAT?
YOU WENT TO HAWAII?
YUP.
MIA NUTS
HUH?
CADAMIA NUTS
I JUST GOT BACK.
WHAT?!
YOU KNOW, HAWAII.
ALOHA.
BUT YOU'VE BEEN **HERE**!
WE JUST WENT FISH-ING!
BUT AFTER THAT, I MADE SOME CALLS AND FOUND A PLANE WITH A LAST-MINUTE CANCEL-LATION.
SO I TOOK IT.

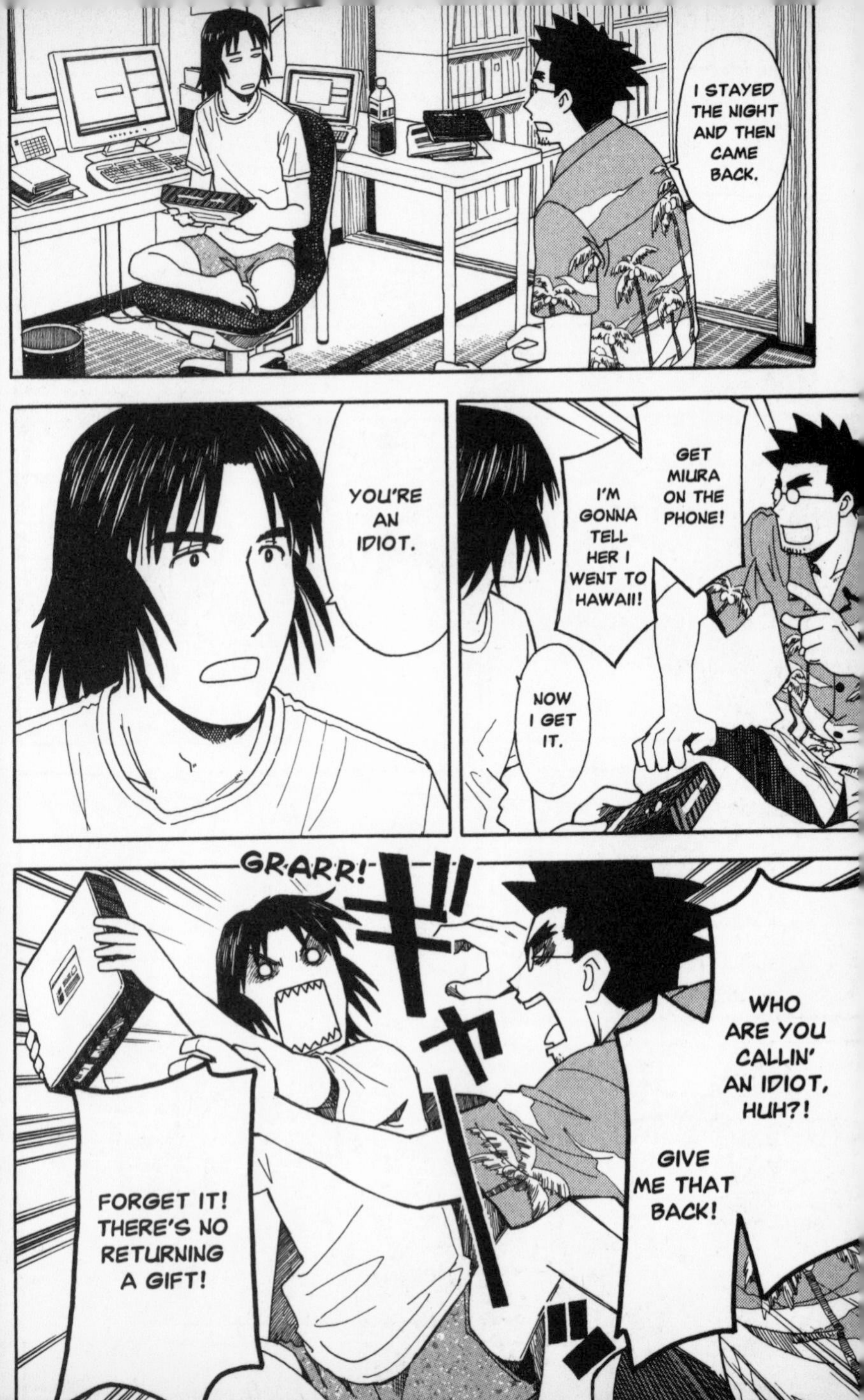
I STAYED THE NIGHT AND THEN CAME BACK.
GET MIURA ON THE PHONE!
I'M GONNA TELL HER I WENT TO HAWAII!
NOW I GET IT.
YOU'RE AN IDIOT.
GRARR!
ギャー
WHO ARE YOU CALLIN' AN IDIOT, HUH?!
GIVE ME THAT BACK!
FORGET IT! THERE'S NO RETURNING A GIFT!

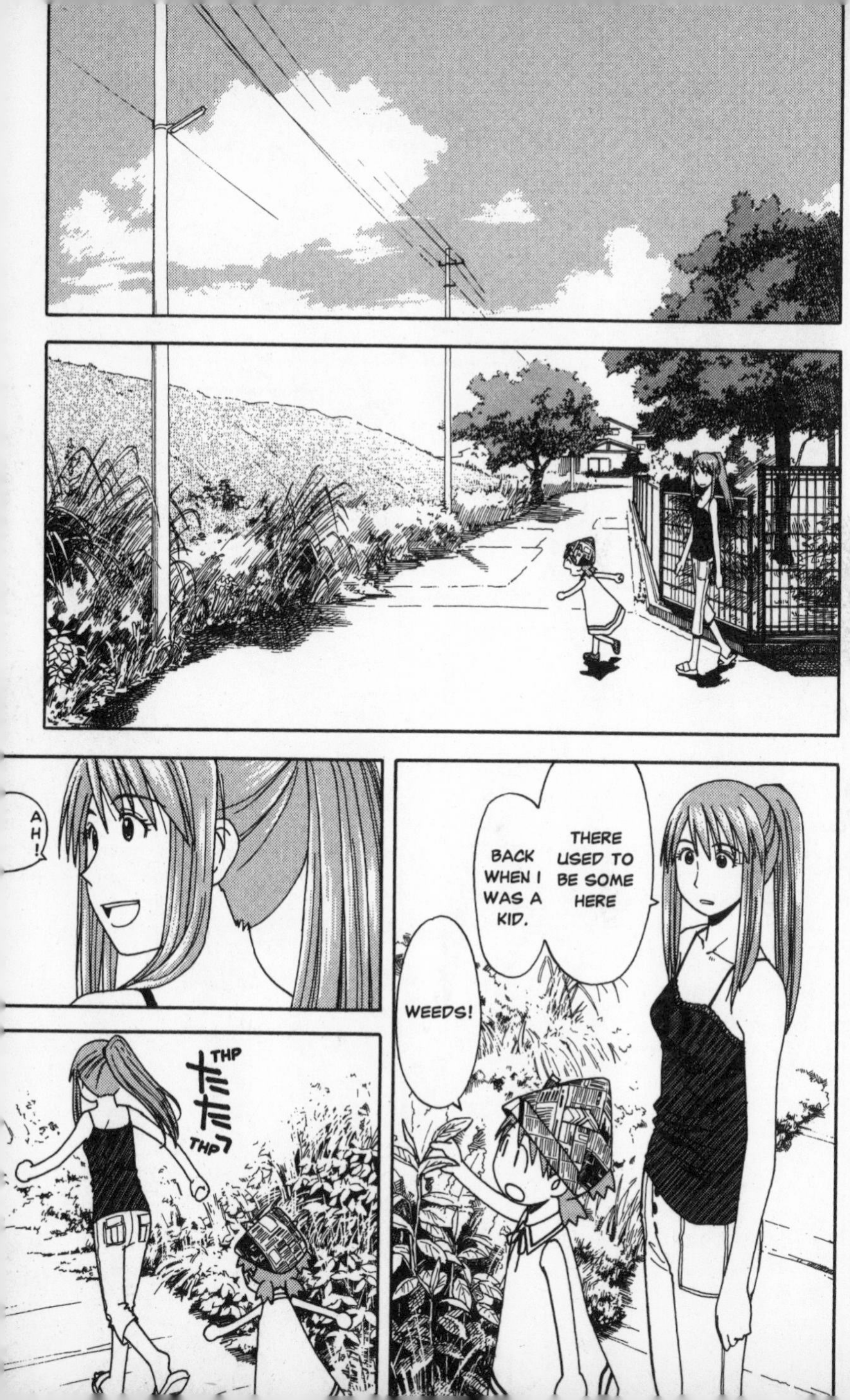
THERE USED TO BE SOME HERE
BACK WHEN I WAS A KID.
WEEDS!
AH!
THP
THP

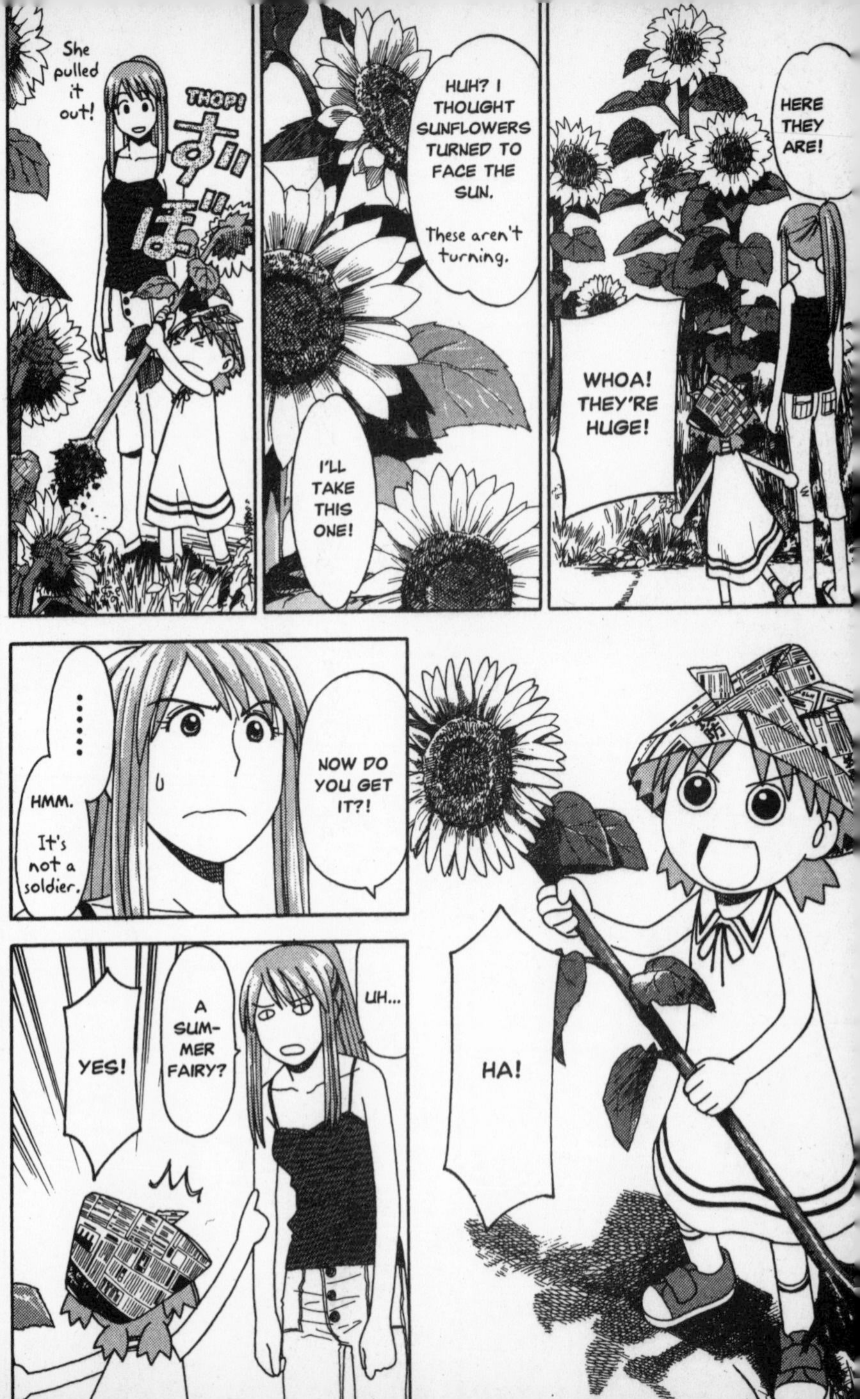
HERE THEY ARE!
WHOA! THEY'RE HUGE!
HUH? I THOUGHT SUNFLOWERS TURNED TO FACE THE SUN.
These aren't turning.
I'LL TAKE THIS ONE!
THOP!
She pulled it out!
HA!
NOW DO YOU GET IT?!
......
HMM.
It's not a soldier.
UH...
A SUM-MER FAIRY?
YES!

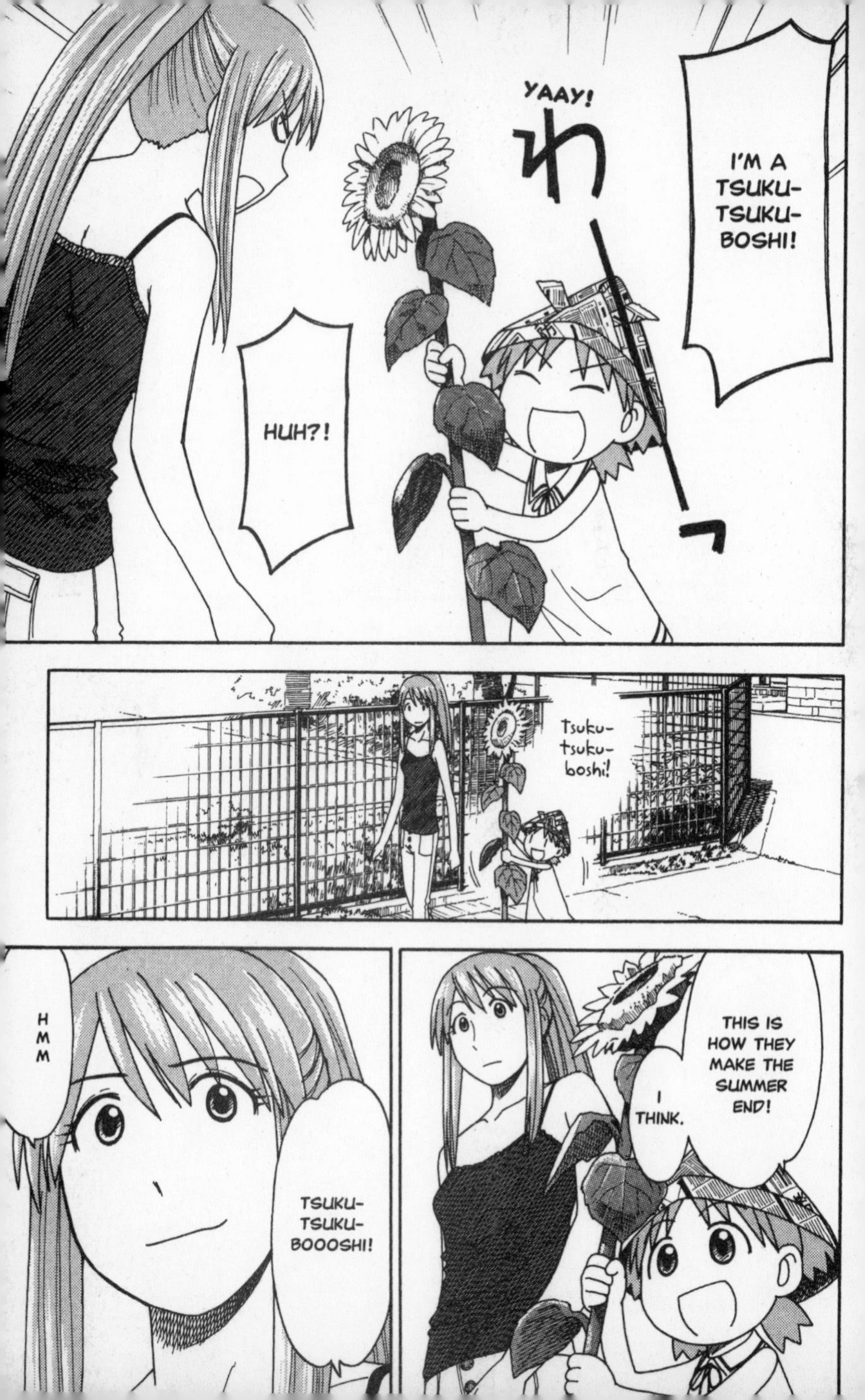
I'M A TSUKU-TSUKU-BOSHI!
YAAY!
わ
HUH?!
Tsuku-tsuku-boshi!
THIS IS HOW THEY MAKE THE SUMMER END!
I THINK.
HMM
TSUKU-TSUKU-BOOOSHI!

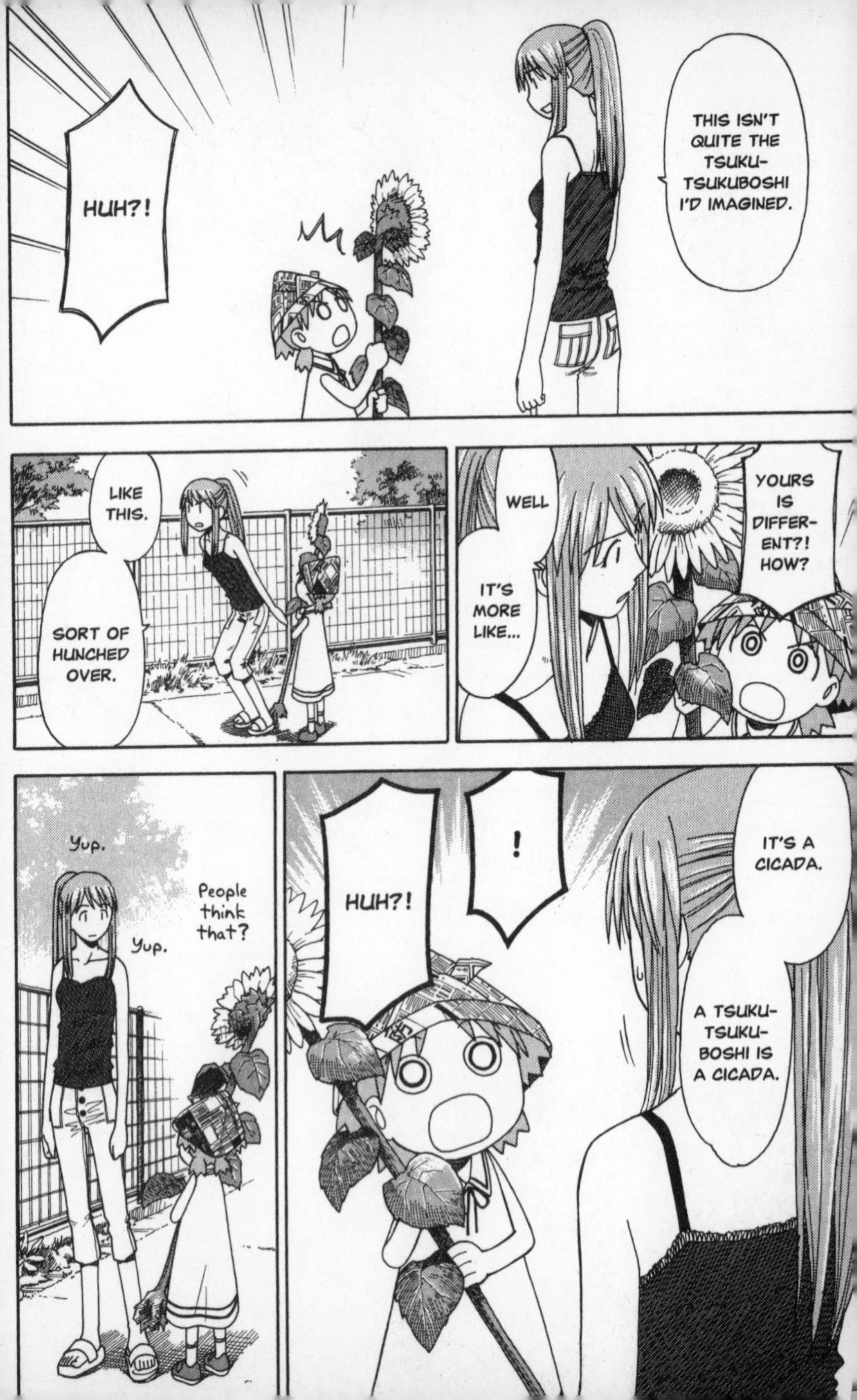
THIS ISN'T QUITE THE TSUKU-TSUKUBOSHI I'D IMAGINED.
HUH?!
YOURS IS DIFFERENT?! HOW?
WELL
IT'S MORE LIKE...
LIKE THIS.
SORT OF HUNCHED OVER.
IT'S A CICADA.
A TSUKU-TSUKU-BOSHI IS A CICADA.
!
HUH?!
Yup.
People think that?
Yup.

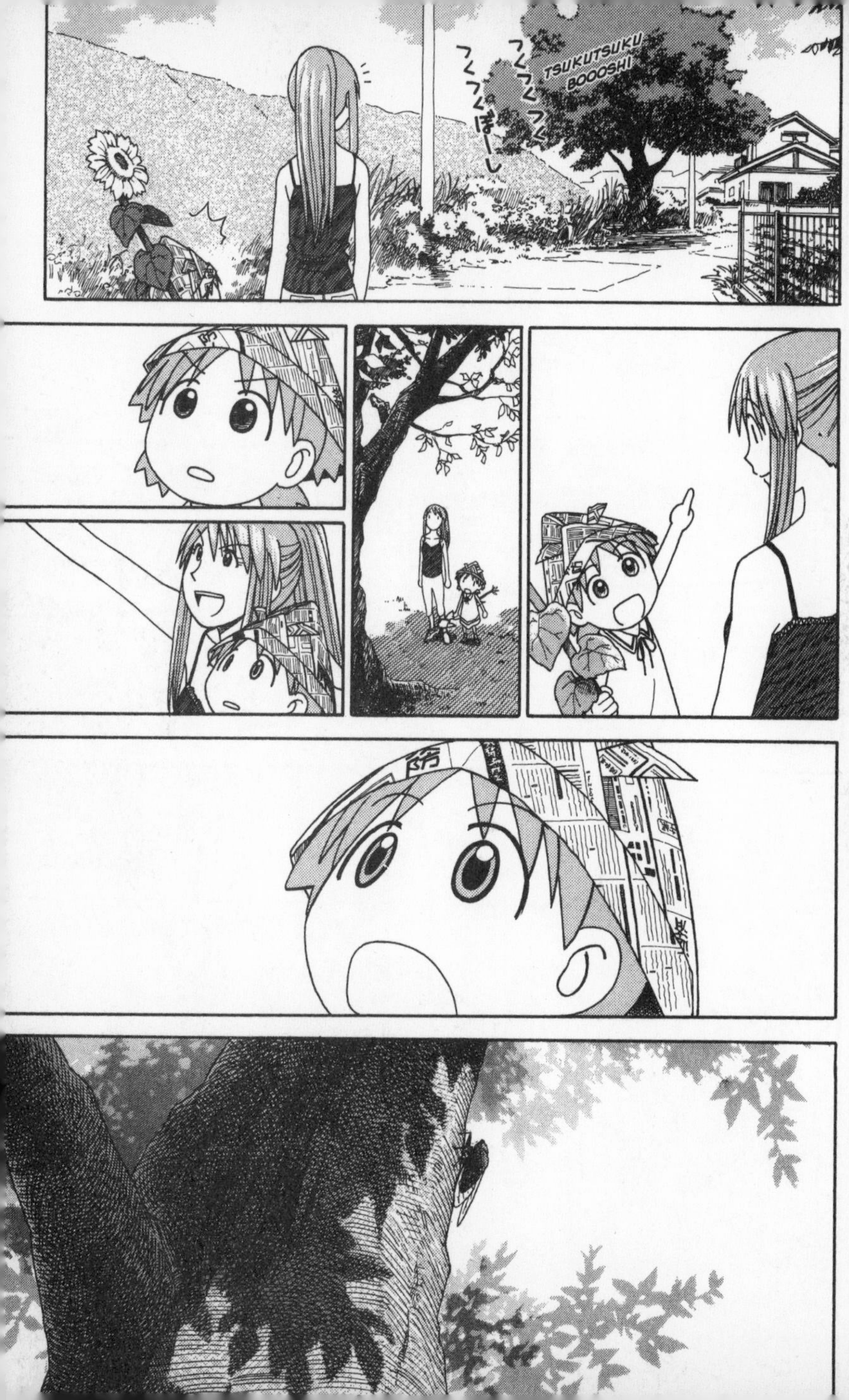
つくつくつくつく
つくつくぼーし
TSUKUTSUKU BOOOSHI

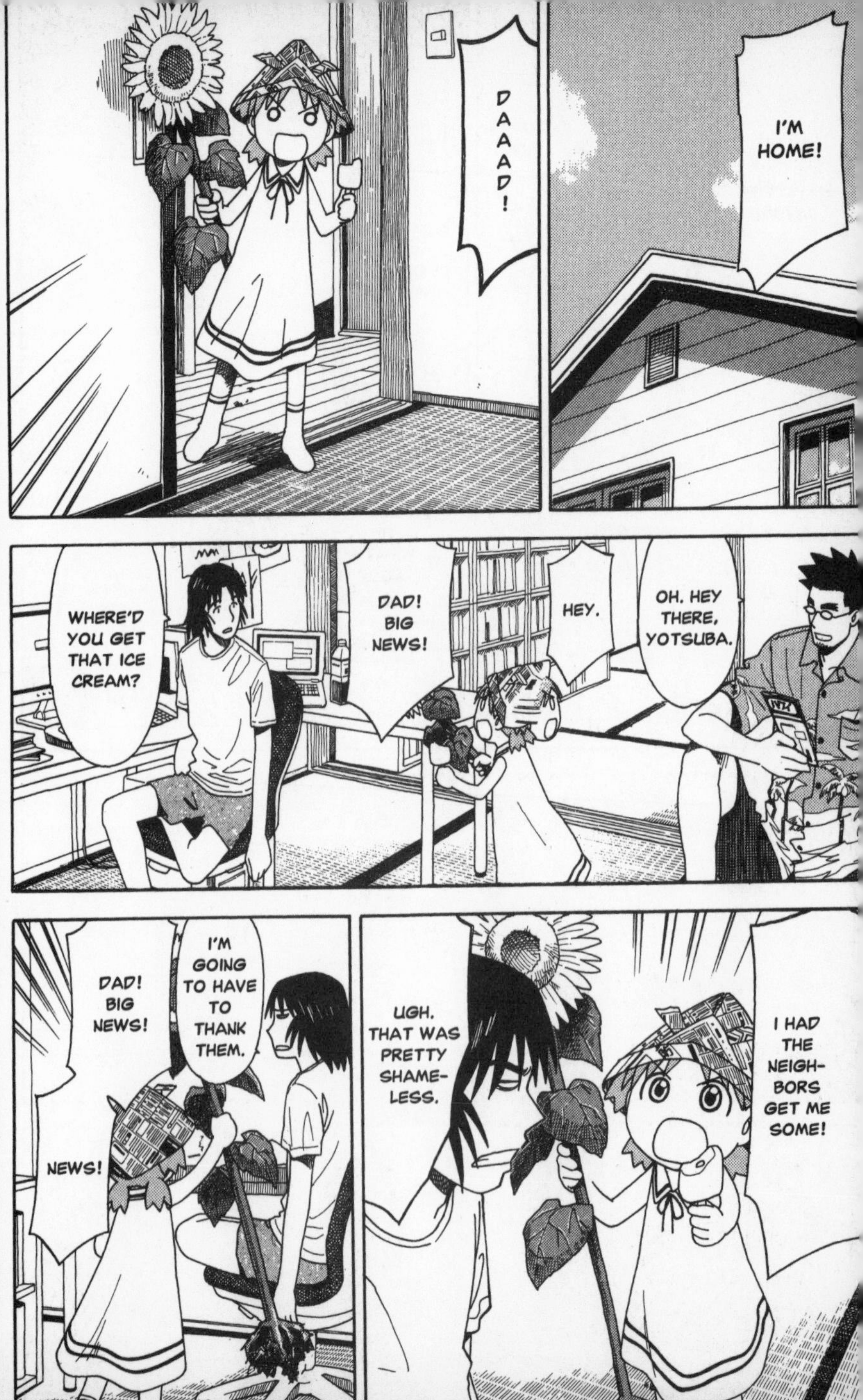
I'M HOME!
DAAAD!
OH. HEY THERE, YOTSUBA.
HEY.
DAD! BIG NEWS!
WHERE'D YOU GET THAT ICE CREAM?
I HAD THE NEIGH-BORS GET ME SOME!
UGH. THAT WAS PRETTY SHAME-LESS.
I'M GOING TO HAVE TO THANK THEM.
DAD! BIG NEWS!
NEWS!

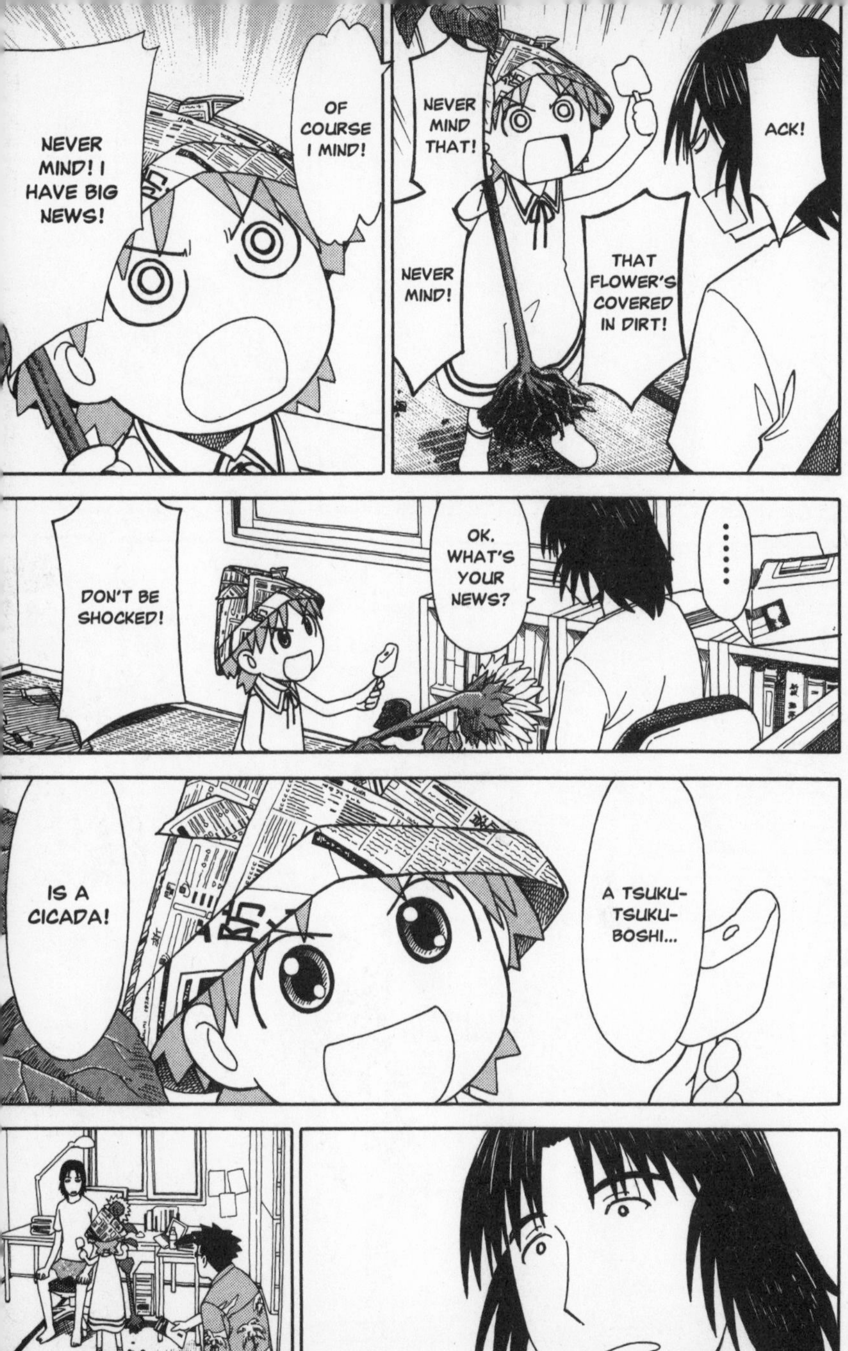
ACK!
NEVER MIND THAT!
THAT FLOWER'S COVERED IN DIRT!
NEVER MIND!
OF COURSE I MIND!
NEVER MIND! I HAVE BIG NEWS!
......
OK. WHAT'S YOUR NEWS?
DON'T BE SHOCKED!
A TSUKU-TSUKU-BOSHI...
IS A CICADA!

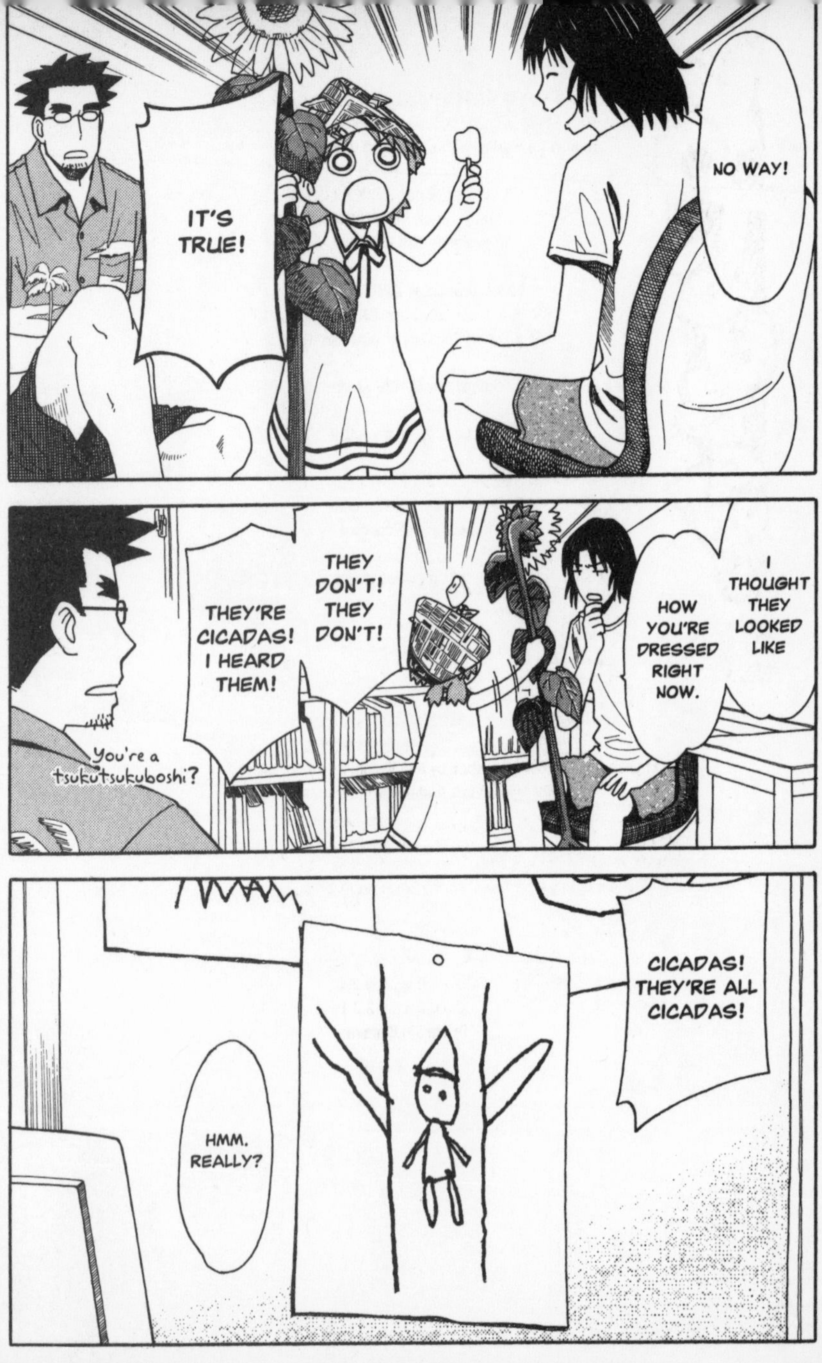
NO WAY!
IT'S TRUE!
I THOUGHT THEY LOOKED LIKE
HOW YOU'RE DRESSED RIGHT NOW.
THEY DON'T! THEY DON'T!
THEY'RE CICADAS! I HEARD THEM!
You're a tsukutsukuboshi?
CICADAS! THEY'RE ALL CICADAS!
HMM. REALLY?

© KIYOHIKO AZUMA/YOTUBA SUTAZIO/MEDIAWORKS
First published in 2005 by Media Works Inc., Tokyo, Japan.
English translation rights arranged with Media Works Inc.

Translator/Editor **JAVIER LOPEZ**
Graphic Artist **SCOTT HOWARD**
Copy Editor **SHERIDAN SCOTT**

Editorial Director **GARY STEINMAN**
Print Production Manager **BRIDGETT JANOTA**
Production Coordinator **MARISA KREITZ**

International Coordinators **MIYUKI KAMIYA & TORU IWAKAMI**

President, CEO & Publisher **JOHN LEDFORD**

Email: editor@adv-manga.com
www.adv-manga.com
www.advfilms.com

For sales and distribution inquiries please call 1.800.282.7202

ADV MANGA™ is a division of A.D. Vision, Inc.
5750 Bintliff Drive, Suite 210, Houston, Texas 77036
English text © 2007 published by A.D. Vision, Inc. under exclusive license.
ADV MANGA is a trademark of A.D. Vision, Inc.

All Rights Reserved. This is a fictional work. Any resemblance to actual events or locales,
or persons, living or dead, is entirely coincidental. Reproduction and, or transmission of
this work in whole or in part without written permission of the copyright holders is unlawful.

ISBN: 978-1-4139-0345-4
First printing, July 2007
10 9 8 7 6 5 4 3 2 1
Printed in Canada

Hyaa!

ENJOY EVERYTHING

to be continued...

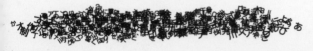

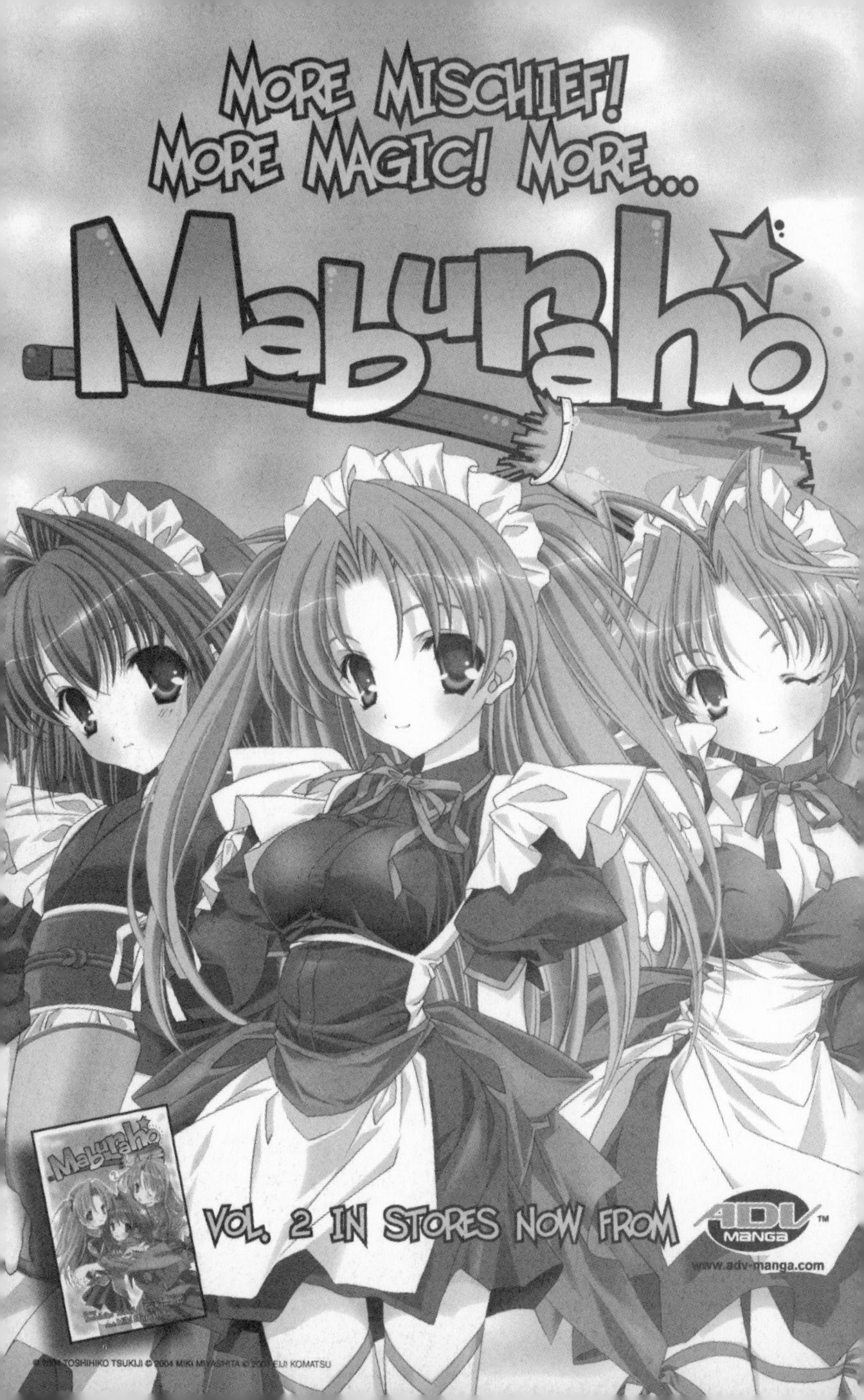
MORE MISCHIEF! MORE MAGIC! MORE...
Maburaho
VOL. 2 IN STORES NOW FROM
ADV MANGA
www.adv-manga.com

ANGEL neo DUST

An innocent prayer at a shrine turns Akito's simple existence upside down. Suddenly a bevy of cute gals enters his life—some claiming to be Emulates who want to "make a contract" with him! What's a boy to do?

SEQUEL TO THE HIT MANGA ANGEL/DUST!

FROM THE PAGES OF NEWTYPE USA!

IN STORES NOW FROM

www.adv-manga.com

© AOI NANASE 2003

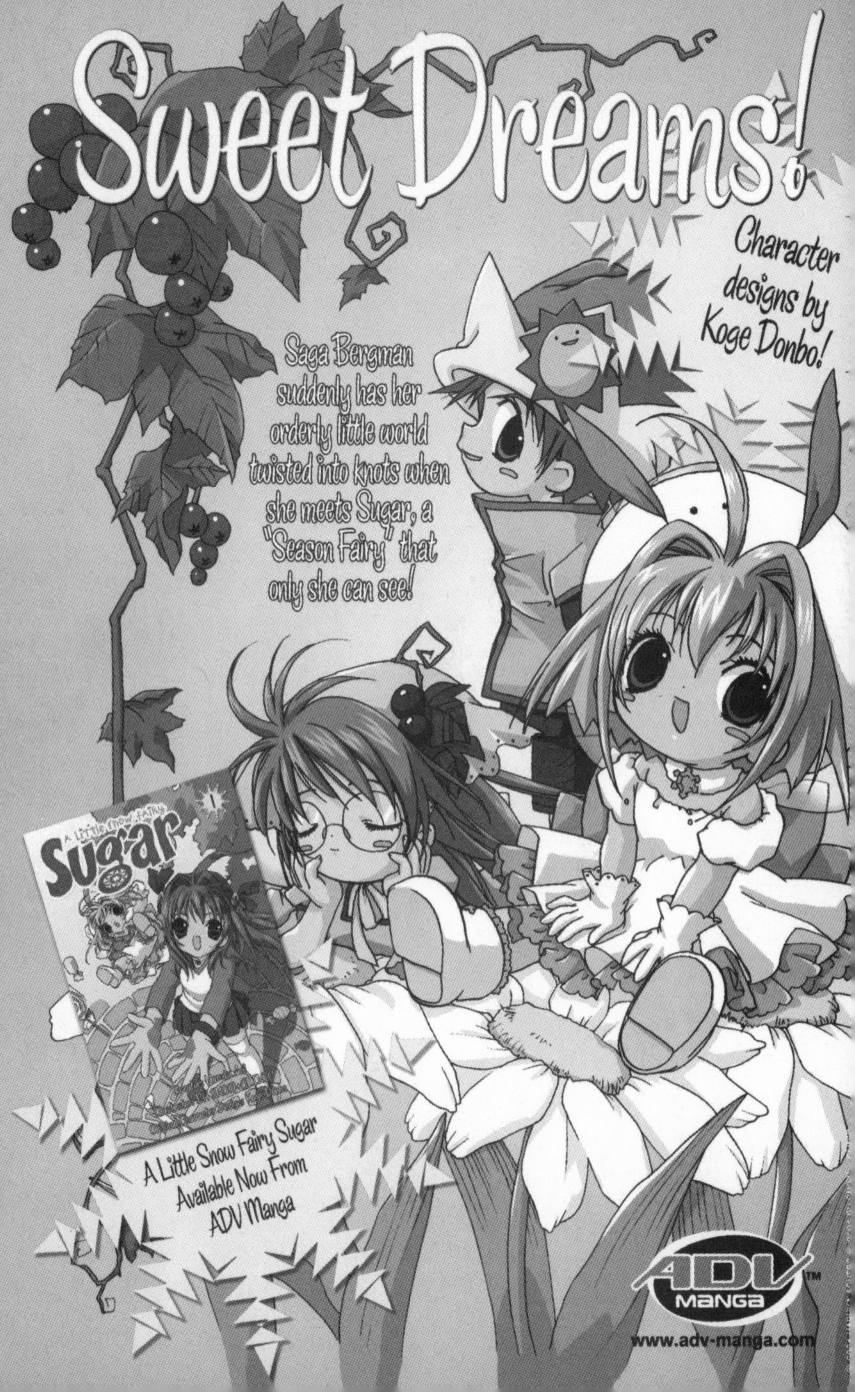

Sweet Dreams!
Character designs by Koge Donbo!
Saga Bergman suddenly has her orderly little world twisted into knots when she meets Sugar, a "Season Fairy" that only she can see!
Sugar
A Little Snow Fairy Sugar Available Now From ADV Manga
ADV Manga
www.adv-manga.com

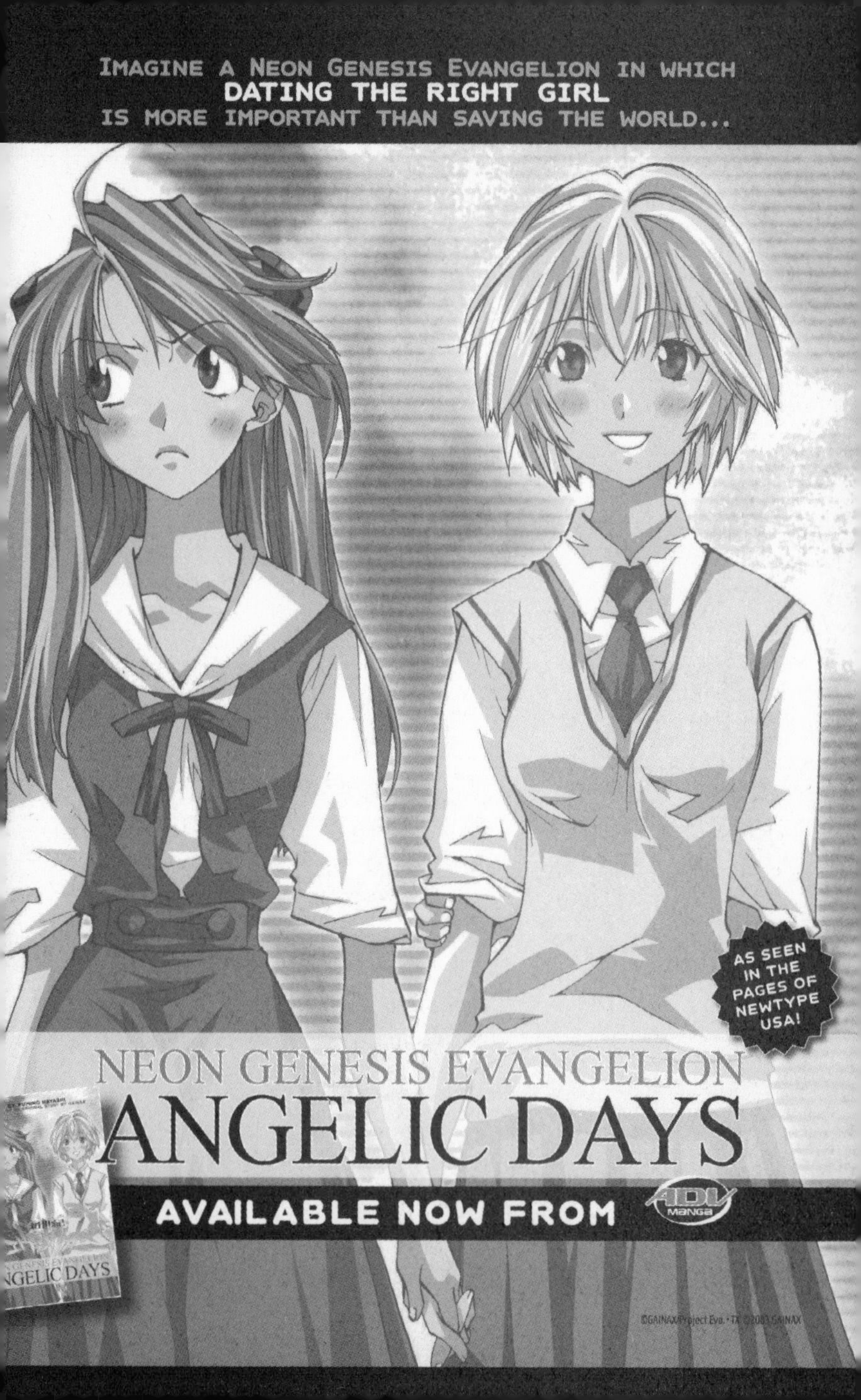

IMAGINE A NEON GENESIS EVANGELION IN WHICH
DATING THE RIGHT GIRL
IS MORE IMPORTANT THAN SAVING THE WORLD...
AS SEEN IN THE PAGES OF NEWTYPE USA!
NEON GENESIS EVANGELION
ANGELIC DAYS
AVAILABLE NOW FROM
ANGELIC DAYS
©GAINAX/Project Eva. • TX ©2003 GAINAX

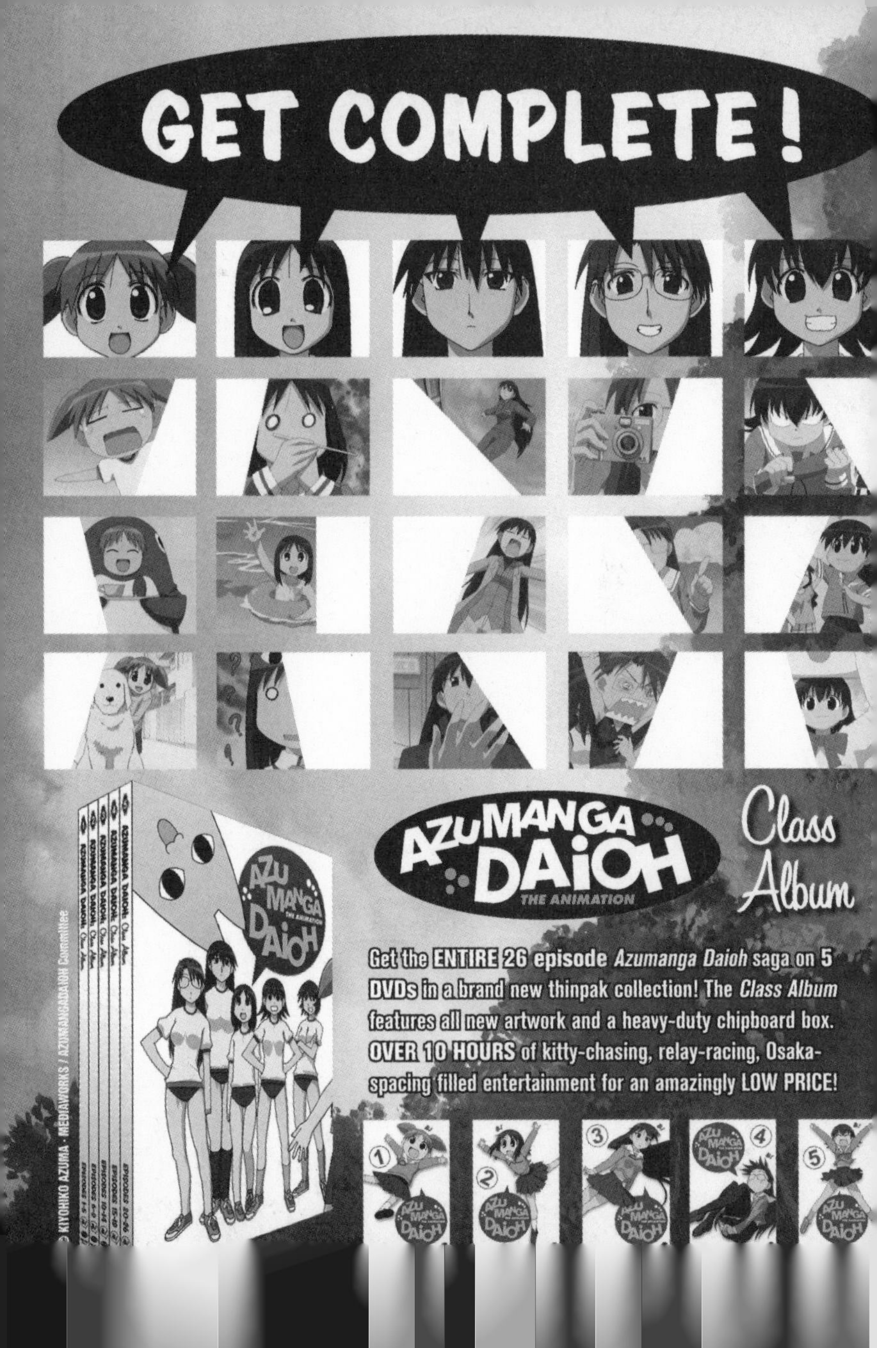
GET COMPLETE!
AZUMANGA DAIOH
THE ANIMATION
Class Album
Get the ENTIRE 26 episode Azumanga Daioh saga on 5 DVDs in a brand new thinpak collection! The Class Album features all new artwork and a heavy-duty chipboard box. OVER 10 HOURS of kitty-chasing, relay-racing, Osaka-spacing filled entertainment for an amazingly LOW PRICE!
© KIYOHIKO AZUMA · MEDIAWORKS / AZUMANGADAIOH Committee

WE'RE CALLING FROM INSIDE THE HOUSE!
YOU ASKED FOR IT!
YOU DEMANDED IT!
NOW YOU GOT IT!
BETTER WATCH IT!
ANIME NETWORK
©2007 ANIME NETWORK
IN OVER 40 MILLION HOUSEHOLDS
FIND YOURS
WWW.FINDANIMENETWORK.COM